THE THREEFOLD LOGIC OF ADVANCED ARCHITECTURE

CONFORMATIVE, DISTRIBUTIVE, AND EXPANSIVE PROTOCOLS FOR AN INFORMATIONAL PRACTICE 1990-2020

MANUEL GAUSA – JORDI VIVALDI

Published by
Actar Publishers
New York, Barcelona

IAAC
Institute for Advanced Architecture of
Catalonia, Barcelona

Authors
Manuel Gausa
Jordi Vivaldi

Collection / n-cities
Director / Manuel Gausa

Guest Contributor
Areti Markopoulou

Proofreading and Editing
Angela Kay Bunning

Distribution
Actar Distribution

NEW YORK
440 Park Avenue South, 17th Floor
New York, NY 10016, USA
T +1 2129662207
salesnewyork@actar-d.com

BARCELONA
Roca i Batlle 2-4
08023 Barcelona, Spain
T +34 933 282 183
eurosales@actar-d.com

ISBN 978-1-948765572

This volume was produced with the PRA 2018 contribution of the Department of Architecture and Design of UNIGE.

Financed with Research funds 2019-2020 IAAC - Institute for Advanced Architecture of Catalonia

Special thanks:
Angela Kay Bunning
Gic-Lab DAD-UNIGE: N. Canessa / G. Tucci / A. Ronco-Milanaccio / M. Pitanti / F. Vercellino
IAAC founders and Direction Team

Published in 2021

Università di Genova | DAD DIPARTIMENTO DI ARCHITETTURA E DESIGN

IaaC Institute for advanced architecture of Catalonia | BARCELONA

ACTAR

This work proposes a threefold cultural narrative whose interactive and informational logic differs from that of modernity and postmodernity. It positions three different *ethos* by critically approaching the architectural side of a cultural mutation that has been affecting the Western experimental areas of knowledge and practice since the end of the last century. A transformative process constituted by a constellation of transdisciplinary manifestations, accelerations, turns, shortcuts and clusterizations that by no means can be read under one single epistemological framwork.

Rather than approaching the practice of architecture focusing on its disciplinary inner specificity, this book approaches the research of experimental architecture focusing on its extra-disciplinary entanglements. It argues that a vast multiplicity of fields of knowledge participates in a cultural endeavour modulated through three protocols -forms of action- that singularize three decades: Conformative Protocols (1990-2000), Distributive Protocols (2000-2010) and Expansive Protocols (2010-2020).

These three periods shouldn't be read as three hermetic and concatenated monades, but as three different modulations of the same narrative, that is, as three overlapping and coexisting systems whose peaks of intensity occur in three different decades.

However, the purpose of this book is not limited to unveiling the *ethos* of these three conjugations. It aims also at using this framework as a "time-field", a narrative map that moves from the classificatory to the cartographical in order to vectorize the last 30 years of experimental architecture.

This book argues that this threefold set of protocols represents the progressive attempt to constitute critical interiorities "looking for" and "produced through" interactions that are increasingly more intimate and whose agents are increasingly more diverse. A tendency oriented towards the consolidation of an "intimacy between strangers" that highly resonates with the cultural and technological landscape in which experimental architecture operates.

INDEX

0. FRAMEWORK

_008_ **INCIPIT: CIRCUMSTANCE AND INTENTION**
Manuel Gausa - Jordi Vivaldi

_012_ **INTRODUCTION: CONFORMATIVE, DISTRIBUTIVE, EXPANSIVE**
Jordi Vivaldi - Manuel Gausa

_034_ **1. CONFORMATIVE PROTOCOLS**

_042_ **THE TOPOLOGICAL CONDITION: OVERLAPPING LAYERS AND MODELLING FIELDS**
Manuel Gausa

_042_ 1. OVERLAPPING LAYERS
_056_ 2. TOPOLOGICAL PATTERN CONDITIONS
_090_ 3. MODELLING FIELDS

_104_ **COLORARIUM: TOPOLOGICAL SPACE AND RELATIONAL SUBJECT: THE CONTINUOUS FLOOR**
Jordi Vivaldi

_123_ **2. DISTRIBUTIVE PROTOCOLS**

_130_ **THE ECOLOGICAL CONDITION: CONNECTING NETWORKS AND PROPAGATING ATMOSPHERES**
Manuel Gausa

_130_ 1. CONNECTING NETWORKS
_134_ 2. ECOLOGICAL CONDITION
_152_ 3. OTHER NETWORKS
_164_ 4. PROPAGATING ENVIRONMENTS

_188_ **THE ECOLOGICAL CONDITION: CONNECTING NETWORKS AND PROPAGATING ATMOSPHERES**
Jordi Vivaldi

_188_ 1. THE ECOLOGICAL CONDITION
_198_ 2. CONNECTING NETWORKS
_207_ 3. PROPAGATING ATMOSPHERES
_218_ 4. TRANSFERENCES

_220_ **3. EXPANSIVE PROTOCOLS**

_228_ **THE XENOLOGICAL CONDITION: MEDIATING AGENTS AND PERFORMING MATTER**
Jordi Vivaldi

_228_ 1. THE XENOLOGICAL CONDITION
_246_ 2. MEDIATING AGENCIES
_274_ 3. PERFORMING MATTER
_296_ 4. XENO-SURREALISM

_308_ **COLORARIUM: AUTOM-ACTING AGENTS & PERFORMING MATTERS UNDER AN ACTANT XENOLOGICAL CONDITION**
Manuel Gausa

_338_ **4. ENDING CONSIDERATIONS**

_340_ **SYNTHESIS: THE 4(+1) IN FACTORS**
Manuel Gausa

_358_ **PERSPECTIVES: TOWARDS A LIMIT-SPACE**
Jordi Vivaldi

5. AFTERWORD

_368_ **COLLECTIVE INTELLIGENCE DESIGN**
Areti Markopoulou

MANUEL GAUSA - JORDI VIVALDI

INCIPIT
Circumstance and Intention

I

As we write, politics both in the Western and Eastern world are marked by wild eruptions of xenophobia, intolerance and misogyny, exacerbated concentrations of wealth, hate and racism, homophobia, private and corporate avarice, surveillance capitalism, willful obliviousness towards the persecution of minorities and fierce denials of climate change.[1]

In light of these reactionary positions, a set of pro-democratic, antiracist and xeno-feminist counter-politics of direct action and mass protest is urgently needed. Architecture offers a powerful channel to provide not just an implacable opposition to fascist, neo-liberal and anti-democratic practices, but also a space to shape "fluid politics" such as gender-abolitionism, anti-naturalism or techno-materialism. The critical reflection and dissemination of innovative future-based architectural practices emphasizing this direction are crucial in an architectural scene whose corporate register is void of a radical political agenda transcending calligraphic gesticulations, computational mannerisms and solipsistic discourses.

II

This book has been simmering during several years in the cauldron of a knowledge in action. It has been forged through encounters with practitioners and researchers, experiences with artists, designers and students, conversations, transdisciplinary readings, polymorphic audiovisuals, presentations, openings, lectures, symposiums. A composite of sustained interactions that in the last years has crystallised in lectures, papers and interviews, and that now is articulated through the present book.

This work proposes a threefold cultural narrative whose interactive and informational nature differs from that of modern and postmodern logics. It positions three different *ethos* by critically approaching the architectural side of a cultural mutation that has been affecting the Western experimental areas of knowledge and practice since the end of the

_1. Jane Bennet, *Influx and Efflux: Writing up with Walt Whitman* (Durham: Duke University Press Books, 2020).

last century. A transformative process constituted by a constellation of transdisciplinary manifestations, accelerations, turns, shortcuts and clusterizations that by no means can be read under one single epistemological umbrella. In this sense, rather than approaching the practice of architecture focusing on its disciplinary inner specificity, this book approaches the research of experimental architecture focusing on its extra-disciplinary entanglements. It argues that a vast multiplicity of fields of knowledge participates in a cultural endeavour modulated through three protocols -forms of action- with a twofold particularity: first, its operative intensifications occur in three different decades, and, second, each protocol ramifies in a discrete and a continuous conjugation:

- Conformative Protocols stand out in the decade 1990-2000, operating under a discrete register based on "overlapping layers" and under a continuous register based on "modelling fields".

- Distributive Protocols stand out in the decade 2000-2010, operating under a discrete register based on "connecting networks" and under a continuous register based on "propagating atmospheres".

- Expansive Protocols stand out in the decade 2010-2020, operating under a discrete register based on "mediating agents" and under a continuous register based on "performing matter".

These three protocols shouldn't be read as three hermetic and concatenated monades, but as three different modulations of the same narrative; three modes of action that coexist during the last 30 years but whose peaks of intensity occur in three different decades.

However, the main purpose of this book is not limited to unveiling the *ethos* of these three conjugations. It aims also at using this framework as a "time-field", a narrative map that moves from the classificatory to the cartographical in order to vectorize the last 30 years of experimental architecture. This essay argues that this threefold set of protocols represents the progressive attempt to constitute critical interiorities "looking for" and "produced through" interactions that are increasingly more intimate and whose agents are increasingly more diverse. A tendency oriented towards the consolidation of an "intimacy between strangers" that highly resonates with the cultural and technological landscape in which experimental architecture operates.

The authorship of this book is twofold. It belongs to two complicit voices associated with two different generations. On the one side, Manuel Gausa, born on the cusp of the 60s and actively engaged with the architectural traffic between the 90s and the beginning of the 2000s. On the other side, Jordi Vivaldi, born on the cusp of the 90s and committed to the philosophical and architectural production of the 21st century. The formation of both voices at the ETSAB in Barcelona and their subsequent involvement with the foundation and/or research of the IAAC (Institute for Advanced Architecture of Catalonia) is not negligible since it defines a great part of the explorative gaze they share.

The double nature of this authorship has an impact on the structure of this book. While the research is divided into three chapters that account for the three proposed periods, each one is articulated through the combination of two different formats: a long essay and a complementary corollary which are written by one author or the other according to his affinity with each period.

This research is firmly associated with the IAAC's TAK area (Theory and Advanced Knowledge), directed by the authors. It represents the construction of a synthetic vision that by no means aims to elaborate an exhaustive inventory. Instead, it conjures up a limited number of experimental projects and ideas whose mode of action indicates the emergence and consolidation of a new era in the experimental realm; a composite of open, tentacular and informational narratives firmly entangled with the 21st century and not exempt of political controversy. In spite of this contemporary focus, this research does not ignore certain echoes coming from the classical worlds of the Renaissance, Enlightenment and Romanticism. It also reverberates with some of the postmodern revisions and, of course, with many of the ideological and technological transformations that the modern order inscribed in the 20th century, which, for better or worse, still resonate in our current experimental realm.

III

On December 17, 1903, more than a century ago, the Wright brothers' plane took flight for the first time over the beaches of Kitty Hawk. At nearly the same time, *The Great Train Robbery* by Edwin S. Porter was being screened. It was the first film that explicitly revealed the depth of the frame and subjective editing.

Three years earlier, in 1900, Sigmund Freud had published *The Interpretation of Dreams*, opening the century with a new conception of the psyche and the world. Only two years later, in 1905, Albert Einstein published his fundamental article on the Special Theory of Relativity. Einstein confirmed the break with the former separated notions of space and time, and their definitive link within a new space-time characterized by relative positions.

One year later, in 1906, Henry Ford was getting the "Model T" ready, fostering mass mobility and assembly-line production while materializing Taylor's efficiency techniques and William James's pragmatic theories. And, finally, in 1907, Pablo Picasso finished "Les Demoiselles d'Avignon", the painting that would identify "cubism", i.e., the analytical division of the object and its fragmentation into multiple contrasting facets.

In barely five years there was a coincidence of decisive contributions destined to transform the scientific, technical and intellectual landscape left by the 19th century. The development of those advances would consolidate a new type of operative logic applied to the definition and construction of space.

The classic "symbolic" logic had been overcome and substituted by a more material, objective and pragmatic logic that was qualified as "modern". Thus, modernity celebrated an apparently more rational - but no less deterministic - form of action arising from a new planimetric, relational and sequential vision of space. It operated through a notion of "mechanics" that was abstract in its form and serial in its production, associated with a positivistic – if not severe or "stripped down" – interpretation of reality itself.

IV

In the mid 20th century, decisive advances occurred simultaneously in different areas of knowledge. The 1960s witnessed the transmission of multiple images in space through the introduction of the television: the "monofocal" projected image of cinema's big screen exploded into a myriad of small screens distributed across the territory. Real and virtual scenarios – and messages – started to coexist and overlap, a phenomena reflected by Marshall McLuhan in *Understanding Media* (1964) or Guy Debord in *Société de l'espectacle*

(1964). Shortly thereafter, in 1969, the Internet was born – the first network, Arpanet – based on military and academic interfaces connecting different research centers.

In 1961, Murray Gell-Mann's study of elemental particles and the computational development of quantum physics closely preceded the publication, in 1963, of Edward Lorenz's text on non-periodic flows. The document had a decisive influence on chaos theory as well as on James Forrester's 1969 definition of "dynamic systems", whose application to the changeable understanding of nature was put forward by Benoît Mandelbrot in his studies of irregular geometries.

In resonance with these technical and scientific developments, the 1960s anticipated "liquid" conceptions of reality through theories such as Lacan's works on ego and desire, Foucault's structures of power or Deleuze's conceptual folds. While the moon landing in 1969 evoked developmental optimism and the Situationists maps conjured up imaginative indiscipline, the crises post May 68 and the birth of environmental consciousness originated a twofold socio-political attitude: on the one side, a profound desire for transformation, and on the other side, a deep mistrust in the established system.

V

As some attentive observers have probably already sensed, the individual and global relevance of those contributions began to anticipate a new operational logic, opposing both the Prometeic "objectuality" of Modernity and the anti-heroic calligraphy of Post-Modernity. It is constituted as an informed and informational systematic of thinking particularly sensitive to complexity; permeable and impure, symbiotic, perverted, derived from a "multiple" and "multi-layered" perception that by no means can be essentialized through figurative gesticulations.

A logic based on diverse stimuli in mutual interaction, supported by "irregular" processes of change and exchange; interested in multitudes rather than in identities, in experimentation rather than in representation, in miscegenation rather than in domestication, in cartographies rather than in classifications, in plurification rather than in purification. It unfolds a spatial approach that replaces "relative positions" with "interactive dispositions"; a form of action favouring an approach to reality that is operative instead of pragmatic, immersed instead of transcendental. It incorporates unheard-of expressions that are transgressive and paradoxical, hybrid frameworks where the natural implies the synthetic, where the virtual overlaps the physical, where the systematic celebrates the exceptional.

Privileging the emergence of symbiotic pluralities over the design of refined identities reveals an architectural shift from static and figurative gestures towards effervescent and interactive frameworks. The consolidation of this turn has left its trace on the past three decades: its explorations, anticipations, falterings and transitions constitute a breeding ground for action shared by different avenues of investigation and, in particular, by the experimental architecture of the last decades.

The following book is dedicated to this collective adventure.

JORDI VIVALDI - MANUEL GAUSA

INTRODUCTION
Conformative, Distributive, Expansive

I– "ADVANCED" AS A KEYWORD

The *Metapolis Dictionary of Advanced Architecture*, published in 2003, was likely one of the first publications to use the term "advanced". It described the emergence of a new conceptual and conceptive logic[1] that differs both from modern paradigms and from their subsequent postmodern revisions. The definition of the expression "Advanced Architecture" was included in one of the dictionary's first entries, in an initial manifesto:[2]

1– "Advanced architecture" (or urbanism) is to the digital or informational society what modern architecture was to the industrial society: an architecture bound up with interchange, interaction and information; with the capacity for displacement, adaptation and modification; with the dynamic evolution of processes and their associated spatial definition

2– "Advanced architecture" (or urbanism) is an architecture with a humanist bent, made by and for humankind. It is also positivist, with faith in the progress capacity to introduce positive energy into an environment qualified by the optimisation of those instruments, means and technologies developed in the conditions of our informational time.

3– "Advanced architecture" (or urbanism) opts for a state of qualitative change produce through an effective combination of heterogeneous data records, flows and bits of information. In an increasing complex reality, it seeks to work with that complexity: not to limit its effects but rather to multiply its potentials

4– "Advanced architecture" (or urbanism) accepts a greater degree of adaptation, flexibility and mixedness in its responsive actions. Creating more plural – and complex– scenarios in which to combine interaction, innovation and information (...)"

The adoption of the term "advanced" is clearly intentional and has a very specific purpose. Advanced[3] should be understood in the sense of being moved, set forward or in the front. It may also be innovative. To advance is, in fact, to move forward along a course or towards a terminus or goal; but also further a cause or provide ahead of time. To thrust – or project – forward.

_1. The term "logic" does not refer here to the discipline that studies the formal structure of the reasonments, that is, if the conclusion follows from the premises. Instead, the term is used in order to allude to a systematic of thinking, a structured set of principles that guides the development of a practice.
_2. Gausa, Manuel, Vicente Guallart, José Morales, Willy Müller, Fernando Porras, Federico Soriano. *Diccionario Metápolis de la Arquitectura Avanzada* (Barcelona: Actar, 2001), 34.
_3. Ibid. 36.

The term "advanced" is thus not used in the sense of leaving "behind" other architectural narratives under a supposed progressive development of the discipline. Instead, it is conjured up in order to label an architecture which is necessarily projective, that is, propositional and anticipatory. Advanced architecture is experimental architecture, that is, an architecture that aims to resonate with ongoing technological change (industry and technology), with ongoing critical culture (thinking and creation), with ongoing scientific developments (research and exchange) and with ongoing social and ambient interaction (inclusivity and environment).

This desire for a reverberation that is both transdisciplinary and contemporary singularizes advanced architecture and defines its experimental character associated with information, interaction and integration. Precisely for this reason, this research has favoured the identification and treatment of ongoing extra-disciplinary intertwinings over historical endo-disciplinary discussions. Although the latter are by no means minor, the former are particularly relevant in this context; they specify the vocation of advanced architecture and inscribe its speculative character: experimental architecture develops knowledge through transdisciplinary synthesis, assuming the specificity of architecture as the production of spaces within spaces – interiorities – either in the physical or psychological sense.

However, the experimental nature of advanced architecture frequently implies the lack of consolidated built references on a large scale; its constant dialogue with ongoing extra-disciplinary contributions implies, in some cases, the presence of a production that is quick, partial and volatile, closer to the effervescence of the installation or the performance than to the solidity and scale characteristic of that architecture which remains outside the experimental realm. Pavilions, prototypes, apps, houses, wearables or light structures are some of the formats that, together with a number of built constructions on a medium or large scale, are used by advanced architecture in order to orient and respond to its *zeitgeist*.

In recent decades, advanced architecture's logic has been characterised by combining a set of attributes: (1) an Informational Structure (Complexity); (2), an Interactive Framework (Responsivity); (3) an Integrative Vocation (Simultaneity); (4) a Transversal Approach (Multiplicity); (5) an Evolutionary Development (Dynamicity); (6) an Open Order (Flexibility) and (7) a Heterogeneous Condition (Diversity).

Some of these attributes could be identified – with different degrees of intensity – in projects that were part of the cultural landscape of the 1960s and 1970s. Cedric Price's "Fun Palace" (1961) or "The Generator" (1976) anticipate some 21st-century attitudes in their disassemblable, reconfigurable, and smart environments. There are other similar cases, including Arata Isozaki's project for the "Osaka Expo" (1970), with its central computer, or the first software experiments in the 1970s designed by Nicholas Negroponte. Works by Archigram, Superstudio or the Japanese Metabolists would produce and advanced architecture "avantlettre" that shares many of the traits that today vertebrate this practice. Even someone with such intimate ties to the more orthodox Modern Movement like Le Corbusier authors, along with Iannis Xenakis, the "Phillips Pavilion" (1958), well-known in virtue of its acoustic-environmental interaction and proto-parametric design.

However, in spite of these precedents, this research starts at the beginning of the 1990s. As we will see in the following pages, the beginnings of this decade witnesses some of the most relevant technological and socio-cultural transformations of the last century, marking a turning point in the development and consolidation of experimental architecture.

2- CHANGES OF LOGICS, CHANGES OF PARADIGMS

During the past 30 years, the field of experimental architecture has resonated with an amalgam of cultural, political and scientific-technological initiatives. However, the socio-cultural intensity and the technological contributions characteristic of the early 90s is pivotal; its presence underpins a series of creative, intellectual and instrumental clusters that define the turn-of-the-century culture. Certain events are particularly representative.

On 8 December 1991, a call from General Stanislav Shushkievich informed the then-president of the USSR, Mikhail Gorbachev, of the signing of the Belavezha Accords. The dissolution of the Soviet Union was made official internationally, and a few days later Gorbachev publicly announced his resignation and the irrevocable breakup of the USSR.

Two years before, the fall of the Berlin Wall marked the end of the Iron Curtain. The Cold War was over and the reunification of Germany took place during the following year. The event had a global value of peace, unity and fraternity that is still evoked under similar circumstances.

In 1990, Apartheid was officially dismantled in a series of negotiations that culminated in the country's 1994 general election, the first in South Africa held with universal suffrage.

The same year, the military tech project Arpanet was brought to a close, leading to the emergence of what we now know as the Internet. A few months later, in December 1990, the first web browser called the WorldWideWeb (WWW) was built, and for the first time the network was opened to everyday users not affiliated with the military or academia.

The same year also saw the widespread popularization of the Windows operating system. Its windows-based processes, tested in 1985 and 1987, experienced broad commercial success for the first time, definitively consolidating the presence of personal computers in Western households.

Also that same year, the Hubble telescope was put into orbit through a joint project between NASA and the ESA; human's ability to explore the confines of the universe was radically expanded. Within just a few months, fundamental assertions – such as the age of the universe, the existence of black holes or the acceleration of cosmos' expansion – were called into question.

Two years later, in mid-1992, the Earth Summit took place in Rio de Janeiro; the expression "sustainable development", coined just five years earlier, became a fundamental concept and was the focal point of the program Agenda 21: a detailed list of global guidelines agreed upon by 179 governments. It underpinned a series of policies with a marked planetary reach that would be developed thereafter.

All these events were not contingent singularities, but the culmination of well-defined socio-cultural trajectories rooted in the 20th century. In the 1950s, the images projected onto movie screens were multiplied across hundreds of thousands of televisions in homes all over the Western world, anticipating the later democratization of computers and the popularization of the Internet. In addition, the computational development of quantum physics, chaos theory and the system dynamics proposed by Jay Wright Forrester underpinned the complex environments of the 1990s. The foundation of the Club of Rome marked the beginning of the environmental concerns that culminated in the Earth Summit of 1992, and later in the Kyoto protocols that entered into force in 2005.

Something similar happened with the discovery of the structure of DNA filaments in 1961, with an echo in the foundation of the "Genome Project" in the 1990s, which completed the sequencing of the human genome in 2006. Finally, Foucault's structures, Derrida's deconstruction, Situationists' cartographies and Deleuze's folds made a decisive contribution, in the 1970s and 80s, along with May '68, to the rise of multiculturalism and alternative media characteristic of the end of the 20th century.

In that sense, the technological, intellectual, political and socio-cultural scenario that was consolidated at the beginning of the 1990s could not have been more conducive to the development and propagation of the relational and operational logic that will vertebrate advanced architecture. The end of the Cold War, the creation of the European Union, the end of Apartheid, the popularization of the Internet, the generalization of personal computers, the rise of mobile devices, the proliferation of environmental agreements on a planetary scale, the explosion of digital art or the expansion of globalization promoted a renewed condition that will certainly reverberate in the experimental architecture of the turn-of-the-century.

Nevertheless; what would all this mean in the field of experimental architecture? And, above all, to what extent did this architecture constitute a renewed cultural approach and not just the umpteenth epigone of the Modern Movement?

3- BEYOND POSTMODERNISM AND DECONSTRUCTIVISM

While the failure of the modern epic was being affirmed by critics such as Colin Rowe or Aldo Rossi, both Postmodernism and Deconstructivism proclaimed themselves as alternatives. However, their development did not result in the innovative cultural movement that had been presaged by their defenders: whereas Postmodernism evolved rapidly from a critical and transgressive movement into a complacent and historicist discourse, Deconstructivist's evocative imaginary was quickly exhausted in a lyrical but sterile formal repertoire.

Legitimated by models derived from memory, history or language, Postmodernism encouraged a revisionist and critical reading of the Modern Movement. In its colourful architectural register, Post-modern compositional evocativeness, called on to "sweeten" the crudity of modern abstractions, emerged as a palliative measure aiming at being corrective and liberating at the same time. However, in a conservative political context promoted by figures such as Thatcher and Reagan, the postmodern lyric was soon transformed into a new corporate style. Its formal language resulted in a design method combining standardized functional production with a singularized iconic design; celebrating historicist imaginary and local contextualism, minimizing the power of technology while quashing any desire for innovation. Whereas the Modern Movement flourished during the economic push for social-democratic development of the post-war period, Postmodernism matured in the neoliberal economic boom of the early 1980s, dissolving a few years later in the waters of its self-imposed calligraphic monotony.[4]

Setting itself apart from the ironic but repetitive images of Postmodernism, Deconstructivism delved into a lyrical formal repertoire which was no less evocative and metaphorical than Postmodernism's gesticulations. In resonance with the Modern Movement, deconstructivism preserved its fascination with abstract forms, eluding any literal reference to history or tradition. It also rekindled a technological imagery: materials such as steel,

_4. Mary McLeod, "Architecture and Politics in the Reagan Era: From Postmodernism to Deconstructivism," in *Architecture Theory since 1968*, ed. Michael Hays, (New York: Columbia Books of Architecture, 2000), 696.

glass and corrugated metal provided progressive aesthetics to its constructions, together with a controversial and polemical rhetoric. However, like Postmodernism, Deconstructivism rejected some of the main premises of the Modern Movement; its agenda did not include functionalism, structural rationalism or, most notably, any profound faith in a promising social future. One of the main causes of this phenomena consisted in its lyric approach to technology; rather than reading it as an operative tool to transform society, deconstructivism conjugated technology as an allegory, as a representation alluding to a cutting edge and apocalyptic future. Under this umbrella, the role of the architect acquired a new dimension; while this figure was exalted by the Modern Movement as a Promethean leader and celebrated by Postmodernism as a glamorous "vedette de salon", Deconstructivism followed in the footsteps of Foucault and Barthes's famous pronouncements on the "death of the author", condemning the notions of intentionality, originality and truth, with no less linguistic ostentation. In spite of this apparent rejection of authorship, there was a subversive, semantically alternative, tendency in Deconstructivism. However, it was undermined by a contradiction with its pursuit of institutional, financial and elitist cultural recognition. Paradoxically, the rhetoric of the death of the author did not seem to detract one bit from the practices of personal promotion and self-affirmation that were both highly criticized and all too common in the most historicist vein of Postmodernism.[5]

Both turn-of-the-century movements accurately detected the weaknesses of the Modern Movement; its instrumental use of extreme rationality, the simplicity of its teleology and its blind faith in technological progress were called into question. However, neither Postmodernism nor Deconstructivism committed to upholding strong social concerns; both accepted the fundamentally formal value of their proposals, independent of the economic and social processes within which they would be implemented. Historical or deconstructive postmodern architecture did not reach beyond the pure play of forms, whether through the cult of image or the celebration of surface. Its content became a rapidly consumable product because it advocated for total independence from other dimensions of architecture, such as program, structure, technique, production or financing. Oblivious to the question of an alternative ideological stance, fundamental social issues such as equity, ecology, gender, poverty or technology were also ignored on an operative level. In this isolation, both movements lost out on vital tools for transcending the borders of academic audiences and causing a broader impact on society.

Although what we have previously defined as Advanced Architecture might possess similar features to those described above, it differs profoundly in its conceptual approach. Far from an exercise of introspection, its vocation is open and relational, rooted in a transdisciplinary framework. It shares with postmodern thought a special attention to openness and diversity, but not as an additive and relativistic complexity conjugated through collage or composition. Its desire for complexity has an integral and integrative – compressive – intent, derived from an order that is at once open, oriented and processual. It is dynamic and extroverted, heterogeneous in its content and flexible enough to integrate contributions from other disciplines such as biology, computer science or sociology. It coincides with deconstructivist thought – and even with the Modern Movement – in a profound fascination with the possibilities derived from technology's imaginary. However the meaning and use given to those possibilities is radically different in each case.

_5. Ibid, 698.

On the one hand, the Modern Movement apparently venerated technology because of its capacity for serial production. Its consequent cost reduction was essential in spreading production to all corners of the world, thus fulfilling an implicit desire for universality. However, a great part of this idealisation was due to machines' symbolic capacity to evoke progress; as it was later criticized by Reyner Banham and in opposition to the work of Buckminster Fuller, modern architecture was subordinated to the Filebo's volumes characteristic of early 20th-century cars and ships, replicating its formal representation but not its operative presentation.[6]

On the other hand, Deconstructivism replaced machines with mechanics: technology was not instrumentalized in order to attend to social demands, but rather to mechanically resolve the extreme forms demanded by Deconstructivism's apocalyptic gestuality.

In Advanced Architecture's logic technology is not meant to evoke human progress or to sustain daring volumes. Instead, the carnal technologies consolidated in the last decades are orchestrated for another purpose: the multiplication, intensification and plurification of interactivity. However, this term shouldn't be reduced to human interactivity; it also encompasses a wide variety of species, including biological, ecological, algorithmic, robotic and geological beings. Under this umbrella, technology is no longer read as a mechanical artefact, but as a fluid device that is both recombinatory and ambivalent.

4– SHIFTING CONDITIONS, SHIFTING PERSPECTIVES

While Postmodernism and Deconstructivism were exhausting their formal repertoire in an attempt to consolidate an alternative to Modernism's failure, the aforementioned events that took place in the 1990s were suggesting the possibility of another operative logic of action. The objectual, dividing, mechanical and cumulative aims of Modernity were left behind in order to embrace a holistic praxis; a form of action aiming at producing intimate relations between strangers, that is, capable of integrating dissimilar agents through a multiple and overlapping approach to reality: plural, interactive and open, comfortable with the temporary and the unstable, and above all, capable of accepting the hyper-specificity of the information age without losing the ability to orient itself within the uncertainty characteristic of open systems. These processes, brilliantly anticipated by Lyotard's exhibition "Les Immatériaux" (1985), refer back to the increasingly diverse, dynamic and ultimately "impure" condition of our context, a condition that we might qualify as more "informal" precisely because of being more "informational", more sensitive to the capacity for interaction in between species, agents, conditions and events.

This change of condition implies a change of perspective; from an unambiguous, analytical, segmented and partitioned view, accustomed to classify the world into closed-off categories, we have moved - we are moving - towards a synthesizing approach, called on to tune into and vectorize various stimuli, messages, species, agents and requests. This also implies decisive changes in established social, creative and scientific disciplines, and the field of experimental architecture is not an exception. Under this umbrella, the last 30 years have witnessed the emergence and consolidation of an approach that is called on to replace classical delineating composition and modern objectual position with contemporary interactive disposition. From outlining stable and singular forms in space, most of

_6. Reyner Banham, *Teoría y diseño en la primera era de la máquina* (Barcelona: Paidós, 2015), 321.

the experimental architecture of the last decades aims at formulating transdisciplinary and multispecie processes through a notion of space whose architectural conception has been replaced; rather than being understood as an "a priori receptacle" that is iconic, figurative and episodic, architectural space is now approached by experimental practices as an "active environment" that is recombinatory, processual and performative.

Contrasting with the habitual and more disciplinary descriptive accounts, the notion of architectural form as a figurative, typological or semantic trace is no longer the foundation for current research. "Form" is understood here as "formation" and as "formulation", as "flexible and topological negotiation", that is, as the result of an open process, impure and variable. In this sense, the "dynamic revolutions" taking place today only confirm the definitive *coup de grâce* for figurative, uni-referential and closed-off readings, for strictly disciplinary linguistic assessments and exemplary principles.

5- TRANSVERSALITIES AND OPEN LOGICS

Throughout these pages, a transdisciplinary reading of recent experimental architecture has been unfolded based not only on chronicles of events and "best" architectural practices, but also on a multi-phased and multi-focal interpretation of the contemporary context. An approach aiming to associate the last years of experimental architecture with the current scientific, socio-cultural, philosophical and artistic conception of space-time. It proposes a theoretical framework – a shared territory – for the multiple and ongoing manifestations of a new informational, conceptual and design action. However, it is not for the purpose of building up a universal corpus for referencing processes, as would be the case of an "inventory", but aiming at critically networking them through a threefold cartography. This approach refers back to similar efforts and experiences intended to connect the local translation of events, that is, their precise materialization, with the global cultural understanding of reality. Indeed, this is a cross-cutting inclination, given its transversal nature, that also permeated a particular "history of criticism", from Veyne to Virilio and from Kübler or Giedion to, at a stretch, Jencks. In the tracing of this complex cartography, the old Newtonian and Einsteinian paradigms have come up against the challenge of a more dynamic and slippery universe, where most processes are extraordinarily undisciplined and ultimately remit to non-linear behaviors derived from their own dynamic nature. Classic Space and Time (Absolute) and modern Space-Time (Relative) have been succeeded by a more dynamic and complex Space-Time-Information (Interactive). It is ultimately more open in its manifestations, and it illustrates the shift from the former (classic) idea of composition and the (modern) idea of position to that of (informational) disposition, constituting thus one of the main premises of this book.

Instrumentalizing this capacity for establishing a "projective and operative link" in between different spheres of knowledge, requires the identification of cross-cutting routes, intimate correspondences and fine-tuned trajectories. It implies making maps for exploration and action; maps that let us move away from the classificatory towards the cartographic,[7] being at the same time documentative and narrative, referring back to the process of exploration, selection and articulation that is implicit in any design process.

Maps understood then not as "representations" but as "re-presentations", that is, not as aseptic registers but as the vectorized reconstructions of an ambivalent and plural

_7. Dolphijn, Rick and Iris van der Tuin, *New Materialism* (Open Humanities Press, 2012), 112.

reality.[8] Many of today's cultural concerns, in fact, tie in with these considerations: from mathematics to biology and from genetics to physics, their impact is directly implicated in the "comprehension" and "compression" of an open order that is more interactive and infrastructural, but also more indeterminate and informal. A systematic of design producing a set of dynamics involving times, spaces and scales that ultimately refer to the notion of milieu; an "environment" that operates as an open, dynamic, multiple and multi-scalar field of forces, opposed to an empty and figurative "receptacle". As such, these dynamics call for a spatial approach constituted as a dispositional agent rather than as a compositional background; it is a dynamic and dynamizing "disposition" capable of "reacting" and "eliciting a reaction" at the same time.

6- TIMEFIELDS

The identification and positioning of this experimental spatial approach resonates with ongoing developments coming from different disciplines. The critical identification of its encounters and disencounters is crucial in order to evaluate the relevance of recent experimental architecture as a cultural construct capable of problematizing our contemporary period. To that effect, this book takes a twofold approach.

On the one hand, it lays out a diachronic interpretation, focusing on the operative variations that have taken place over the last three decades. On the other hand, it presents a synchronic interpretation, revealing its resonances with its cultural, ecological, algorithmic, geological or biological "others". In that vein, this book operates through the identification of a series of multidisciplinary clusters of events linked together by their conformative, distributive or expansive nature. This double demand, diachronic and synchronic, requires the use of a temporal framework that can stretch beyond the limitations inherent in a merely cumulative method; rather than a "time-line", what is needed is a "time-field".

Time's systematisation has frequently aimed at establishing correspondences between its passage and the variation of socio-cultural customs. Traditionally, two time structures have prevailed: time as time-cycle and time as time-line. The former was particularly common in antiquity: the Aztec sun stone, the Buddhist cycle of Samsära and the ancient Greek Orphism are just some examples of this recursive temporal structure. But in the West, and especially since the advent of Christianity, the seriality of the latter has been cemented as the main means of historical reading, vastly transcending its religious original framework; it was actually the incipient atheism of 19th-century positivism which, through figures such as Hegel, Marx, Darwin or Morgan, led to the apogee of this linear approach. However, in the 20th century the linear structuring of time lost some of its sway. Authors like Ilya Prigogine, Manuel De Landa, George Kubler or Jean Baudrillard defended – in different ways – an understanding of time that is neither circular nor linear, but topological (time-field). Here, one unbreakable assertion remains in force: the Second Law of Thermodynamics imposes a single direction for time based on the inevitable increase of entropy in the system. However, the fluctuations, turbulences and densifications characteristic of topological states generate situations of indetermination which resemble those of a chaotic system. As opposed to a circular repetition or a linear progress, historical processes are the product of the collective crossing of various critical

_8. *"What we know about the mutation we are carrying out is really little (...). We know with certainty that we are oriented with maps that do not yet exist (...) but until we take the trip we will not be able to know if (the ones we draw here are reliable, precise or useful (to understand the globality of the process) ".* Alessandro Baricco, The Game (Barcelona, Anagrama, 2018), 21.

thresholds. Thus, the three periods presented in this book shouldn't be read as monadic eras separated by Braudelian divisions, but as "intensifications" of multidisciplinary events sharing the same (conformative, distributive or expansive) protocol, that is, mode of action. This approach neither eclipses the singularity of each intensification nor does it imply that historical processes are uniform or random; there are no grounds to posit a single historical atmosphere in which everything moves together in lockstep. Instead, the contribution of this book follows a different path: it aims at vectorizing these historical processes, that is, it aims at reconstructing them from inside through a critical narrative, a cultural excavation progressing hand in hand with the development of advanced architecture. According to the authors previously mentioned and in opposition to linear or circular frameworks, historical processes follow a topological scheme. Under this umbrella, time is understood not as a time-cycle or as a time-line, but as a time-field in which variable and interdisciplinary intertwinings take center stage. And yet, representing events using a non-linear framework does not imply that they are interpreted from a position of relativism; on the contrary, the potential of a system based on attractors, flows, currents, densifications, clusters, disturbances, thresholds and thickenings lies precisely in reconciling this relational richness with a critical vectorization of the ensemble. Italo Calvino describes a similar map of pressures when when he writes the following:

"Lovers' reading of each other's bodies (of that concentrate of mind and body which lovers use to go to bed together) differs from the reading of written pages in that it is not linear. It starts at any point, skips, repeats itself, goes backward, insists, ramifies in simultaneous and divergent messages, converges again, has moments of irritation, turns the page, finds its place, gets lost. A direction can be recognized in it, a route to an end, since it tends toward a climax, and with this end in view it arranges rhythmic phases, metrical scansions, recurrence of motives."[9]

Tentacular but directional, open but vectorized, multiple but oriented. The notion of time-field moves away from the classificatory towards the cartographical; precisely because of its simultaneous conjugation of the plural and the intentional, timefields are used in this book in order to approach the following key question: How have the specific attributes of experimental architecture evolved in relation to the socio-cultural and scientific-technological development characteristic of the turn of the century?

7. CONFORMATIVE, DISTRIBUTIVE, EXPANSIVE

This book argues that over the past 30 years, experimental architecture has been intertwined with its contemporary cultural landscape through three protocols: conformative protocols (C), distributive protocols (D), and expansive protocols (E). The term "protocol" refers to a mode of action; it is an apparatus of organization, a decentralized means via which to guide the formation of artistic, technological and socio-political constructs. It is thus a vigorous directional force within an open system, a projective set of translocal operations that "can evolve to suit specific contexts, whilst retaining sufficient determining characteristics to remain more or less recognizably itself"[10]. Although all three protocols share the same open and interactive vocation, each one combines those principles in a different way, resonating with the lines of research more accentuated by each decade. Although we may make out examples of all three protocols at any point

_9. Italo Calvino, *If on a Winter's Night a Traveller* (London: Harcourt Brace International, 1998), 56.
_10. Helen Hester, *Xenofeminism* (Cambridge: Polity Press, 2018), 112.

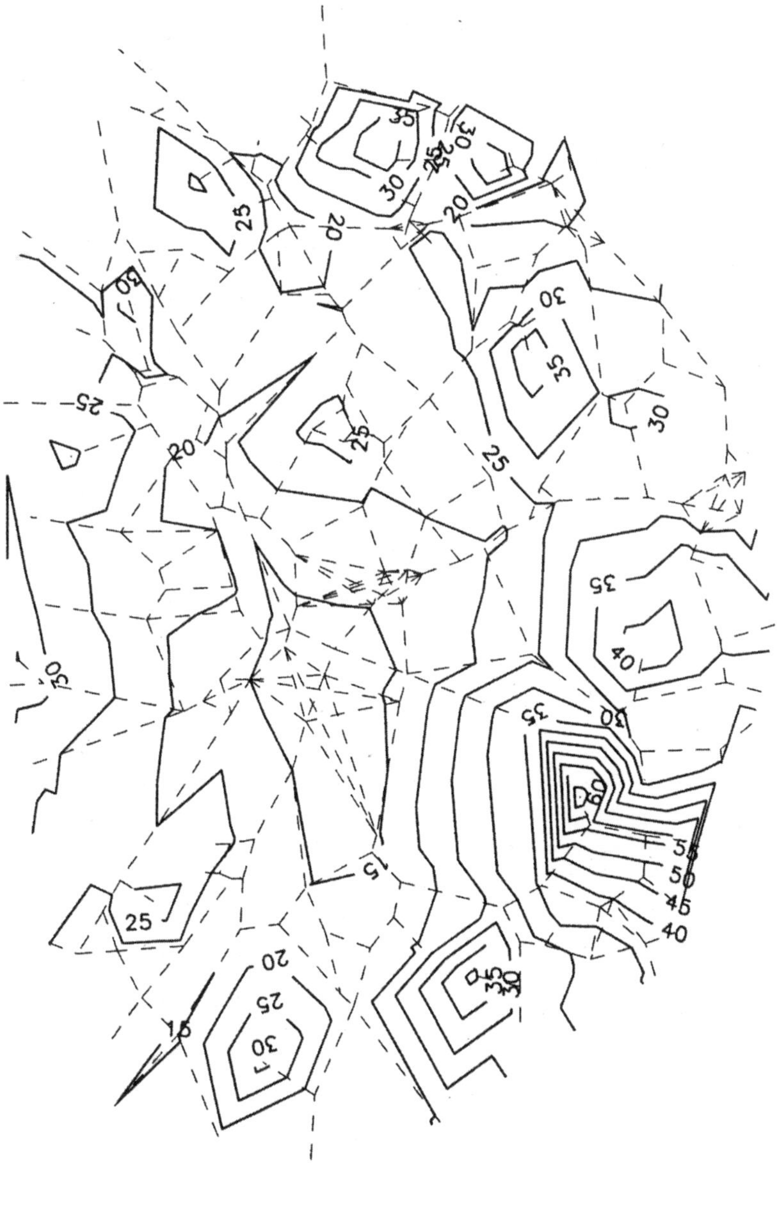

Map of dynamic settlements in Africa; Sybille Becker, *Arch +*, 1994.

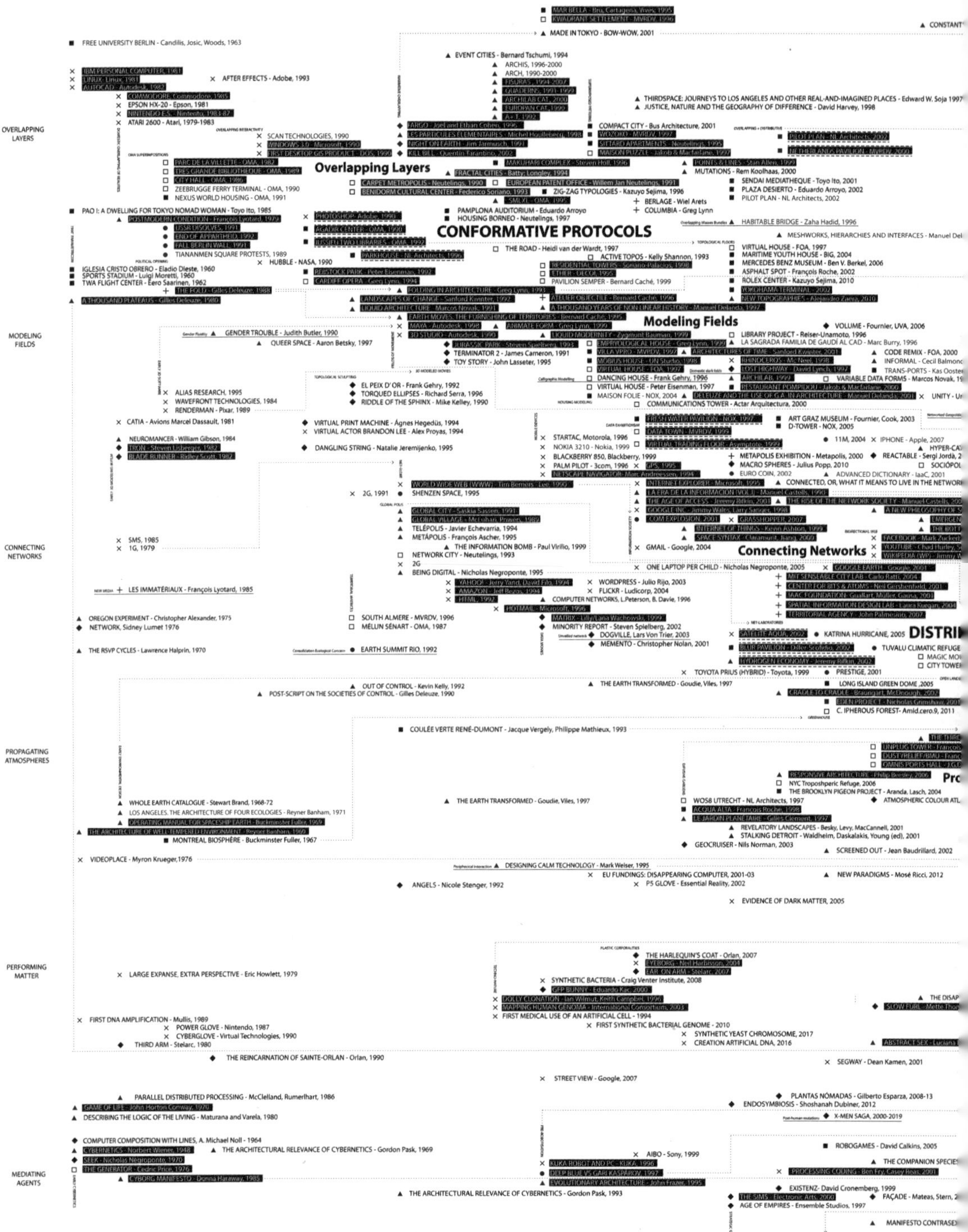

CENTRAL ITEMS
TRANSITIONAL ITEMS
- ■ BUILT BUILDINGS
- □ NON-BUILT BUILDINGS
- ▲ PUBLICATIONS
- + EXHIBITIONS & SCHOOLS
- ◆ ART
- × TECHNOLOGY & SCIENCE
- ● SOCIOPOLITICS

Moving from the classificatory towards the cartographical, this timefield operates as a narrative map of pressures and *décalages*; it circumvents the desire for exhaustivity, universality and consensus characteristic of modern taxonomies by critically imbricating a limited and multidisciplinary number of items whose presence underpins the threefold narrative proposed by this book. Thus, this map is ideological: instead of taking inventory of a raw litany of facts by instrumentalizing time in the additive register of *Kronos* and his filicide voracity, it critically positions a set of events into an irregular but oriented temporal regime. The latter's tentacular consistency is traversed by all sorts of currents, densifications, ramifications, disturbances, thresholds, swirls, traces and thickenings; the minute register of their vectorisation by the conformative, distributive and expansive logics associated here with the advanced architecture of the last 30 years constitutes the leitmotiv of this cartographical endeavour.

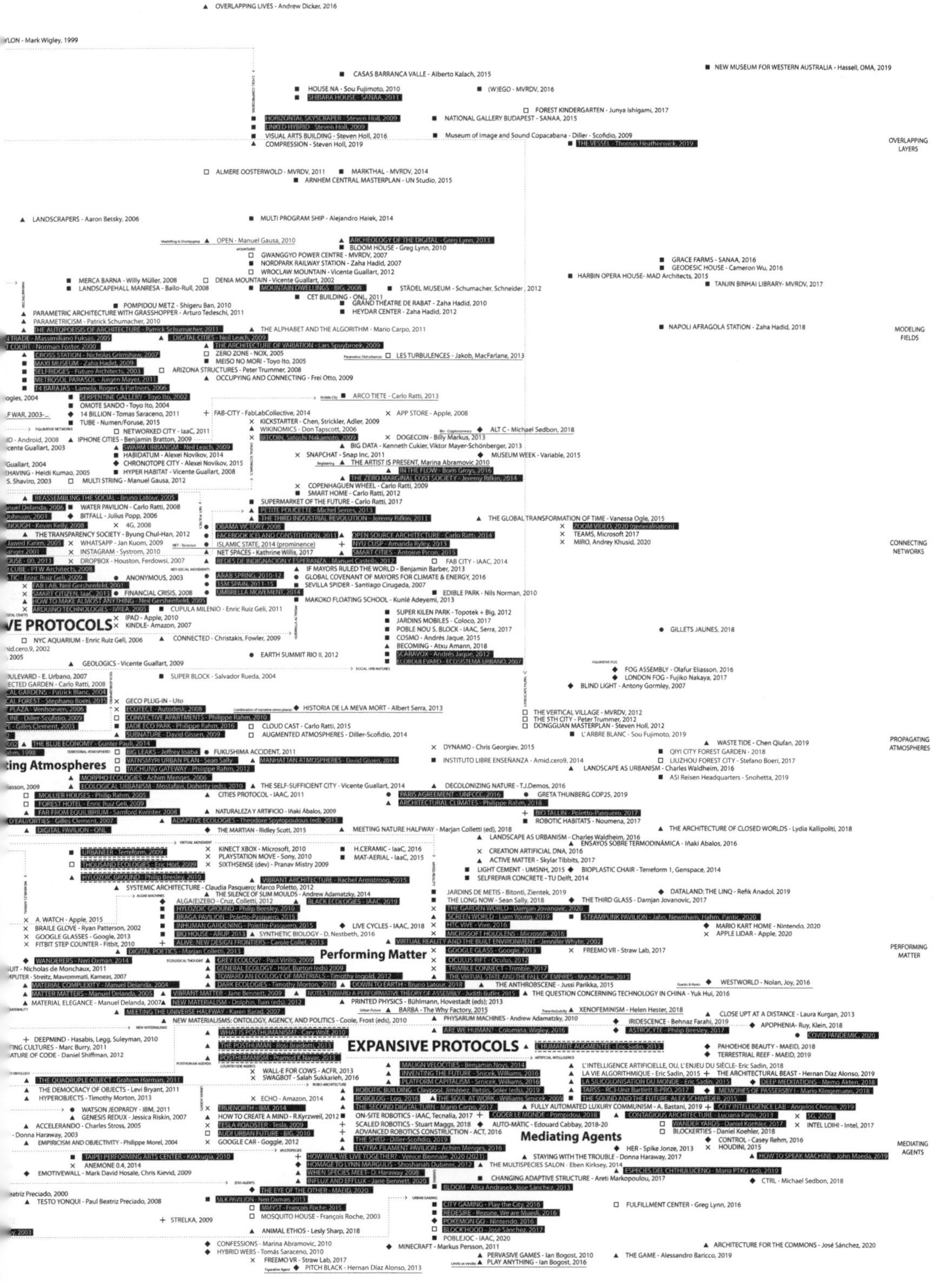
OVERLAPPING LIVES - Andrew Dicker, 2016
CASAS BARRANCA VALLE - Alberto Kalach, 2015
NEW MUSEUM FOR WESTERN AUSTRALIA - Hassell, OMA, 2019
HOUSE NA - Sou Fujimoto, 2010
(W)EGO - MVRDV, 2016
SHIBARA HOUSE - SANAA, 2011
FOREST KINDERGARTEN - Junya Ishigami, 2017
HORIZONTAL SKYSCRAPER - Steven Holl, 2009
NATIONAL GALLERY BUDAPEST - SANAA, 2015
LINKED HYBRID - Steven Holl, 2009
VISUAL ARTS BUILDING - Steven Holl, 2016
Museum of Image and Sound Copacabana - Diller - Scofidio, 2009
COMPRESSION - Steven Holl, 2019
THE VESSEL - Thomas Heatherwick, 2019
OVERLAPPING LAYERS
ALMERE OOSTERWOLD - MVRDV, 2011
MARKTHAL - MVRDV, 2014
ARNHEM CENTRAL MASTERPLAN - UN Studio, 2015
LANDSCRAPERS - Aaron Betsky, 2006
MULTI PROGRAM SHIP - Alejandro Haiek, 2014
OPEN - Manuel Gausa, 2010
ARCHEOLOGY OF THE DIGITAL - Greg Lynn, 2013
BLOOM HOUSE - Greg Lynn, 2010
GWANGGYO POWER CENTRE - MVRDV, 2007
NORDPARK RAILWAY STATION - Zaha Hadid, 2007
WROCLAW MOUNTAIN - Vicente Guallart, 2012
GRACE FARMS - SANAA, 2016
GEODESIC HOUSE - Cameron Wu, 2016
HARBIN OPERA HOUSE - MAD Architects, 2015
TANJIN BINHAI LIBRARY - MVRDV, 2017
MERCA BARNA - Willy Müller, 2008
DENIA MOUNTAIN - Vicente Guallart, 2002
LANDSCAPEHALL MANRESA - Ballo-Rull, 2008
MOUNTAIN DWELLINGS - BIG, 2008
STÄDEL MUSEUM - Schumacher, Schneider, 2012
CET BUILDING - ONL, 2011
POMPIDOU METZ - Shigeru Ban, 2010
GRAND THEATRE DE RABAT - Zaha Hadid, 2010
PARAMETRIC ARCHITECTURE WITH GRASSHOPPER - Arturo Tedeschi, 2011
HEYDAR CENTER - Zaha Hadid, 2012
PARAMETRICISM - Patrick Schumacher, 2010
THE AUTOPOEISIS OF ARCHITECTURE - Patrick Schumacher, 2011
THE ALPHABET AND THE ALGORITHM - Mario Carpo, 2011
NAPOLI AFRAGOLA STATION - Zaha Hadid, 2018
MODELING FIELDS
TRADE - Massimiliano Fuksas, 2005
DIGITAL CITIES - Neil Leach, 2009
COURT - Norman Foster, 2000
THE ARCHITECTURE OF VARIATION - Lars Spuybroek, 2009
CROSS STATION - Nicholas Grimshaw, 2007
ZERO ZONE - NOX, 2005
LES TURBULENCES - Jakob, MacFarlane, 2013
MAXI MUSEUM - Zaha Hadid, 2009
MEISO NO MORI - Toyo Ito, 2005
SELFRIDGES - Future Architects, 2003
ARIZONA STRUCTURES - Peter Trummer, 2008
METROSOL PARASOL - Jurgen Mayer, 2011
OCCUPYING AND CONNECTING - Frei Otto, 2009
T4 BARAJAS - Lamela, Rogers & Partners, 2006
SERPENTINE GALLERY - Toyo Ito, 2002
ARCO TIETE - Carlo Ratti, 2013
OMOTE SANDO - Toyo Ito, 2004
14 BILLION - Tomas Saraceno, 2011
FAB-CITY - FabLabCollective, 2014
APP STORE - Apple, 2008
TUBE - Numen/Foruse, 2015
KICKSTARTER - Chen, Strickler, Adler, 2009
NETWORKED CITY - IaaC, 2011
WIKINOMICS - Don Tapscott, 2006
ALT C - Michael Sedbon, 2018
IPHONE CITIES - Benjamin Bratton, 2009
BITCOIN - Satoshi Nakamoto, 2009
DOGECOIN - Billy Markus, 2013
SWARM URBANISM - Neil Leach, 2009
BIG DATA - Kenneth Cukier, Viktor Mayer-Schönberger, 2013
HABIDATUM - Alexei Novikov, 2014
SNAPCHAT - Snap Inc, 2011
MUSEUM WEEK - Variable, 2015
CHRONOTOPE CITY - Alexei Novikov, 2015
THE ARTIST IS PRESENT, Marina Abramovic 2010
HYPER HABITAT - Vicente Guallart, 2008
IN THE FLOW - Boris Groys, 2016
MULTI STRING - Manuel Gausa, 2012
THE ZERO MARGINAL COST SOCIETY - Jeremy Rifkin, 2014
COPENHAGUEN WHEEL - Carlo Ratti, 2009
SMART HOME - Carlo Ratti, 2012
REASSEMBLING THE SOCIAL - Bruno Latour, 2005
SUPERMARKET OF THE FUTURE - Carlo Ratti, 2017
WATER PAVILION - Carlo Ratti, 2008
PETITE POUCETTE - Michel Serres, 2013
BITFALL - Julius Popp, 2006
THE THIRD INDUSTRIAL REVOLUTION - Jeremy Rifkin, 2011
THE GLOBAL TRANSFORMATION OF TIME - Vanessa Ogle, 2015
4G, 2008
OBAMA VICTORY, 2008
ZOOM VIDEO, 2020 (generalisation)
THE TRANSPARENCY SOCIETY - Byung Chul-Han, 2012
FACEBOOK ICELAND CONSTITUTION, 2011
OPEN SOURCE ARCHITECTURE - Carlo Ratti, 2014
TEAMS, Microsoft 2017
WHATSAPP - Jan Kuom, 2009
ISLAMIC STATE, 2014 (prominence)
NYU CUSP - Amanda Ryley, 2013
MIRO, Andrey Khusid, 2020
INSTAGRAM - Systrom, 2010
NET SPACES - Kathrine Willis, 2017
SMART CITIES - Antoine Picon, 2015
CONNECTING NETWORKS
DROPBOX - Houston, Ferdowsi, 2007
REDES DE INDIGNACION Y ESPERANZA - Manuel Castells, 2012
FAB CITY - IAAC, 2014
ANONYMOUS, 2003
ARAB SPRING, 2010-12
IF MAYORS RULED THE WORLD - Benjamin Barber, 2013
15M SPAIN, 2011-15
GLOBAL COVENANT OF MAYORS FOR CLIMATE & ENERGY, 2016
FAB LAB, Neil Gershenfeld, 2001
SEVILLA SPIDER - Santiago Cirugeda, 2007
SMART CITIZEN, IaaC, 2013
FINANCIAL CRISIS, 2008
UMBRELLA MOVEMENT, 2014
EDIBLE PARK - Nils Norman, 2010
HOW TO MAKE ALMOST ANYTHING - Neil Gershenfeld, 2005
MAKOKO FLOATING SCHOOL - Kunlé Adeyemi, 2013
ARDUINO TECHNOLOGIES - IVREA, 2005
CUPULA MILENIO - Enric Ruiz Geli, 2011
SUPER KILEN PARK - Topotek + Big, 2012
IPAD - Apple, 2010
JARDINS MOBILES - Coloco, 2017
VE PROTOCOLS
KINDLE - Amazon, 2007
POBLE NOU S. BLOCK - IAAC, Serra, 2017
GILLETS JAUNES, 2018
COSMO - Andrés Jaque, 2015
NYC AQUARIUM - Enric Ruiz Geli, 2006
CONNECTED - Christakis, Fowler, 2009
BECOMING - Atxu Amann, 2018
SCARAVOX - Andrés Jaque, 2012
EARTH SUMMIT RIO II, 2012
ECOBOULEVARD - ECOSISTEMA URBANO, 2007
GEOLOGICS - Vicente Guallart, 2009
FOG ASSEMBLY - Olafur Eliasson, 2016
SUPER BLOCK - Salvador Rueda, 2004
LONDON FOG - Fujiko Nakaya, 2017
BLIND LIGHT - Antony Gormley, 2007
GECO PLUG-IN - Uto
ECOTECT - Autodesk, 2008
HISTORIA DE LA MEVA MORT - Albert Serra, 2013
THE VERTICAL VILLAGE - MVRDV, 2012
CONVECTIVE APARTMENTS - Philippe Rahm, 2010
THE 5TH CITY - Peter Trummer, 2012
JADE ECO PARK - Philippe Rahm, 2016
CLOUD CAST - Carlo Ratti, 2015
DONGGUAN MASTERPLAN - Steven Holl, 2012
SUBNATURE - David Gissen, 2009
AUGMENTED ATMOSPHERES - Diller-Scofidio, 2014
L'ARBRE BLANC - Sou Fujimoto, 2019
THE BLUE ECONOMY - Gunter Pauli, 2014
WASTE TIDE - Chen Qiufan, 2019
PROPAGATING ATMOSPHERES
BIG LEAKS - Jeffrey Inaba
FUKUSHIMA ACCIDENT, 2011
DYNAMO - Chris Georgiev, 2015
QIYI CITY FOREST GARDEN - 2018
VATNSMYRI URBAN PLAN - Sean Sally
MANHATTAN ATMOSPHERES - David Gissen, 2014
INSTITUTO LIBRE ENSEÑANZA - Amid.cero9, 2014
LIUZHOU FOREST CITY - Stefano Boeri, 2017
ting Atmospheres
TAICHUNG GATEWAY - Philippe Rahm, 2012
LANDSCAPE AS URBANISM - Charles Waldheim, 2016
MORPHO ECOLOGIES - Achim Menges, 2006
ASI Reisen Headquarters - Snohetta, 2019
ECOLOGICAL URBANISM - Mostafavi, Doherty (eds), 2010
THE SELF-SUFFICIENT CITY - Vicente Guallart, 2014
DECOLONIZING NATURE - T.J.Demos, 2016
MOLLIER HOUSES - Philip Rahm, 2005
CITIES PROTOCOL - IAAC, 2011
PARIS AGREEMENT - UNFCCC, 2016
GRETA THUNBERG COP25, 2019
FOREST HOTEL - Enric Ruiz Geli, 2009
ARCHITECTURAL CLIMATES - Philippe Rahm, 2018
FAR FROM EQUILIBRIUM - Samford Kwinter, 2008
NATURALEZA Y ARTIFICIO - Iñaki Ábalos, 2009
BIO TALLIN - Poletto-Pasquero, 2017
D'EAU/ORTIES - Gilles Clement, 2007
ADAPTIVE ECOLOGIES - Theodore Spyropoulous (ed), 2013
ROBOTIC HABITATS - Noumena, 2017
DIGITAL PAVILION - ONL
THE MARTIAN - Ridley Scott, 2015
MEETING NATURE HALFWAY - Marjan Colletti (ed), 2018
THE ARCHITECTURE OF CLOSED WORLDS - Lydia Kallipoliti, 2018
LANDSCAPE AS URBANISM - Charles Waldheim, 2016
ENSAYOS SOBRE TERMODINÁMICA - Iñaki Ábalos, 2016
URBANEER - Terreform, 2009
KINECT XBOX - Microsoft, 2010
H.CERAMIC - IaaC, 2016
CREATION ARTIFICIAL DNA, 2016
PLAYSTATION MOVE - Sony, 2010
MAT-AERIAL - IaaC, 2015
ACTIVE MATTER - Skylar Tibbits, 2017
THOUSAND ECOLOGIES - Eric Hörl, 2009
SIXTHSENSE (dev) - Pranav Mistry 2009
LIGHT CEMENT - UMSNH, 2015
BIOPLASTIC CHAIR - Terreform 1, Genspace, 2014
SELFREPAIR CONCRETE - TU Delft, 2014
HYLOZOIC GROUND - Philip Beesley, 2010
VIBRANT ARCHITECTURE - Rachel Armstrong, 2015
SYSTEMIC ARCHITECTURE - Claudia Pasquero; Marco Poletto, 2012
THE SILENCE OF SLIM MOULDS - Andrew Adamatzky, 2014
JARDINS DE METIS - Bitonti, Zientek, 2019
DATALAND: THE LINQ - Refik Anadol, 2019
ALGA(E)ZEBO - Cruz, Colletti, 2012
BLACK ECOLOGIES - IAAC, 2019
THE LONG NOW - Sean Sally, 2018
THE THIRD GLASS - Damjan Jovanovic, 2017
HYLOZOIC GROUND - Philip Beesley, 2010
THE GARDEN WORLD - Damjan Jovanovic, 2020
BRAGA PAVILION - Poletto-Pasquero, 2015
SCREEN WORLD - Liam Young, 2019
STEAMPUNK PAVILION - Jahn, Newnham, Hahm, Pantic, 2020
A. WATCH - Apple, 2015
INHUMAN GARDENING - Poletto-Pasquero, 2015
LIVE CYCLES - IAAC, 2018
HTC VIVE - Vive, 2016
MARIO KART HOME - Nintendo, 2020
BRAILE GLOVE - Ryan Patterson, 2002
BIO HOUSE - ARUP, 2013
SYNTHETIC BIOLOGY - D. Nestbeth, 2016
MICROSOFT HOLOLENS - Microsoft, 2016
APPLE LIDAR - Apple, 2020
GOOGLE GLASSES - Google, 2013
ALIVE: NEW DESIGN FRONTIERS - Carole Collet, 2013
VIRTUAL REALITY AND THE BUILT ENVIRONMENT - Jennifer Whyte, 2002
FITBIT STEP COUNTER - Fitbit, 2010
DIGITAL POETICS - Marjan Colletti, 2013
Performing Matter
GOOGLE GLASS - Google, 2013
FREEMO VR - Straw Lab, 2017
PERFORMING MATTER
WANDERERS - Neri Oxman, 2014
GREY ECOLOGY - Paul Virilio, 2009
OCULUS RIFT - Oculus, 2012
UIT - Nicholas de Monchaux, 2011
GENERAL ECOLOGY - Hörl, Burton (eds) 2009
TRIMBLE CONNECT - Trimble, 2017
PUTER - Streitz, Mavrommati, Kameas, 2007
TOWARD AN ECOLOGY OF MATERIALS - Timothy Ingold, 2012
THE VIRTUAL STATE AND THE FALL OF EMPIRES - Mychilo Cline, 2013
MATERIAL COMPLEXITY - Manuel Delanda, 2004
DARK ECOLOGIES - Timothy Morton, 2016
DOWN TO EARTH - Bruno Latour, 2018
THE ANTHROBSCENE - Jussi Parikka, 2015
WESTWORLD - Nolan, Joy, 2016
MATTER MATTERS - Manuel Delanda, 2005
VIBRANT MATTER - Jane Bennett, 2009
NOTES TOWARD A PERFORMATIVE THEORY OF ASSEMBLY - Judith Butler, 2015
THE QUESTION CONCERNING TECHNOLOGY IN CHINA - Yuk Hui, 2016
MATERIAL ELEGANCE - Manuel Delanda, 2007
NEW MATERIALISM - Dolphin, Tuin (eds) 2012
PRINTED PHYSICS - Bühlmann, Hovestadt (eds); 2013
MEETING THE UNIVERSE HALFWAY - Karen Barad, 2007
BARBA - The Why Factory, 2015
XENOFEMINISM - Helen Hester, 2018
CLOSE UPT AT A DISTANCE - Laura Kurgan, 2013
NEW MATERIALISMS: ONTOLOGY, AGENCY, AND POLITICS - Coole, Frost (eds), 2010
PHYSARUM MACHINES - Andrew Adamatzky, 2010
IRIDESCENCE - Behnaz Farahi, 2019
APOPHENIA - Ruy, Klein, 2018
WHAT IS POSTHUMANISM? - Cary Wolf, 2010
ARE WE HUMAN? - Colomina, Wigley, 2016
ASTROCYTE - Philip Beesley, 2017
DEEPMIND - Hasabis, Legg, Suleyman, 2010
COVID PANDEMIC, 2020
TING CULTURES - Marc Burry, 2011
THE POSTHUMAN - Rosi Braidotti, 2013
EXPANSIVE PROTOCOLS
L'HUMANITÉ AUGMENTÉE - Eric Sadin, 2013
PAHOEHOE BEAUTY - MAEID, 2018
ATURE OF CODE - Daniel Shiffman, 2012
POSTHUMANISM - Pramod K.Nayar, 2013
TERRESTRIAL REEF - MAEID, 2019
MALIGN VELOCITIES - Benjamin Noys, 2014
L'INTELLIGENCE ARTIFICIELLE, OU, L'ENJEU DU SIÈCLE - Eric Sadin, 2018
WALL-E FOR COWS - ACFR, 2013
INVENTING THE FUTURE - Srnicek, Williams, 2016
LA VIE ALGORITHMIQUE - Eric Sadin, 2015
THE ARCHITECTURAL BEAST - Hernan Díaz Alonso, 2019
SWAGBOT - Salah Sukkarieh, 2016
PLATFORM CAPITALISM - Srnicek, Williams, 2016
LA SILICOLONISATION DU MONDE - Eric Sadin, 2016
DEEP MEDITATIONS - Memo Akten, 2018
THE QUADRUPLE OBJECT - Graham Harman, 2011
ROBOTIC BUILDING - Claypool, Jiménez, Retsin, Soler (eds) 2019
TARSS - RC3 Unit Bartlett B-PRO, 2017
MEMORIES OF PASSERSBY I - Mario Klingemann, 2018
THE DEMOCRACY OF OBJECTS - Levi Bryant, 2011
ROBOLOG - Log, 2016
THE SOUL AT WORK - Williams Srnicek, 2009
THE SOUND AND THE FUTURE - ALEX SCHWEDER, 2015
HYPEROBJECTS - Timothy Morton, 2013
ECHO - Amazon, 2014
THE SECOND DIGITAL TURN - Mario Carpo, 2017
FULLY AUTOMATED LUXURY COMMUNISM - A. Bastani, 2019
CITY INTELLIGENCE LAB - Angelos Chronis, 2019
WATSON JEOPARDY - IBM, 2011
TRUENORTH - IBM, 2014
ON-SITE ROBOTICS - IAAC, Tecnalia, 2017
CODER LE MONDE - Pompidou, 2018
CONTAGIOUS ARCHITECTURE - Luciana Parisi, 2013
5G, 2020
GENESIS REDUX - Jessica Riskin, 2007
HOW TO CREATE A MIND - R.Kyrzweil, 2012
SCALED ROBOTICS - Stuart Maggs, 2018
AUTO-MATIC - Edouard Cabbay, 2018-20
WANDER YARDS - Daniel Koehler, 2017
INTEL LOIHI - Intel, 2017
ACCELERANDO - Charles Stross, 2005
TESLA ROADSTER - Tesla, 2009
ADVANCED ROBOTICS CONSTRUCTION - ACT, 2016
BLOCKERTIES - Daniel Koehler, 2018
Donna Haraway, 2003
AUDI URBAN FUTURE - BIG, 2010
Mediating Agents
CONTROL - Casey Rehm, 2016
EMPIRICISM AND OBJECTIVITY - Philippe Morel, 2004
GOOGLE CAR - Goggle, 2012
THE SHED - Diller-Scofidio, 2019
HER - Spike Jonze, 2013
HOUDINI, 2015
MEDIATING AGENTS
ELYTRA FILAMENT PAVILION - Achim Menges, 2016
TAIPEI PERFORMING ARTS CENTER - Kokkugia, 2010
HOW WILL WE LIVE TOGETHER? - Venice Biennale, 2020 (2021)
STAYING WITH THE TROUBLE - Donna Haraway, 2017
HOW TO SPEAK MACHINE - John Maeda, 2019
ANEMONE 0.4, 2014
HOMAGE TO LYNN MARGULIS - Shoshanah Dubiner, 2012
THE MULTISPECIES SALON - Eben Kirksey, 2014
EMOTIVEWALL - Mark David Hosale, Chris Kievid, 2009
WHEN SPECIES MEET - D. Haraway 2008
ESPECIES DEL CHTHULUCENO - Maria PTKQ (ed), 2019
INFLUX AND EFFLUX - Jane Bennett, 2020
CHANGING ADAPTIVE STRUCTURE - Areti Markopoulou, 2017
CTRL - Michael Sedbon, 2018
THE EYE OF THE OTHER - MAEID, 2020
eatriz Preciado, 2000
BLOOM - Alisa Andrasek, José Sánchez, 2013
TESTO YONQUI - Paul Beatriz Preciado, 2008
SILK PAVILION - Neri Oxman, 2013
MMYST - François Roche, 2015
CITY GAMING - Play the City, 2016
FULFILLMENT CENTER - Greg Lynn, 2016
MOSQUITO HOUSE - François Roche, 2003
REDESIRE - Rezone, We are Muesli, 2016
STRELKA, 2009
POKEMON GO - Nintendo, 2016
ANIMAL ETHOS - Lesly Sharp, 2018
BLOCK'HOOD - José Sánchez, 2017
POBLEJOC - IAAC, 2020
CONFESSIONS - Marina Abramovic, 2010
MINECRAFT - Markus Persson, 2011
ARCHITECTURE FOR THE COMMONS - José Sánchez, 2020
HYBRID WEBS - Tomás Saraceno, 2010
PERVASIVE GAMES - Ian Bogost, 2010
THE GAME - Alessandro Baricco, 2019
FREEMO VR - Straw Lab, 2017
PLAY ANYTHING - Ian Bogost, 2016
PITCH BLACK - Hernan Díaz Alonso, 2013

over the last 30 years, this book argues that the main intensifications of each protocol are strung together, densified and intensified following the order described above.

The notion of protocol is thus stretched by a twofold tension:

On the one hand, each of the three protocols has its own references, tools, and strategies. In this sense they can be considered as autonomous scenarios, universes in themselves.

On the other hand, the three protocols share common attributes and therefore they can be read as derivatives of a larger logic: the open and interactive logic associated with what we have defined here as advanced architecture.

Each protocol conjugates thus advanced architecture's logic in a different way:

1. Informational Structure (Complexity)

C: Information as Parameter
D: Information as Indicator
E: Information as Experience

2. Interactive Framework (Responsivity)

C: Interaction in between Programs
D: Interaction in between Environments
E: Interaction in between Species

3. Integrative Vocation (Simultaneity)

C: Integration through Overlapping & Modelling
D: Integration through Connecting & Propagating
E: Integration through Mediating & Performing

4. Transversal Approach (Multiplicity)

C: Transversality based on Layers & Fields
D: Transversality based on Networks & Environments
E: Transversality based on Agents & Matter

5. Evolutionary Development (Dynamicity)

C: Evolution by Formulation
D: Evolution by Collaboration
E: Evolution by Symbiosis

6. Open Order (Flexibility)

C: Openness based on Dispositions
D: Openness based on Clusterings
E: Openness based on Platforms

7. Heterogeneous Condition (Diversity)

C: Heterogeneity as Topology
D: Heterogeneity as Ecology
E: Heterogeneity as Xenology

As we mentioned earlier, the fact that different protocols coexist, interact and overlap neither negates their differences nor equalizes them into a homogeneous magma. It also does not imply that they are not oriented: it does not prevent them from being explained (although not exhausted) a posteriori via an underlying narrative. Although this book sets out on a search for attractors, densifications, flows and clusters, it does not forgo proposing an underlying vector orienting all those events.

In that sense, the three chapters that follow are based on an approach that is simultaneously synchronic and diachronic.

– Synchronic, to argument how each of the three architectural set of protocols has been able to create a "recognizable scenario", which, despite its uniqueness, is able to establish relationships with other scenarios.

– Diachronic, to argument how, even though elements of different protocols intersect, overlap and even blend together, their centers of gravity are linked sequentially in a specific chronological order, resonating with the variation of its surrounding socio-technological framework.

The next chapters expose how, since the 1990s and in resonance with its technological and socio-cultural landscape, experimental architecture has been modulated through three protocols while progressively articulating a form of interaction whose actants are increasingly diverse although its entanglement are increasingly intimate.

If we approach the development of these intertwinings, generated and consolidated during the past 30 years, into decades, we can correlate them to the three poles already mentioned, being unfolded each one of them through a discrete and a continuous register:

A: Conformative Protocols (1990-2000): Overlapping Layers & Modelling Fields.

B: Distributive Protocols (2000-2010): Connecting Networks & Propagating Atmospheres.

C: Expansive Protocols (2010-2020): Mediating Agencies & Performing Matter.

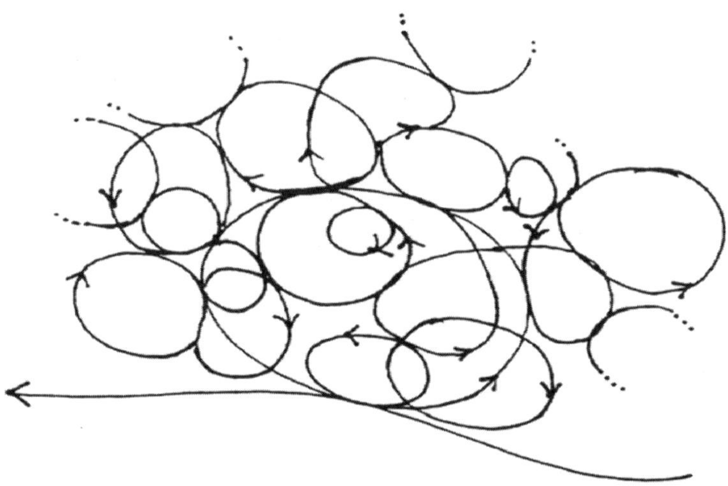

Diagrams of energy flows and exchanges; Mae Wan Ho, 1997.

A- CONFORMATIVE PROTOCOLS AND THE TOPOLOGICAL CONDITION

After years of historical revisionism and instrumental calligraphy, the final decades of the 20th century were marked by the impact of the new digital universe and its heavy computational component. Under this umbrella, conformative protocols operate through morphological transformations; formal variations associated with the recognition of the irregular patterns and mutable processes of the city it-self understood as a dynamic and non-linear system. The main first open devices of this period are linked with this epitomical condition of the project as a resonating and transferring "map-inductor" related with the new accelerated and dynamic urban conditions themselves. The notion of conformation implies an understanding of form as "matter in movement", that is, as a process of becoming. In this sense, conformation is thus con-formation, the action of gathering a set of distinct forms under one single formulation. To conform means to apply a set of forces; a group of pressures and draggings that is not expressed through clear and distinct figures, but through a dynamic amalgam of frames that documents the applied forces. Conformative architecture manipulates these systemic fluctuations through two main formal actions that consist in overlapping layers and modelling fields, that is, in superimposing discrete strata and deforming continuous volumes. Rather than introducing Platonic and apriori forms, conformative architecture works with open and a posteriori spatial formulations; continuous variations controlled through a set of geometric parameters.

During the 90s, the exploration of this open and irregular architectural configuration – and its diagrammatic potential- deeps in the capacity of synthesis of the device/diagram as an informational "cartography": it maps the conditions, solicitations, fluctuations and oscillations that occur in a space associated with patterns compression, evolution and transfer. Under this umbrella, two main factors characterized the decade of the 90s, particularly the second half. On the one hand, an interest in approaching reality through a cross-cutting and multi-layered reading. On the other hand, an interest in the construction of propositional responses capable of translating this urban, territorial and cultural shift into new design approaches. In this sense, some technological contributions had a decisive impact: the consolidation of "Windows" in the 1990s with its multi-layered interface, the arrival of the first PC laptops by IBM, Commodore and Acer, and the generalisation in the 90s of software like AutoCAD (1982), GIS (1990) and SCANNER (1984-90) expressed the "symptoms" of a new mode of action; they promoted the emergence of new anti-typological spatial responses that were less taxonomically predictable or predetermined, but more complex, hybrid and "multi-formatted".

These formal articulations can be found in architectural projects such as Rem Koolhaas' "Jussieu" (1992), MVRDV's "Wozoko" (1997) or Greg Lynn's "Embryological House" (1997-2002), but also in other disciplines during the same years: Lynch's domestic folds, Barry Le Va's open structures or Houellebecq's murky narratives exemplify the "correlative difference" characteristic of conformative protocols and its contrast with picturesque's "added difference". A multi-layered and fluctuant approach whose conceptualization was supported by publications like Koolhaas-Mau's *S, M, L, XL*, Bernard Tschumi's *Event Cities* collection (from 1994 to 2010), Bernard Caché's *Earth Moves* (1995), Manuel Delanda's *A Thousand Years of Non-Linear History* (1997) Stan Allen's *Points + Lines: Diagrams and Projects for the City* (1999), Greg Lynn's *Animate Form* (1999), Cecil Balmond's *Informal* (1999), Sandford Kwinter's *Architectures of Time* (2001) and Manuel Gausa's *Open-Space-Time-Information* (2010) and *Open(ing)* (2019).

Most of these architectural explorations proposed new types of spatial configurations, crystallizing in multi-faceted and fluid constructions. Topological geometries were fundamental for its production; growths, twinnings, meshes, fields, topographies and reliefs were widely explored through the software released during those years, such as "Catia V4-V5-3D Modeling" (1996-98), "Maya 3D-Modeling & Animation" (1998), "Rhinoceros "(1994) or "Adobe Photoshop" (1990). Open models and irregular patterns, along with deployed hyper-surfaces, came together to delve into aspects of inter-scalar transversality and inter-temporal dynamism. This resulted in, on the one hand, the formulation of anti-typological "dispositifs" (anti-types or hybrids) and, on the other, the generation of fluid and fluctuating forms in which information operated as a geometrical parameter. At the end of the 1990s, two lines of action seemed to be recognisable in many of the experiences tested:

– A tactical-practical line of action, strategic and operational, interested in manipulating the "codes" of the inertial productive system itself, that is, its standards. This line aims at disrupting them, modulating its parameters through new conceptual and intentional bases such as combinatorial games, programmatic multilayers or anti-typological manipulations.

- A genetic-experimental line of action, kinetic and productive, interested in proposing a dynamic and procedural generation of architectural morphologies. It operates through a "genetic of forms", that is, a formulation that resonates with procedural and material bases such as parameterization, algorithmic formulation, topological fluctuation or numerical conceptions.

Both lines - synthesized in the publications *S,M,L,XL* by Rem Koolhaas and Bruce Mau, (1994) and *Animated Form* by Greg Lynn, (1998) - will further reverberate in the construction of a new thought that in the 90s was embryonic.

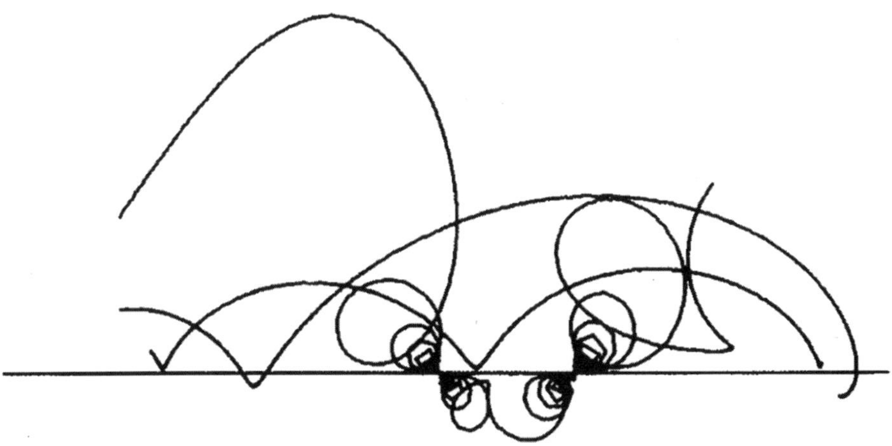

A force as an open vector of beams, hops, and loops; Cecil Baldmond, 1999.

B- DISTRIBUTIVE PROTOCOLS AND THE ECOLOGICAL CONDITION

Following the pioneering approaches of the 1990s, the first decade of the 21st century was characterized by the consolidation of new technological advances and new conceptual tools aiming at implementing open coordinational processes. In resonance with the generalisation of the Internet and its impact on the economic, social and cultural spheres, the experimental architecture of the early 20th century resonates with Latour's actants: an entity is what it "modifies, transforms, perturbs, or creates". However, rather than establishing a system of relations (topology), distributive protocols establish relations between systems (ecology): they conjugate operative clusters capable of transferring resources between different mediums.

Thus, instead of introverted formulations, trascendental essences or metaphoric references, distributive architecture establishes social, economic and energetic transferences. Under this umbrella, information is not a geometric parameter, but a territorial indicator: it in-forms and measures the impact established on the territory not only in terms of recognizable and physical shapes, but also and especially in terms of energetic, hydrothermal and socio-economic transfers.

Distributive architecture produces these transversal links through connecting networks and propagating atmospheres, that is, through linking discrete webs and disseminating continuous environments. These coordinational articulations can be found in Diller-Scofidio's "Blur Pavilion" (2002), Enric Ruiz Geli's "Mediatic" (2010) or Phillippe Rahm's "Jade Eco Park" (2012), but also in other disciplines during similar years: Julius Popp's informational art-works, Gunter Pauli's Blue Economy or Gilles Clement's planetarian gardens exemplify the extroverted nature of distributive protocols, contrasting with conformative protocols' introverted vocation.

Interconnection, sensorization, data optimization, intelligent interfaces, responsive devices, etc. In the early 21st century, the dispositifs of a-scalar transfer that were characteristic of much of the research in the mid-1990s no longer seemed necessary; in their place emerged an approach intended to combine not just sense and sensibility but sensorization and sensory perception.

This coordinational conceptualization was supported by publications such as Bruno Latour's *Reassembling the Social* (2005); Steven Johnson's *Emergence* (2001); Manuel Castells' *The Rise of the Network Society* (2010); Jeremy Rifkin's *The Age of Access* (2000); *The New Culture of Hyper-Capitalism* (2000); Braungarts and Mac Donough"s *Cradle to Cradle* (2003); Richard Florida's *Cities and the Creative Class* (2005); Hensel and Menges' *Morpho Ecologies* (2006), Gausa, Guallart and Müller *Hyper Catalunya, Territories of Research* (2003), Nikos Komninos' *Intelligent Cities and Globalisation of Innovation Networks* (2007) and Vicente Guallart's *Self-Sufficient City* (2010).

The technological contributions of that decade resonated with those arguments: the progress made in the evolution of computers and specially the emergence and consolidation of networking technologies amplified the scope of distributive protocols. Some examples of it are the generalisation of the Internet, the use of "Fab-Labs" and 3D-printing, the launch of "Arduino" in 2005, the appearance in early 2000 of the first personal digital assistants (PDAs) and the spread, starting in 2007, of mobile applications and smartphones (2003 – first "Blackberry", 2007 – "iPhone", 2008 – "Samsung Galaxy" (2010). This development was quickly consolidated with the arrival of networked platforms such as "Yahoo" (2000-2002), "Google" (2002), "LinkedIn" (2004-2007), "Facebook" (2005), "YouTube" (2006), "Twitter" (2008) or "Amazon-Kindle" (2007). These cases contributed to the emergence of a networked framework for relationships and exchanges that was not only "virtual" in its operational definition, but "real" in its effects in socio-economic, cultural and environmental terms.

Besides, the 2000s would see the consolidation of a new type of thinking more sensitive to a holistic integration between anthropic systems and ecological systems, physical networks (mobility, accessibility), informational networks (social and cultural) and natural networks (eco-systemic).

The Rio Agendas (1992 and 2002) reinforced by various meetings and appointments (2005 Kyoto Protocol, 2007 Climate Change Panels, 2008 Green Economy Proposals) allowed us to understand the fundamental notion of Sustainability associated with the importance of the informational processing equation <4+1> IN Factors: Information, Interaction, Integration (intelligence) and Innovation.

Virtual networks of global informational connections and ecological networks of local environmental connections could thus be combined in a new type of approach that, in any case, responded to that capacity for holistic interaction previously mentioned.

Under this umbrella, the growing importance of networks, the progressive incidence of real-time data processing and the emergence of environmental sensorization was quickly associated with one polemical concept that had a big impact in the following years: the notion of smart cities. Its emergence, based on digital nets, webs, (hyper)links and matrices, but also on parametric indicators and environmental sensors, combined distributive models of transfer and responsiveness on a territorial scale. It resulted, on the one hand, in new connective (infra-, intra-, info- and eco-structural) nets and, on the other, in an environmentally sensitive approach that emphasized self-sufficiency, eco-efficiency and sustainability. However, as we will see later in detail, the agendas of smart cities were in most cases too attached to the particular interest of the corporations that provided the required technology for their operations, losing a great part of the concept's emancipatory power.

The design of networked inhabited environments, the implementation of territorial approaches associated with sustainability agendas and the sensorization of urban infrastructures characterized many of the projects undertaken during this period. In this sense, distributive architecture conjugates these territorial and multidimensional transfers through an interaction that occurs not only within a single medium but in between different mediums: it promotes an inner and outer sensorial relationality aiming to establish energetical, informational and social intertwinings with its territory.

In this sense, the exploration of a new eco-social activism aims at co-defining and co-producing our habitats; it proposes a new sensitive form of interaction -empathic or eco-empathic- in order to approach scenarios of global deficit: political conflicts, geo-economic threats, climate change or social inequalities are a decisive part of the advanced architecture of this period.

C- EXPANSIVE PROTOCOLS AND THE XENOLOGICAL CONDITION

The second decade of the 21st century is characterized in experimental architecture by the consolidation of a twofold line of thought that was shyly insinuated since the end of the 20th century. It consists, on the one side, in recognizing the agency of ecological, biological, geological and algorithmic others, and, on the other side, in the establishment of multispecie and operative entanglements in between these agents. As a consequence, and together with the exponential development of "carnal technologies", the nature of spaces, contexts, media and species is radically expanded through symbiotic entanglements.

Under what we define as a xenological condition, intimate relations in between strangers are favoured: rather than autopoietic identities, expansive architecture aims for simpoeitic multitudes, that is, operative tunings in between ecological, biological, geological and algorithmic others. In resonance with the rise of Artificial Intelligence, Haraway's multispecies composts and Sadin's antrobology, expansive architecture assumes Braidotti's post-human subject: the human being becomes a moveable assemblage within a common life-space that s/he never masters nor possesses but merely inhabits together with a non-human community. Rather than unfolding a design framework based on geometric transformations or territorial transferences, expansive architecture produces multispecies enrichments, that is, symbiotic associations whose impact reverberates at multi-scalar distances and questions the notion of nature itself.

Under this umbrella, expansion implies miscegenation; it establishes bastard interlacements that do not constitute an additive and exceptional event, but an impure and tentacular regime that participates in a number of sequences increasingly permeating our daily life. Expansive architecture orchestrates these miscegenations by mediating agents and performing matter, that is, by crossing discrete species and synthesizing continuous substances. These symbiotic articulations characterize Phillip Beesley's "Hylozoic Ground" (2010), Nery Oxman's "Silk Pavilion" (2013) or François Roche's "MMYST" (2015), but also other disciplines of the same period: Neil Harbisson's cyborg constitution, Spela Petric's vegetal otherness or IBM's neuro-processors exemplify the desire for "operative multitudes" characteristic of expansive protocols.

The launch of hyper-personalized prosthetic devices such as watch computers, augmented reality glasses or smart shoes, but also and especially the generalisation of artificial intelligence, robotic structures and bio-technological processes consolidates the presence of what we define as "carnal" technology: rather than celebrating the sacred distance and consequent untouchability of modern technics, carnal technology is intimate, subtle and profound, adhered or injected into the body rather than exterior to it. It provides a technological haptic framework that introduces technical efficiency in recreational activities, although not always permitting a real emancipation from the established power, as we will see in detail in the third chapter. In this sense and under the controversial label of accelerationism, a certain techno-optimism is being emphasized over the too-narrow scope of folk politics and its frequent reactionary approach to technology.

Central issues characteristic of Expansive Protocols have been addressed by theoretical publications of this decade such as Bruno Latour's *Down to Earth* (2017), Mario Carpo's *The Second Digital Turn* (2017) Carlo Ratti and Joseph Grima *Open Source Architecture Manifesto* (2012), Nick Srnicek's *Platform Capitalism* (2016), Haraway's *Staying with the Trouble* (2018), Barad's *Meeting the Universe Halfway* (2007), Braidotti's *The Posthuman* (2015), Dolphijn and Van der Tuin's *New Materialism* (2012), Alessandro Baricco's *The Game* (2019) or Eric Sadin's *L'humanité augmentée* (2013).

Maps of cross-cutting fissures ans seams in mineral mass; Pablo Gumiel, 1996.

Links, keys, nodes and connections; Douglas R.Hofstadter, *Gödel-Esher adn Bach*, 2000.

In resonance with these theoretical, technological and artistic contributions, Expansive Protocols blur the division, on the one side between passive matter and active form, and on the other side, between autonomous agents and objective environment. Thus, agents and matter define focal points respectively approached from an interest in multispecies multitudes and a desire for ubiquity and responsivity. Following Latour's notion of the "Terrestrial," the environment is no longer approached as an exterior framework occupied by the agents that inhabit it, but it is conceived as the ongoing co-existentence among a litany of species.

8. INTIMACY BETWEEN UNKNOWNS

Conformative, Distributive and Expansive protocols constitute a narrative taxonomy whose borders are viscous and slippery. Rather than being established as a Braudelian segmentation, it is orchestrated as a field of references, a framework that, despite its tentacular and open nature, positions a specific vector of interpretation: it argues that through these 30 years and under the three protocols described earlier, the notion of "interaction" varies in a twofold sense; although its participants are increasingly diverse, paradoxically its interrelation is increasingly intimate.

The last 30 years of experimental architecture are thus the progressive attempt to produce critical interiorities that promote and are promoted by Lynn Margulis' "long-lasting intimacy of strangers"[11], that is, profound and operative entanglements among mutually unknown collectives: algorithmic, biological, geological and ecological species whose symbiotic intertwinings produce an architectural miscegenation that no longer fits into Modernity's epistemic classifications.

This tendency is shyly pioneered by the inner programmatic interaction of Conformative Protocols, opposing the functional zonification characteristic of the Modern Movement. Distributive Protocols increase the diversity and profundity of this interaction by connecting ecosystems rather than programs: their entanglements add factors such as temperature, pollution, humidity or pressure in order to operatively intertwin artificial and natural environments. Expansive protocols radicalize this tendency by promoting operative associations in between species. Rather than intertwining programs or environments, Expansive Protocols sintonize multitudes; its symbiotic entanglements disembogue in an "intimacy in between unknowns" that orients the experimental architecture characteristic of the last decade.

As we will see in the following chapters, all three protocols harbor the desire of impacting the multidisciplinary cultural scenario of our times; an attitude that reclaims, in fact, the role of architecture as a socio-political, creative and technological endeavor that critically produces spaces within spaces, that is, inhabitable interiorities. Under this formal specificity, architecture defines our habitats and environments, but it inevitably advocates as well for certain attitudes and practices whose impact transcend the architectural discipline; by resonating with its socio-cultural and technological landscape, experimental architecture has the potential of being decisive in the cultural and political vectorization of our *zeitgeist*.

_11. "Lynn Margulis knew a great deal about "the intimacy of strangers," a phrase she proposed to describe the most fundamental practices of critters becoming-with each other at every node of intraaction in earth history". Donna Haraway, Staying with the Trouble (London: Duke University Press, 2016), 60.

CONFORMATIVE PROTOCOLS 1990-2000

The Topological Condition:
Overlapping Layers and Modelling Fields

OVERLAPPING LAYERS

TOPOLOGICAL CONDITION

MODELLING FIELDS

COLORARIUM

Conformative protocols operate through morphological transformations. Modern and postmodern concepts such as semantics, standardisation, calligraphy or eclecticism are replaced by topological processes based on a set of multiscalar formulations. In resonance with the advent of the computational revolution, the experimental architecture of the late 80s and 90s explores the potential of Deleuze's expression "anexact yet rigorous": rather than introducing platonic and apriori forms, conformative architecture works with open and a posteriori spatial formulations, that is, continuous variations controlled through a set of geometric parameters.

The notion of conformation (or configuration, as another associated term) implies an understanding of form as "matter in movement", as a process of becoming. Under this umbrella, conformation is thus con-formation, the action of gathering a set of distinct forms under one single framework. To conform means to apply a set of forces; a group of pressures and draggings that is not expressed through gesticulative and frozen figures, but through a formulative amalgam of frames documenting the applied forces. Conformative architecture manipulates these systemic fluctuations through two main formal actions that consist in overlapping layers and modelling fields, that is, in superimposing discrete strata and deforming continuous volumetries.

These formal articulations can be found in Koolhaas' "Jussieu" (1992), MVRDV's "Wozoko" (1997) or Lynn's "Embryological House" (1997-2002), but also in other disciplines during the same years: Lynch's domestic folds, Barry Le Va's open structures or Houellebecq's murky narratives exemplify the "correlative difference" characteristic of conformative protocols and its contrast with picturesque's "added difference". Under this umbrella, space is conceived as "continuous yet heterogeneous", promoting a programmatic interaction that opposes the functional zonification characteristic of modernity.

1. Information as a "Parameter"
Information operates as an abstract geometric parameter. Its content does not refer to any external agent, but to the internal properties that define architecture's morphology. The algorithmic articulation characteristic of non-standard serialities permits a systematic management of information. It operates via parametric functions that oppose traditional notational systems, independently of its analogical or digital nature.

2. Interaction in between "Programs"
Interaction consists in a combination of programs internal to its architecture. It rarely implies the inclusion of the site as an operational element beyond its morphological attributes, and it usually does not approach the user beside its volumetric and generic presence. The spatial richness provided by the topological geometries characteristic of this architecture favours the coexistence of several programs and their functional interplay.

3. Transversality through "Layers" & "Fields"
Layers and Fields are two formal resources that produce spatial difference under one single system of relations. In spite of its common articulation through forces and movements in process, both tools differ in their formal nature: while Layers are discrete elements that are superposed and compressed, Fields are continuous morphologies that are stretched and deformed.

4. Integration through "Overlapping" & "Modelling"
Overlapping and Modelling are two formal processes that produce sets of non-standard series. Both are defined by the formal differentials produced in between the items of their sequences, but differ in their mode of action: while overlapping consists in a morphological and functional superposition of discrete layers, modelling consists in a morphological and functional transformation based on the inherent continuity of foldings and bendings.

5. Evolution by "Formulation"

Formulation produces formal familiarity through a common algorithmic structure. The systematic alteration of its parameters results in a process of variation based on the production of difference oriented towards a specific target. It accounts for the perpetual development of a form-becoming. Its codified nature constructs forms that oscillate in between similarity and difference, opposing both the mechanical identicality of modern mass production and the calligraphic diversity of postmodern relativism.

6. Openness through "Dispositions"

Disposition consists in a combinatory system of potentials: it articulates multiple trajectories and mutations operating under a space-time-information continuum. It opposes the classic notion of composition and the modern notion of position: while the former alludes to an essentialist conception of space as a separate and transcendent entity, the latter refers to relative, free, and reciprocal relations in between entities under a spatio-temporal coordinate system.

7. Heterogeneity as "Topological"

A topology consists in a system of relations that doesn't account for metric distances but for the organization of an object. Under this framework, variations are not arbitrary, but the end product of systematic relationships; a single organization contain many possible structures, and consequently it permits the application of continuous transformations on a geometrical entity without altering its main organization.

■ MAR BELLA - Bru, Car
□ KWADRANT SETTLEM
▲ MADE IN TOKYO - BO

■ FREE UNIVERSITY BERLIN - Candilis, Josic, Woods, 1963

▲ EVENT CITIES - Bernard Tschumi, 1994
▲ ARCHIS, 1996-2000
▲ ARCH, 1990-2000
▲ FISURAS , 1994-2007
▲ QUADERNS, 1991-1999
▲ ARCHILAB CAT., 2000
▲ EUROPAN CAT.,1990
▲ A+T, 1992

× IBM PERSONAL COMPUTER, 1981
× LINUX- Linux, 1981
× AUTOCAD - Autodesk, 1982
× AFTER EFFECTS - Adobe, 1993
× COMMODORE, Commodore, 1985
× EPSON HX-20 - Epson, 1981
× NINTENDO E.S. - Nintento, 1983-87
× ATARI 2600 - Atari, 1979-1983

DOMESTIC OVERLAPPING OF REALITIES

NARRATIVE OVERLAPPING

SUPERIMPOSED PATTERNS

OVERLAPPING LAYERS

OVERLAPPING INTERACTIVITY
× SCAN TECHNOLOGIES, 1990
× WINDOWS 3.0 - Microsoft, 1990
× FIRST DESKTOP GIS PRODUCT - DOS, 1990

◆ FARGO - Joel and Ethan Cohen, 1996
▲ LES PARTICULES ÉLEMENTAIRES - Michel Houllebecq, 1998
◆ NIGHT ON EARTH - Jim Jarmusch, 1991
◆ KILL BILL - Quentin Tarantino, 2002
■ COM
■ WOZ
■ SITTA
□ MAIS

OMA SUPERIMPOSITIONS
□ PARC DE LA VILLETTE - OMA, 1982
□ TRÈS GRANDE BIBLIOTHEQUE - OMA, 1989
□ CITY HALL - OMA, 1986
□ ZEEBRUGGE FERRY TERMINAL - OMA, 1990
■ NEXUS WORLD HOUSING - OMA, 1991

Overlapping Layers

■ MAKUHARI COMPLEX - Steven Holl,
▲ FRACTAL CITIES - Batty; Longley, 1994
□ CARPET METROPOLIS - Neutelings, 1990
□ EUROPEAN PATENT OFFICE - Willem
□ BENIDORM CULTURAL CENTER - Federico Soriano, 1993
■ ZIG-ZAG TYPOLOGIE
▲ SMLXL - OMA, 1995

■ PAO I: A DWELLING FOR TOKYO NOMAD WOMAN - Toyo Ito, 1985
▲ POSTMODERN CONDITION - François Lyotard, 1979
● USSR DISOLVES, 1991
● END OF APPARTHEID, 1992
● FALL BERLIN WALL, 1991
● TIANANMEN SQUARE PROTESTS, 1989

1960' PARAMETRICISM

POLITICAL OPENING

× PHOTOSHOP- Adobe, 1990
■ AGADIR CENTER - OMA, 1990
■ JUSSIEU TWO LIBRARIES - OMA, 1992
■ PARKHOUSE - NL Architects, 1996
× HUBBLE - NASA, 1990

■ PAMPLONA AUDITORIUM - Eduardo Arroyo
■ HOUSING BORNEO - Neutelings, 1997

CONFORMATIVE PROTO

□ THE ROAD - Heidi van der Wardt, 199
□ ACTI
□ RESIDENTIAL TOWER
□ ETHER - DECOI, 1995
□ PAVILION SEMPER - B

■ IGLESIA CRISTO OBRERO - Eladio Dieste, 1960
■ SPORTS STADIUM - Luigi Moretti, 1960
■ TWA FLIGHT CENTER - Eero Saarinen, 1962
+ THE FOLD - Gilles Deleuze, 1988
▲ A THOUSAND PLATEAUS - Gilles Deleuze, 1980

■ REBSTOCK PARK - Peter Eisenman, 1992
□ CARDIFF OPERA - Greg Lynn, 1994
▲ FOLDING IN ARCHITECTURE - Greg Lynn, 1993
▲ LANDSCAPES OF CHANGE - Sanford Kwinter, 1992
▲ LIQUID ARCHITECTURE - Marcos Novak, 1991
▲ EARTH MOVES. THE FURNISHING OF TERRITORIES - Bernard Caché, 19
+ ATELIER OBJECTILE -
▲ A THOUSAND YEARS

MODELING FIELDS

Gender Fluidity ▲ GENDER TROUBLE - Judith Butler, 1990
▲ QUEER SPACE - Aaron Betsky, 1997

× MAYA - Autodesk, 1998
× 3D STUDIO - Autodesk, 1990
▲ ANIMATE FORM - Greg Lynn, 1999
▲ LIQUID MODERNITY

FIELDS OF MOVEMENT

◆ JURASSIC PARK - Steven Spielberg, 1993
◆ TERMINATOR 2 - James Cameron, 1991
◆ TOY STORY - John Lasseter, 1995
□ EMPR
■ VILLA
■ MOBI
□ VIRTU
□ DANC
□ VIRTU
■ MAIS

3D MODELED MOVIES

EARLY 3D SOFTWARE

TOPOLOGICAL SCULPTING
◆ EL PEIX D'OR - Frank Gehry, 1992
◆ TORQUED ELLIPSES - Richard Serra, 1996
◆ RIDDLE OF THE SPHINX - Mike Kelley, 1990

Calligraphic Modelling

HOUSING MODELING

× ALIAS RESEARCH, 1995
× WAVEFRONT TECHNOLOGIES, 1984
× RENDERMAN - Pixar, 1989

× CATIA - Avions Marcel Dassault, 1981

◆ VIRTUAL PRINT MACHINE - Ágnes Hegedüs, 1994
× VIRTUAL ACTOR BRANDON LEE - Alex Proyas, 1994
◆ DANGLING STRING - Natalie Jeremijenko, 1995

MOBILE DEVICES

DATA

× STARTAC, Motorola,
× NOKIA 3210 - Nokia,
× BLACKBERRY 850, Bl
× PALM PILOT - 3com,
× NETSCAPE NAVIGAT

▲ NEUROMANCER - William Gibson, 1984
◆ TRON - Steven Lisberger, 1982
◆ BLADE RUNNER - Ridley Scott, 1982

EARLY 3D MODELING IN FILM

NET-GLOBE

× WORLD WIDE WEB (WWW) - Tim Berners - Lee, 1990
× 2G, 1991
● SHENZEN SPACE, 1995

GLOBAL POLIS
▲ GLOBAL CITY - Saskia Sassen, 1991
▲ GLOBAL VILLAGE - McLuhan, Powers, 1989
▲ TELÉPOLIS - Javier Echevarria, 1994
▲ METÁPOLIS - François Ascher, 1995
▲ THE INFORMATION BOMB - Paul Virilio, 1999
□ NETWORK CITY - Neutelings, 1993
× 2G
▲ BEING DIGITAL - Nicholas Negroponte, 1995

CONNECTING NETWORKS

× SMS, 1985
× 1G, 1979

NEW MEDIA + LES IMMATÉRIAUX - François Lyotard, 1985

TERRITORIAL MATRICES

× YAHOO! - Jerry Yand, David Filo, 1994
× AMAZON - Jeff Bezos, 1994
× HTML, 1992
× HOTMAIL - Microsoft, 1996
× WOR
× FLIC
▲ COMPUTER NETWOR

▲ OREGON EXPERIMENT - Christopher Alexander, 1975
◆ NETWORK, Sidney Lumet 1976

□ SOUTH ALMERE - MVRDV, 1996
□ MÉLUN SÉNART - OMA, 1987

◆ MATRIX - Lilly/Lana W
◆ MINORITY REPORT -
Unveiled network ◆ DOG
◆ MEN

DATA MOVIES

▲ THE RSVP CYCLES - Lawrence Halprin, 1970

Consolidation Ecological Concern ● EARTH SUMMIT RIO, 1992

▲ OUT OF CONTROL - Kevin Kelly, 1992
▲ POST-SCRIPT ON THE SOCIETIES OF CONTROL - Gilles Deleuze, 1990
▲ THE

■ COULÉE VERTE RENÉ-DUMONT - Jacque Vergely, Philippe Mathieux,

PROPAGATING ATMOSPHERES

EARLY ENVIRONMENTAL DESIGN

▲ WHOLE EARTH CATALOGUE - Stewart Brand, 1968-72
▲ LOS ANGELES. THE ARCHITECTURE OF FOUR ECOLOGIES - Reyner Banham, 1971
▲ OPERATING MANUAL FOR SPACESHIP EARTH - Buckminster Fuller, 1969
▲ THE ARCHITECTURE OF WELL-TEMPERED ENVIRONMENT - Reyner Banham, 1960
■ MONTREAL BIOSPHÈRE - Buckminster Fuller, 1967

▲ THE EARTH TRANSFORMED - Goudie, Viles, 1997

× VIDEOPLACE - Myron Krueger,1976

Peripherical interaction ▲ DESIGNING CALM TECHNOLOGY - Mar
× EU

◆ ANGELS - Nicole Stenger, 1992

▲ OVERLAPPING LIVES

Vives; 1995
MVRDV, 1996

▲ CONSTANT'S NEW BABYLON - Mark Wigley, 1999

2001

S.HOLL COMPRESSIONS

▲ THIRDSPACE: JOURNEYS TO LOS ANGELES AND OTHER REAL-AND-IMAGINED PLACES - Edward W. Soja 1997
▲ JUSTICE, NATURE AND THE GEOGRAPHY OF DIFFERENCE - David Harvey, 1998

TY - Bus Architecture, 2001
OVERLAPPING + DISTRIBUTIVE
MVRDV, 1997 ■ PILOT PLAN - NL Architects, 2002
RTMENTS - Neutelings, 1995
ZLE - Jakob & Macfarlane, 1997 ■ NETHERLANDS PAVILION - MVRDV, 2000
▲ POINTS & LINES - Stan Allen, 1999
▲ MUTATIONS - Rem Koolhaas, 2000
telings, 1991 ■ SENDAI MEDIATHEQUE - Toyo Ito, 2001
yo Sejima, 1996 ■ PLAZA DESIERTO - Eduardo Arroyo, 2002
BERLAGE - Wiel Arets ■ PILOT PLAN - NL Architects, 2002
COLUMBIA - Greg Lynn
Overlapping Masses Bundles ▲ HABITABLE BRIDGE - Zaha Hadid, 1996

Conformative Protocols

▲ ALMERE OOSTERW
▲ LANDSCRAPERS - Aaron Betsky, 2006 ■ MU
Modeling & Overlapping ▲ OPEN - Manuel Gau

LS

▲ MESHWORKS, HIERARCHIES AND INTERFACES - Manuel Delanda, 1998

TOPOLOGICAL FLOORS
□ VIRTUAL HOUSE - FOA, 1997
OS - Kelly Shannon, 1993 ■ MARITIME YOUTH HOUSE - BIG, 2004
no-Palacios, 1998 ■ MERCEDES BENZ MUSEUM - Ben V. Berkel, 2006
■ ASPHALT SPOT - François Roche, 2002
Caché, 1999 ■ ROLEX CENTER - Kazuyo Sejima, 2010
■ YOKOHAMA TERMINAL - 2002
Caché, 1996 ▲ NEW TOPOGRAPHIES - Alejandro Zaera, 2010
LINEAR HISTORY - Manuel Delanda, 1997

MOUNTAINS
□ GW
■ NOR
□ WR
■ MERCA BARNA - Willy Müller, 2008 □ DENIA MOUNTAIN -
■ LANDSCAPEHALL MANRESA - Bailo-Rull, 2008 ■ MO

PARAMETRICISM
■ POMPIDOU METZ - Shigeru Ban, 2010
▲ PARAMETRIC ARCHITECTURE WITH GRASSHOPPER - Arturo Tedeschi, 2011
▲ PARAMETRICISM - Patrick Schumacher, 2010
▲ THE AUTOPOEISIS OF ARCHITECTURE - Patrick Schumacher, 2011 ▲ THE

Modeling Fields

◆ VOLUME - Fournier, UVA, 2006
nt Bauman, 1999 □ LIBRARY PROJECT - Reiser-Unamoto, 1996
CAL HOUSE - Greg Lynn, 1999 ▲ LA SAGRADA FAMILIA DE GAUDÍ AL CAD - Marc Burry, 1996
MVRDV, 1997 ▲ ARCHITECTURES OF TIME - Sanford Kwinter, 2001 ▲ CODE REMIX - FOA, 2000
SE - UN Studio, 1998 ✕ RHINOCEROS - Mc Neel, 1998 ▲ INFORMAL - Cecil Balmond, 2002
SE - FOA, 1997 Domestic dark folds ◆ LOST HIGHWAY - David Lynch, 1997 ■ TRANS-PORTS - Kas Oosterhuis, 2001
USE - Frank Gehry, 1996 ▲ ARCHILAB, 1999 □ VARIABLE DATA FORMS - Marcos Novak, 1999
SE - Peter Eisenman, 1997 ■ RESTAURANT POMPIDOU - Jakob & Macfarlane, 2000
E - NOX, 2004 ▲ DELEUZE AND THE USE OF G.A. IN ARCHITECTURE - Manuel Delanda, 2001 ✕ UNITY - Unity Technologies, 2004
COMMUNICATIONS TOWER - Actar Arquitectura, 2000

■ MILAN TRADE - Massimiliano Fuksas, 2005 ▲ DIGITAL CITIES - Neil Leach, 2009
■ GREAT COURT - Norman Foster, 2000 ▲ THE ARCHITECTURE
■ CROSS STATION - Nicholas Grimshaw, 2007 □ ZERO ZONE - NOX, 2
■ MAXI MUSEUM - Zaha Hadid, 2009 ■ MEISO NO MORI - To
■ SELFRIDGES - Future Architects, 2003 □ ARIZONA STRUCTURES - Peter Trum
■ METROSOL PARASOL - Jürgen Mayer, 2011 ▲ OCCUPYING AND C
■ T4 BARAJAS - Lamela, Rogers & Partners, 2006
■ SERPENTINE GALLERY - Toyo Ito, 2002
■ OMOTE SANDO - Toyo Ito, 2004

FRESH WATER PAVILION - NOX, 1997 ■ ART GRAZ MUSEUM - Fournier, Cook, 2003 Networked Geopolitics ● II GULF WAR, 2003-... ◆ 14 BILLION - Tomas Saraceno, 2011 + FAB-CITY - FabLabCo
■ D-TOWER - NOX, 2005 ■ TUBE - Numen/Foruse, 2015 ✕ KICK
DATA TOWN - MVRDV, 1999 FIGURATIVE NETWORKS □ NETWORKED CITY - IaaC, 2011 ✕ WIK
● 11M, 2004 ✕ IPHONE - Apple, 2007 ✕ ANDROID - Android, 2008 ◆ IPHONE CITIES - Benjamin Bratton, 2009 ✕ BITC
VIRTUAL TRADING FLOOR - Asymptote, 1999 ▲ HYPER-CATALUNYA - Vicente Guallart, 2003 ▲ SWARM URBANISM - Neil Leach, 2009
, 1999 + METAPOLIS EXHIBITION - Metapolis, 2000 ◆ REACTABLE - Sergi Jordà, 2003 ■ HABIDATUM - Alexei Novikov, 2014
GPS, 1995 ◆ MACRO SPHERES - Julius Popp, 2010 □ SOCIÓPOLIS - Vicente Guallart, 2004 ◆ CHRONOTOPE CITY - Alexei Novikov, 2015
Andreessen, 1994 ● EURO COIN, 2002 ▲ ADVANCED DICTIONARY - IaaC, 2001 ◆ MISSBEHAVING - Heidi Kumao, 2005 ■ HYPER HABITAT - Vicente Guallart, 2008
INTERNET EXPLORER - Microsoft, 1995 ▲ CONNECTED, OR, WHAT IT MEANS TO LIVE IN THE NETWORK SOCIETY - S. Shaviro, 2003 □ MULTI STRING - Manuel Gausa, 2012

DIGITAL ECONOMICS

LA ERA DE LA INFORMACIÓN (VOL.I) - Manuel Castells, 1990
THE AGE OF ACCESS - Jeremy Rifkin, 2001 ▲ THE RISE OF THE NETWORK SOCIETY - Manuel Castells, 2000 ▲ REASSEMBLING THE SOCIAL - Bruno Latour, 2005
GOOGLE INC - Jimmy Wales, Larry Sanger, 1998 ▲ A NEW PHILOSOPHY OF SOCIETY - Manuel Delanda, 2006 ■ WATER PAVILION - Carlo Ratti, 2008 ■ SU
.COM EXPLOSION, 2001 ✕ GRASSHOPPER, 2007 ▲ EMERGENCE - Steven Johnson, 2001 ◆ BITFALL - Julius Popp, 2006 ▲ PE
▲ INTERNET OF THINGS - Kevin Ashton, 1999 ▲ THE BOTTOM IS NOT ENOUGH - Kevin Kelly, 2008 ✕ 4G, 2008 ▲ THE
▲ SPACE SYNTAX - Claramunt, Jiang, 2000 BIDIRECTIONAL WEB ✕ FACEBOOK - Mark Zuckerberg, 2004 ▲ THE TRANSPARENCY SOCIETY - Byung Chul-Han, 2012 NET-POLITICS ● OBAMA VICTORY, 2
GMAIL - Google, 2004 ✕ YOUTUBE - Chad Hurley, Seteve Chen, Jawed Karim, 2005 ✕ WHATSAPP - Jan Kuom, 2009 ● FACEBOOK ICELAN

Connecting Networks

✕ WIKIPEDIA (WP) - Jimmy Wales, Larry Sanger 2001 ✕ INSTAGRAM - Systrom, 2010 NET - Terrorism ● ISLAMIC STATE, 201
▲ NET SPACES - Kathr
ONE LAPTOP PER CHILD - Nicholas Negroponte, 2005 ✕ GOOGLE EARTH - Google, 2001 ■ WIKIHOUSE - 00, 2011 ✕ DROPBOX - Houston, Ferdowsi, 2007 ▲ REDES DE INDIGNA
- Julio Rijo, 2003 + MIT SENSEABLE CITY LAB - Carlo Ratti, 2004 ■ WATER CUBE - PTW Architects, 2008 NET-SOCIAL MOVEMENTS
orp, 2004 + CENTER FOR BITS & ATOMS - Neil Gershenfield, 2001 ■ MEDIA TIC - Enric Ruiz Geli, 2009 ● ANONYMOUS, 2003 ● ARAB SPRING, 201
son, B. Davie, 1996 + IAAC FOUNDATION - Guallart, Müller, Gausa, 2001 ✕ FAB LAB, Neil Gershenfield, 2001 ● 15M SPAIN, 2011-1
+ SPATIAL INFORMATION DESIGN LAB - Laura Kurgan, 2004 NET-BUILDINGS ✕ SMART CITIZEN, IaaC, 2013 ● FINANCIAL CRISIS, 2008 ● UMBRELLA MOVEM
ki, 1999 + TERRITORIAL AGENCY - John Palmesino, 2007 ✕ HOW TO MAKE ALMOST ANYTHING - Neil Gershenfield, 2005
NET-LABORATORIES DIGITAL CRAFTS ✕ ARDUINO TECHNOLOGIES - IVREA, 2005 ■ CUPULA MILENIO - Enric Ruiz Geli, 2
pielberg, 2002 ✕ IPAD - Apple, 2010
rs Von Trier, 2003 ✕ SATELITE AQUA, 2002 ● KATRINA HURRICANE, 2005

DISTRIBUTIVE PROTOCOLS

✕ KINDLE- Amazon, 2007
Christopher Nolan, 2001 ■ BLUR PAVILION - Diller-Scofidio, 2002 ● TUVALU CLIMATIC REFUGEES, 2009 □ NYC AQUARIUM - Enric Ruiz Geli, 2006 ▲ CONNECTED - Christakis, Fowler, 2
□ MAGIC MOUNTAIN - Amid.cero.9, 2002
▲ HYDROGEN ECONOMY - Jeremy Rifkin, 2002 □ CITY TOWER - Ken Yeng, 2005 ● EAR
✕ TOYOTA PRIUS (HYBRID) - Toyota, 1999 ● PRESTIGE, 2001 ▲ GEOLOGICS - Vicente Guallart, 2009
OPEN LANDSCAPES
ANSFORMED - Goudie, Viles, 1997 ■ LONG ISLAND GREEN DOME ,2005 ■ ECO BOULEVARD - E. Urbano, 2007 ■ SUPER BLOCK - Salvador Rueda, 200
▲ CRADLE TO CRADLE - Braungart, McDnough, 2002 ■ UNEXPECTED GARDEN - Carlo Ratti, 2008
■ EDEN PROJECT - Nicholas Grimshaw, 2001 ■ VERTICAL GARDENS - Patrick Blanc, 2004 TECH-ATMOSPHERES
□ C. IPHEROUS FOREST- Amid.cero.9, 2011 ■ VERTICAL FOREST - Stephano Boeri, 2015 ✕ GECO PLUG-IN - Uto
GREENHOUSE ■ SPORT PLAZA - Venhoeven, 2006 ✕ ECOTECT - Autodesk, 2008 Combination of narrative
■ HIGH LINE - Diller-Scofidio, 2009 □ CONVECTIVE APARTMENTS - Philippe Rahm, 2010 □ CLO
▲ THE THIRD LANDSCAPE - Gilles Clement, 2003 ■ JADE ECO PARK - Philippe Rahm, 2016 □ AU
□ UNPLUG TOWER - François Roche, 2002 ■ SUBNATURE - David Gissen, 2009
□ DUSTYRELIEF/BMU - François Roche, 2002 ▲ THE BLUE ECONOMY - Gunter Pauli, 2014
□ OMNIS PORTS HALL - J.G.Décosterd, Rahm, 1998 TERRITORIAL ATMOSPHERES □ BIG LEAKS - Jeffrey Inaba ● FUKUSHIMA ACCIDE
DIFFUSIVE GARDENS
▲ RESPONSIVE ARCHITECTURE - Philip Beesley, 2006

Propagating Atmospheres

□ VATNSMYRI URBAN PLAN - Sean Sally ▲ MAN
□ NYC Troposhperic Refuge, 2006 □ TAICHUNG GATEWAY - Philippe Rahm, 2012
■ THE BROOKLYN PIGEON PROJECT - Aranda, Lasch, 2004 ▲ MORPHO ECOLOGIES - Achim Menges, 2006
□ WOS8 UTRECHT - NL Architects, 1997 ◆ ATMOSPHERIC COLOUR ATLAS - Olafur Eliasson, 2009 ▲ ECOLOGICAL URBANISM - Mostafavi, Doherty (eds), 2010 ▲ THE
■ ACQUA ALTA - François Roche, 1998 □ MOLLIER HOUSES - Philip Rahm, 2005 ▲ CITIES PROTOCOL -
▲ LE JARDIN PLANÉTAIRE - Gilles Clement, 1997 □ FOREST HOTEL - Enric Ruiz Geli, 2009
▲ REVELATORY LANDSCAPES - Besky, Levy, MacCannell, 2001 ▲ FAR FROM EQUILIBRIUM - Samford Kwinter, 2008 ▲ NATURALEZA Y ARTIF
▲ STALKING DETROIT - Waldheim, Daskalakis, Young (ed), 2001 ■ JARDIN D'EAU/ORTIES - Gilles Clement, 2007 ▲ ADAPTIVE ECOLOGIES - Theodore S
◆ GEOCRUISER - Nils Norman, 2003 ▲ DIGITAL PAVILION - ONL ◆ THE MARTIAN - Ridle
▲ SCREENED OUT - Jean Baudrillard, 2002
VIRTUAL MOVEMENT
995 ■ URBANEER - Terreform, 2009 ✕ KINECT XBOX - Mic
S: DISAPPEARING COMPUTER, 2001-03 ▲ NEW PARADIGMS - Mosé Ricci, 2012 ✕ PLAYSTATION MOV
P5 GLOVE - Essential Reality, 2002 □ THOUSAND ECOLOGIES - Eric Hörl, 2009 ✕ SIXTHSENSE (dev) -
▲ HYLOZOIC GROUND - Philip Beesley, 2010 ▲ VIB
✕ EVIDENCE OF DARK MATTER, 2005 WEARABLES ARRIVAL ▲ SYSTEMIC ARCHITECTURE - Claudia Pasquero; Marco
ALGAE MACHINES ▲ THE SILENCE OF SLIM
◆ ALGA(E)ZEBO - Cruz, Colletti, 2012
■ HYLOZOIC GROUND - Philip Beesl

CONFORMATIVE PROTOCOLS
1990-2000

THE TOPOLOGICAL CONDITION: OVERLAPPING LAYERS AND MODELLING FIELDS

Manuel Gausa

1. OVERLAPPING LAYERS

1.1. Mutations-Reevaluations

1.2. Caution and Looking Backward

1.3. Another Form, Another Place: The Outskirts as Myth

1.4. Dispersions and Discohesions

1.5. The Turn-of-the-Century City

1.6. Metropolis-Metapolis: A Vibrating Territory

1.7. New Records: Evolving Maps

2. TOPOLOGICAL PATTERN CONDITIONS

2.1. "Space-Time-Information"

2.2. Composition-Position-Disposition (Order-Form-Organization)

2.3. Dynamic Trajectories: Other Geometries, Other Fluctuant Patterns

2.4. Diagrams and Epitomes. Scalar Leaps

2.5. "Maps & Fields" of Forces: Intersections and Hybridizations

3. MODELLING FIELDS

3.1. Fields of Movement: Fluctuations and Animations

3.2. Network Frameworks

3.3. Wagers and New Paradigms: A New Para-theory for Post-Postmodernity

COLORARIUM: TOPOLOGICAL SPACE AND RELATIONAL SUBJECT: THE CONTINUOUS FLOOR

Jordi Vivaldi

1. FIGURATION AND FIGURATIVE

2. TOPOLOGICAL SPACE

3. THE RELATIONAL SUBJECT

4. THE CONTINUOUS FLOOR

5. RISKS AND MENACES: ARCHITECTURE AS AN EFFECT

MANUEL GAUSA

CONFORMATIVE PROTOCOLS 1990-2000

The Topological Condition: Overlapping Layers and Modelling Fields

I- OVERLAPPING LAYERS

I.I Mutations-Reevaluations

In the final third of the 20th century, the city (its new dimensions, its mutations, its transformations and definitions) became the main focus of the turn-of-the-century cultural and architectural debate.This was proof of the scale of the dynamics that had been unleashed in just a few decades, in which the urban process had experienced a spectacular and, at the same time, unexpected scalar leap – both conceptually and in size – resulting from its own accelerated, entropic mutation.

These dynamics had seen the old limits of what had, for years, been defined as a "city" fall away, faced with the new scales of a new "urban-territorial" space where presences and absences, valences and latencies, consolidated fabrics and denatured spaces, dense cores and ambiguous edges, mixed growths and blended grounds would coexist.[1]

Vast residential estates and hard industrial boundaries, large connective infrastructures and new productive structures were revealed as the generic elements in a progressive urban expansion mechanics that ended up laying bare the crisis of the modern yearning for rational order and functional planning, specialized zoning and sectorized organization, as alternative paradigms to more figural and/or traditional ones.

Turn-of-the-century urban culture was increasingly perplexed and disarmed by what Ian McHug defined as the "uncontrolled growth spectrum of the contemporary city. [2]

_1. Manuel Gausa, "Metrópolis>Metápolis: Nuevas mapificaciones para la ciudad contemporánea", *Quaderns* no. 213 (1996), 102.
_2. Ian McHug, "Scaping from planning and world building", www.ianmachugh.wordpress.com

This scenario replaced the old idea of "centrality", continuous radiation, coherence and linear development, with a set of autonomous, discontinuous, heterogeneous and apparently incoherent structures, open to constant entropic evolutions.

Given the disciplinary perplexity in the face of scenarios that seemed impossible to accept with systemic and grammatical clarity, the mystique of a necessary "turning back" or "return to the past" was the most generalized response:

– A "return to the origins" (to a sacred and protectionist "architecture of the city") as a possible line of action: an option based on the recovery of memory as a motto ("history is rich in lessons"), in the semantic attention to context as an argument, in the control of form as a goal, and in the appreciation of an idealized "center" as an essential model, in which the linguistic apparatus and formal eclecticism would be the foundations for sustaining an ambiguous postmodern ideology of relativist conviction and a more or less explicit dialogue with history.

– Or a "return to dogma", to conceptual abstraction, to the positioned and positional object, to essential design, to formal (dry, succinct, functional) minimalism, to an articulating structuralism, as the substantive foundations for a possible "neo-modern", more or less alternative, ideology.

That was the instrumental basis for a compound urbanism rooted in the safety of codes and tried-and-true catalogs: notes and annotations describing the meticulous definition of a morphology recovered through the calligraphic and/or rhetorical use of design (and details) or through the plastic and positional conception of volume, in which the neo-figurative (i.e., formal) nature of the proposals was particularly important.[3]

1.2 Caution and Looking Backward

In fact, in the shared ideology of much of the revisionist official urbanism of the late 1970s and much of the 1980s/90s, the longing for a "reconstructed urban space" was the main *common goal* for quite some time. A period that was going to see rise and consolidate, worldwide, all the baggage of "postmodern" eclectic relativism – of essentially guarantee and vocationist vocation – favored in large part by the social and cultural confusion that would, in effect, suppose major economic crises of the mid-70s and the collapse of the entire modern epic based on optimistic confidence and developmental and ideological *progress*. The upheaval of the mid-1970s and early 80s – and the different political and social movements that coincided with it – (although less present in the media than events today) had decisive consequences not only in the global development of the planet but in a certain shift in the direction of urban thinking, management and conception during the final third of the 20th century. Its generalized acceptance (framed by the oil crisis of the 1970s, the announcement of incipient industrial reconversions, tensions in the Middle East, and the final effects of post-colonialism) definitively ushered in the end of an era that had arisen from the immediate postwar period, characterized by a shared sentiment of renewed euphoria and confidence in a potential modern construction of progress.

Operative caution and a revision of values ("conversation with history"), although latent since the late 1960s, ultimately ended up replacing, in a new framework of uncertainty, the indeterminate idea of innovation with the more reassuring notion of continuity.

Discretion and moderation, weighted management and *possibilist* pragmatism, reconstruction and/or recreation, tradition and habit, pre-existence or experience (as consolidated

_3. Michael Batty, "Sobre el crecimiento de la ciudad", *Fisuras* no. 5 (1997), 6.

or consensual assets) and a certain focus on the local context as a close and familiar framework for action, were the keys to a critical, pragmatic and "realistic" period, which – with varying results – ended up determining not only many of the urban references but also the most important pedagogical, productive, creative and cultural models of the time.

A concentration on issues of typology, of morphology, of layout, in short, which served as the preferred refuge for those turn-of-the-century revisionist dogmas that had emerged as a reaction to the anathematized formal, and also spatial, rupture brought about by modernity. Dogmas based on the recovery of a longed-for urban harmony addressed from the strict compositional control of building construction, in particular, and urban "traditional planning", in general.

The subtle preference for compositional figuration, for evocative outlines, for a linguistic eclecticism of light (or explicit) historical references, characterized many of the main instrumental tendencies of the time, combining – with particular commercial success – productive (modern) mechanics and reproductive (retro-classical or postmodern) calligraphy.

This return to a symbolic, gravitational "center", recovered or recreated locally (and through localism) was the main contribution to a new formal-urban debate. For most of the 1980s, it shifted between the final throes of Italian theory (Rossi's "form of the city", Gregotti's "realist-type" *genius loci*, the environmental factors of the Milanese School, etc.) or the "pop-post" and "post-pop" re-propositions by a critical-positivist like Venturi or a critic-nihilist like Tafuri and, ultimately, the fortunes – for a good part of the decade – of Kenneth Frampton's famous "critical regionalism", so prestigious in areas characterized by a signified identity: Catalonia, Porto, Ticino, Flanders, etc. This new theoretical framework was called on to replace the old universal ideologies with a practical, domestic, contextual pragmatism that would have a short (and effective) range, in times of uncertainty and past refuges and its main source of inspiration came from the models supported by the "finest" urban tradition. A line blessed by an actively belligerent disciplinary culture that was to base its main source of inspiration on those models supported by the urban "best tradition".[4]

1.3 Another Form, Another Place: The Outskirts' Myth.

Given the different figurative expressions – broadly "postmodern" or softly "eclectic" – displayed by this defensive rearguard which took the evocation of an ideal and referential (civic, cohesive, harmonic) center as its main model, but, also, faced with a dreamy eagerness to recover "lost paradises", the critical reaction propitiated at the time by certain theoretical positions was to return to the rigorous foundations of a more objective and abstract universe, related not only to the icons of history but also to the manifestations of a contemporary civilization with a strong expressive component.[5]

It is in this context that we should interpret the interest manifested by the investigations produced in the mid-1980s regarding a "new" narrative landscape: that of the periphery as an "alternative scenario": a myth and a cliché at the same time.[6]

Contrasted with the decadent harmony of a recreated history, and contrasted with the impossible sentimentality of the traditional city, the periphery became an alternative "new landscape" ("a landscape without pre-established qualities").[7]

_4. Ignasi Solà-Morales, *Fer la ciutat, fer l'arquitectura* (Barcelona: Editorial Alain, 1994), 401.
_5. The "new objectivity" advocated by Quaderns d'Arquitectura i Urbanisme (Quaderns) was going to confront the urban lyric of the traditional city with the "metropolitanism" of the emerging city.
_6. Dietmar Steiner, "Vielleicht eine Biographic der Peripherie", *Daidalos* no. 15 (1993).
_7. Marcel Meili, "Periferia. Una carta desde Zürich", *Quaderns,* no. 177 (1988).

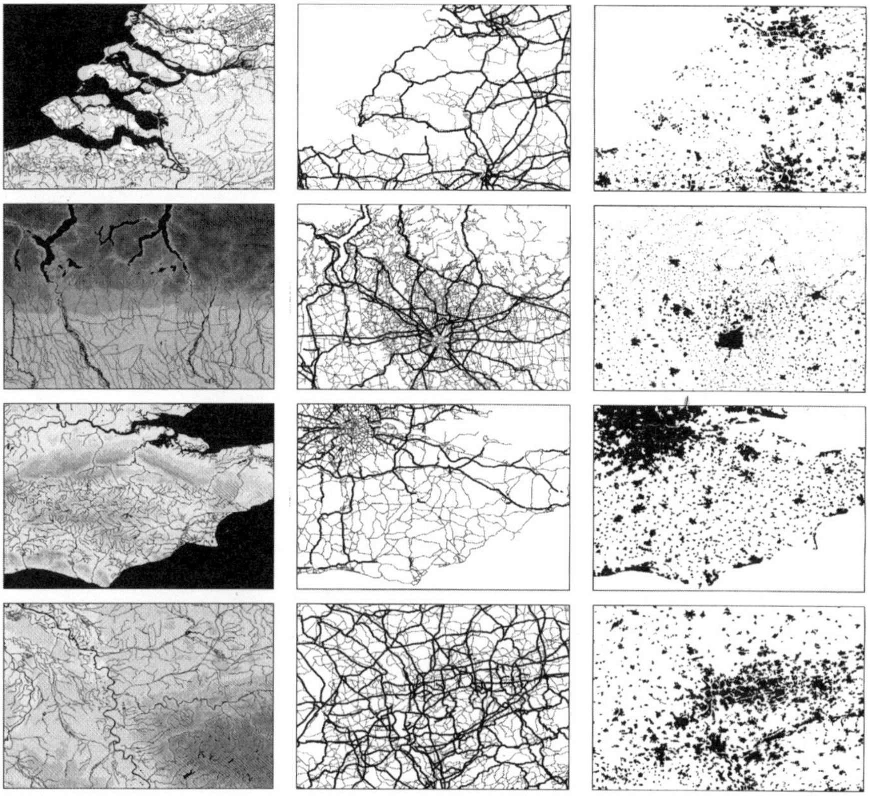

Processes of interrelation among infrastructural nets and urban sprawl spattering in different city-regions: the Rijn-Schelde delta, the Milan region, Kent Metropolis and the Ruhr Valley. According to MUST S/A Lab (in *De Verkenning Van de Hoeksche Waard*).

During a good part of the 80s and 90s, it was upheld as the "impossible" dream of a "possible" – as in "interrupted" – lost modernity: the poetic setting of a failed city (defective in its concretion, clumsy, conflictive, tense, out of harmony) but which could still potentially be re-interpreted and instrumented. It allowed for contrasting the evocative model of the historic city, with the rigor and austerity, the abstract intensity and the "latent" (and open) condition of a modern city that could be reevaluated and reformulated.[8]

The subtle borderline between the outskirts in the 1980s as an alternative "cultured landscape" – a potentially "expectant" space of latencies but also of valences – and the suburbs of the 1960s as a political scenario for social indictment – lacking, conflictive, belligerent, socially "resistant" – outlined an ambiguous space of contradictions and intersections at the same time. However, the very idea of the outskirts as a "border landscape" (or perimeter) continued to underlie and thrive in their nature as "ex-centric". As the end of the 80s and the beginning of the 90s, however, that notion of a peripheral perimeter was changing to make way for a more diffuse, more dynamic, ambiguous and *fractalized* scenario in its expressions and manifestations.

_8. Frederick Barthelme, "Estar en el error", *Quaderns,* n° 177 (1988).

1.4 Dispersions and Discohesions

The generalized increase in new transformation phenomena associated with how the impact of mobility and communication at a distance affected territorial occupation, the appearance of new "networked territorialities", the refocusing of cities in suburbs, demographic explosions and real estate growth – with the resulting residential, productive or leisure-related suburban developments (without necessarily being connected to one another) – the emergence of overgrown "world-cities" and specialized ghettos (occurring on all spatial and social levels) and, in short, the appearance of new urban "para-" and "meta-" forms of irregular development, brought about local and global transformations that seemed not to have been anticipated, addressed or foreseen by an urban science that was locked into the linear imposition/composition of traditional models that were often self-contained.

The less-than-flexible repercussions of planning that was meticulously detailed and managed, but with hardly any capacity for evolution and/or adaptation (as well as the contingent development of infrastructural support systems produced only based on circumstantial connections, which, as a result, were insufficiently integrated into – and joined with – an authentic strategic organization of the city-territory "beyond the limits"), not only seemed not to have been anticipated, but seemed not to respond to the demands of accelerate dynamic processes that were constantly up against a discipline – and a figuration – that held fast to the old rules of a static/esthetic condition and that it could only be conveniently approached from its own procedural and relational logic.[9]

In that sense, whereas the dichotomy between a "center frozen in history" and an "expectant periphery" – handled so well by planners like Marcel Smets, Bruno Fortier, Joan Busquets or Manuel de Solà Morales from his important "Urbanism Laboratory" – was, for a certain time, a revitalizing leitmotiv for turn-of-the-century urban planning, it also ended up limiting the debate to a kind of aesthetic confrontation between two figurative landscapes (the morphological continuity of the historical city versus the objectual freedom of modern growth), reducing the perception of – and the approaches to – space to a problem of forms: old or new forms for scenarios – interior fabrics or perimeter boundaries – which were situated, in any case, within the familiar framework of what was traditionally understood as a "city": a recognizable and coherent, univocal enclosure,[10] whose geometry had nonetheless begun to unravel, evidencing more and more explicitly the accelerating dynamic nature of urban systems and their new "geo-urban" dimension.[11]

Growing sprawl of large conurbations: polycentric structures described through fractal geometries.
Urban dispersion related to an ideal compact circle of the same occupied area (in *Arch+* no. 121, 1994).

_9. See the magazine Urbanisme n° 262, and the issues 109, 110 y 112 of the magazine Arch+, 1991-92.
_10. Juan Manuel Fernandez Alonso, "Arquitectura y urbanismo para el territorio contemporáneo," *BAU*, no. 14 (1996).
_11. The term geo-urbanity is introduced by the author in Manuel Gausa, Guallart, Vicente; Müller, Willy, HiCat. Hiper-Catalunya. Territoris de recerca (Barcelona: Ed. Actar, 2003).

Territorial Sprawl Plankton: Steven HOLL: "Edge of a City" in *Pamphlet Architecture* no. 13.

1.5 The Turn-of-the-Century City

The very idea of the "city" could not be associated (as it had been at the beginning of the decade) with a single place (center or periphery, area or region) or a specific form, not even with a single state of evolution, but with the diverse evolutions of a dynamic system, constantly changing, open to the interactive combination of different simultaneous states, phases and experiences.[12]

The turn of the century confirmed the evidence of a spectacular scalar leap (paradigm shift) in the definition of our living spaces and social spaces – our habitats – associated with the rapid increases in mobility and communication over (long) distances, the delocalization of exchanges, and the growing capacity for the material and technological transformation of our milieu associated with the accelerated increase in mobility, communication at (long) distance, the de-location of exchanges and the increasing material and technological capacity of transformation of our medium(s.

A global process tied in, at the same time, with the expansion of the digital sphere and the growing possibility of effectively combining complex, simultaneous and overlapping parameters of information.

The assimilation of this new – global, holistic, multiple – capacity called on to process informational and spatial (variable and differential, dynamic and evolving) interactions in increasingly complex frameworks of exchange, was one of the great social and cultural revolutions of this new era.

This accelerated increase in mobility and exchange conditions was going to show, in an increasingly explicit way, the dynamic nature of urban systems and their new "geo-urban" dimension, materializing that transfer between centuries of the old city enclosure (*Wall City*) to the new dispersed city (*Sprawl City, Ink-Stain City, Spot City* or *Patchwork City* according to various authors).[13]

The old compact urban machine gave way to a more irregular and scattered structure. The old cohesive (essentially coherent) city gave way to a new simultaneous (differentially consistent) multi-city. The progressive development of mobility, communication, transport and information,shifted the contemporary city toward a new form of self-planning and self-organization in which the increasing "freedom of movement" in space – displacement, access and occupation – ultimately gave rise to a new type of artificial, fluctuating, non-linear poly-constructions. Curiously enough, they were not that different from the more "natural" – and unplanned – constructions, characteristic of most of the distributions, occupations and spontaneous groupings (dynamic in their configuration) present in nature.

The old paradigms of rigid urban architectural disciplines drawing on the approach to old urban planning – delineating or functionalist, zoning or formalizing, managing and/or regulating – showed their limitations when faced with progressively unpredictable, complex and shifting developments, associated with the growing capacity to process, exchange (and transform) information that was increasingly simultaneous and (de)localized – both geographically and socially, spatially and temporally.

The objective of many of the analyses, essays and approaches of the late 20th century dedicated to recognizing this new fragmented, heterogeneous and apparently unstructured reality, in mutation, was not only to record its plural manifestations (those of an increasingly multi-faceted and diverse organism, that was potentially richer and – also

_12. Sabine Kraft, "La périphérie: mobilité et projet urbain" in *V.V.A.A : Construire la ville sur la ville*, Catalogue Europan (1995)
_13. Willem Jan Neutelings, "Patchwork City", *AD-Architectural Design*, no. 2/4, vol 64 (1994).

Nile Ole LUND: Dreaming of your own home, *Collage*, 1975

– more threatening) or to describe the apparent chaos and wild growth of the urban milieu from a simple angle of fascination. Instead, they attempt to come to terms with and make use of the structural and infrastructural processes that define these developments (which are often disquieting, because they are irregular) and progressively disperse them.

Complexity, diversity, discontinuity, irregularity and, in any case, – local and global – interaction among phenomena, processes, structures and configurations, are some of the new parameters for definition in use at the turn of the century, demonstrating the obsolescence of most urban planning models carried over directly from situations in the past – which are more linear and apparently stable because they are excessively deterministic.

The dynamic simulations already within reach (as we will see later) thanks to the development of digital computing, helped to demonstrate how the city tends to manifest itself as a variable, complex and interactive system, that could only be interpreted through the accumulation of multiple, simultaneous and often contradictory actions: *stages, states and strata*.

A progressively diversified "multi-layer" system produced by the complex interaction between diverse, discontinuous, non-permanent and overlapping – coexisting – information and realities that were continually changing, distorting, altering, transforming – and reinterpreting – the developmental patterns that defined and whose strength would lay precisely in that constant capacity for renewal and modernization, construction and recycling.[14]

_14. Manuel Gausa, "Metrópolis>Metápolis", *Quaderns* no. 213 (1996), 102.

1.6 Metropolis-Metapolis: a Vibrating Territory

The contemporary *n-city* or *multi-city* could not be approached (or thought about) in terms of a single (stable) "place" or a (pre-established) "form"; or in terms of a "singular" evolutionary stage (or a unique – more or less ideal or coherent – "movement"). A real and virtual scenario at the same time that would no longer be a form – or it would not be just a form – but rather a complex system of relationships based on simultganeous informational layers that would define it (physical but also demographic, biological, economic, cultural, political, etc.) and large structural networks that would link it (transport, energy, information dissemination, financial movements, etc.): a new "urban-territorial" scenario that appears as an algorithmically fluctuating structure in which more flexible systematic, elastic, permeable, deformable and topological matritial orders could be recognized.[15]

This new *multicity* or the new *multilayered Metapolis*, (to use the term coined by François Asher in 1995)[16] was posited as an increasingly "flexible" organism that was difficult to continue subjecting to the closed and static formulas (forms and models) old planning and that, on the contrary, it would respond to parameters of a strangely informal (for informational) order that, as in any dynamic development, would tend to evolve freely and spontaneously. Parameters that allow us to guess a new type of organization related to global "topological schemes" (which, at all scales and at all levels, in these processes would be inferred) but, also, with "informational" processes of interaction, whose unstable nature and irregular pretend it was important to recognize in turn.

The "rich and complex nature" of this new *n-city* resided in that shift from a city essentially understood as a form to a city understood as a system: as a dynamic and informational system: a system of relationships and interactions between layers and networks of information – real and virtual, material and immaterial. This "relational" rather than "formal" potential of the new city (tending toward more polyfaceted, plural, complex and open structures) expressed a new and radical change of paradigms in which

– the old "stable" condition of urban life progressively gave way to a definitely more dynamic (unstable-evolving) condition.

– the old closed (regular) geometries were replaced by new, more flexible and differential, more open and irregular topologies.

– the old linear (complete and deterministic) models gave way to other non-linear (incomplete and indeterminate) models

– the old notion of form (object) was expanded to the notion of process (system).

The conclusion to that scenario was the necessary adoption of a different kind of tools for analysis that were capable of studying the city, not as a "fabric" or an "object" but as an open process of exchange; a flexible and "dis-dense" process – which is discontinuous and dense at the same time, as well as irregular and connected, diverse and disperse.

Approaching this new reality – the result of mobility, exchange, migration and precise communication – required a persistent attention to "multi-layer" factors of simultaneity, capable of proposing "descriptions" and "evolutions" of the system and within it: occupational, demographic, environmental and cultural parameters, as well as parameters of connectivity and use, etc. served as the foundation for possible "evolving cartographies", Cartographies where the city appeared synthesized – compressed – into basic "levels" of

_15. Michael Batty, "Sobre el crecimiento de la ciudad", *Fisuras* no. 5 (1997), 6.
_16. François Asher, *Métapoles ou l´avenir des villes* (París: Ed. Odile Jacob, 1995)

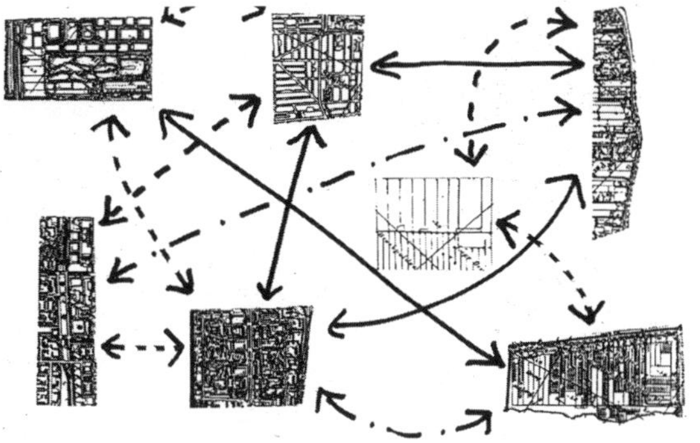

The metapolitan n-city or "multicity" is a complex system generated through the simultaneity of information layers and interconnected networks in constant interaction. Willem Jan Neutelings: *The Carpet Metropolis*, 1995.

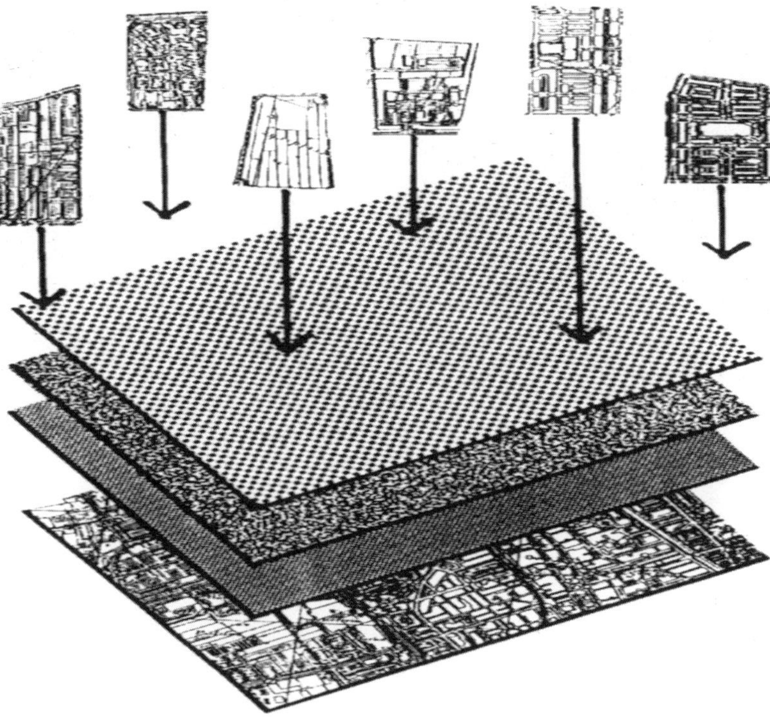

information" (informational layers of relational nets) that could potentially be activated in – and through – different suitable tactical combinations.

The adventure of this new urban approach tied in with architectural conception and the digital and informational revolution was shared by a whole generation of ideas, research and investigations driven by the same prospective intent that combined transversal strategies with new holistic approaches in the pursuit of an effective mapping and a new type of (intentional / informational) cartography for a new type of more complex (multilayer and multi-scalar, dynamic and multidimensional) hyper-urban scenario.

April 24th1990- Launch of Hubble, first data-satellite orbit.

1.7 New Records: Evolutive Maps

The launch of the Hubble Space Telescope in 1990 – as the first "processor" of geo-referenced information – highlighted this new multilevel and multilayer condition (real and virtual, material and immaterial, formal and informational) of a system – the urban sphere – in terms of multi-localized processes of exchange – and mapping.

The city could be approached, thus, as a dynamic and informational system, of relationships and interactions, (of layers of information and networks of relationships) in which diversity and simultaneity, multi-scalar complexity and inter-scalar transversality, could be recognized using the new GIS systems (launched in 1991) and the first sequential Scanner readings (marketed in 1993).[17]

Whereas the territory was no longer represented using systems based on fixed landmarks or static plans, to be replaced by models using aerial photogrammetry, and then satellite images, (where the new "real" space, paradoxically, was outlined based on the "virtual" space of "information" and "telecommunication").

The scanspace of radars and lasers and its digital translation, are the best example to demonstrate the move beyond "figural" space (and the associated conception of time) not only as an effect of an eventual abstract and "de-territorialized" logic, but also as a manifestation of technological development itself – of a prospective and evolving form of representation, that is informational, and *processual* (in terms of "processes" and "processing" data).[18]

A new digital, informational space was revealed as a synthetic, (mathematical, parametrized) space, but it is also concrete (modelable, manipulable, singularizable).

The idea of visualization and representation led, in this new smart cartography, associated with the pioneering digital programs, to the "capacity for projection, combination and modification": a characteristic that is promoted by the progressive sophistication of information and its manipulation (or edition) associated with new technological tools.[19]

Whereas in traditional plans governed by formal logics, the drawings that were generated tended to be identified with a – more or less literal – "composed" whole, in the new digital documents – the famous GIS, for example – graphic elements are no longer literal translations of reality; rather they are graphic "meta-forms" (synthetic maps, diagrams or combinatory matrices) intended to represent vectors associated with the topological characteristics of the systems they are addressing.[20]

The introduction of techniques of movement and time into digital programming allowed for working with "abstract syntheses" and "concrete evolutions", i.e., with dynamic simulations and parametric processes associated with variables that can be modified in keeping with successive prospective options. The old static figurations of representation gave way to virtually dynamic sets of evolution referred to basic instructional rules (devices / *dispositifs*) and possible combinations of movements (dispositions) in which relations and actions, programs and scenarios would be merged.[21]

_17. Xavier Costa, "Topometries", in Costa, Xavier and Laura Kurgan, *You are Here: Architecture and Information Flows* (Barcelona: MACBA, 1995)

_18. Mario Gandelsonass, "The Exurban Observer," *Quaderns* no. 213 (1996), 152.

_19. Josep M. Fargas and Papazian, Pegor, "Territory and Modeling," *Quaderns* no. 194 (1992), 90.

_20. Josep M. Fargas and Papazian, Pegor, "Territory and Modeling," *Quaderns* no. 194 (1992), 90.

_21. "Maps will be territories of representation, simulation or recreation. They will construct, not reproduce. They will be open, connectable in all their dimensions (with the potential to be subject to constant modifications). The value of abstraction, with a generative, evolutionary and productive sense, will be evident in them." Francisco Porras, "Editorial," *BAU* no. 014 (1996).

Geographical Information Systems (GIS): digital maps of land use and topo-projections (in *Quaderns* n. 194, 1982)

Cartographies transformed into vectorized (processual and, perhaps, intentional) records, to be used in generating – i.e., selecting, hierarchizing, but above all recognizing and combining, in order to manipulate them and make them operative – layers of information, rather than representation.

The aim, then, was not to produce only forms "in" space but to formulate (to map out) processes (programs and/for movements) "between" spaces: outlines, diagrams, ideograms, or infograms, patterns and frameworks, matrices or dynamic grids emerged, in this initial phase of research, as "open records" of an itinerary, which like real or virtually evolving trajectories, allowed for recognizing processes – and the phenomena associated with them – with the potential to change, to grow and to develop; combining the global abstraction of systematization and the local figuration of contingencies (*generative trajectories and resolutive maneuvers*).

Whereas the old idea of analog, figurative and literal representation (associated with classical representation) had promoted a type of compositional cartography – regulatory and dividing – intended to delineate (and regulate) the limits, the restrains and the "contours" of things – and their physical ties "in" the plane – and whereas the idea of typological, abstract and determinate planning (associated with modern reproduction) had called for a more positional kind of cartography (oriented toward linking and positioning the modern "volume-object", as a functional mechanism, "above" the plane) this new contemporary

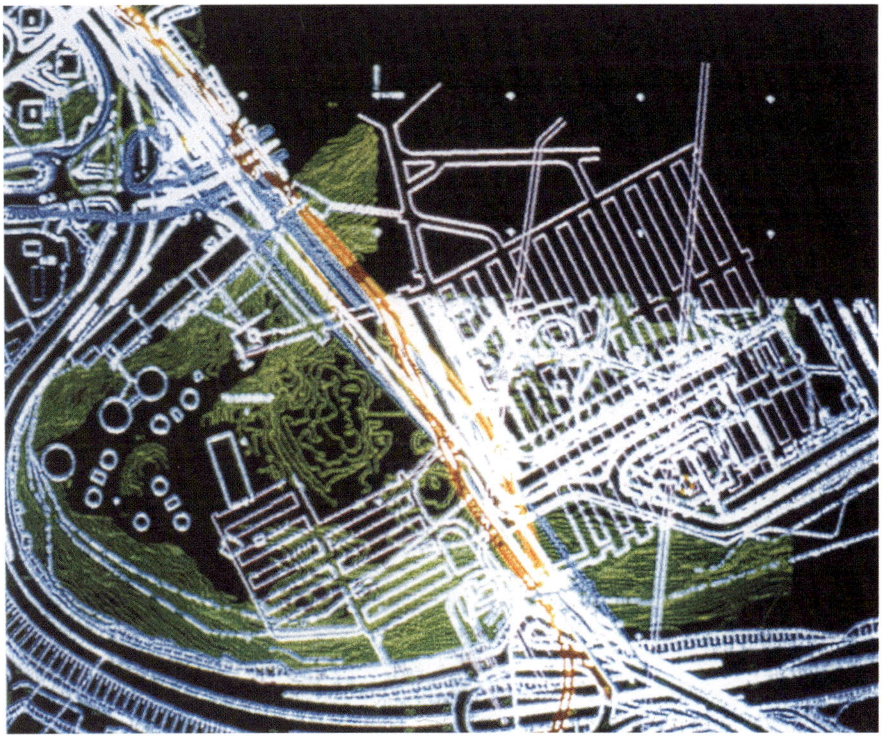

Overlapping urban structures and underground infrastructures (in *Vag-OchVattenbyggaren*, 4, 1990)

diagrammatic synthesis (dynamic, informational and combinatory) required a new kind of dispositional, compressive and processual cartography, with the potential to process data and map processes at the same time.[22]

Where classical representation outlined figures and modern representation produced objects, contemporary representation mapped processes. Processes, in fact, as opposed to events. [23]

The exponential access to the possibility of understanding better – thanks to the new computer programs – models and patterns of/between complex and variable evolutionary processes (fractals, flows, crowds, deployments and clustering, etc.) as well as the capacity to better analyze the dynamic systems themselves and to synthesize and condense their own evolutionary, variable, inaccurate and unpredictable projections into possible "consensus figures" (*strange attractors,* such as basic and *open instructions* or *protocols*, at the same time) made it possible to compress in inductive *informational instructions* of schematic compression, the diversified layers of intentional analysis - or the infinite irregular variations - of multiple levels of/and trajectories summarized in possible models or protocols, "cito" and "kino" diagrammatic.

_22. Fernandez Guerra Juan has similar works in relation to this facts.
_23. This text is related with the chapter 3 of the publication: Manuel Gausa, *Open(ing), Space-Time-Information* (Barcelona: Actar, 2018).

1990, first personal computers of Macintosh, perfecting the micro-processing and windows systems.

2- TOPOLOGICAL PATTERN CONDITIONS

2.1 Space-Time-Information

After years of historical revisionism and instrumental calligraphy (both modern and post-modern) the final decades of the 20th century were characterized, in effect, by the initial impact of the new digital universe and its marked computational component.

In that sense, the early years of the 90s were characterized by the intellectual assimilation of this procedural, but also "urban-territorial", scalar leap, with a comprehensive scope (the city no longer as a recognizable form but as a complex, informational, social, economic, spatial and cultural process) that was intensified by mobility and communication and extended beyond the landscapes typical of the old dichotomies between "center" and "periphery".

Territorial mutations, migratory flows, immaterial processes, infrastructural connections and spatio-temporal interaction systems emerged as substantive phenomena of a shift in scenario(s) coinciding with the first manifestations of the digital – computational or informational – revolution and its growing (universal and personal) capacity to process, manage, visualize and synthesize complex information in potential interaction.

In 1981, IBM introduced its Personal Computer, practically the first PC format – with the COMMODORE 64 (IBM 5150 model, 4.77 MHz, Intel 8080) – based on Microsoft MS-DOS microprocessors.

1990, First Atari videogame digital device consoles.

The IBM PC was going represented an absolute change in approach to the computational universe, which had, until then, been housed in "laboratory" settings (large shared machines) but little by little began optimizing both size and features (the IBM 1400 and CD 6600 series, for example).

A year later, in 1982, *Time* magazine gave its commemorative issue the explicit title "Machine of the Year", in reference to the PC, in place of the usual "Man of the Year", foreshadowing the great revolution that the advance seemed to presage on a technological and productive level.

During the 1980s, the impact of the computational devices only increased, although it was limited to operating systems that were perceived more like faster and more efficient calculators or typewriters.

At the beginning of the 1990s, however, another substantial advance took place: Macintosh perfected its micro-processing systems and introduced the laptop, and Apple launched its Laptop in 1990 – initially to limited success, but its impact on the market quickly increased. The factors of portability, speed, adaptability and access to a complex and pliable approach to the environment, combined to facilitate a real change in the management and perception of our environment, which spread rapidly with the consolidation of Windows-based operating software throughout the 1990s (Windows 3.0-1990 / Windows NT-1995 / Windows XP-2000).[24]

_24. See "History of Computing" in www.wikipedia.org/wiki/History_of_computing and "Digital Computing - Dictionary definition of Digital Computing | Encyclopedia.com: FREE online dictionary".

The old classical mono-focal vision or the modern relativistic (or planar) vision – still with a recognizable referential basis – had progressively made way for a more dynamic and complex perception of reality: first with cinema as a focused moving image; then with television, as the first domestic screen with the ability to combine inhabited reality and observed reality; and, later, with the "processing windows" characteristic of a new type of interface called on to demonstrate not only multi-layer but also procedural condition of a new type of multiple and multiplied ("multi-type and multi-level") scenarios that had such a profound influence on the pioneering experiments of the moment.[25]

The development of the first "video games" (with the ATARI-1980 and NINTENDO-1985 consoles and the first PlayStation-1995), as well as the sophistication of advertising and spatial effects in the media, augmented the combined experience of referent reality (acting) and experiential virtuality (fluctuating).

The former "topical" space is replaced by an increasingly "teletopical" one, where the real time of broadcasting an event blends together with the real space of the event itself, where the heterogeneous perception of experiences and scenarios – "projected" and simultaneous, virtual and real – tends to overlap with the apparent calm of stability, stabilization and the established.[26]

Sudden slips and shifts between the commonplace and the extraordinary, the predictable and the surprising, the stable and the ephemeral, the familiar and the foreign; between the artificial – because it is strange – and the "strangely natural"... because it is artificial.

This slippery, atonal channel-hopping or zapping condition implies a new type of perception, which is, in turn, related to a new experience of change and exchange – of informational interaction, in short – that is often created during situations of relocation and clashing.[27]

Simultaneity and brevity, dynamism and instability, irregularity and dispersion are some of the many variables related to the transformation and overlapping of more *polyphasic* "new scenarios", but also to the transformation that is apparent in the current cultural framework, which is more sensitive to the compatible multiplication and combination of different cultural, social and spatial realities; to this vague mixture of coexistences and *inter-weavings*, of relationships and *de-familiarizations* between the universal and the particular, the systematic and the contingent, the domestic and the public, the real and the virtual, the natural and the artificial – in short, between the commonplace and the extraordinary – which tends, increasingly, toward articulating situations and experiences (of one's own and others) translating this decided loss of stability and "positional" essentiality and its substitution with a new more multi-faceted "hyper-scenario" composed of multiple situations, conflicts and tensions, but also possible qualitative re-evaluations – and reinventions.[28]

The fall of the Berlin Wall summed up the confirmation of a time of pluralities, intersection, simultaneities and diversities, of heterogeneities and multiplicities, surprisingly intermingled and/or interwoven, which was faithfully translated in publications like *Mille*

_25. Alessandro Baricco, *The Game* (Barcelona: Ed. Anagrama, 2018).

_26. Vicente Guallart, "Architecture by Software," *Quaderns*, no. 203 (1995).

_27. Francisco Jarauta, "Tensiones del arte y la cultura contemporáneos en las sociedades tardocapitalistas," in *V.V.A.A: Otro marco para la creación* (Madrid: Ed. Universidad Complutense, 1994).

_28. This text is related with the chapters 3 (Records) and 4 (Territories) of the publication: Manuel Gausa, *Open(ing), Space-Time-Information* (Barcelona: Ed. Actar, 2018).

1989, the fall of the Berlin Wall (Mauerfall), parallel to the digital era birth was an essential event that marked the fall of the iron curtain (and the deterministic and positional duality capitalism-communism) opening the door to a more complex and ambivalent interpretation of the history.

Plateaux by Deleuze and Guattari (1980) or *A Thousand Years of Non-Linear History* by Manuel De Landa (1997), with its multi-layer interpretation of history.

The films of the decade by Quentin Tarantino (*Reservoir Dogs*-1992, *Pulp Fiction*-1994, *Kill Bill* -2004) or by Jim Jarmush (*Night on Earth*-1991) proposed mixed scenarios, within manipulated complex realities (far from the eclectic postmodern collage, they narrated a new type of non-linear complexity that was woven, oriented and processed all at once).[29]

Others films, like *Edward Scissorhands* (Tim Burton, 1990), *Blue Velvet* (David Lynch, 1990), *Mulholland Drive* (David Lynch, 2001), Fargo (Ethel & Joel Cohen, 1996) or *Coffee and Cigarettes* (Jim Jarmusch, 2003) explored this meeting between the ordinary and the extraordinary, the everyday and the uncertain, which represents the shift toward a more polyfocal (transversal and sequential) perspective and shows clear ties, as we have already pointed out, with the first attempts to register a more complex reality (Windows-1990, GIS-1991, Scanner-1993) and with the instrumental, formal and spatial research associated with "multi-layer" digital software programs such as "Autocad", launched in 1983 and implemented throughout the following decade (or other first graphic software of expressive manipulation (Vectorworks 1985-2000 "Nemoscheck", "Illustrator" 1987, "Photoshop", 1990, "Indesign" 1999).[30]

In short, a new conceptual and operational revolution was beginning to take place. A revolution associated with the multiple and complex logics of n-realities (cities, societies, milieux, networks, spaces, scenarios, etc.) understood as complex multi-environments in interaction.

The old stable approach to our environment gave way to a new fluctuating, dynamic and non-linear approach in a complex system of relationships and interactions.

2.2 Composition-Position-Disposition (Order-Form-Organization)

Classical space and modern "space-time" were followed by an *inform(ation)al* space-time, which created greater instability and indetermination in our understanding of the universe – greater informality – but which also allowed for comparing it to a great catalyst for impulses and demands in a possible interactive "co-participation" between processes with local definitions and global developmental frameworks.

The study of nonlinear dynamic systems revealed, increasingly rapidly, the possibility of considering another type of more open order, defined beyond the traditional idea of order as a closed control of processes. A more "disordered" order, fundamental to the understanding of certain scenarios (environments of coexistence), which – as we have been demonstrating – maximize their irregular effects due to an increase in the phenomena of mobility and exchange, and an increase in the degree of interaction between the varied information that has an impact on them.

Both classical space and time and modern space-time manifested a readily apparent desire for substantive stability in the first (or for, suggested, "metaphorical displacement", in the second).

Against the traditional idea of order that had influenced the classical interpretation of space (based on the idea of "composition" as a hierarchical relationship, but also as a cohesive, closed off, predictable figuration between parts), modern thought presented

_29. Other references can be suggested, evidently, but these ones are clearly explicit.
_30. See specially the interesting timeline of the Computer History Museum in https://www.computerhistory.org/ Op.cit

In Jarmush, *Night on the Earth*, 1992: five short multi-layered encounters of overlapping realities occur in five taxis on the same night in Los Angeles, New York, Rome, Paris and Helsinki.

COMPOSITION
Linear Logic - Classical Order

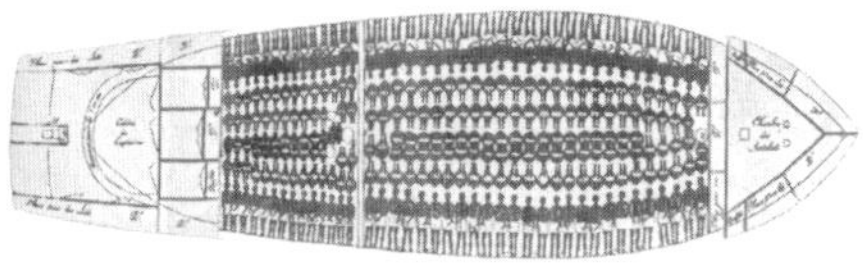

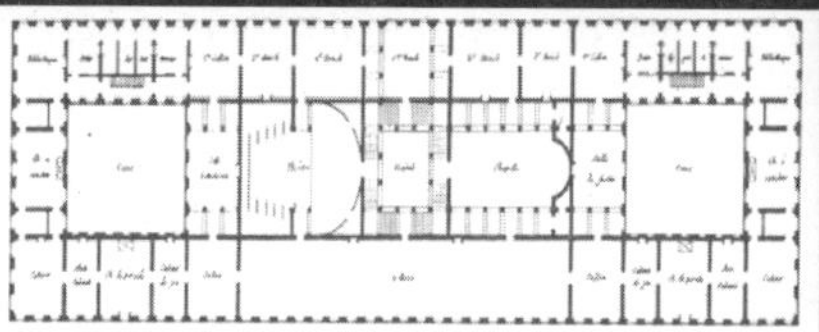

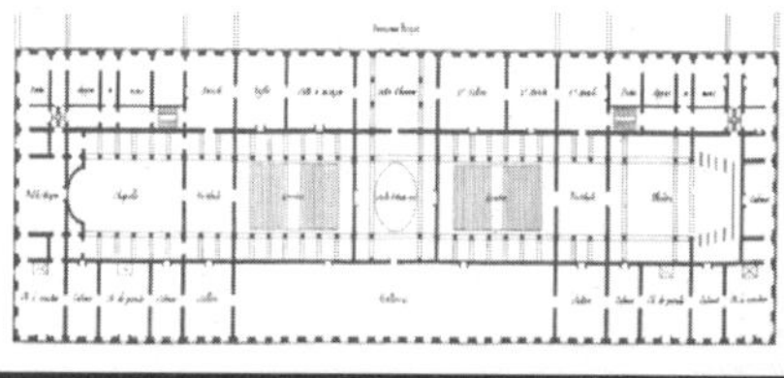

POSITION
Neo-Linear Logic - Modern Order

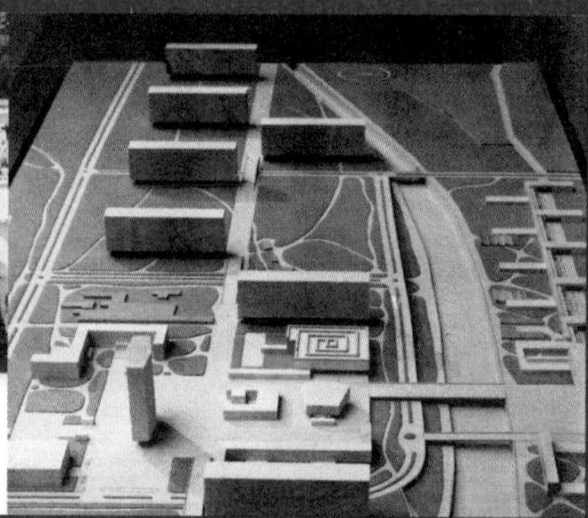

DISPOSITION
Non-Linear Logic - Informational Order

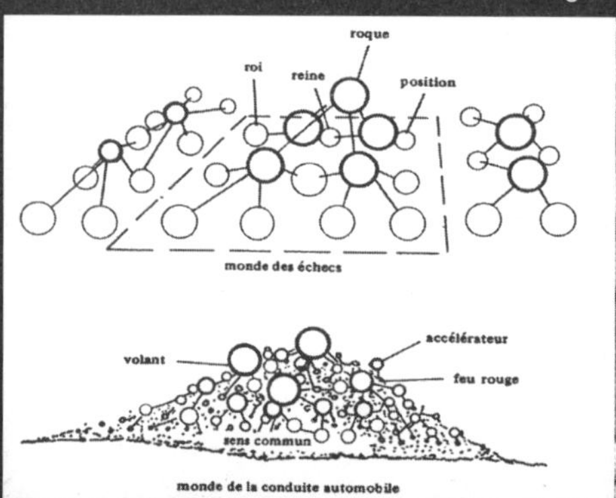

Classical Composition, Modern Position, Informational Disposition (as flexible formulation)
From left to wright: Slaves Ship, and *Urban Palace* (Durand) // A. Resnais: *Last Year at Marienbad*, 1961 and Saint Dié Le Corbusier, 1948) // Dynamic growth and crowd (A. Goula, 1998). *Fuzzy Logic Diagrams*

an alternative "new order" associated with a relativist interpretation of space and time, based on "spatial position" as a freer, though no less strict – fixed, measurable – link between objects. Position as organization, but also as an unalterable, affiliation principle (in harmony with the "ideological" – dogmatic – moment of modern space-time) that is more fragmented, though no less deterministic. [31]

Contemporary space-time emerged, however, as an increasingly variable, changeable and open landscape – of interconnected (and/or interconnected) messages – which possessed, in information and in its open capacity for interaction, a new dimensional vector.

A combinatory and differential space-time-information; informational, then, rather than essential or material; digital rather than analog or mechanical; operative rather than ritual or functional; probable rather than regulated or exact; strategic and tactical rather than symbolic or dogmatic; changeable rather than "eternal" or fragmented; reactive rather than "evocative" or "autonomous"; interactive (simultaneous and multiple) rather than absolute or relative.

This (technological, instrumental, perceptive, conceptual) shift in logic at the turn of the century, the new digital revolutions, and the new idea of time associated therewith, favored the revelation of this new – more elastic – *inform(ation)al* order, no longer based on compositions or on positions, but on dispositions; dispositions that are open to variation, to individuality and to diversity, but also to an exchange and an interaction that are both global and local at the same time.

We could say that if in the field of projection / representation the ancient classical (purist) or modern (depurative) abstraction had marked much of the history of architectural discipline today, however, a new type of abstraction (more "impure") emerges – compressive and comprehensive, condenser, operative – called to combine and synthesize new scenarios of analysis, action and interpretation of the notions of "condition, situation and solicitation, that is, information".

In this context, the emergence, at the end of the 20th century, of a clear paradigm shift in architectural thinking was entirely understandable: moving away from an architecture that had been based, for a long time, on a static logic, the turn of the century led toward an architecture based on a decidedly and definitively dynamic logic... more impure, irregular and ultimately interactive... in an interaction with a medium, a context, a society, and a creative and scientific culture attuned to the diversity and complexity of a decisively informational space-time...

A new type of "alternative" – or advanced – logic derived from the conditions of a new informational time and associated with the key Informational factors of:

Complexity (Multiplicity), Interaction/Interactivity (Exchange), Transversality (Relationality / Inter-Connectivity), Dynamicity (Evolutivity), Simultaneity (Combinatoriality), Adaptability (Flexibility), Diversity (Heterogeneity/Irregularity) and Reactivity (Responsivity).

Factors that would be associated with this new, more open logic, in that it is more unrestricted, more relational and more interactive. A more open logic, which was no longer that of classical metaphysical continuity – or that of postmodern calligraphy (associated with a coveted composition of space), nor that of modern functional objectuality (associated with a certain position in space) but that of a new, contemporary "dispositional interactivity" (associated with a possible disposition between spaces).[32]

_31. Stan Allen, *Points + Lines: Diagrams and Projects for the City* (Princeton: Ed. Princeton Architectural Press, 1999).
_32. Manuel Gausa, *Open(ing), Space-Time-Information* (Barcelona: Ed. Actar, 2018), 293.

Whereas modern space, in its day, implied a shift from the idea of composition, as regulation, to that of position, as a correlation, contemporary space revealed a new shift from the idea of position to that of disposition: as an operative "decision/instruction" but, also, as a possible combination of "arranged" and "interconnected" positions and information, based on a more open, reactive, extroverted and, ultimately, dispositional "attitude" and "aptitude". A flexible and operational "agencement"[33] in which the idea of order as a "stabilized control" would yield to a new conception more "differentially" and "responsively" relational. The new capacity for connection and interaction between the physical and the virtual, i.e., for combining and processing multiple and differential scenarios, messages and information, lent a new importance to the idea of change as (inter)change (between layers of information) and, therefore introduced increased complexity (and impurity) into this progressive capacity for interaction between "data", "codes", "messages", "programs", "conditions" and "solicitations".

If the object of classical composition was the (symbolic or metaphysical) reproduction of what came before, and if the object of modern position was the (functional) production of what was new, the object of contemporary disposition had to be the (interactive) co-production of the simultaneous, real and/or virtual. From a new type of architectural thinking – and design – called on to celebrate, articulate and foster diversity, and make it interact. That could be the ultimate condition of architectural design: generating – and materializing – relationships in space, not just forms in it. Therein lies the innovative potential of a new pioneering focus for project design.

That of an architecture that can express its own movements, but also the variety of information and demands that call for it... and shape it. Capable of working beyond boundaries and beyond – traditional – dichotomies: architecture and landscape, city and territory...[34]

2.3 Dynamic Trajectories: Other Geometries, Other Fluctuant Patterns

Not just the survey of the complex city, but also the architecture associated with it, required a type of multiple spatiality focused, in those initial moments of investigation, on the creation of "n-dimensional maps" not only for registering and prospecting, but also for defining the possible correlated "n-differential" strategies: "informational" (tendential) maps, but which were also "slanted" (intentional) maps of the city and/in the territory.

(Combinatory) maps and (relational) strategies capable of selecting, in this pioneering moment – in a more synthetic (conceptual) rather than parametric (numeral) way – relevant messages and conditions from a multiple reality, processing them, registering them, synthesizing them operatively in order to better "condense" their respective levels of "incidental information" and immanent interaction.

The analysis of the complex processes of *space-temporal-informational interaction* referred to a new type of structures with remarkable levels of self-regulation and self-organization: in more or less stable "settlements" (groupings), and in more temporary "deployments" (distributions), the geometric characteristics associated with these structures and the

_33. We use the term "agencement" as "assemblage", a contractual organization in a similar, but not identical, way to how it is used by Deleuze and Guatarri. In Deleuze and Guatarri, agencement is the term used to describe the "complex" of material singularities and production processes that produce the expressive traits, which are characteristic of a material culture. See: Gilles Deleuze and Guattari, Félix, *A Thousand Plateaus* (Minneapolis: Ed. University of Minnesota Press, 1987).
_34. "I've always been interested in the 'trans' particle. This transit from one into another, not to another, internally." Pablo Palazuelo and Power, Kevin, "Form as Research: A Conversation", *Quaderns,* no. 218 (1997), 42.

"formal" patterns that could be deduced from them helped reveal the topological, open and irregular definition of those fluctuating trajectories, through their most recurrent parameters – and possible characteristics[35].

Beyond any hypothetical formal parallelism, the greatest interest in these geometries lies in their incomplete morphology, characteristic of a process in progress, and their very constitution – internal, multi-scalar and recursive – which is adapted to the strange condition of transfer generated between different combinations and degrees of emergence ("emptiness-fullness-link", "positioning-distancing-itinerary", "occupation-spacing-access", "point-surface-line").

"Recursiveness" between different transitive scales and "distributive complexity" between different generative processes seem to be the main characteristics of those variable, differential and substantially irregular geometries, called on to combine their own inductive frameworks in varying trajectories and/or bypasses (loops, folds, spirals and fluctuations or oscillations of movement). [36]

The developments of fractal or pseudo-fractal geometry were revealed, in that context as particularly suited to design "reverberating" forms and structures, in which any scalar response would possess evidence of the whole.

This inter-scalar property, of cross-cutting recurrence or reverberation, appeared closely linked with the first pioneering investigations, associated with the exploration of new conformative systems in that they suggested a possible scalar "transfer" or "hand-off" between systems, with a broad level of formal variation (as opposed to a strict "morphological analogy") between architectural formulation and dynamic configuration.

The notion of recurrence – more so than self-similarity – effectively expressed this "induction criteria" or "nuclear instruction" in and of the system, which allowed for its movements to be summarized, condensed and/or compressed through certain synthetic figures, or criteria for action.

These abstract figures (or better schematic lines of forces) like diagrammatic trajectories (inductive or generative, called "initiators" by Mandelbrot), also responded, at the same time, to this indeterminate and determinate condition inherent in configurations that are essentially multi-programmatic and evolving.[37]

Most of these new (complex, open and irregular) formulations could effectively refer back to certain codes or patterns of "a-scalar transfer" as possible abstractions of synthesis and representation, understood as strategic (rather than formal) criteria for action.

We can talk of maps of synthesis or diagrammatic formulations, understood as possible basic codes for generation and evolution, called upon to adjust, transform and, definitively, to change.[38]

2.4. Diagrams and Epitomes. Scalar Leaps

Complex and simultaneous movements and events (defined, as indicated, by layers and information networks) did not prevent the processes from being referred to possible evolutionary structures associated with flexible development vectors (or "evolution-

_35. Josep M. Fargas and Papazian, Pegor, "Territory and Modeling," *Quaderns* no. 194 (1992).
_36. "We can affirm that there is a fractal conception and geography of nature. These are based on the concept of self-similarity or recursivity, a property for which small parts they look alike... "
Benoît Mandelbrot, *Los objetos fractales* (Barcelona, Tusquets, 1897).
_37. Ivar Ekeland, *Le Chaos* (Paris: Ed. Flammarion, 1995), 107.
_38. Peter Saunders, "Nonlinearity – What It Is and Why It Matters," *Architectural Design 9/10*, vol. 67 (1997).

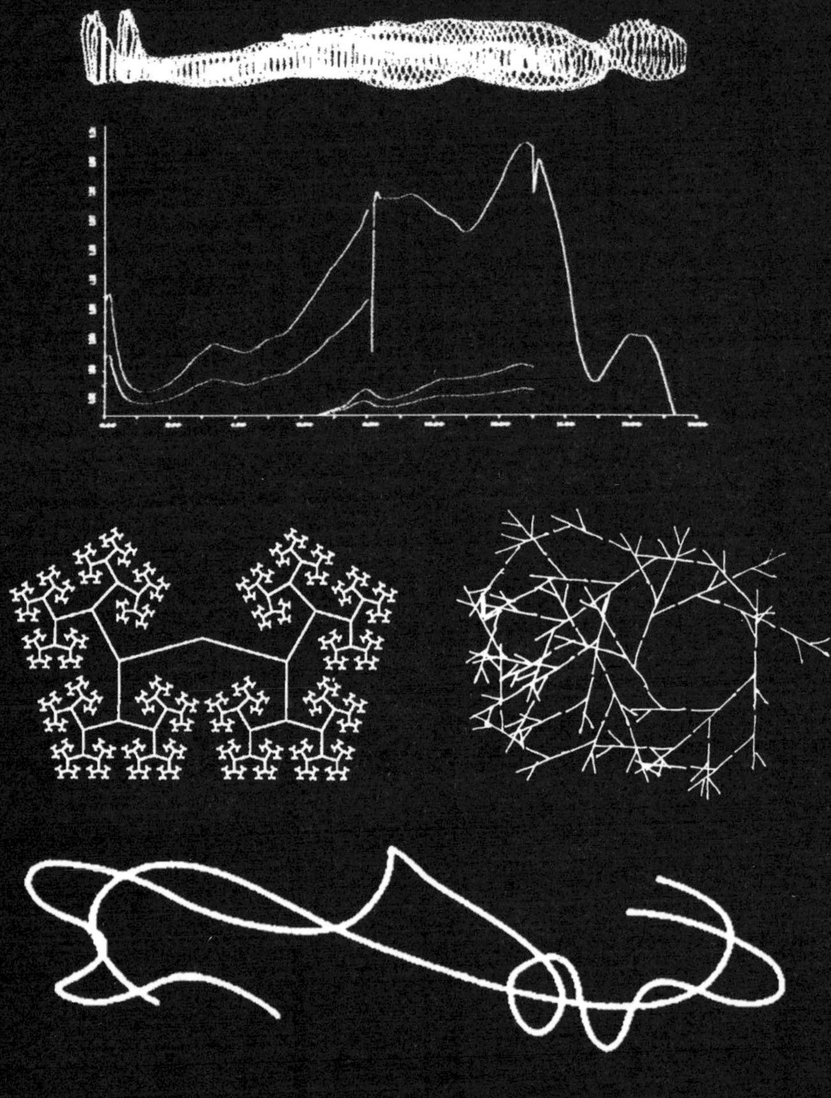

Diagrams and maps of synthetic recognition. From up to down, from left to wright.
– Pioneering computerized images of a human body. Scanner map of slices and a synthesized section (in *National Geographic*, vol. 153, no.3, 1978).
– Fractal spiral evolution in ramifications and broccoli rhizome diagram (in Benoît MANDELBROT, Les Objets Fractals)
– Lorenz curve, abstract diagram (in Peter SAUNDERS: "Nonlinearity – What It Is and Why It Matters," *AD Architectural Design 9/10*, vol. 67, Sept. Oct. 1997).
– Rectification diagram of a curve of current.
– Diagram by Paul Klee referenced by Gilles Deleuze in *The Fold*.

ary patterns") described in possible "trajectories compressors "(" compressions "of the system itself, its dynamic structures and its operational movements) translated into possible maps - or diagrams - of synthesis. In that sense, during much of the 1990s the exploration of a new type of more open and irregular architectural configuration and its ties to the diagrammatic potential (as informational "compression/induction") delved into the diagram's capacity for synthesis as a virtual "map" or synthetic "cartography" of information, but also of conditions, demands and possible (plural and differential) fluctuations or oscillations in space (and between spaces).

The diagram was revealed as the graphic representation of the multiple *progresses of a process in progress* recorded using "compression", "abstraction" and "simulation" all at once.[39]

Based on these premises, it is worth considering the important contributions of certain architectural research generated at the turn of the century, which had that ability to instrumentalize this "dispositional", a-scalar and multi-scalar potential of the diagram and relate it to the synthetic (and dynamic) cartographies of the city, strategically reinterpreted.

Design dynamics with the ability to respond to the specific demands of the local sphere – place, program, uses, etc. – and to connect them with the possible generic components (more strategic than figurative) that define the global scenario in which the design will be inscribed. *Dispositifs (dispositional-devices)* that mobilize (and oriented) local – concrete – information based on patterns of global disposition (frameworks for generation) which, in turn, refer to other superior characteristics inherent in urban processes and in those other dynamic space-time systems that tend to be found therein.

Underlying this attempt to synthesize scalar relationships and multi-scalar relationships diagrammatically as maneuvers that can combine multiple, resonant and transferring potentials, we find the operative logic of certain attempts directed at promoting the development of possible trajectories of production and connection between typical processes and scenarios and/or complex scenarios, but also between general conditions and particular conditions; never in a metaphorical or allegorical way, but conclusively and resolutely strategically: generative "resonant" trajectories, conceived as virtual "compressions" of a multi-city that was demonstrated to be a conclusively explicit mechanism for combining (and conjugating) heterogeneous information into devices that are both generic and contingent at the same time: information that was interpreted, in this early research, as – different and differential – programs, models, configurations, messages and requests rather than as data or parametric indicators.[40]

The complex contemporary city appeared, at the time, as the most evident manifestation of the progressive dynamic and informational condition of our environment, which lay beneath its complex and irregular nature.

It is not surprising, then, that the conceptual transformation of contemporary design would tend – during the initial period of trials and reformulations in the 1990s as a pioneering moment – to be oriented toward the investigation of anti-typological relationship mechanisms that might strategically "resonate" with (rather than "evoke" or "reproduce") the processes that would come to structure the new "multi-polis" today, in order not only to assimilate them but to reinterpret them instrumentally. Forcing design to move beyond a reading that was sometimes excessively focused on circumstances,

_39. This text is related with the chapter 7 (Diagrams) of the publication: Manuel Gausa, *Open(ing), Space-Time-Information* (Barcelona: Ed. Actar, 2018).
_40. Ibid. See also chapter 6 (Dispositions) of the same publication.

in order to connect with the open processes of the city, which have their own scalar transversality, substantive irregularity, and topological variety, as the most immediate manifestation of a new more complex and more dynamic spatial conception, attempting to address urban configurations themselves, associating them with new – urban and, also, social – progressively "heterogeneous", but also "heterodox" design mechanisms.[41]

Probably the two main proposals for the Villette Park, those of Tschumi and OMA, would constitute the first "starting shots" of all these adventures, combining post-modern "event" concepts with matrix-diagrammatic processes.

Devices (*dispositifs*) that adapt to a place and "refer" back to a city ("resonating" and "transferring" with it); and in referring back to the city – to those generic scenarios and operative movements that synthesize it – they allude to the dynamic processes that make it up (both abstract global processes and contingent – specific – local processes), thus creating a strange "loop of meanings" between "recognition maps" (information maps) and "action maps" (battle maps) as possible "operative diagrams".

Maps of the tensions that suggest them and maps of the "generative instructions" (and generated trajectories) that define them.[42] "Multi-Layering Maps", therefore, of a multiple city - "meta-territorial" - approached more from the registration and superposition of various territories of relationship (and synergy) than from mere physical contiguity and / or proximity and where architectural design appears as a possible "local map" of the "global scenario" – an "a-scalar" synthesis of a definitively "multi-scalar" city.

An epitome – a "concentrate", a "compression" – of its own dynamics of development; but also a transfer: a *glocal* (local and global) energy interchange, in synergy with the place but also capable of transferring it to other scenarios "beyond" the limits defined by the context, in a highly significant "scalar leap" between systems and subsystems in process, which connects with a new type of "typological repertoires" associated not only with the strategies of urban re-evaluation and reactivation we discussed earlier but also with their implicit (local and global) potentials for configuration. With their variable conditions of density, of spacing and/or articulation but, also, of intersection, interweaving and encounter (between fabrics and weavings, between architectures and landscapes, between cities and geographies).[43]

Movements conceived using strategies of volumetric agglomeration (or unfolding); meshed connection (or retraction); superficial undercurrents (or folds); in other words, movements of concentration, linking and/or expansion, which referred to other "space-time" fluctuations characteristic of the dynamic systems associated with them ... and related to them.

Movements and dispositional strategies that attempted to respond to conditions of building concentration and density, meshing and infrastructural articulation, and even superficial (spatial) hollowing out and "emptying", which tended to be defined as:

– Complex growths and re-growths (offshoots or sprouts):

manifested preferably as, essentially vertical, localized movements of condensation, concentration and accumulation (unfolding), including such significant projects as OMA / Rem Koolhaas ("Hague City Hall", 1986-87 / "Netherlands Dance Theater," Den Hague 1987), Steven Holl ("Edges of a City", "Proposal for Dallas-Fort Worth", 1990 / "Resi-

_41. Ibid. See also chapter 1 (Surveys) of the same publication.
_42. Ibid. See also chapter 7 (Diagrams) of the same publication.
_43. Ibid. See also the chapters 1 (Surveys), 7 (Diagrams) and specially 6 (Dispositions)

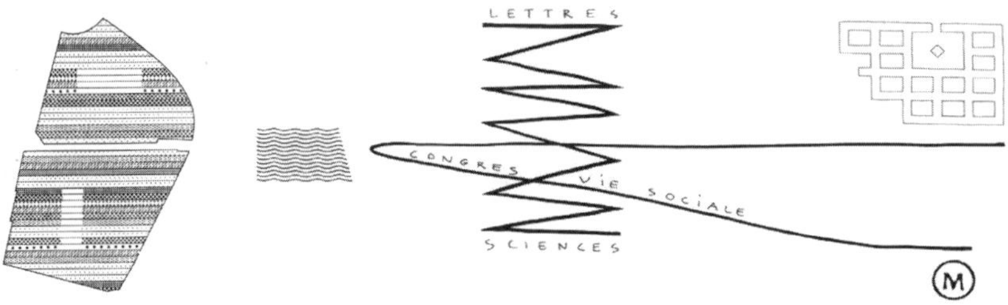

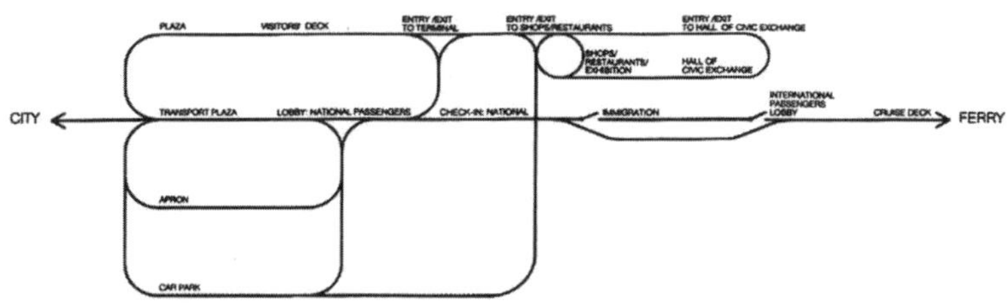

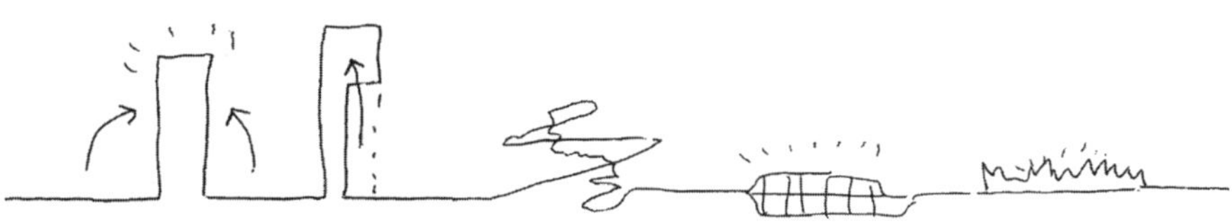

The operative condition of the "diagram-ideogram" as a (tactical) response associated with a possible (strategic) logic: a synthetic trajectory bringing together "recognition", "diagnostic" and "response" into a "device-criteria" for action-disposition to a trajectory of "folding, refolding and/or unfolding".
From up to down
– OMA: Ideogram for the second Jussieu Library competition, Paris, 1993. 7.27.
– FOA: Diagram for Yokohama Station: Program organization, 1995
– njiric& njiric. Ideogram for the Baumax shopping center, Maribor, 1998.
– MVRDV: Diagrammatic trajectory for the Villa VPRO building, Hilbersum, 1995/97.
– OMA-Rem Koolhaas: Different strategic devices for urban restructuration (*De Architect* n. 12,1994).

dential complex in Makuhari", 1994-96 / "Bellevue Art Museum," Washington USA, 1997-2000), Neutelings-Riedijk ("IJ Apartment tower," Amsterdam, 1993/1998 / "Prinsenhoek Building", Sittard, 1992-1995), MVRDV, Maas-De Vries-Van Rijs ("Mixed Megastructure", Europan II, Berlin, 1990 / "WoZoCo", Amsterdam, 1996) and in Spain those of Eduard Bru & Serra-Cartagena-Vives ("Poblenou Seafront", Barcelona, 1995) or S & Aa, Soriano-Palacios ("Benidorm Cultural Center & Auditorium", Alicante, 1993) among others.

– Meshes and Grids (flexible weavings and inter-weavings):

manifested as linear bundles or matrix circuits or braided knots of structural articulation and/or connection (folding), including transition projects as the Bernard Tschumi's and OMA's matrixes for La Villette Park (1982-85), or paradigmatic proposals of OMA-Rem Koolhaas ("Zeebrugge Ferry Terminal", 1990 / "Mixed Residential Complex", Fukuoka, 1993 / "Eurolille", Lille, 1990-1994), Kazuyo Sejima, ("Zig-Zag typologies", "Metropolitan Housing Studio", 1996), Willem Jan Neutelings ("De Ring Culture", Rotterdam 1988 / "European Patent Office" , Den Hague, 1991), MVRDV ("L-Loop", Combined Ring Prototypes, Almere, 1996-1998 / "Residential Complex Hoornse Kwadrant", Delft, 1996) NL archs., ("Parkhouse", Amsterdam, 1996 / "Flat City Residential Complex," Leidsche Rijn, 1997), Adriaan Geuze & West 8 ("Borneo Sporenburg", Amsterdam, 1993-1996) UN studio-Van Berkel & Bos ("Project for the Yokohama Ferry Terminal", 1995 / "Houses in Borneo Sporenburg", Amsterdam, 1996) or of Actar Arquitectura in Spain ("Residential complex in Monte Hacho", Ceuta, 1998) among others.

– Topographies and Topometries (ground and reliefs):

manifested as enclaves or "operative surfaces", associated with new city/landscape equations (folds), including projects such as OMA-Rem Koolhaas ("Hotel complex in Agadir," Morocco, 1990 / "Proposal for the Jussieu Library", Paris, 1992), FOA, Zaera-Moussavi ("Yokohama Ferry Terminal", 1996-2000 / "Myeongdong Cathedral", Seoul, 1995), Roche & DSV & SIE ("Topographies de Pli", 2001), MVRDV, Maas-van Rijs-de Vries ("Villa VPRO", Utrecht, 1993-1997 / "Dutch Pavilion Hannover" 2000), UN studio-Van Berkel & Bos ("Moebius House," Het Gooi, 1993-97), njiric & njiric ("Residential Landscapes", Den Bosch and Schwerin, 1994 and Glasgow, 1996), Francis Soler ("New Walloon Parliament", Namur, 1995), Kazuyo Sejima ("Multimedia Studio in Gizu", Tokyo, 1996), Plot, Bjarke Ingels-Julien de Smedt ("Youth center and Sailing Club", Copenhagen 2004), Kas Oosterhuis and NOX ("Water Pavilion", Neeltje Jans, 1997) and in Spain such emblematic projects as Actar Arquitectura, ("Graz-Maribor, Operational Topographies", 1998-2000 / "Sociopolis Project", 2003-2004), S & Aa, Soriano-Palacios ("Residential Geography", Europan 4, Bilbao Auditorium, 1996), Vicente Guallart ("House on the City Limits", Valencia, 1995-96 / "House of Seven Summits", Valencia, 1998), Eduardo Arroyo-NO. Mad Architecture ("Auditorium and Convention Center, Pamplona", 1998) or Willy Müller ("Old Breakwater Proposal", Barcelona, 1998) among others.

Publications such as *Open: Space-Time-Information, The Metapolis Dictionary of Advanced Architecture* or, more indirectly, the different issues of the magazine *Fisuras* or the ArchiLab catalogs, help to re-trace this taxonomic logic of "offshoots" and "sprout"; of "weavings" and "interweavings; of "topographies" and "reliefs", which, more than strict classifications, associate the projects with possible generative "scenarios". Scenarios that can be approached as "keys for action", and which allow for "instrumentalizing" certain generic potentials of the city.

Diagrammatic-devices linked with a possible taxonomy of the generic nature of the city as a dynamic system with operational patterns (combinable keys, rather tan closes-off categories) leads to adaptable strategies in/and specific trajectories and formulations (in Manuel Gausa, *Housing*, New Alternative, New Systems, Barcelona,

Diagrams of "field conditions". A paradigmatic taxonomic map of urban and natural patterns.
(in Stan Allen: *Points, Lines, Diagrams and Projects for the City*, N Y, Princeton Architectural Press, 1998)

Some examples of encounters between "architecture" "landscape" and "site-fields" .
- O.M.A.-Rem Koolhaas: City Hall, The Hague (1986-1987).
- Steven Holl: Edge of a City, Proposal for Manhattan (1990).
- S&Aa (Soriano-Palacios), Benidorm Cultural Centre and Auditorium (Alicante, 1993).
- FOA (Zaera-Moussavi): Entrance to the Myeongdong Cathedral (Seoul, 1995).
- Aranguren-Gallegos, Benidorm Cultural Centre and Auditorium (Alicante, 1993).

The images illustrate the hybrid condition of "operational topographies" or "*reliefs*". The condition of "ground is shifted in height" toward a roof that becomes a relational landscape. From top to bottom:
– Eduardo Arroyo (NO. Mad Arquitectura): Pamplona Auditorium, 1998
– Actar Arquitectura. Sociopolis Project, 2003-2004
– Willy Müller, Mercat de les Flors (Barcelona, 2009)

From top to bottom:
– Vicente Guallart. House on the Edges of the City (Valencia, 1995-96)
– njiric&njiric. Baumax Shopping Center (Maribor, 1998) //
– MVRDV (Maas-van Rijs-de Vries). Villa VPRO (Utrecht, 1993-1997).

Two exemples of folding and multilayer formats:
General views and relation with urban landscapes.
Left: MVRDV, Villa VPRO, Hilversum 1996-97.
Right: BIG, Mountain Dwellings, Copenhagen, 2006 (Source C. Portal)
Although the BIG project was built 10 years later, it remains linked with the 90s "antitypological" research of OMA and MVRDV

Strategies for concentration and containment, strategies for hybridization and transition can be contemplated based on their ability to define specific urban (or pseudo-urban) development processes, in order to activate "fields of forces", to interconnect scales, to connect distances, to focus tensions, to emphasize rhythms, to highlight vectors, to combine information, but, above all, to induce developments capable of articulating (and conveying) diverse and heterogeneous information, experiences and events (programs, uses, models, etc.). Spaces of "accumulation", spaces of "connection" and spaces of "expansion" translate into a new kind of toolkit with the capacity to work with possible – multi-layer – "mixed combinations" associated with the possibility of conceiving richer and more ambivalent dispositional systems for the construction and occupation of the ground.

Folding, refolding, unfolding: many of the architectural explorations linked to this propositional approach – associated with a more dynamic and complex, less linear conception of form – attempted to propose new types of spatial configurations with more open, more differential and irregular, more topological and topo-morphic geometries, connected – as we have pointed out – with the dynamics characteristic of a city and an environment in transformation and its anti-typological (i.e., multiple and multi-faceted) translation in the form of growths and twinning, meshes and networks, topographies and reliefs, etc.

2.5. "Maps & Fields" of Forces: Intersections and Hybridizations

New urban and architectural repertories lnked also, with a new type of morphology resulting from the exploration of new patterns and new software (Catia V4-V5-3D modeling-1996-98, Maya 3D-Modeling & Animation-1998, Photoshop, launched in 1990 , etc.) associated with flexible, variable and adaptable geometries, understood as new dynamic and fluctuating fields.[44]

The launch of the highly versatile graphic software Photoshop (1991) favored experimentation with a new type of complex and intertwined patterns but, above all, with a new type of non-linear geometries (topological structures) in combined processes of stamping, folding and layering associated with possible deformations, extensions, elongations, compressions and stretches of a (spatial, architectural, graphic or objectual) form, which no longer appeared as a pure, fixed, essential figure but as an evolutionary trajectory in a "field" of forces, but also of intersections, cuttings and fluctuations.

A "between" spaces (between physical "fields" and "fields" of information), based on a new type of structure that is "anti-typological", because "multi-typological". [45]

As Alejandro Zaera-Polo pointed out:[46]

"*These days, occupying a new spatial position can be as important as maintaining an ideological position was for the avant-garde. If the amount of information produced in the late capitalist era has devalued representation as a vehicle for communication, the traditional systems of*

_44. In fact in the two publications GAUSA, Manuel (2010): Open, Espacio-Tiempo-Información, Barcelona-New York, Actar and GAUSA, Manuel (2018): Open(ing), Space-Time-Information, Barcelona-New York, Actar, these flexible taxonomy is developed as a first essay to combine topological movements, city pattern processes and open combinatory trajectories for a new kind of anti-typological architectural spatial devices.

_45. See specially the interesting timeline od the Computer History Museum in https://www.computerhistory.org/ Op.cit.

_46. Alejandro Zaera-Polo: "Orden desde el caos," in *Exit* no. 1 (1993), 23.

MVRDV (Maas-De Vries-Van Rijs): WoZoCo 100 unit building (Amsterdam, 1996)

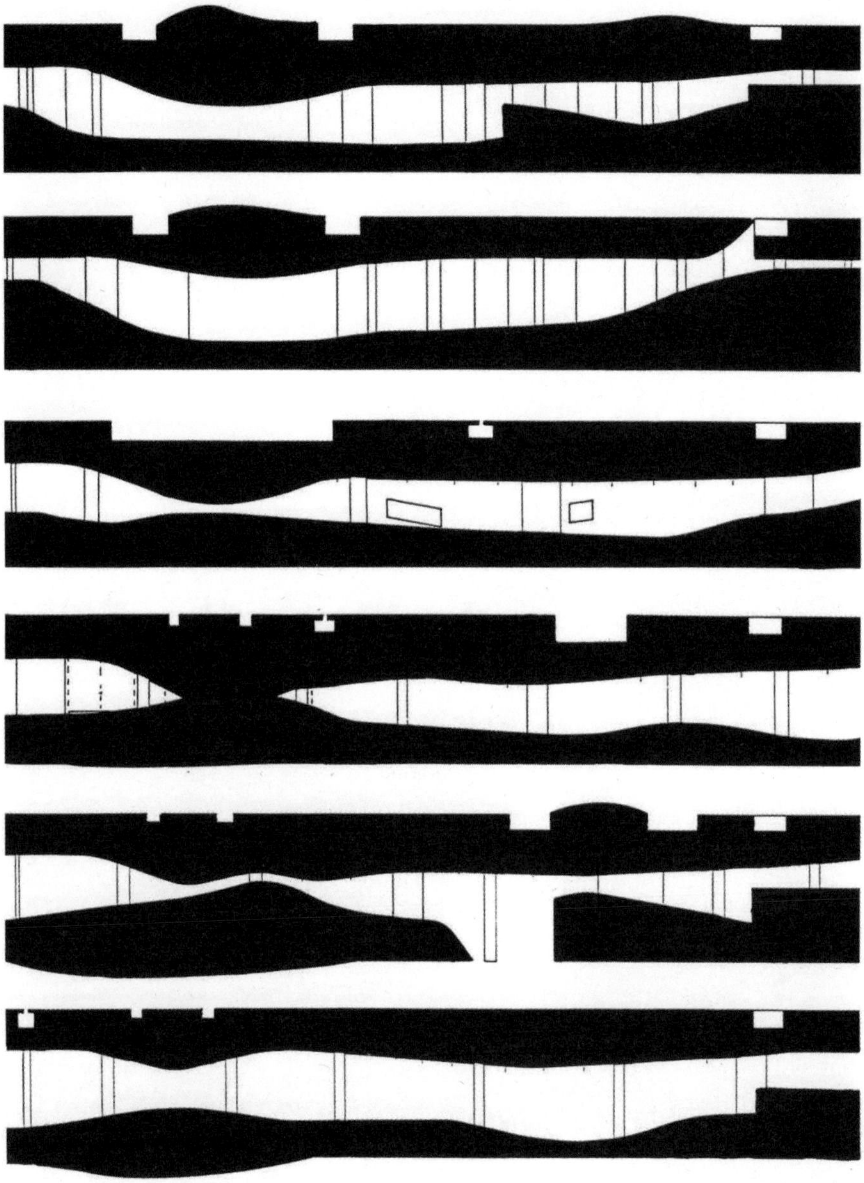

It is interesting to compare the "*compressed landscape*" of OMA's first experimentations with multi-layers and un unfolding-topos in Agadir Hotel (1990) and the multi-layering urban programmatic maps of the Yokohama Urban Studio (1992) with the stacked nature of the Holland Pavilion for the World's Fair of Hannover 2000 (MVRDV-Maas-van Rijs-de Vries, 2000).

Two examples of strategic folding or stretching *multi-layer field-adaptations*:
Moebius House (UN-Studio-Van Berkel & Bos, Het Gooi, The Netherlands, 1993-1997)
Parkhouse Parking-Mall (NL archs. /Carstadt (Amsterdam, 1996)

meaning or values can be replaced by a new type of material or spatial organizations that serve as the foundation for communication, exchange and consensus."

The design responses that we have highlighted aimed to respond in a pioneering and creative way to those challenges, setting themselves up as (reactive and operative) "dispositional" strategies" with the capacity to synthesize information (understood as "programming" and, above all, as "demands") while tuning in to the environment(s) at the same time – presenting themselves as both "structural systems" and as "formalizing processes", characteristic of a time of transition, between (disciplinary) cultures and new (transdisciplinary) formulations.

Folding, refolding, unfolding... twinning, stacking, cuttings, grafts, point to recent "anti-compositional" mechanisms, which translate this desire to propose more direct and "un-subjected" (more open) actions in harmony with the interpretation of an increasingly com-

Relational and connective synergeic clusters; Onion Scan Report, 1997.

plex space that can only be approached effectively from the standpoint of synchronization and the active organization of layers and networks that are overlapping and differentiated at the same time.

The understanding of the idea of "place" as an active, fluctuating, unstable, ultimately dynamic) milieu (or environment) (contemplated beyond its old semantic connotations: what has habitually been called "context") invites the exploration of this new fluctuating nature of the old "locus" and its new evolving manifestations as a virtual "field of forces", as a scenario for intersection and interaction (between conditions, between scales, between programs, between "natures").

Place appears as an increasingly less stable and ritual environment, less genuine and literal, which can only be understood based on the assumption of a vibratory framework of "layers" (or levels) of information in movement (a "field of forces and information") requiring new exploration and new tools for action.[47]

_47. See the chapters 7 (Topographies, Intermediate Epilogue, p. 668) in: Manuel Gausa, *Open(ing), Space-Time-Information* (Barcelona: Ed. Actar, 2018).

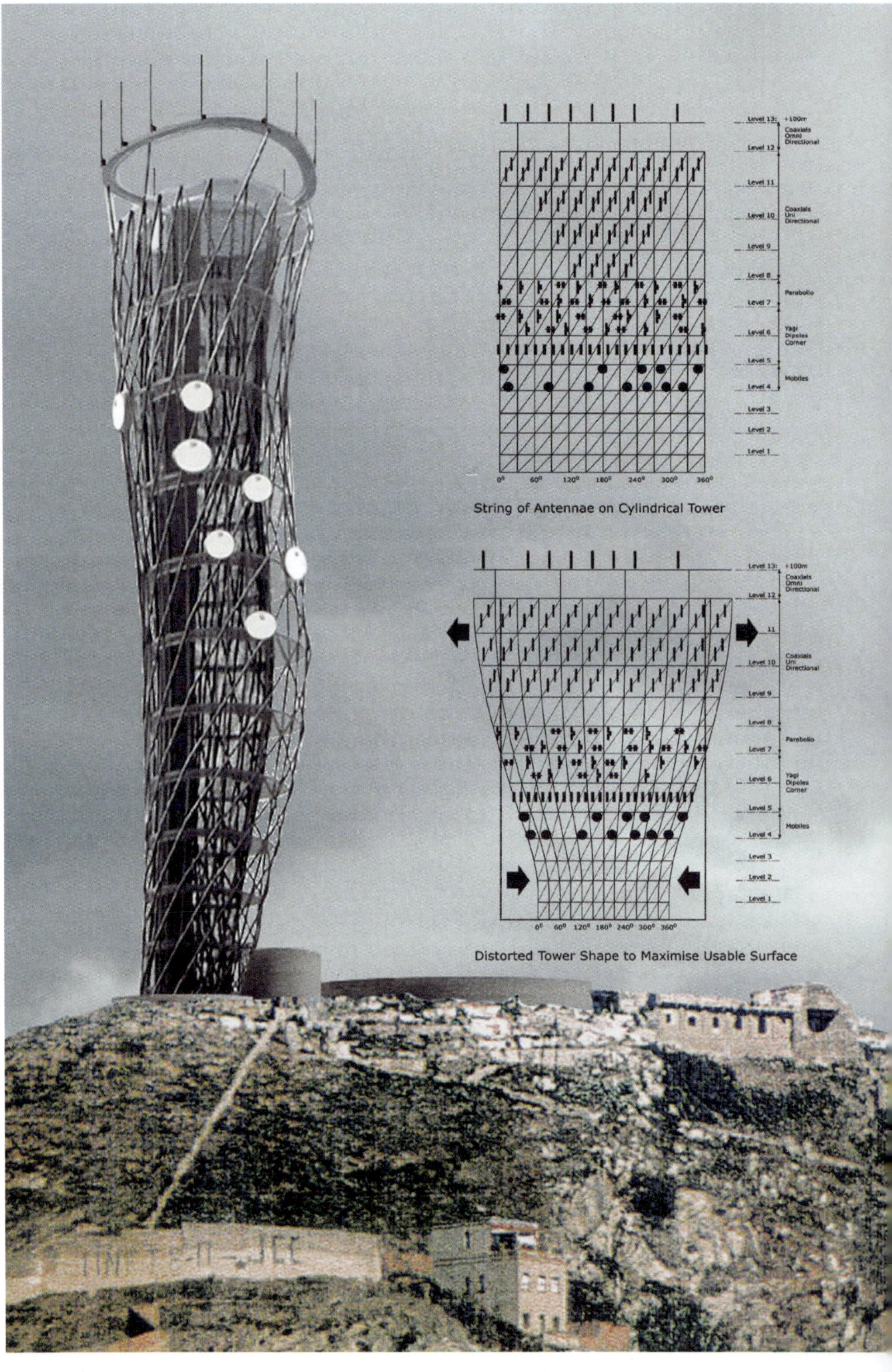

String of Antennae on Cylindrical Tower

Distorted Tower Shape to Maximise Usable Surface

The aim is not to omit the site, place or context – to reject it or redeem it – but to pay attention to its atonal music and its reverberating sounds.

Actar Arquitectura: Communications tower, Turó de la Rovira (Barcelona, 2000).

S&Aa (Soriano-Palacios): Residential towers, Barakaldo, Europan 5 (Bilbao, 1998).

Mixtures, manipulations and cross-breedings that are associated with this interactive, multi-level capacity, similar to functional and/or dispositional hybridization that can be explored using manipulation programs like Photoshop.

At the same time, they allude to the progressive acceptance of mixtures (cross-breeding and blending) that are unauthorized or impure – in short, diverse and irregular – as an interactive condition of the "new".

The awareness of this "agreed-upon" – but not necessarily "united" – diversity reflects the emergence of a new more permeable, more elastic – more open – "logic" between experiences and scenarios that are interposed and superimposed, mixed and intertwined at the same time.

The classical idea of "communion" – as a stable link between coherence and cohabitation – makes way progressively for the notion of connection – or interconnection – as a flexible and varied relationship among variable and differentiated "n-identities": a relationship that is more suited to this "diachronic synchronicity" – purer and more cross-bred – among behaviors and event, between places, spaces and scenarios (both individual and collective, singular and plural, natural and artificial) which tends to fit in with a new conception of diversity as an irregular network "of" – and "between" – differentiated processes, which are both in accord and interconnected at the same time.

Formulations, interpretations – and expressions – that presented a new kind of more open and intriguing combinations, generated between different informational conditions, situations and solicitations. They manifested this "plural" (and often heterodox, surprisingly "anti-natural") condition, translated into possible multi-layer apparatuses capable of interweaving and connecting, for example, "figure" and "ground", "empty" and "full", "structure" and "infrastructure", "nature and artifice", in the same dispositional strategy but, also, in a strange hybrid union between the conventional and the transgressive, the systemic and the singular, the alternative and the operative, in short.

Anti-typological *natufices* – cross-breedings, cuttings, paradoxes and/or hybridizations – constituted renovation approaches that moved between morpho-genetic researches and operative strategies.

Experiments that could, in turn, be interpreted as individual trials (generated, above all, by some of the most enterprising new professional teams of the moment) in an attempt to express the "symptoms" of this new logic in progress and to summarize them through new anti-typological spatial responses that were less taxonomically predictable, less pre-determined, more complex and "multi-formatted"; responses that a series of publications, like *S, M, L, XL* (Rem Koolhaas-Bruce Mau, 1995), *FARMAX: Excursions on Density* (MVRDV, 1998), P*oints + Lines: Diagrams and Projects for the City* (Stan Allen, 1999), *Architectures of Time: Toward a Theory of the Event in Modernist Culture* (Sanford KWINTER 2001) or *The Metapolis Dictionary of Advanced Architecture* (Gausa-Guallart-Morales-Müller-Porras-Soriano, 2001/2003 and *Open, Space-Time-Information,* (Manuel Gausa, 2005-2010) helped to conceptualize.

Combinations intended to disrupt the orthodox (and secular) divisions and codes of the discipline, coupling dissimilar concepts ("above and below", "exterior and interior", "figure and ground", "public and private", "volume and surface", "building and landscape", "landscape and infrastructure", "infrastructure and building", etc.) in new hybrid unions – or "couplings" – which (as we have pointed out) allude to the interactive, *inform(ation)al* and

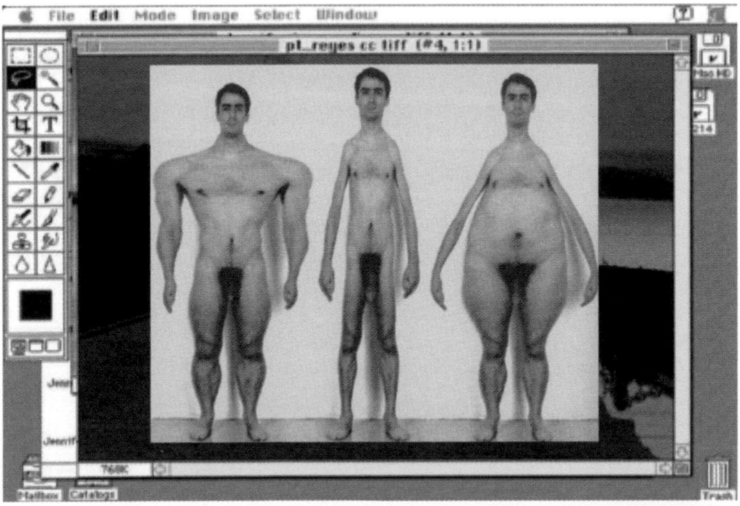

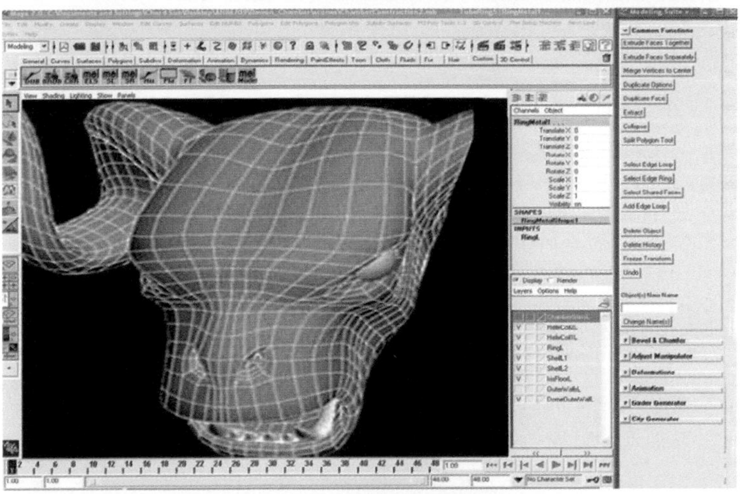

Top: Released in February 1990 as a graphic product, Photoshop allowed the first stretch deformation experiments.
Center. Launched in 1997 Autodesk Maya was initially a software for 3D graphic special effects, animation and simulation, awarded an Oscar thanks to its enormous impact on the film industry (*Jurasic Park, The Abbyss, Terminator 2,* etc.)
Bottom: The new Ria de Bilbao with the Guggenheim Museum (Frank Gehry, 1997).

extroverted nature of the order and form (and the associated factors and parameters) that we are concerned with here.[48]

From the famous roof-ground of F.O.A.'s "Yokohama Ferry Terminal" (a "surface", but also "a landscape above another landscape, "fullness as emptiness", "building as ground") to the impossible cantilevers in MVRDV's "WoZoKo" building (a "conglomerate", but also "a vertical growth, horizontally"; from the hybrid configuration of W.J. Neutelings' "Residential complex" in Sittard (a "conglomerate" too, but also a "compatible coupling of incompatible genes") to the continuous fluctuation of O.M.A.'s "Jussieu Library", or the multi-layered unfolding of MVRDV's "Villa VPRO" (an "enclave", but also an "expanding retreat"; from the strange "weightlessness" of Toyo Ito's "Sendai Mediatheque" (a frame, but also "a structure of – and above – voids", a "dissolved matter") to the fluid profile of Frank Gehry's "Guggenheim Museum" ("a liquid matter", but also the virtual sublimation of an immaterial "field" of forces); or from the ambiguous nature of the "grafts" by Duncan Lewis and François Roche ("a building like a landscape") to the "Vertical Gardens" by Adriaan Geuze & West 8 ("a landscape like a building"), the true cultural dimension of contemporary design is rooted in its capacity to formulate "new and strange paradoxes" – rebellious trajectories – where, for example:

"The roof of a building can be, at the same time, its main floor"; "a growth can sprout horizontally"; "a building can also be nature"; "a conjunction can be understood as a disjunction"; "different overlapping levels can become a single unfolded level"; "matter can be fluid"; or "weightlessness can be supported by dematerialization".

This would be not just a linguistic action, since the goal is not just to explore language, syntax, or poetic metaphor. The true meaning of this type of architectural paradox lies in its capacity to generate new "experiences", new "structures", and new spatial "natures; which are decidedly strategic and operative; precise and transgressive, unobstructed and expressive at the same time.[49]

Spatial trajectories with the ability to respond to local demands and to synthesize possible global information (formulations and statements). New operative paradoxes, then, for a new architecture called upon to generate complex processes using mechanisms which are often simple.Experiences particularly interested in exploring, in that first moment of search, new models, new patterns and new geometries (more open and / by topological) from, on the one hand, attention to the multiple dimension of the n-city, such as paradigm directly associated with complex systems and, on the other, from the exploration of the new digital animation (3D-Fields) as a complementary paradigm associated with dynamic systems.

_48. Ibid. See the chapters 12 (Intrigues and Paradoxes, p. 709).
_49. Ibid. pp. 735-739.

Next page: FOA- Zaera- Moussavi. Yokohama Ferry Terminal (2002). The iconic Image from the competition (1995). Wright: scan of the different structural sections conceived by Over Arup (Cecil Balmond) for the fluctuant cover-ground of the competition.

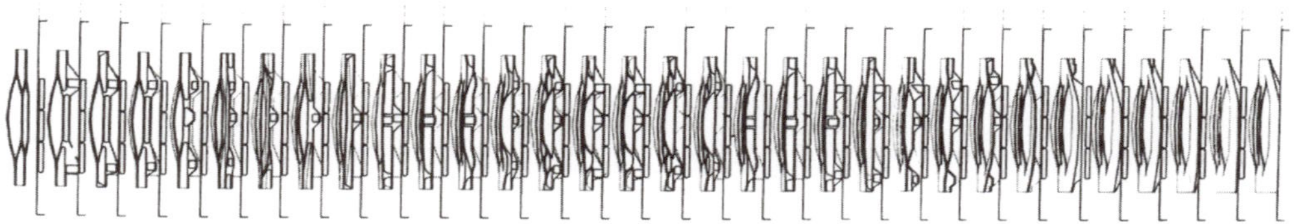

3- MODELLING FIELDS

3.1. Fields of movement: Fluctuations and Animations

The notions of "field" or "environment" understood as dynamic frameworks or atmospheres ties in with this ability to recognize and articulate "localized stimuli" and, at the same time, to express logics and actions which are "deployed" in trajectories that are – actually or virtually – reactive and evolving, generators of movements that are processed synthetically.[50]

A dispositive, understood as an "open field" of movement within another "open field of forces", is not dissolved or camouflaged; it does not impose itself; it does not appropriate. It "reacts" with the (physical and virtual, material and immaterial) environment, inserting itself flexibly into the milieu in order to generate cross-cutting responses that are local and global, plural and specific, reactivating it and re-informing it at the same time.

Both the idea of "field" and the idea of place or environment exist on the basis of linking together ambiguous relationships between reaction and interaction, between independence and interconnection, between "medium and mediator".[51]

Then, the project appears as a virtual "field of forces", infiltrating another "field of forces". With, in and between them, there are exchanges of energy, material and/or information. Its condition is that of a relational, operative and flexible system, inscribed in a global synergic and synesthetic space. [52]

The exploration itself with an elastic geometry like the topological one allowed to influence the adaptable and elastic capacity of the architectural form, turned into a response formed by internal and external forces rather than formed by aesthetic-disciplined predetermines.

In the mid-1990s the first applications of operative programs such as CATIAV1 andV5 3D Modeling (1995-1996) and MAYA 3D Modeling Animation (1996-1998) initially intended for use in film animation made it possible, in symbiosis with computational developments, to model and animate complex mesh-like forms using variable and fluctuating matrices.

Films like *Jurassic Park* (Steven Spielberg, 1990), *Terminator 2* (James Cameron, 1994) or *Toy Story* (John Lasseter, Walt Disney, 1994), the first successful films created with new digital technologies, illustrated the ongoing development of software and the experimentation taking place using those operative tools, both in special effects and in digital animation (from the tropical universe of video games to the new real-virtual cinematographic scenography) and its rapid translation into spatial and architectural experimentation in new fluctuating fields of evolution.

_50. Stan Allen: "Distributions, Combinations, Fields", *The Berlage Cahiers*, no. 5 (1996) 72.

_51. "Fields are shaped as scale-less entities, which can only be defined by certain 'limit' principles, either via coordinates or nets. They are generic configurations, which both relate and articulate specific 'events' at the same time, enriching themselves with the information from specific scenarios, programs, occurrences, interests.
They are, 'forces of risk' and they are always in a state of transformation. They are always 'in movement', in constant development; they are never reconstructed; they are dynamic and complex and they relate with a progressive process of change. [...] Architecture as a field of support, as a density of vectors, as a cluster of links, as an intensity of fields of forces attends to implementations, influences, links, attractions and repulsions; simultaneously.
It attends to the milieu as an essential artifice, taking on the category of 'milieu', whether through 'stamping' (architecture as superficial curves, the expression of a concept), 'gradients' (continuous structures read as pulses of density), 'nets' (architecture as links and nodes of transmission) or 'protrusions-peaks" (discontinuities and peculiarities). Architecture-milieu; milieu and architecture."
Fernando Porras: "Editorial," *BAU*, no. 014 (1996).

_52. Silvia Molina: "El espacio intermedio visual-virtual," in *V.V.A.A (1995): Entorno. Sobre el espacio y el arte* (Madrid: Editorial Complutense, 1995), 51.

FOA (Zaera-Moussavi): Virtual House, 1996-1997

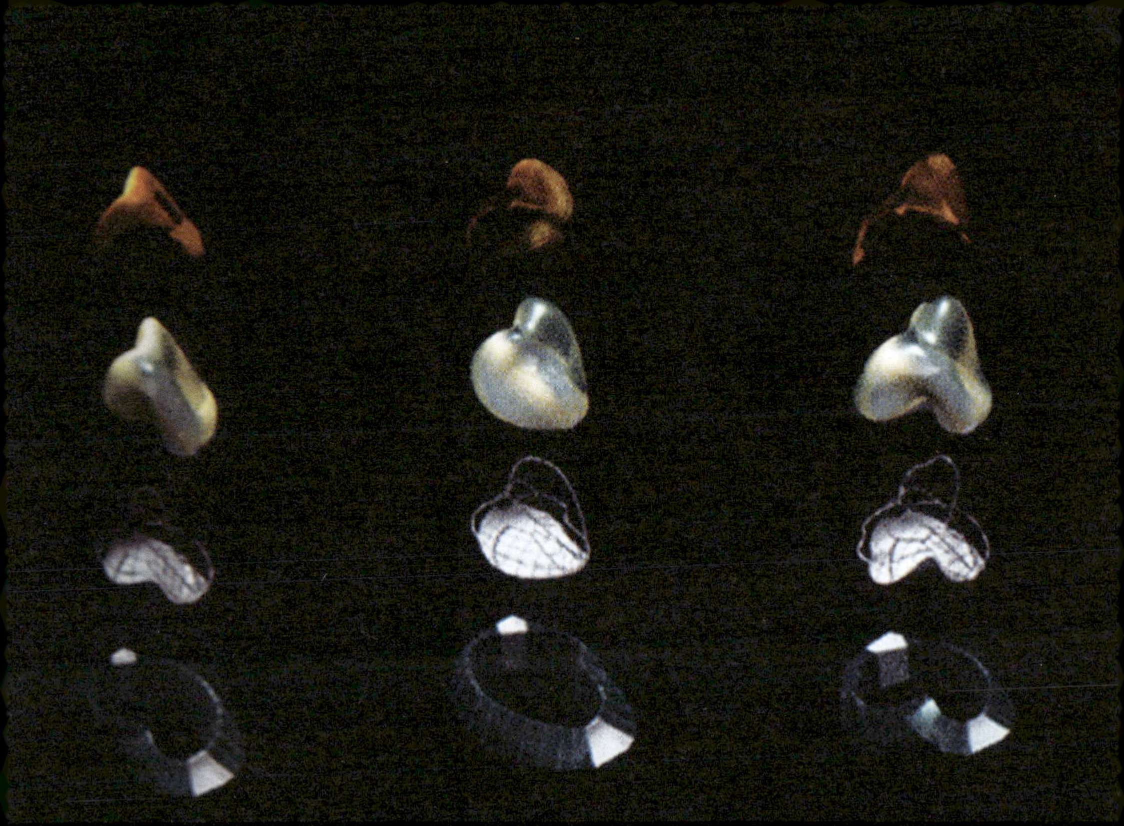

Different experiment with Animated Forms, 1998.
Examples of open movements with chains of events. Different "*bubbles*" examples and genetic trajectories for the Greg Lynn Embryological House (1997-2001) and the Cardiff Bay Opera House, 1998

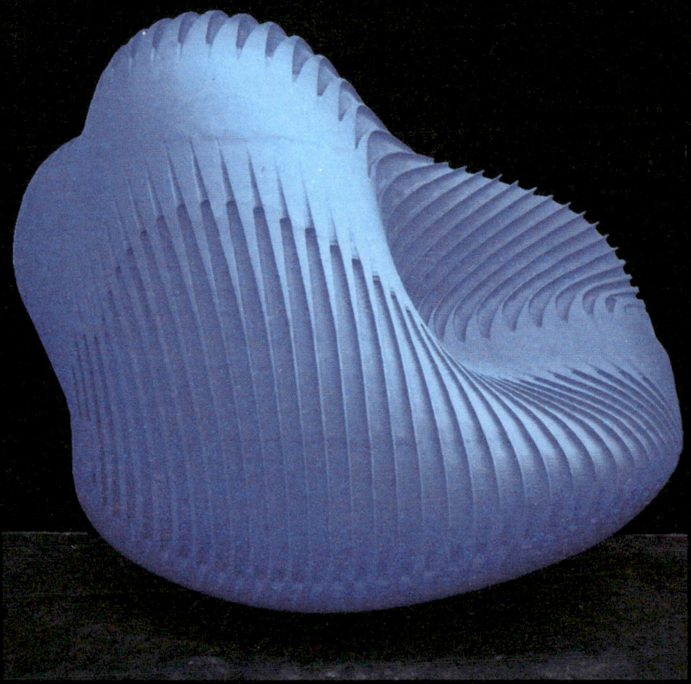

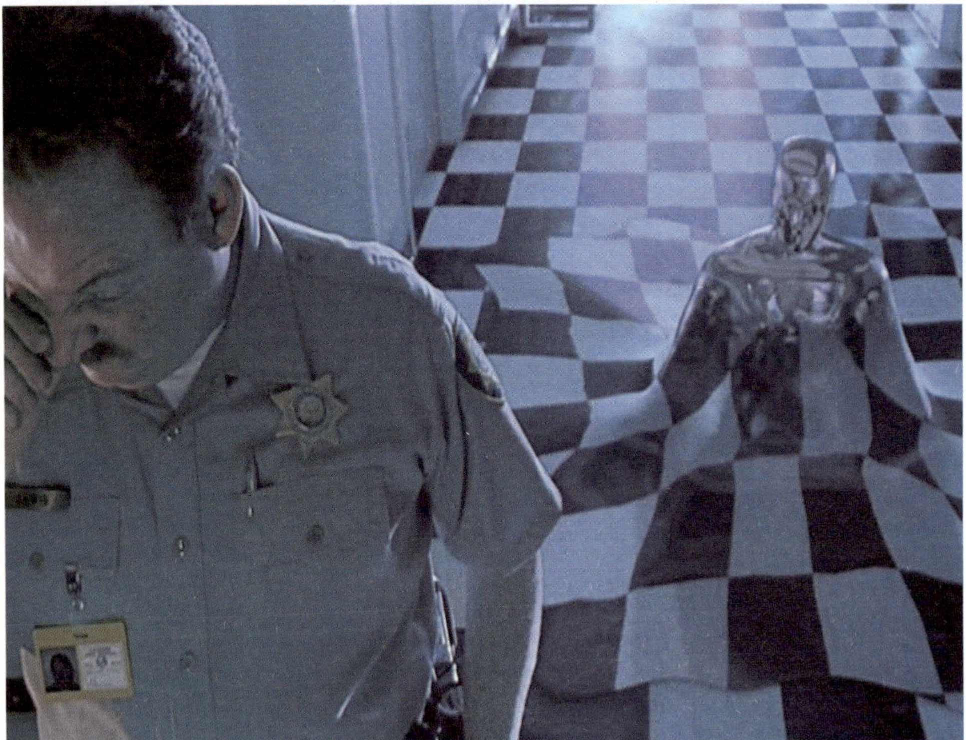

Folding and field-adapted topological "*camouflages*":
Terminator 2 (James Carpenter, 1991), with spetial effects of deforming bodies and matters.
Les Turbulences, FRAC-Centre, Orléans (Jakob-MacFarlane, 2013)

Pioneering proposals like the ones by Marcos Novak (*Liquid Forms*, 1997-2000, explicitly related to the essays on *Liquid Modernity* by Zygmunt Bauman, 1995), Bernard Cache (*Field Territories and Earth Moves*, 1995), Karl Chu (*Complex Organic Forms*, 1997) and in particular Greg Lynn (*Animated Form*, 1998) synthesized this experimentation with a new "genetics of form" tied into dynamic inter-relational fields (3DFields), orienting the new architectural research towards a new operative thinking based on the flexible, responsive and adaptive capacity of architectural form, modeled on a new type of informational environments.[53]

The exploration of a new multi-layer and multi-scale (multi-level) definition for new urban environments but also of a new topological, elastic, variable and differential condition, would mark many of the trials produced at the time still faced with some particularly conservative cultural, academic and productive environments that would continue to assimilate the operative to the predetermined (the guaranteed, the already tested and approved).

New models, new patterns and new geometries (more open and/or topological) based, on the one hand, on an attention to the multiple dimensions of the n-city (as a paradigm directly associated with complex systems) and, on the other, on the exploration of the new digital animation (as a complementary paradigm associated with dynamic systems) translated into the exploration of a new multi-valent – multi-layer and multi-scale (multi-level) – definition, associated with the new urban environments, but also with a new, more flexible, variable and differential topological condition that would characterize many of the first efforts produced at the time, still up against particularly conservative cultural, academic and productive environments that continued to assimilate the operative to what was built or already "pre-determined" (guaranteed, rehearsed pre-approved).

At the end of the 1990s two lines of action were discernible in many of the experiments taking place.

– One line of action was more "tactical-practical" – or more "strategic-operative" – interested in the ability to manipulate the "codes" of the system itself – its inertias, its standards – in order to disrupt it, parameters based on more conceptual and purposeful, more expressive foundations (combinatorial games, programmatic mixing and hybridization, anti-typological manipulation, paradoxical expression, plastic forcefulness).

– Another line of action was more "genetic-experimental" or "kinetic-productive", interested in the capacity to propose a new dynamic generation of architectural form and formulation, based on new technological, scientific, procedural foundations (evolving parametrization, algorithmic formulation, topological fluctuation, numerical conception, etc.).

Both lines (summarized in *S,M,L,XL* by Rem Koolhaas and Bruce Mau, 1994 and in *Animated Form* by Greg Lynn, 1998) will continue to coexist and acknowledge one another in the construction of a new way of thinking that is still embryonic and just emerging, which different media and gatherings like Metápolis or Archilab, (in which both tendencies appeared broadly reflected) helped to recognize.[54]

_53. See "History of Computing" in www.wikipedia.org/wiki/History_of_computing
and "Digital Computing - Dictionary definition of Digital Computing | Encyclopedia.com: FREE online dictionary". www.encyclopedia.com. Retrieved 2017-09-11. Op. cit.

_54. These concepts are developed in the part 6 (Outcomes) of the publication: Manuel Gausa, *Open(ing), Space-Time-Information* (Barcelona: Ed. Actar, 2018).

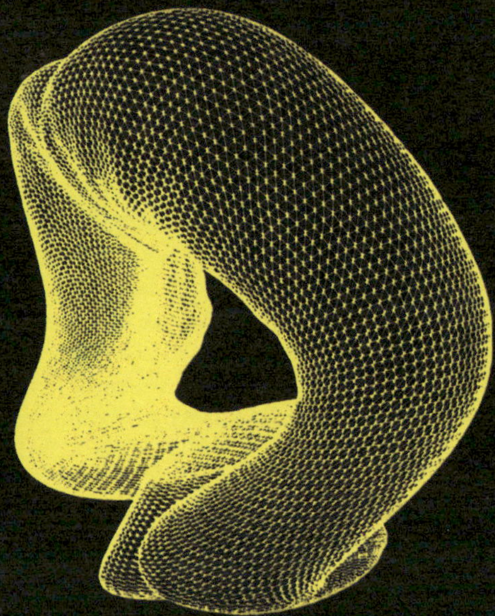

Examples of animated forms or new genetic conformations in interacting fields, with different adaptative answers produced through deformation and fluctuation on the basis of "typological matrices" facilatated by the new Maya and Rhino software.

Bernard Cache, fluctuant geno-form (*AD, Architectural Design* n. 9/10, vol. 67, Sept-Oct, 1997)
33– Karl S. Chu (X Kavya). Genetic Space-Phylogon 1, 1998.

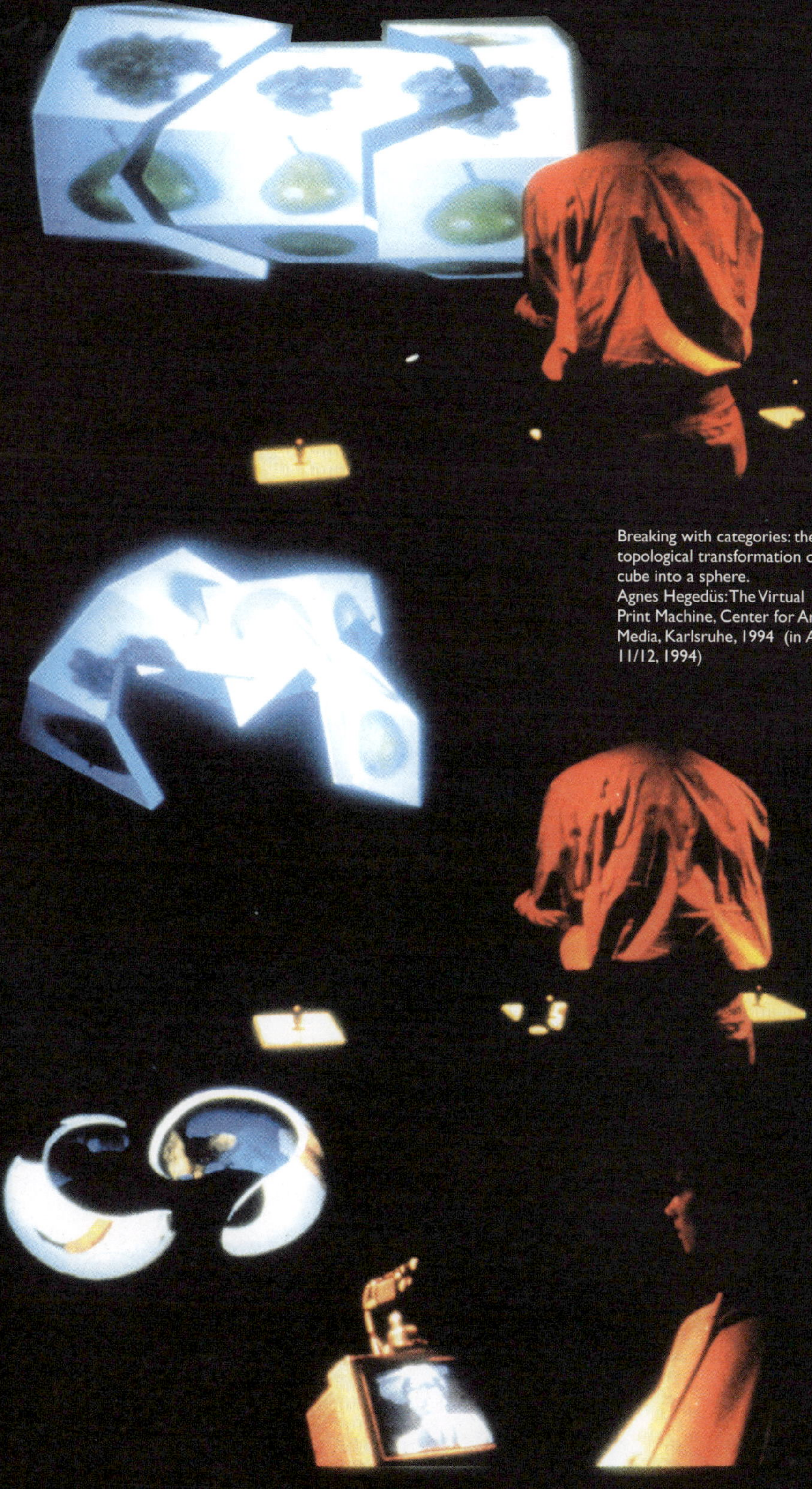

Breaking with categories: the topological transformation of a cube into a sphere.
Agnes Hegedüs: The Virtual Print Machine, Center for Art & Media, Karlsruhe, 1994 (in *AD* n. 11/12, 1994)

2001, New York, September 11th. A new global and networked era with unpredictible non-linear effects.
Advanced Architecture projects for the Ground 0 Competition (2002)
– NOX (Lars Spuybroek) design.
– Greg Lynn with FOA, UN Studio, Reiser + Umemoto, Kevin Kennon Architects and Imaginary Forces (Ground 0. 2 Pase II proposal)
– FOA´s Phase I studies (Ground 0.1)

Marcos Novak, *Variable Data Forms*, 1999. Author of the text *Liquid Architectures in the Cyberspace* in M. BENEDIK, *Cyberspace first steps* (MIT Press, 1991), so close to Zygmunt BAUMAN's *Liquid Modernity* (Cambridge, Polity, 2000). Novak's new genetics of form were meant to express the first steps of a time of fluctuations and (fuzzy) behaviors, spaces and configurations.

3.2. Networked Frameworks

On more than one occasion,[55] we have argued that this, more or less conscious, more or less spontaneous, drive for research characterized a new "framework for action" generated more as a virtual network for explorations and complicities than as a real binding (or dogmatic) common structure: a framework that would indeed demonstrate the possibility of generating a new and possible "collective adventure" beyond simple showy collectionism or an endogamic brand image. Much of the turn of the century and the beginning of our current century has been characterized by a growing awareness of this new propositional initiative and the attempt to articulate it, to track it and materialize it in a possible, more or less shared, "narrative" that is "more inclosing than decidedly imposing". A new framework for a network of concerns (and explorations), based on exchanges from a distance, intersecting stimuli, shared readings, mutual interests, feeding and feedback – which are more or less conscious and/or convergent – present, on the other hand, in various fields of knowledge (economy, art, science, technology) which required a new theoretical construction – something that is not always available and, as such, is often addressed and approached by professionals who are generally and vocationally "committed to action". In this sense, we could talk about a certain "para-theory" developed by "para-theoreticians" who, aside from "producing" and "designing" – doing – would also talk, write and debate – think – about urban, spatial, formal and even moral issues ... concerning architectural attitudes and ethics... The contribution of new spaces for diffusion and stimulus, for the intersections and encounters most engaged with disciplinary renewal, was fundamental to proposing (in an interwoven way) a certain shared interpretation of the post-postmodern project.

Publications like *Quaderns, Fisuras, A+T,* or *Circo* in Spain, Arch+ in Germany, *Archis* in Holland, etc.; platforms like "Actar Publishers" (Barcelona-New York); meet-ups and *forums* such as "Europan" or "Archilab" in France; the importance of the researches that have been promoted in this way, and in these years, in certain educational centers as the Berlage Institute in Amsterdam (founded in 1990 by Herman Hertzberger, oriented by Wiel Arets since 1995, and directed by Alejandro Zaera-Polo – 2002- 2005), in the Graduate School of Architecture, Planning and Preservation of the New York Columbia University (in the Dean period of Bernard Tschumi – 1998-2003 –) or in an incipient SCIARC directed by Neil Denari from 1997 and by Eric Owen Moss from 2002 and in the renovation of the Units Studios in the AA of London or in the openness and leadership of Peter Cook and Peter Hall in the Bartlett School of the 1990s, were specially incident in this new architectural and design revaluation that was understanding the end of the Post-Modern period and the beginning of a more complex spatial, hyperrelational and transversal thinking.

In this context, the importance of a collective action like the one developed by Metápolis in Barcelona (meetings, publications, spaces for debate, and teacher training) was to express, perhaps like no other, that willingness to communicate and celebrate a new ideology, expressed explicitly in the *Metapolis Dictionary of Advanced Architecture* and in the foundation of the "IAAC" (Institute for Advanced Architecture of Catalonia) during the early years of the 20th century, a manifesto (an intentional vocabulary) that explicitly revealed the emergence of a new architectural logic related to the information society, and the digital and computational revolution.[56]

Next page: Data Landscapes and new natures. Ramon Prat: graphic photomontage (in *Quaderns* n. 217, 1997-98)

_55. Manuel Gausa, *Open(ing), Space-Time-Information* (Barcelona: Ed. Actar, 2018).

_56. The IAAC (Institute for Advanced Architecture of Catalunya) was founded officially in 2003 but started its activities on 2001 as IAAM (Institute for Advanced Architecture - Metapolis).

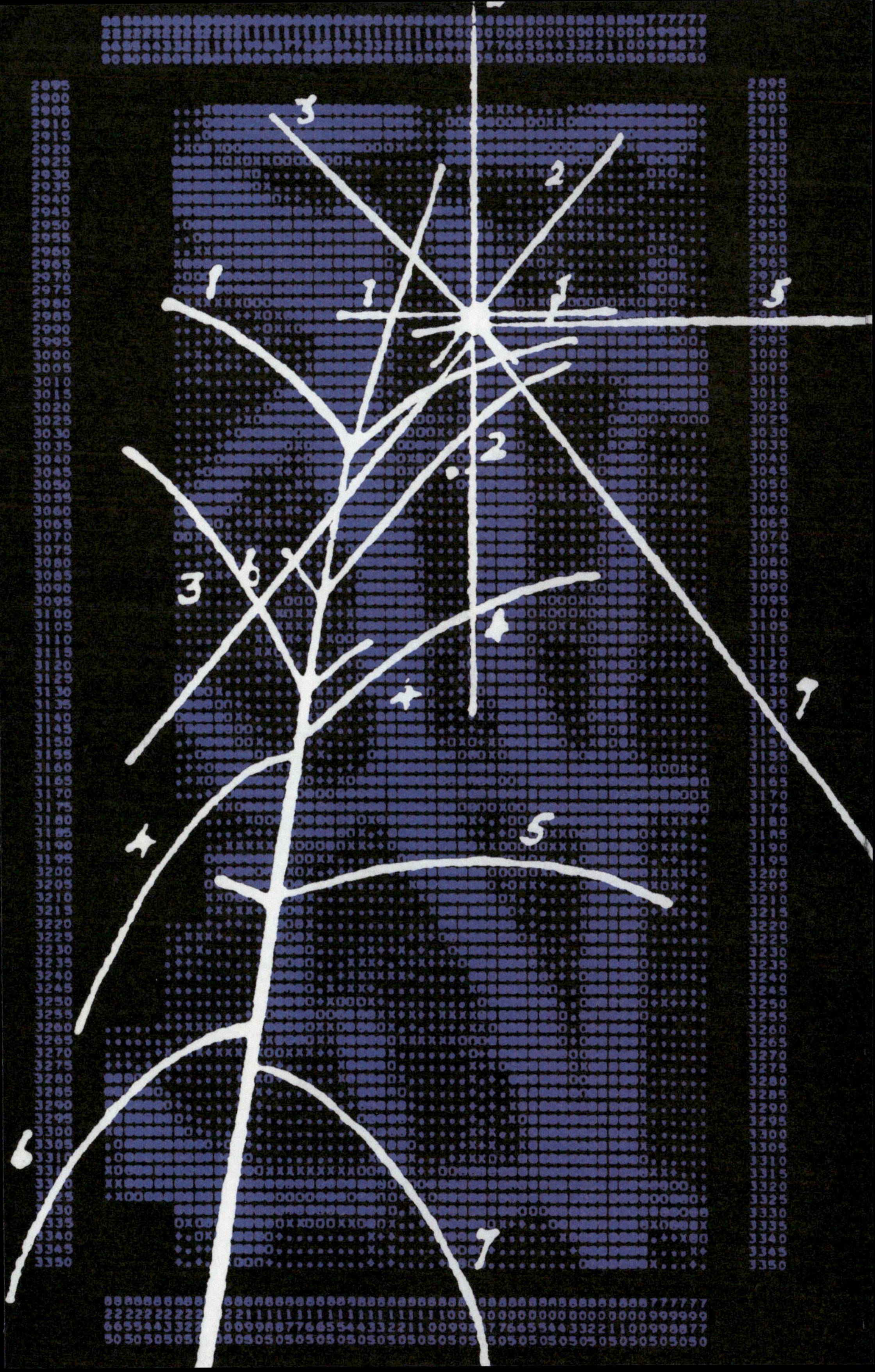

3.3. Wagers and New Paradigms: A New Para-theory for the Post-Postmodernity[57]

The turn of the century and the emergence of a new, more communicated, diverse and cosmopolitan scenario of technological and social transformations, but also a new conception of the idea of progress (not as the imposition of a new universal order but as the re-activation and re-information of reality) helped demonstrate the need for a return to research and innovation more as a shared prospection in and by different disciplinary fields than as a new independent "purpose". It was an intellectual and cultural commitment that aimed to characterize a new era in research that would more open, plural, restless, interactive and – above all – optimistic, in its moral and conceptual foundations.

For many of the new emerging players at the time, what was taking place at the turn of the century – and was later cemented – was the pioneering explosion of a new operative, advanced or informational logic, which was decidedly innovative in its ideas of order, form, and geometry, and in its materialization and organization. A logic associated with the acceptance of complexity, transversality, the capacity for interaction, the dynamic condition of processes and, ultimately, a desire for openness and relational adventure, called on to create intersections, encounters, hybridizations, mixtures and exchanges between spaces and information. This critical-propositional – or critical-proactive – reaction of a generation more motivated by the construction of a new horizon (and a new operative logic) than by the recreation of ancient arcadias or dogmas, or by the construction of isolated "icons", was fundamental to understanding, for example, the differences between the generation of the 1990s and the generation immediately before, from the 1980s.

Although that generation was pioneering in renewing modes and methods, it continued to confide not only in an apparent "conceptual formality", implicit in its concepts and designs, but, above all, in a determined purpose (professionally more profitable) to see itself claimed as an "intellectual elite" – vocationally and culturally officialized as a design "brand" or "signature", rather than as an authentic "collective field" of research, designated to accept proximity to power only based on the proximity to ideas.

Evidently, the temptation to fall into the diva-ism and iconographic virtuosity of the generation that dominated in the 1980s – which, with few exceptions (read Koolhaas, Tschumi and, perhaps, Ito), after having opened the door to the critical surmounting of post-modernity, abandoned all attempts at shared research to embrace individual significance (and individual "brand marketing") – also ended up influencing the new protagonists of the 1990s, in a long phase of iconographic consumption that colored most of the end of the 20th century. However, the defense not only of an architecture but, also, of a society, a culture – and a city – that would be more heterogeneous and complex, more multiple and multifaceted, richer and more plural in their manifestations, led, in the early 90s, to many significant experiments in which a certain social, and disciplinary, ideology could be seen that was called on to generate complicities, with an ongoing belief in the ability to conceive a shared scenario – and an associated habitat – which could be expressed as a place that was not only more dignified but, also, more stimulating, more imaginative, varied and definitively positive (and positivized) at the same time. In the late 1980s and early 1990s, some of the most interesting experiments in the European international scene attempted – perhaps as a response to the progressive tendency toward the description of panoramas rather than true theoretical stances – to conjugate this two-fold aspect

_57. Mosé Ricci, *Nuovi Paradigmi / New Paradigms* (Trento: List Laboratorio Editoriale Internazionale, 2012).

(theorizing and active, diffusing and projective), laying the foundations for a new critical and productive action understood more as an operative toolkit than as a mere neutral position. Professionals who ended up writing, reflecting and debating on what they did not see reflected in the "theory" or in the descriptive chronicles for use (scholarly or simply historiographic annotations...). [58]

Para-theory like the *para-military*... In that sense, we could talk about a certain "para-theory" developed by "para-theoreticians" who, aside from "producing", "mading" and "designing" – doing, but also talking, writing and debating, that is thinking – about urban, spatial, formal and even moral issues ... concerning architectural attitudes and ethics... With regard to this interest in doing and thinking, creating and narrating, producing and writing, designing and interpreting – in other words, in "manifesting" – a certain optimistic idea of the world, it is worth mentioning the importance of different forums for exchange and connection where there was a stimulating "renewing energy", forged through theoretical concerns and clear research experiences, (although they often lacked any real global interpretation).

In any case, during the 1990s, those forums gave rise to the first physical materialization of that other type of more "virtual" encounter, constituted by advanced networks for exchange and research on an international scale. The entire architectural debate in the final decade of the 20th century settled between the small-minded defense of a resistant universe, that is still subject to fixed and stabilized parameters of order which are often not without a certain purist puritanism (what is "coherent" as a guarantee of "order") , and the intuition (and acceptance) of a dynamic universe – ultimately more "restless" and impure – associated with more open, flexible and permeable trajectories with the ability to combine variation and interaction, mixture and change, and therefore singularity, irregularity and impurity. Dynamism, multiplicity, interaction, transversality, in short; the complexity of processes, of programs, and of combined and processed information; networked information and interactions... threads with which the beginnings of the 21st century were to be woven. [59]

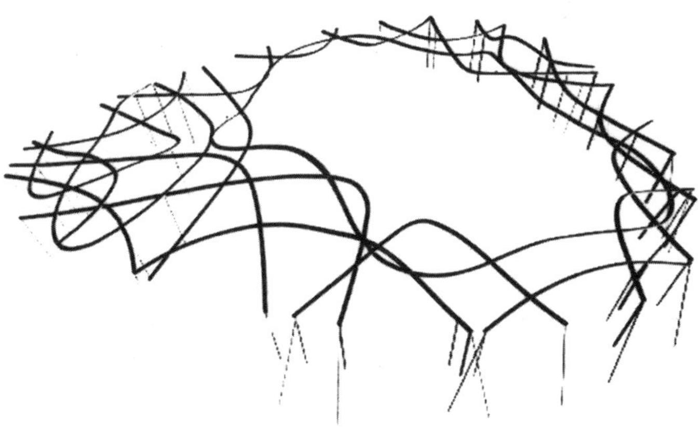

Cecil Balmond. Variable structural schemes for the Chemnitz Stadium from a dynamic and differentially braided trajectory (in Cecil Balmond, *Informal*, New York, Prestel Publishing, 2002)

_58. These concepts are in: Manuel Gausa, *Open(ing), Space-Time-Information* (Barcelona: Ed. Actar, 2018).
_59. Ibid.

JORDI VIVALDI

COLORARIUM
Topological Space and Relational Subject: The Continuous Floor

I- FIGURATION AND FIGURATIVE

In his book *Francis Bacon: The Logic of Sensation* (1981), Deleuze distinguishes between the terms "figuration" and "figurative".[1] For the French philosopher, the first expression refers to a form that maintains a certain relationship with the object it represents. On the contrary, the second expression, instead of the representation of a form, is a matter of capturing forces: it documents the meeting between the physical stuff of painting (canvas, paint, painting, painter) and a series of forces (both physical and psychological). Therefore, and in its condition as a "record" of those forces, the human figure is no longer expressed in a "clear and distinct" way, as if it was a direct representation. On the contrary, it is blurred, becoming an amalgam of contours that are not intended to create a defined and understandable form, but rather to document the forces affecting it.

The difference between figuration and the figurative is fundamental in order to understand the consolidation in the 90s of conformative protocols as a mode of action. Modern and postmodern figurational concepts such as semantics, symbolism, evocation, gesture or language are no longer operational tools: they don't engage with the *zeitgeist* characteristic of a turn of the century that headed down a different path. With the advent of the computational revolution, the experimental architecture of the 1990s is no longer an architecture of "Filebian solids", but an architecture of "topological processes". It is a dynamic, systematic and fluctuating architecture, but above all, it is a relational architecture that is circumscribed within a specific ontological framework: true reality is no longer found in the discrete individuality of substances, but in an underlying continuum of forces.

In resonance with this metaphysical framework, the topological spatiality characteristic of this decade and the relational subject associated with the end of the XX century establish certain correspondances that impact in one of the most primary architectural elements: the floor and its vertical layout. The singularity of the floor as part of an architectural whole is derived from the fact that, in contrast to other parts like walls, windows, pillars, or stairs, the floor is a necessary condition for the production of any kind of interiority within a gravitational scenario. Its absence is inconceivable. The reason lies in the performative nature of its presence: the floor can hardly be reduced to a mere contingency whose value is accidental. On the contrary: the layout of the floor tends to go unnoticed; it is not made an issue because its presence is so essential that it is accepted acritically as a given, as that what Heidegger would define with the german term *Zuhandenheit*.[2]

_1. Peter Eisenman, *Ten Canonical Buildings 1950-2000*, (New York: Rizzoli, 2008), 73.

_2. Together with the hammer, the floor is one of the most common examples that is used in order to explain the Heideggerian concep of "readiness-to-hand" (Zuhandenheit). Readiness-to-hand is manifested in its purest form when the user uses the tool without thinking about the tool at all, which is precisely the case of the floor.

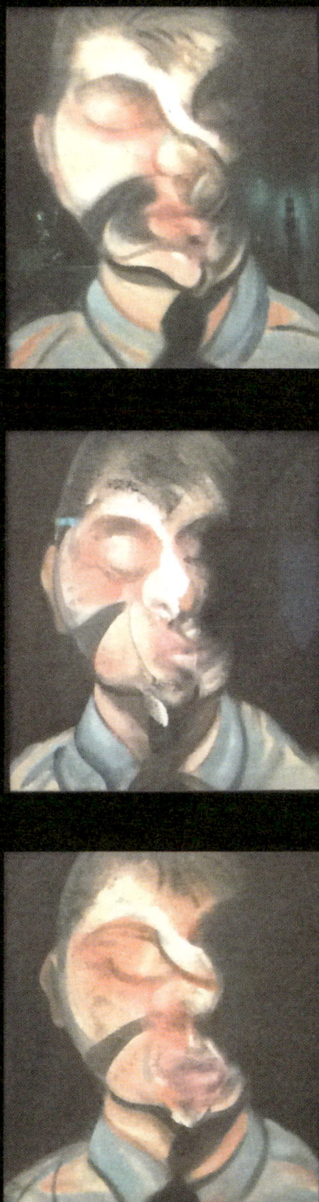

_"Self-Portrait"; Francis Bacon, 1973.

However, its participation as diagram is fundamental: the layout of the floor does not qualify space only through formal categories, but also through performative ones given its peculiarity of being in constant contact with us.

The applications of this ontological approach are not exclusive to architecture, but shared by cultural contributions of a different nature: Deleuze's multiplanar readings, Lynch's domestic folds, Barry Le Va's multi-layered structures or Houellebecq's murky viscosities are good examples of it. Under this cultural scenario, architecture operates via topological thought: it dissolves the independence of the architectural object, bringing it closer to a holistic field of intensities, flows, emergences and singularities. In contrast to the devotion to fracture characteristic of Deconstructivism, to the eclecticism related to Post-modernism or to the objectuality assumed by Modernism, multiplicity became the new totem for advanced architecture.

2- TOPOLOGICAL SPACE

Deleuze defines the notion of multiplicity as a series of structures in which all of the elements are determined reciprocally according to a specific organization. As such, the elements are united by relationships, and this union is at the root of their holism, understood as a system in which all the parts depend on each other because they are determined reciprocally. That is precisely what Deleuze seems to argue when he writes that "the reality of the virtual consists of the differential elements and relations along with the singular points which correspond to them. The reality of the virtual is structure."[3] Here, Deleuze refers to the concept of structure as what remains invariant despite experiencing changes on its surface. That is precisely what a topology is: an invariant structure that is also capable of undergoing variations in its metric properties. As Lars Spuybroek writes in his book *The Architecture of Continuity*, a topology "understands that a single organization may contain many possible structures (invariants), because an object can change its features and shape without changing its organization."[4] It follows that an architecture of variation does not necessarily imply a free architecture, much less one that is out of control. On the contrary, it is an architecture whose variations are controlled by a specific system. In that sense, the architecture of "blobs", which is so characteristic of some late-20th-century work, is based on uncontrolled variations and therefore are problematic under this framework: in a topological architecture, the elements are a result, i.e., a product of relationships as opposed to something a priori.

The digital technologies of the 1990s and the posterior digital manufacturing technologies were fundamental to engage in a dialogue, from an architectural point of view, with these reflections. The emergence of software such as Catia, Rhinocerous, Photoshop, and 3D Studio allowed for the manipulation of topological spaces with the precision demanded by what Mario Carpo calls "the notational bottleneck". The digital manufacturing technologies that appeared some time later, such as 3D printing, laser cut or milling, made it possible to convert digital forms into empirical reality in an accessible and immediate way. In fact, Deleuze "had famously anticipated this technological shift in his studies of difference and repetition through his dual notion of 'objet' and 'objectile'".[5] The expression objectile was introduced by Deleuze to express a new idea of the object based on Leibniz's mathematics of continuity: differential calculus does not describe objects, but

_3. Gilles Deleuze, *Difference and Repetition,* trans. Paul Patton, (New York: Continuum International Publishing Group Ltd, 2004), 182.

_4. Lars Spuybroek, *The Architecture of Continuity* (Rotterdam: V2/NAi Publishers, 2008), 209.

_5. Mario Carpo, *The Alphabet and the Algorithm*, (Massachussets: MIT Press, 2011), 99.

rather their variations. In this sense, an objectile would be a "function that contains an infinite number of objects". Each individual object is one crystallization of a mathematical algorithm that is common to all. Bernard Cache developed the objectile concept in his book *Earth Moves* from 1995, where he defines it as a new concept of the technical object – not mass produced mechanically, but digitally and based on variations of non-standard series. As such, the emergence of the continuous in the field of architecture in the 1990s occurred through multiple complicities, including the computational revolution that took place during that decade, the topological thinking of Deleuze and Guattari, the recovery of Leibniz's mathematics of continuity, and a reaction against the formal language characteristic of the 1980s.

This topological thinking, understood as a holistic system, is the geometric foundation that fuels the continuous spaces of the 1980s and 1990s. They are difficult to explain without referring to Deleuze's ideas of topology and holism, understood as systems of relations. Deleuze's description of a living organism in *Difference and Repetition* is representative of this argument. The French philosopher presents a model based on a relationship between three levels; an internal level defined by its genes; an external level defined by its relationships with other organisms; and a horizontal level defined by the relationships between its internal parts. However, as Levy Briant points out very opportunely, this relational model of the organism leaves out the agent's participation in its own construction.[6] The agent is instead posited as an object that is the effect of the dynamic relationships that occur in its surroundings – in other words, the interactions between environments. That is precisely why the Kantian subject characteristic of Modernity is so different from Deleuze's subject: whereas the former argues for an absolute subject that is incarnated in man, the latter defends a relational subject that takes shape through a system of relationships.

3- THE RELATIONAL SUBJECT

The notion of subject is crucial in order to approach the particular understanding of space proposed by conformative protocols. As Lorens Holm argues,[7] architecture inevitably puts objects in relation to subjects, that is, it produces an spatial apparatus that represents objects to subjects. Under this umbrella, the constitution of the latter not only defines the manner in which space is aprehended, but also the manner in which space is orchestrated in order to be inhabited. In this sense, conformative protocols no longer operate under the cartesian notion of subject, but as we will see in what follows, under the understanding of a fluctuant subject characterized by its relational vocation.

The crisis of the modern absolute subject goes hand in hand with the crisis of the Fordist industrial human. Following on the Renaissance and the Enlightenment, for centuries the modern subject enjoyed an ontologically privileged position. Free, optimistic and deeply positivist, generally speaking the modern subject upheld science and technology as infallible catalysts for progress. However, first, Ricoeur's masters of the school of suspicion, and second, the perverse results of the Second World War, questioned this Promethean narrative, replacing the absolute subject characteristic of modernity with a relational subject. Under this umbrella, notions such as language, power, unconscious, or ideology played a crucial role in a subject's process of construction that was not anymore autonomous and independent.

_6. Levi Bryant, *The Democracy of Objects*, (Michigan: Open Humanities Press 2011), 245.
_7. Lorens Holm. "Architecture and Its Objects" in *Is There an Object-Oriented Architecture?* (London: Bloomsbury Academic, 2020). 64.

The social and technological conditions characteristic of Fordism's default were aligned with this approach. The increases in wage stratification caused by the increment in labour diversification forced the market to diversify. As a result, instead of addressing a uniform market that had called for the strategy of mass-repeating an optimized standard, greater value was placed on the ability to innovate and make production more flexible, like in The Toyota Way with its 5 Whys. The globalization of markets in the 70s cut back on the stabilizing ability of States, since their economies had come to depend on large international flows that were difficult to control. In consequence, capacities for prediction were also reduced, which further discouraged the production of large stocks for mass consumption. In addition, computational productive strategies such as digital manufacturing technologies began to allow for a greater product diversity without the associated high costs of hand-made products. Production became much more flexible, both in terms of time and space, such that "the static organizing principles of Fordist mass society – separation, specialization and mass repetition – were replaced by the dynamic principles of self-organization of the emerging Post-Fordist network society: variation, flexible specialization and networking."[8]

In a intelectual, social and technological context characterized by its fluidity and volatility, the relational subject, ambiguous, weak and relativistic, recognizes that s/he is mediated by a series of linguistic and ideological structures that s/he cannot entirely control. S/he assumes, therefore, that the closest thing to "the Truth" that can be obtained is just one of the multiple perspectives offered by a reality that cannot be exhausted by way of science or technology. The advent of the Information Age invested the relational subject with a more complex, strategic and operative condition. Divided and fluctuating, the relational subject takes on the role of the Baudelairean flâneur-voyeur: open, idle, toughened, and explorer, s/he is not a mere "wandering" ambler, but rather an active part of the topological space through which s/he is moving.

4- THE CONTINUOUS FLOOR

The continuous floor characteristic of many experimental projects of this period conjugates several attributes associated with the emergence of the topological space and the rise of the relational subject previously described. Its main characteristic is that of ambiguity: the floor in Yokohama is figure, but it is also ground; it is façade, but it is also roof; it is surface, but it is also a volume. We are no longer dealing with the abstract and neutral Platonic *chora* exalted by the Modern Movement, but rather with an Aristotelian *topos*: concrete, singular, specific, differentiated.

In relation to the floor's design, the spatial topological framework characteristic of the 90s freed architects from the rigid section of the discrete floor characteristic of Modernity. This resulted in a stimulus for the creation of new techniques for manipulating the floor, which led to an increase in the complexity of its determining factors, its limits and its nature. In that sense, Alejandro Zaera-Polo asserts that "the exploration of the surface of the ground is established as the most unstable and revealing component of the emerging forms of space. [...] Our surface designs don't deal with the absence of ground, but with its redefinition and the creation of a series of techniques: a new discipline of the ground."[9]

_8. Patrick Schumacher, *The Autopoiesis of Architecture*, vol 2, (Wiltshire: Wiley, 2012), 654.
_9. Alejandro Zaera-Polo, "Nuevas topografías. La reformulación del suelo," in *Otra mirada: posiciones contra crónicas*, ed. Manuel Gausa and Ricardo Devesa, (Barcelona: Gustavo Gili, 2010), 116.

In this sense, the nature of continuous floors is fundamentally active. Whereas the discrete floor characteristic of the 1909 Theorem was understood as a foundation that was repeated vertically in an unlimited way, the continuous floor should be understood as a single platform, i.e., a single operating system that does not function as a mere "background", but as a self-referential entity. Under this background, Zaera differentiates discrete floors from continuous floors based on six points:

"Unlike traditional floors, the new floors:
1. are an artificial construction, and not a natural space, from both the physical and the cultural point of view;
2. they are not abstract, neutral or homogeneous, but concrete and differentiated; in other words, they are not figure or ground, but rather operating systems
3. they do not have a particular framework, since the field where they exist is not a fragment, but a differentiated field affected by external processes; in other words, they are inseparable from our intervention;
4. they do not constitute a datum or a point of reference;
5. they are not solid but empty;
6. and their structure is diagonal, as opposed to a structure determined by gravity."[10]

However, besides these disciplinary singularities, the folded or wavy nature of continuous floors has some similarities with the fluctuating subject of the late 20th century. In continuous floors, the singularity of each of the points on the surface leads to a situation in which, according to Eisenman, "no longer is the subject in a one-to-one relationship with another subject but, because of the inclined planes, it views other subjects – and is viewed by them – as objects"[11]. The fact that the one-to-one relationship is lost is not anecdotal: the philosopher Emmanuel Levinas argues that true existence does not lie in oneself as an isolated and unique subject, but in a transcendent subject that is only achieved in time and through the other, but above all, through the "face to face" encounter with the other: "The face-to-face situation would be the fulfillment of time; the overlap of the present in the future is not the event of a single subject, but an intersubjective relationship".[12]

First, Levinas argues for an existence through otherness: i.e., an existence that is such if and only if it opens up to the other. This openness implies a relationship with the other, but it is an asymmetrical relationship, since, according to the french philosopher, one must be responsible for the other without expecting anything in return. It is precisely that gratuity what constitutes an authentic subject. Second, Levinas argues that the face-to-face encounter is the culminating moment of the relationship with the other: absolute alterity occurs through the face, always unique, which can only be approached with infinite responsibility.

In this way, Levinas posits the face-to-face as the only way to recognize an "other subject". While it may seem that there is something metaphorical in Levinas' argument, it is interesting to note how it can be applied to discrete and continuous floors. While discrete floors offer a relationship between absolute subjects that can only occur in a face-to-face encounter, continuous floors transform that relationship into a relationship between fluctuating subjects: depending on their position, the face-to-face encounter disappears,

_10. Ibid.
_11. Peter Eisenman, *Ten Canonical Buildings 1950-2000*, (New York: Rizzoli, 2008), 205.
_12. Emmanuel Levinas, *Le temps et l'autre*, (Paris: Presses Universitaires, 2014), 69.

_"Jussieu-Two Libraries"; Rem Koolhaas, 1992.

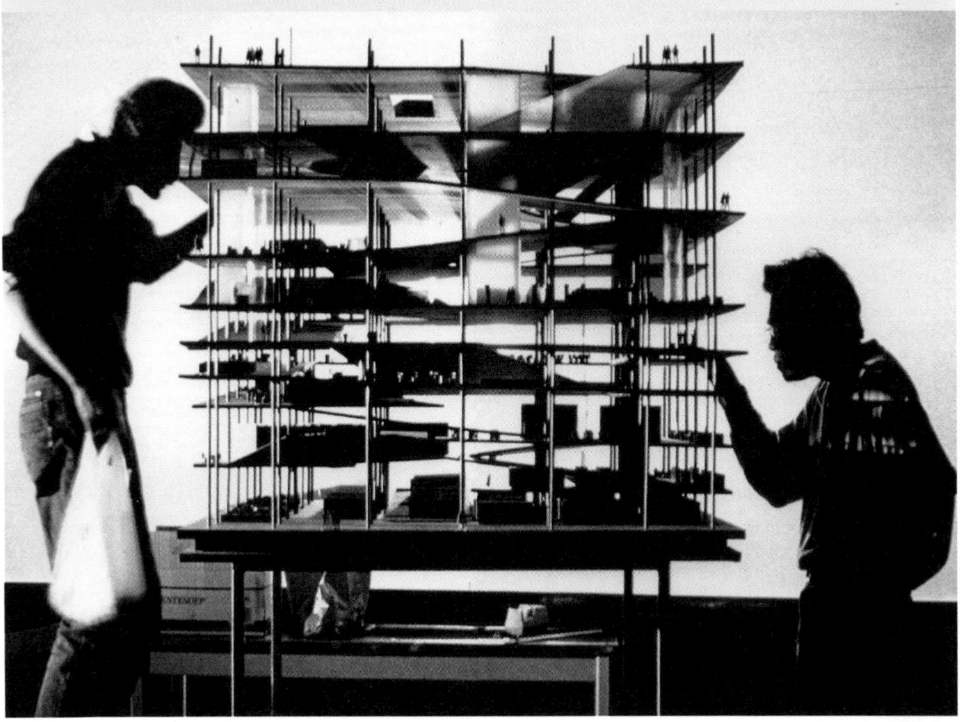

resulting in a mutual objectivation of the other. Here again, and in a very literal way, we see a relationship between the formalization of floors and the conception of the subject, expressed in this case through the experience of the other.

Although continuous floors, as we have just described them, have some precedents dating back a thousand years, and others from the first and second thirds of the 20th century like Le Corbusier's "Saint-Pierre Church" in Firminy (1971 – 2006), their great moment of splendour took place at the end of the 20th century. The reasons for this championing that took place in the 80s and 90s had at least three allies: first, an ontological framework based on a relational subject, second, a sociocultural understanding of the human based on a fluctuating, Toyotist and ambivalent individual, and third, a technological reality with the potential to proliferate difference.

Related in different degrees with the parametricism of the time, there are a series of continuous floors that provide paradigmatic examples of this category. In the design for a "Convention Center" in Agadir, Morocco, from 1990, Koolhaas does not approach the ground as a datum, as it was with the discreteness characteristic of skyscrapers. Nor is it the horizontal didactic continuum of the Cartesian "x" and "y" axes typical of Le Corbusier's open plan; rather the section shifts from generic to figurative: Koolhaas alters the horizontal of the section with the aim of producing a series of artificial undulations. And yet, the floor in the "Convention Center" in Agadir still has a horizontal tendency in that it does not provide movement from one story to the next, but only a "vibration" in the floor level. Something similar happens in FOA's design for "Yokohama Terminal", from 1995. In this case, the continuous floor has a different scale, but it maintains an undulation with a horizontal tendency. Like in Koolhaas' project, there is a strategic formal decision that involves the edges of the floor: in both cases, the edges are dictated by the limits of the site, as if the project would be a piece of a bigger cake.

The decision was not self-evident, however, and Alejandro Zaera-Polo says as much when he asserts that one of the team's doubts was: "Do we place importance on the surface as a constituent element, or on the idea of an arbitrary frame for a limitless surface as a conceptual strategy?"[13] Finally, they decided to define an arbitrary frame, a strategy also used by Sejima in their "Rolex Center" (2004), which contrasts with other more restrained designs by FOA like the "Virtual House" (1995). However, continuous floors are even more peculiar when their tendency is not horizontal but vertical, since their continuity in section is highlighted as a disruptive element in relation to discrete floors. In that sense, the "Mercedes Benz Museum" is a clear example: in a spiral with clear Wrightian reminiscences, the building resolves the entire program in a continuous and unified way.

Alberto Campo Baeza's design for the same competition responds to a similar strategy, although in his case it is an eccentric spiral. And of course, the exercises of single surface floor of Diller Scofidio are among the most representative cases of this category, specially through buildings such as the "Education Center in New York" (2016) or the "Museum of Image and Sound of Rio" de Janeiro (2018). However, the most emblematic project focused on continuous floors is Rem Koolhaas' design for "Jussieu" from 1992. Although it is an eminently vertical project, with a height of 40 meters for a square 60 x 60 meter plan, its warped floors show an evolution that began with the Agadir project. However, unlike Agadir, where the warped slab is still horizontal, as we have seen, the

_13. Alejandro Zaera-Polo, "Nuevas topografías. La reformulación del suelo," in *Otra mirada: posiciones contra crónicas*, ed. Manuel Gausa and Ricardo Devesa, (Barcelona: Gustavo Gili, 2010), 117.

floor slabs of the Jussieu libraries are warped in section so that they rise to reach the slab of the next floor. The section for Jussieu becomes a critique of the "1909 theorem" and the "New York Athletic Club", producing another diagram based, in this case, on the internal continuity of the surfaces.

The fact that the plan is square and that certain heights remains constant between them only serves to further emphasize the curvature of the slabs. In the end, as Eisenman points out, "the only real volumes in the building are the interstitial spaces between floors. These are bounded as figures by the bow and bend of the floor planes, and in that sense can be viewed as residual, while the linking of circulation with the floor planes suggests that a diagram of circulation is its governing form."[14]

The cross section of the project is completely different from a case of discrete floors: we are no longer dealing with the stacked strata of the "New York Athletic Club", or the layered system from the "Parc de la Villette", but the result of slicing a single warped plane. In plan, there is no obvious centripetal or centrifugal tension; there is a diffuse force that avoids disrupting the edge and that translates into horizontal cuts, spirals or inclined slabs. There are some aspects where certain classic notations can still be read, such as the legibility of the four elevations, or the grid of columns. However, these elements do not form the *leitmotiv* of the design; rather they stand out as aspects that, by contrast, emphasize the disciplinary innovations contributed by the vertical use of the continuous floor.

The continuous floor characteristic of topological surfaces uniquely combines a series of spatial attributes that distinguish it from the discrete floor not only in its form but also in its performance:

Mereology: Whole > Parts

To conceive the continuous floor as a single differentiated floor means to consider it as a whole that incorporates all of its parts. In that sense, the parts are entirely subjugated to a whole that determines them through their relationships, thus negating their individuality. Where discrete floors were characterized by the wide autonomy of their parts, continuous floors are characterized by the reduction of their parts to the series of relationships that make up the whole. At the point where all the parts depend on each other by virtue of a system that is determined reciprocally, they form a totality. As Sanford Kwinter suggests, "Every real system is made up of other systems, and they are all continually leaking information to one another in such a way as to link them across a single 'continuum of influence'"[15]. In that sense, where discrete floors constituted a series of distinct and independent worlds (1909 theorem), continuous floors form a single "hyper-connected" and "super-unified" world, rooted in the concept of the field. It "describes a space of propagation, of effects. It contains no material points, rather functions, vectors and speeds. It describes local relations of difference within fields of celerity, transmission or of careering points, in a word, what Minkowski called the world."[16]

_14. Peter Eisenman, *Ten Canonical Buildings 1950-2000*, (New York: Rizzoli, 2008), 206.
_15. Sanford Kwinter, "Landscapes of Change", *Assemblage*, no. 19 (1992), 59.
_16. Sanford Kwinter, "Landscapes of Change: Boccioni's Stati d' animo as a General Theory of Models", Assemblage, no. 19 (1992), 88-89.

Geometry: Topological

Whereas the discrete floor of the skyscraper and the open plan of the Dom-ino scheme are based on rigid and hermetic figures like the triangle, the rectangle or the circle, the geometries of continuous floors are, in Schumacher's words, "animate (dynamic, adaptive, interactive) geometrical entities – splines, nurbs, and subdivs." [17] They form open systems, react to points of attraction and, most importantly, they are connected to one another, which allows for their variability overall.

The type of geometry that best represents these attributes is topological geometry, that is, the branch of mathematics that studies those characteristics of an object that remain invariant despite homeomorphic transformations such as folding, warping or stretching. Topological geometry is, therefore, a geometry of positions rather than a geometry of objects.

Thus, continuous floors are described via topologies. The case of "Yokohama" is emblematic: the tectonic play that develops between the floor and the roof is ultimately a symbiotic exchange, a mechanism that becomes a multi-layered topography, rising and falling along the quay.

Contour: Virtual

If an element is considered to be continuous, we imagine that it is uninterrupted; strictly speaking, then, we should not assume it that has any limits. FOA's "Virtual House" is emblematic in that sense: the moebius strip that forms it does not end at any particular place; on the contrary it twists back into itself. In other projects like "Yokohama", "Agadir" or the "Rolex Center", the limit of the floor is not constituted by a natural limit on the surface (impossible, since the surface in itself is infinite), but by an arbitrary frame.

However, the notion of limit does not necessarily refer to a physical limit: if we understand the horizon as the part of a surface that includes the line that separates the surface from the sky, as seen from our perspective, we realize that the fluctuation of a continuous surface produces multiple horizons, not just one or none. They are apparent limits: when a user reaches this kind of limit, he discovers that he can continue moving forward. In that sense, and as we can see in projects like "Asphalt Spot" of F.Roche (2002) rather than a discrete set of horizons, continuous soils produce a network of horizons, since they are connected to one another through the floor itself, although the connection may be provisionally invisible to the user.

Jeff Kipnis asserts something similar when he writes that, in Jussieu, "the plates are cut and the rims warped, allowing visitors to gaze surreptitiously at others above and below. The effect shatters the ideal horizon line of Dom-ino and folds the fragments back into the space as an eroticized web of partial horizons." [18] Kipnis argues that these horizons are erotic and partial: erotic because of the voyeurism they induce, and partial because their nature is multiple and limited. In contrast to the immateriality and universality characteristic of the horizon of discrete floors, the horizon of continuous floors is essentially the material fragmentation of the modern horizon.

_17. Patrick Schumacher, The Autopoiesis of Architecture, vol 2, (Wiltshire: Wiley, 2012), 654
_18. Jeff Kipnis, *A question of Qualities,* (London: Writing Architecture Series, 2013), 124.

_"Villa VPRO"; MVRDV, 1997.

Arrangement: Field

In his text *La crise de la musique sérielle*, Xenakis criticizes, on the one hand, the seriality of linear polyphony and, on the other hand, the indeterminacy and arbitrariness of John Cage's compositions. As an alternative, Xenakis proposes "stochastic music", understood as "a world of sound-masses, vast groups of sound-events, clouds and galaxies governed by new characteristics such as density, degree of order, and rate of change, which required definitions and calculations using probability theory."[19] In short, it would be what in physics is called a field: i.e., the space-time distribution of one or more physical magnitudes that can be measured around each point in a region of space for each moment in time. Following this definition, a field produces an underlying matrix with the ability to unify a series of elements that behave differently. Stan Allen aptly summarizes the architectural consequences of fields, when he states that "form matters, but not so much the forms of things as the forms between things."[20]

Thus, whereas discrete floors are distributed according to stratification strategies based on the *1909 theorem*, continuous floors arrange their singularities drawing on the notion of the field. The case of Jussieu is emblematic in that regard, not only because of its nature as a continuous surface, but above all because of its implicit references to the Dom-ino diagram: Koolhaas' design incorporates Le Corbusier's schema but does away with its uniform infinity through a finite field of fluctuating interactions.

Growth: Deformation

In his book *SMLXL*, Rem Koolhaas included a photograph where a hand appears lifting up a corner of the floor. It is a didactic image in its contrast with another one, in this case by Le Corbusier, where a hand is shown sliding a prefabricated unit into a structure. Deforming versus sliding. Through this image, the Dutch architect suggests that the surface is no longer a tabula rasa to which assembled elements are added; rather it consists of a variable plane, i.e., an adaptable, foldable element that is part of a vertical continuum. Thus, whereas the growth of discrete floors is founded on a simple exercise of repetition inspired by the serialization of Fordist assembly lines, continuous floors grow through an exercise of variation based on folding and warping strategies. These must respect the fundamental principle of a topology: the univocality of the original form cannot be separated into two distinct elements. Projects like "Yokohama" are the maximum expression of this guiding principle. The deformation of the floor in FOA's design emerges as a fundamental technique for transforming an element that is usually based on a fixed code, like discrete floors, into what Alejandro Zaera-Polo defines as "an active, complete and shifting field". The expression "deformation" loose its negative connotation derived from modern morality: at a time when the objet-type was exalted as an ideal model that should be repeated with the utmost fidelity, any alteration was viewed as heresy. However, continuous floors draw on a much less absolutist vision than was the case for modern proclamations. In that sense, continuous floors as Jussieu take part in a Situationist détournement: they take an object created by the modern system - the Domino schema - and distort its meaning in order to produce a critical and subversive effect.

_19. Iannis Xenaquis, "Towards a Metamusic," *Tempo*, no. 93 (1970), 3.
_20. Stan Allen, "Field Conditions" in Points + Lines, Ed. Princeton Architectural Press, ed. Mark Lamster, (New York: Princeton Architectural Press, 2012), 92.

Figuration: Figure = Ground

Continuous floors no longer take their inspiration from the modern relationships between building and floor based on the opposition between figure and ground. While discrete floors are presented as "ground" because of their condition as lots repeated in section, continuous floors no longer participate in "the definition of the ground as something defined, stable, horizontal, fixed and homogeneous."[21] As a result, it can no longer be seen as mere ground, since its active condition as a platform negates any strictly receptive function. In contrast, continuous floors posit a marked ambiguity between figure and ground, which ends up making them equivalent: ground is figure and figure is ground. Indeed, their status as "operating systems", to quote Alejandro Zaera-Polo relates them further to the landscape condition: i.e., understood as a topographic configuration that simultaneously acts as figure and ground. In that sense, Stan Allen is very clear in asserting that "one of the potentials of the field is to redefine the relation between figure and ground. If we think of the figure not as a demarcated object read against a stable field, but as an effect emerging from the field itself -as moments of intensity, as peaks or valleys within a continuous field- then it might be possible to imagine figure and field as more closely allied."[22] The case of the lower platform in the Agadir project is emblematic: on the one hand, its undulating floor blurs together with the softness of the desert dunes that surround it; while, on the other hand, it highlights its nature as a built floor, whose volume houses a convention center and a public space.

Circulation: Wander

In the 1960s, in the context of the Situationist movement, Guy Debord popularized a series of experiments he called dérives, that is, an urban and targetless "wandering". This activity was framed within the larger context of psychogeography, aimed at understanding how the geographical environment affects people's emotions and behaviour. Dérives result in erratic and seemingly meaningless trajectories, in line with the fluctuating understanding of the subject characteristic of the 20th century. They also stand in direct opposition to the optimized journey of modernity and the understanding of circulation as a mere movement in a "straight line" and "between two points". In that sense, whereas the circulation characteristic of the discrete floor was resolved using a "spine" system based on an optimization of paths in order to minimize travel times, continuous floors produce the opposite effect: in them, circulation becomes a "wandering" experience, a series of "surfing" trajectories that are never repeated and that unfold across the undulations characteristic of a warped slab. Koolhaas describes it when he explains, referring to Jussieu, that its visitor "becomes a Baudelairean flaneur, inspecting and being seduced by a world of books and information by the urban scenario."[23] As such, the inhabitant of a continuous floor can no longer be defined as a "user"; rather he becomes what Walter Benjamin described as an urban explorer: he is a gentleman of the metropolis, seductive and enticeable, but he is also an adventurer, a daring traveler familiar with the streets; there is nothing lazy in his recreational wandering, but rather a great curiosity for the complex richness of the urban landscape.

_21. Alejandro Zaera-Polo, "Nuevas topografías. La reformulación del suelo," in *Otra mirada: posiciones contra crónicas* (Barcelona: Ed. Gustavo Gili, 2010), 116.

_22. Stan Allen, "Field Conditions" in Points + Lines, *Ed. Princeton Architectural Press*, ed. Mark Lamster, (New York: Princeton Architectural Press, 2012), 97.

_23. Rem Koolhaas, *SMLXL*, (New York: Monacelli Press, 1995), 344.

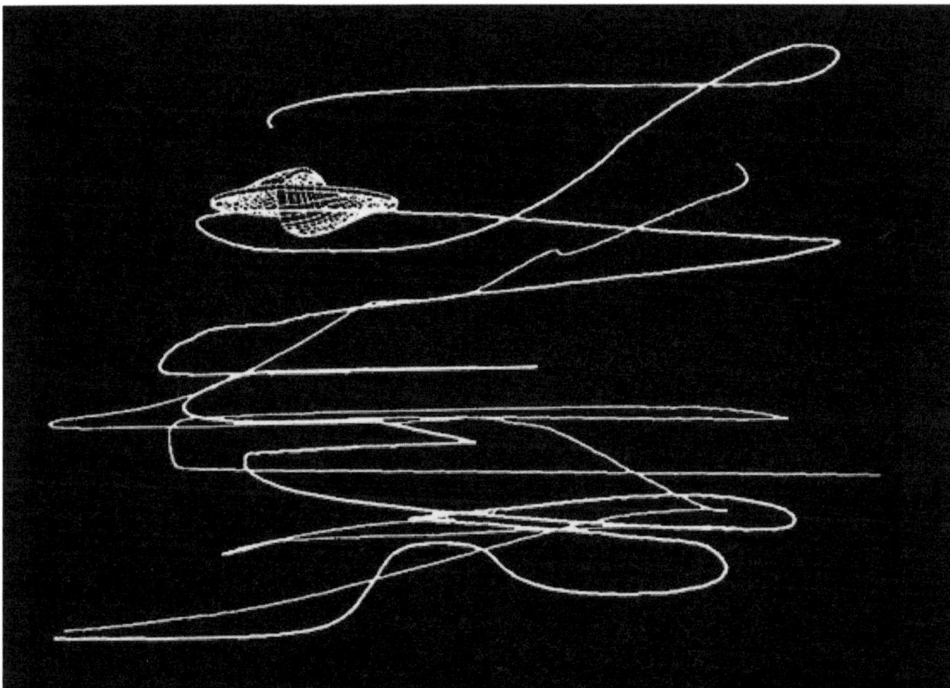

_"Jussieu-Two Libraries' Circulation", Rem Koolhaas, 1992.
_"The Naked City", Guy Debord, 1957.

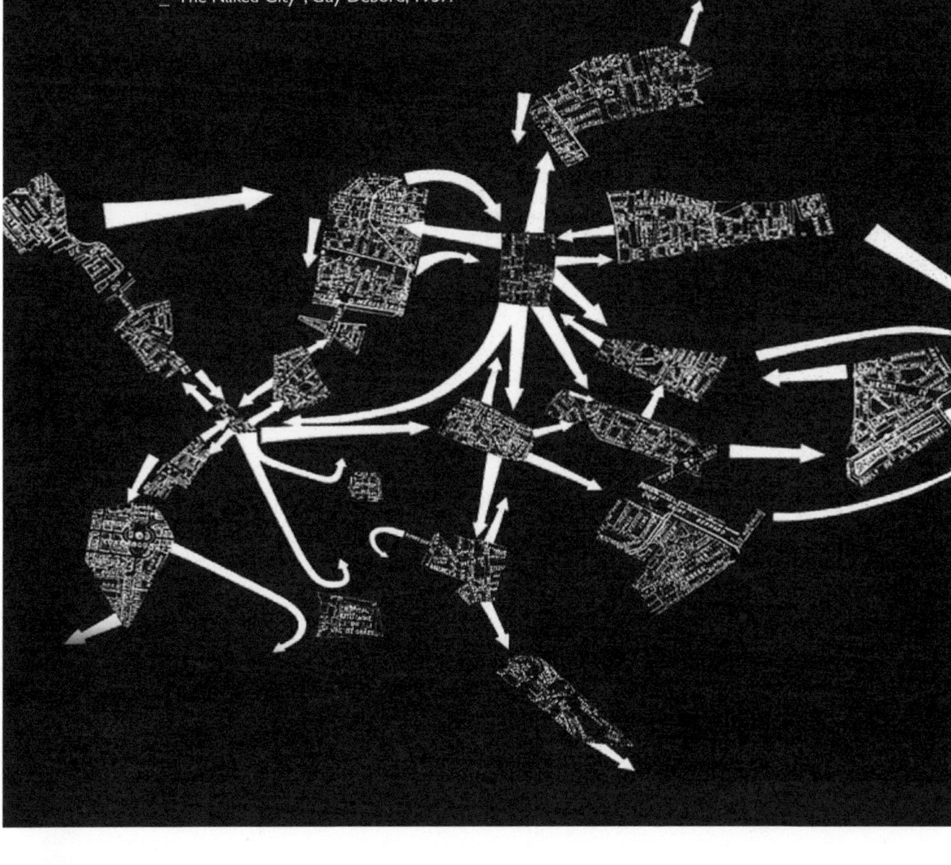

Gaze: Voyeur

The undulations of the continuous ground produce a series of situations in which other subjects can be observed at higher and lower levels. This visual complexity derived from gazes that intersect through all three axes of space, moves away from a gaze whose fundamental trait is the horizontal depth associated with the discrete floor. On the contrary, the undulations of the continuous floor offer situations where a person can watch without being seen; this translates into a sexualized space, where the visitor becomes a veritable voyeur. Jeff Kipnis insists on this when he says that "in his project for the university libraries at Jussieu, the architect revisits Corbusian themes to generate a social setting organized less by the program than by the erotic fantasies of the voyeur."[24] Here, Kipnis seems to be realizing something that Beatriz Colomina had already suggested in her comparison between the centrifugal gaze of the Ville Savoye and the centripetal gaze of Loos' Raumplan. In the latter, the Viennese architect also created sexualized spaces, almost as though they were a series of stages located at different heights. Continuous floors emphasize a sexualization of the gaze, which no longer seeks out the idealized abstraction of the modern horizon, but rather the particular effects of an eroticized environment.

Orientation: Deviation

Discrete floors use an external element as a point of reference – the circulation core – which only through its radical otherness is able to a function as a cosmic connection between the different autonomous worlds that are repeated in section. The elevator appears as a space shuttle, a transitional capsule that allows for the "impossible leap" between worlds. It constitutes a rite de passage; a sliding limbo and a "no-man's land" where one can only await the arrival of the new world. The core operates as a transcendent reference that serves as an axis of spatial orientation for the user. In contrast, continuous floors are put forward based on the idea of an immanent reference – in other words, a reference that is established inherently, from the floor itself. Indeed, in continuous floors the surface itself has the ability to unify all the events and circumstances that come to pass in the building; based on its role as a continuous unified system, it can structure and mediate all the different aspects that appear on its surface. As such, users' orientation in space is derived from the direction and magnitude of the slope at any given point on the surface, since that is the source of their specificity. From there, what will be relevant to the user will be the angle between the line of gravity relative to his body and the intersecting angle of the surface at the point where he is standing. The magnitude of that deviation emerges as the unique specificity for each point on the surface and consequently as an element of orientation.

Interiority: Gradiation

The fact that, in the continuous floor, figure and ground – understood traditionally as interior and exterior, respectively – are fused into a single continuum has consequences that reach beyond the strictly formal sphere. The blurring of hard borders affected by the continuous floor also implies the elimination of the edges that purposefully separated the interior from the exterior in the discrete floor. While both concepts remain valid in the sense that an absolute interior and an absolute exterior do, in fact, exist, the two categories are no longer opposites within a binary structure; rather, they are the two endpoints of a gradual structure.

_24. Jeff Kipnis, *A question of Qualities*, (London: Writing Architecture Series, 2013), 125.

Looking closely at the case of Yokohama, we see how, along the path from the outside to the inside, there are several moments characterized by ambiguity: i.e., conditions of exteriority and interiority overlap analogically.

5- RISKS AND MENACES: ARCHITECTURE AS AN EFFECT

In spite of constituting a new formal and performative *episteme* for architecture, the relational nature of conformative protocols has recently been challenged by what David Ruy has defined as a "return to (strange) objects"[25]. This position resonates with the emergence of Graham Harman's Object-Oriented Ontology, whose central statement affirms that although the cosmos may be populated with an infinity of objects, they come in only two kinds: "the real object that withdraws from all experience, and the sensual object that exists only in experience".[26] Objects have a unified reality that cannot be reduced to its parts or to its effects.

Although it is too early to evaluate the impact that this shift is having on architecture, most of its protagonists coincide in the fact that concepts such as "becoming" frequently pushed architecture to become a surrogate for the ground "in which buildings were often reduced to an outcome of real or imagined contextual forces",[27] that is, a trickle-down effect of an underlying system which is supposed to constitute the true relevant reality - whether it be social, economic, formal, cultural, etc. In the radicalization of its integrating intent, architecture would end up dissolving into a uniform world of flows and relationships. In contrast to the internal and external granularity occurring in the classic and modern object, conformative protocols promote just the opposite: they produce an internal fusion through which traditionally separated parts such as roof, structure and façade form a single whole, and they also operate an external fusion, in which design and context form a "reactive" continuum.

Accepting this radical relationism is problematic: if an element is exhausted in the sum of the relationships that make it up, it is hard to understand what constitutes its specificity in relation to the continuum from which it is emerging. To that effect, something must overstep the relationships inherent to that object, rendering it irreducible to its context or to its processes of emergence. The current architectural revival of the notion of object resonates with this ontological position by seeking for a formal and ideological vocabulary emphasizing ruptures, separations and breaks, but also nestings, groupings and chunks; it leaves behind the topological modulations characteristic of conformative protocols in order to speculate with autonomous and differentiated architectural objects that are irreducible to its surroundings. The ongoing challenge of the most formalistic contemporary architecture is to establish a new type of clusterizations constituted by a set of elements whose interrelations do not totalize them under one single continuum. Rather than assuming its subjugation into an underlying field of forces, its specificity in relation to its context is promoted as an operative tool of differentiation and emancipation. This exploration unveils a formal condition that is no longer continuous or discrete, but rather continuous while discrete: it is supported by the topological thinking of the first conformative systems and, at the same time, it avoids its totalization into a single continuum by combining it with a singular revival of the discrete.

_25. David Ruy, "Returning to (Strange) Objects", *Tarp Architecture Manual* (2012).
_26. Graham Harman. The Quadruple Object (Winchester: Zero Books, 2011), 49.
_27. Tom Wiscombe, "Discreteness, or Towards a Flat Ontology of Architecture", *Project: A Journal for Architecture*, no. 3 (2014), 40.

Fluctuant spaces with first dynamic, reactive and interactive sensor configurations
NOX-Kaas Osterhuis: H20. Pavilion, Neeltjejans, 1997 (*Quaderns* n. 218, 1999).

DISTRIBUTIVE PROTOCOLS

2000-2010

The Ecological Condition:
Connecting Networks and Propagating Atmospheres

ECOLOGY

CONNECTING NETWORKS

PROPAGATING ATMOSPHERES

Distributive protocols operate through coordinational processes. In resonance with the consolidation of Internet and its impact on the economical, social and cultural spheres, the experimental architecture of the early XX century resonates with Bruno Latour's actants: an entity is that what it "modifies, transforms, perturbs, or creates". However, rather than establishing a system of relations (topology), distributive protocols establish relations in between systems (ecology): they conjugate operative clusters capable of transferring resources in between different mediums. Thus, rather than introverted formulations, trascendental essences or metaphoric references, distributive architecture establishes social, economic and energetical transferences. In this scenario, information is not a geometrical parameter, but an environmental indicator: it in-forms and measures the impact established on the territory not only in terms of recognizable and physical shapes, but also and especially in terms of energetic, hydrothermal and socio-economic modulations.

Distributive architecture produce these transversal links through connecting networks and propagating atmospheres, that is, through linking discrete webs and disseminating continuous ambiences. These coordinational articulations can be found in Diller-Scofidio's "Blur Pavilion" (2002), Geli's "Mediatic" (2010) or Rahm's "Jade Eco Park" (2012), but also in other disciplines during similar years: Julius Popp's informational art-works, Gunter Pauli's Blue Economy or Gilles Clement's planetarian gardens exemplify the extroverted nature of distributive protocols, contrasting with conformative's introverted vocation. Distributive architecture conjugates these territorial and multidimensional transfers through an interaction that occurs not only within a single environment but in between different environments: it promotes an inner and outer sensorial relationality resulting in energetical, informational and social intertwinings.

1. Information as an "Indicator"
Information operates as an environmental indicator. Its value does not refer to a geometrical internal condition that has been abstracted in a formula, but to the hydro-thermic, social and energetic properties of the mediums in which architecture operates. An indicator informs architecture based on the different frameworks in which it is embedded, promoting an extroverted operativity.

2. Interaction in between "Environments"
Architecture is here understood not as a multi-programmatic enclosed entity encrusted in a generic context, but as a specific environment that interacts with outer specific environments. It produces an operative and measurable set of social, economic, and energetic transferences, providing a non-metaphorical interaction with other mediums.

3. Transversality through "Networks" & "Atmospheres"
Networks and Atmospheres operate as two distributive tools that permit systematic articulations in between several mediums, independently of their sociological, ambiental or economical nature. In spite of their common dynamism and multidimensionality, both resources differ in their constitution: while Networks are built by nodes and links, Atmospheres are conformed by particles and proximities.

4. Integration through "Connecting" & "Propagating"
Connecting and Propagating produce social, economical and ecological integration under an architectural framework. In spite of their common extroverted vocation and their shared transversal development, both processes differ in their formal constitution: While "Connecting" produces discrete links that alternate in between on and off, "Propagating" manages continuous gradients that permit multiple positions.

5. Evolution by "Collaboration"
Collaboration implies the operative co-presence of external entities that coordinate its common activity under the persecution of a common target. Therefore, collaboration as an evolving architectural practice does not proceed through the internal process characteristic of formulative strategies, but through the combination of a large number of external entities whose massive coordinational requirements are managed by Big Data processes.

6. Openness based on "Clusters"
A cluster is composed by a set of entities whose open cooperation permits to decrease costs and increase productivity in relation to a closed disposition. Its distributional logics imply a particular formal order; it is based on aggregates or grumes whose networked operativity promotes the production of environmental transfers.

7. Heterogeneity as "Ecological"
An Ecology is not a system of relations (topology), but a set of relations in between systems. Under this framework, diversity is not based on establishing relations in between its inner morphologies, but on relating to the outer environmental, social and economical mediums in which architecture operates. Ecology is therefore inherently extroverted: it implies the resonance of a collection of mediums, in which architecture is one of them.

ULTURAL CENTER - Federico Soriano, 1993
ZIG-ZAG TYPOLOGIES - Kazuyo Sejima, 1996
PLAZA DESIERTO - Eduardo Arroyo, 2002
PILOT PLAN - NL Architects, 2002
SMLXL - OMA, 1995
BERLAGE - Wiel Arets
COLUMBIA - Greg Lynn
PAMPLONA AUDITORIUM - Eduardo Arroyo
HOUSING BORNEO - Neutelings, 1997
Overlapping Masses Bundles
HABITABLE BRIDGE - Zaha Hadid, 1996

CONFORMATIVE PROTOCOLS

MESHWORKS, HIERARCHIES AND INTERFACES - Manuel Delanda, 1998
A, 1992
TOPOLOGICAL FLOORS
THE ROAD - Heidi van der Wardt, 1997
VIRTUAL HOUSE - FOA, 1997
- NL Architects, 1996
ACTIVE TOPOS - Kelly Shannon, 1993
MARITIME YOUTH HOUSE - BIG, 2004
RESIDENTIAL TOWERS - Soriano-Palacios, 1998
MERCEDES BENZ MUSEUM - Ben V. Berkel, 2006
man, 1992
ETHER - DECOI, 1995
ASPHALT SPOT - François Roche, 2002
1994
PAVILION SEMPER - Bernard Caché, 1999
ROLEX CENTER - Kazuyo Sejima, 2010
FOLDING IN ARCHITECTURE - Greg Lynn, 1993
YOKOHAMA TERMINAL - 2002
OF CHANGE - Sanford Kwinter, 1992
ATELIER OBJECTILE - Bernard Caché, 1996
NEW TOPOGRAPHIES - Alejandro Zaera, 2010
ITECTURE - Marcos Novak, 1991
A THOUSAND YEARS OF NON LINEAR HISTORY - Manuel Delanda, 1997
EARTH MOVES. THE FURNISHING OF TERRITORIES - Bernard Caché, 1995

Modeling Fields

VOLUME - Fournier, UVA, 2006
MAYA - Autodesk, 1998
ANIMATE FORM - Greg Lynn, 1999
LIBRARY PROJECT - Reiser-Unamoto, 1996
MILAN
3D STUDIO - Autodesk, 1990
LIQUID MODERNITY - Zygmunt Bauman, 1999
LA SAGRADA FAMILIA DE GAUDÍ AL CAD - Marc Burry, 1996
GREAT
JURASSIC PARK - Steven Spielberg, 1993
EMPRYOLOGICAL HOUSE - Greg Lynn, 1999
ARCHITECTURES OF TIME - Sanford Kwinter, 2001
CODE REMIX - FOA, 2000
TERMINATOR 2 - James Cameron, 1991
VILLA VPRO - MVRDV, 1997
INFORMAL - Cecil Balmond, 2002
TOY STORY - John Lasseter, 1995
MÖBIUS HOUSE - UN Studio, 1998
RHINOCEROS - Mc Neel, 1998
TRANS-PORTS - Kas Oosterhuis, 2001
3D MODELED MOVIES
VIRTUAL HOUSE - FOA, 1997
Domestic dark folds
LOST HIGHWAY - David Lynch, 1997
Calligraphic Modelling
DANCING HOUSE - Frank Gehry, 1996
ARCHILAB, 1999
VARIABLE DATA FORMS - Marcos Novak, 1999
- Frank Gehry, 1992
VIRTUAL HOUSE - Peter Eisenman, 1997
RESTAURANT POMPIDOU - Jakob & Macfarlane, 2000
LIPSES - Richard Serra, 1996
MAISON FOLIE - NOX, 2004
DELEUZE AND THE USE OF G.A. IN ARCHITECTURE - Manuel Delanda, 2001
UNITY - Unity Technolo
HE SPHINX - Mike Kelley, 1990
HOUSING MODELING
COMMUNICATIONS TOWER - Actar Arquitectura, 2000
Networked Geopolitics
II GULF
gnes Hegedüs, 1994
FRESH WATER PAVILION - NOX, 1997
ART GRAZ MUSEUM - Fournier, Cook, 2003
EE - Alex Proyas, 1994
DATA EXHIBITIONISM
DATA TOWN - MVRDV, 1999
D-TOWER - NOX, 2005
MOBILE DEVICES
STARTAC, Motorola, 1996
11M, 2004
IPHONE - Apple, 2007
ANDROID
NOKIA 3210 - Nokia, 1999
VIRTUAL TRADING FLOOR - Asymptote, 1999
HYPER-CATALUNYA - Vic
Jeremijenko, 1995
BLACKBERRY 850, Blackberry, 1999
METAPOLIS EXHIBITION - Metapolis, 2000
REACTABLE - Sergi Jordà, 2003
PALM PILOT - 3com, 1996
GPS, 1995
MACRO SPHERES - Julius Popp, 2010
SOCIÓPOLIS - Vicente G
NETSCAPE NAVIGATOR- Marc Andreessen, 1994
EURO COIN, 2002
ADVANCED DICTIONARY - IaaC, 2001
MISSBEH
NET-GLOBE
WORLD WIDE WEB (WWW) - Tim Berners - Lee, 1990
INTERNET EXPLORER - Microsoft, 1995
CONNECTED, OR, WHAT IT MEANS TO LIVE IN THE NETWORK SOCIETY - S.
SHENZEN SPACE, 1995
LA ERA DE LA INFORMACIÓN (VOL.I) - Manuel Castells, 1990
THE AGE OF ACCESS - Jeremy Rifkin, 2001
THE RISE OF THE NETWORK SOCIETY - Manuel Castells, 2000
GLOBAL CITY - Saskia Sassen, 1991
GOOGLE INC - Jimmy Wales, Larry Sanger, 1998
A NEW PHILOSOPHY OF SOCIETY - Man
GLOBAL VILLAGE - McLuhan, Powers, 1989
.COM EXPLOSION, 2001
GRASSHOPPER, 2007
EMERGENCE - Steven Jo
TELÉPOLIS - Javier Echevarria, 1994
INFORMATION SOCIETY
INTERNET OF THINGS - Kevin Ashton, 1999
THE BOTTOM IS NOT EN
METÁPOLIS - François Ascher, 1995
BIDIRECTIONAL WEB
SPACE SYNTAX - Claramunt, Jiang, 2000
FACEBOOK - Mark Zuckerberg, 2004
THE INFORMATION BOMB - Paul Virilio, 1999
GMAIL - Google, 2004

Connecting Networks

YOUTUBE - Chad Hurley, Seteve Chen, J
NETWORK CITY - Neutelings, 1993
WIKIPEDIA (WP) - Jimmy Wales, Larry Sa
2G
ONE LAPTOP PER CHILD - Nicholas Negroponte, 2005
GOOGLE EARTH - Google, 2001
WIKIHO
BEING DIGITAL - Nicholas Negroponte, 1995
MIT SENSEABLE CITY LAB - Carlo Ratti, 2004
WATER
YAHOO! - Jerry Yand, David Filo, 1994
WORDPRESS - Julio Rijo, 2003
CENTER FOR BITS & ATOMS - Neil Gershenfield, 2001
MEDIA
AMAZON - Jeff Bezos, 1994
FLICKR - Ludicorp, 2004
IAAC FOUNDATION- Guallart, Müller, Gausa, 2001
HTML, 1992
COMPUTER NETWORKS, L.Peterson, B. Davie, 1996
SPATIAL INFORMATION DESIGN LAB - Laura Kurgan, 2004
NET-BUILDINGS
HOTMAIL - Microsoft, 1996
TERRITORIAL AGENCY - John Palmesino, 2007
ERE - MVRDV, 1996
MATRIX - Lilly/Lana Wachowski, 1999
NET-LABORATORIES
DIGI
RT - OMA, 1987
MINORITY REPORT - Steven Spielberg, 2002
SATELITE AQUA, 2002
KATRINA HURRICANE, 2005

DISTRIBUTIV

Unveiled network
DOGVILLE, Lars Von Trier, 2003
DATA MOVIES
MEMENTO - Christopher Nolan, 2001
BLUR PAVILION - Diller-Scofidio, 2002
TUVALU CLIMATIC REFUGEES, 2009
MIT RIO, 1992
MAGIC MOUNTAIN - Am
HYDROGEN ECONOMY - Jeremy Rifkin, 2002
CITY TOWER - Ken Yeng,
TOYOTA PRIUS (HYBRID) - Toyota, 1999
PRESTIGE, 2001
OPEN LANDSCAPES
TROL - Kevin Kelly, 1992
THE EARTH TRANSFORMED - Goudie, Viles, 1997
LONG ISLAND GREEN DOME ,2005
ECO BO
Gilles Deleuze, 1990
CRADLE TO CRADLE - Braungart, McDnough, 2002
UNEXPE
EDEN PROJECT - Nicholas Grimshaw, 2001
VERTIC
C. IPHEROUS FOREST- Amid.cero.9, 2011
VERTIC
GREENHOUSE
SPORT
COULÉE VERTE RENÉ-DUMONT - Jacque Vergely, Philippe Mathieux, 1993
HIGH L
THE THIRD LANDSCAP
UNPLUG TOWER - François Roche, 200
DUSTYRELIEF/BMU - François Roche, 20
OMNIS PORTS HALL - J.G.Décosterd, Ra
DIFFUSIVE GARDENS
RESPONSIVE ARCHITECTURE - Philip Beesley, 2006

Propagat

NYC Troposhperic Refuge, 2006
THE BROOKLYN PIGEON PROJECT - Aranda, Lasch, 2004
THE EARTH TRANSFORMED - Goudie, Viles, 1997
WOS8 UTRECHT - NL Architects, 1997
ATMOSPHERIC COLOUR ATLAS - Olafur Eli
ACQUA ALTA - François Roche, 1998
LE JARDIN PLANÉTAIRE - Gilles Clement, 1997
REVELATORY LANDSCAPES - Besky, Levy, MacCannell, 2001
STALKING DETROIT - Waldheim, Daskalakis, Young (ed), 2001
JARDIN
GEOCRUISER - Nils Norman, 2003
SCREENED OUT - Jean Baudrillard, 2002
Peripherical interaction
DESIGNING CALM TECHNOLOGY - Mark Weiser, 1995
EU FUNDINGS: DISAPPEARING COMPUTER, 2001-03
NEW PARADIGMS - Mosé Ricci, 2012
ANGELS - Nicole Stenger, 1992
P5 GLOVE - Essential Reality, 2002
EVIDENCE OF DARK MATTER, 2005
PLASTIC CORPORALITIES
THE HARLEQUIN'S COAT - Orlan, 2007
EYEBORG - Neil Harbisson, 2004
TECHNO-NATURE
EAR ON ARM - Stelarc, 2007
SYNTHETIC BACTERIA - Craig Venter Institute, 2008
SPACES
GFP BUNNY - Eduardo Kac, 2000
THE DISAPPEARING COM
DOLLY CLONATION - Ian Wilmut, Keith Campbel, 1996
SLOW FURL - Mette Thomsen, 2008
MAPPING HUMAN GENOMA - International Consortium, 2003
FIRST MEDICAL USE OF AN ARTIFICIAL CELL - 1994
FIRST SYNTHETIC BACTERIAL GENOME - 2010
DELANDA &
SYNTHETIC YEAST CHROMOSOME, 2017
CREATION ARTIFICIAL DNA, 2016
ABSTRACT SEX - Luciana Parisi, 2004
SEGWAY - Dean Kamen, 2001
SCRIP
STREET VIEW - Google, 2007
THE N
PLANTAS NÓMADAS - Gilberto Esparza, 2008-13
OBJECT-ORIENTE
ENDOSYMBIOSIS - Shoshanah Dubiner, 2012
Post-human mutations
X-MEN SAGA, 2000-2019

ANDSCRAPERS - Aaron Betsky, 2006
■ MULTI PROGRAM SHIP - Alejandro Haiek, 2014

Modelling & Overlapping ▲ OPEN - Manuel Gausa, 2010
▲ ARCHEOLOGY OF THE DIGITAL - Greg Lynn, 2013
■ BLOOM HOUSE - Greg Lynn, 2010

MOUNTAINS
□ GWANGGYO POWER CENTRE - MVRDV, 2007
■ NORDPARK RAILWAY STATION - Zaha Hadid, 2007
□ WROCLAW MOUNTAIN - Vicente Guallart, 2012
■ MERCA BARNA - Willy Müller, 2008
□ DENIA MOUNTAIN - Vicente Guallart, 2002
■ HARBIN OPE
■ LANDSCAPEHALL MANRESA - Bailo-Rull, 2008
■ MOUNTAIN DWELLINGS - BIG, 2008
■ STÄDEL MUSEUM - Schumacher, Schneider, 2012
■ CET BUILDING - ONL, 2011
■ POMPIDOU METZ - Shigeru Ban, 2010
■ GRAND THÉATRE DE RABAT - Zaha Hadid, 2010
ARAMETRIC ARCHITECTURE WITH GRASSHOPPER - Arturo Tedeschi, 2011
■ HEYDAR CENTER - Zaha Hadid, 2012
ARAMETRICISM - Patrick Schumacher, 2010
HE AUTOPOEISIS OF ARCHITECTURE - Patrick Schumacher, 2011
▲ THE ALPHABET AND THE ALGORITHM - Mario Carpo, 2011
Aassimiliano Fuksas, 2005
▲ DIGITAL CITIES - Neil Leach, 2009
Norman Foster, 2000
▲ THE ARCHITECTURE OF VARIATION - Lars Spuybroek, 2009
CROSS STATION - Nicholas Grimshaw, 2007
□ ZERO ZONE - NOX, 2005
Parametric Disturbances □ LES TURBULENCES - Jakob, MacFarlane, 2013
AAXI MUSEUM - Zaha Hadid, 2009
■ MEISO NO MORI - Toyo Ito, 2005
ELFRIDGES - Future Architects, 2003
□ ARIZONA STRUCTURES - Peter Trummer, 2008
AETROSOL PARASOL - Jürgen Mayer, 2011
▲ OCCUPYING AND CONNECTING - Frei Otto, 2009
4 BARAJAS - Lamela, Rogers & Partners, 2006

Distributive Protocols

■ SERPENTINE GALLERY - Toyo Ito, 2002
Mobile City ■ ARCO TIETE - Carlo Ratti, 2013
■ OMOTE SANDO - Toyo Ito, 2004
3-... ◆ 14 BILLION - Tomas Saraceno, 2011
+ FAB-CITY - FabLabCollective, 2014
× APP STORE - Apple, 2008
■ TUBE - Numen/Foruse, 2015
× KICKSTARTER - Chen, Strickler, Adler, 2009
IGURATIVE NETWORKS
□ NETWORKED CITY - IaaC, 2011
▲ WIKINOMICS - Don Tapscott, 2006
Bio - Cryptocurrency ◆ ALT C - Michael Sedbon, 2018
d, 2008 ▲ IPHONE CITIES - Benjamin Bratton, 2009
× BITCOIN, Satoshi Nakamoto, 2009
× DOGECOIN - Billy Markus, 2013
lart, 2003
▲ SWARM URBANISM - Neil Leach, 2009
DIGITAL ECONOMICS
▲ BIG DATA - Kenneth Cukier, Viktor Mayer-Schönberger, 2013
■ HABIDATUM - Alexei Novikov, 2014
× SNAPCHAT - Snap Inc, 2011
◆ MUSEUM WEEK - Variable, 2015
)04 ◆ CHRONOTOPE CITY - Alexei Novikov, 2015
Registering ▲ THE ARTIST IS PRESENT, Marina Abramovic 2010
Heidi Kumao, 2005
■ HYPER HABITAT - Vicente Guallart, 2008
▲ IN THE FLOW - Boris Groys, 2016
2003 □ MULTI STRING - Manuel Gausa, 2012
▲ THE ZERO MARGINAL COST SOCIETY - Jeremy Rifkin, 2014
× COPENHAGUEN WHEEL - Carlo Ratti, 2009
■ SMART HOME - Carlo Ratti, 2012
EASSEMBLING THE SOCIAL - Bruno Latour, 2005
■ SUPERMARKET OF THE FUTURE - Carlo Ratti, 2017
ida, 2006 ■ WATER PAVILION - Carlo Ratti, 2008
NET-POLITICS
▲ PETITE POUCETTE - Michel Serres, 2013
)01 ◆ BITFALL - Julius Popp, 2006
▲ THE THIRD INDUSTRIAL REVOLUTION - Jeremy Rifkin, 2011
▲ THE GLOBAL TRANSFORMATION OF TIME - Va
Kevin Kelly, 2008
× 4G, 2008
● OBAMA VICTORY, 2008
× ZOOM VIDEO, 2
HE TRANSPARENCY SOCIETY - Byung Chul-Han, 2012
● FACEBOOK ICELAND CONSTITUTION, 2011
▲ OPEN SOURCE ARCHITECTURE - Carlo Ratti, 2014
× TEAMS, Micros
m, 2005 × WHATSAPP - Jan Kuom, 2009
NET - Terrorism ● ISLAMIC STATE, 2014 (prominence)
+ NYU CUSP - Amanda Ryley, 2013
× MIRO, Andrey K
× INSTAGRAM - Systrom, 2010
■ NET SPACES - Kathrine Willis, 2017
▲ SMART CITIES - Antoine Picon, 2015
2011 × DROPBOX - Houston, Ferdowsi, 2007
▲ REDES DE INDIGNACIÓN Y ESPERANZA - Manuel Castells, 2012
□ FAB CITY - IAAC, 2014
W Architects, 2008
NET-SOCIAL MOVEMENTS
▲ IF MAYORS RULED THE WORLD - Benjamin Barber, 2013
Ruiz Geli, 2009
● ANONYMOUS, 2003
● ARAB SPRING, 2010-12
● GLOBAL COVENANT OF MAYORS FOR CLIMATE & ENERGY, 2016
B LAB, Neil Gershenfeld, 2001
● 15M SPAIN, 2011-15
■ SEVILLA SPIDER - Santiago Cirugeda, 2007
127
MART CITIZEN, IaaC, 2013
● FINANCIAL CRISIS, 2008
● UMBRELLA MOVEMENT, 2014
■ EDIBLE PARK - Nils Norman, 2010
OW TO MAKE ALMOST ANYTHING - Neil Gershenfield, 2005
■ MAKOKO FLOATING SCHOOL - Kunlé Adeyemi, 2013
RDUINO TECHNOLOGIES - IVREA, 2005
■ CUPULA MILENIO - Enric Ruiz Geli, 2011
GUERRILLA ACTIVISM
■ SUPER KILEN PARK - Topotek + Big, 2012

ROTOCOLS

× IPAD - Apple, 2010
× KINDLE- Amazon, 2007
■ JARDINS MOBILES - Coloco, 2017
■ POBLE NOU S. BLOCK - IAAC, Serra, 2017
/C AQUARIUM - Enric Ruiz Geli, 2006
▲ CONNECTED - Christakis, Fowler, 2009
■ COSMO - Andrés Jaque, 2015
002
▲ BECOMING - Atxu Amann, 2018
● EARTH SUMMIT RIO II, 2012
■ SCARAVOX - Andrés Jaque, 2012
▲ GEOLOGICS - Vicente Guallart, 2009
■ ECOBOULEVARD - ECOSISTEMA URBANO, 2007
SOCIAL URB-NATURES
FIGURATIVE FOO
- E. Urbano, 2007
TECH-ATMOSPHERES
■ SUPER BLOCK - Salvador Rueda, 2004
DEN - Carlo Ratti, 2008
◆ BLIND LIGHT
NS - Patrick Blanc, 2004
LANDSCAPE PILING
- Stephano Boeri, 2015
× GECO PLUG-IN - Uto
nhoeven, 2006
× ECOTECT - Autodesk, 2008
Combination of narrative atmospheres ◆ HISTORIA DE LA MEVA MORT - Albert Serra, 2013
Scofidio, 2009
□ CONVECTIVE APARTMENTS - Philippe Rahm, 2010
□ THE VERTICAL VILLAGE - MVR
ement, 2003
■ JADE ECO PARK - Philippe Rahm, 2016
□ CLOUD CAST - Carlo Ratti, 2015
□ THE 5TH CITY - Peter Trumme
□ DONGGUAN MASTERPLAN - S
▲ SUBNATURE - David Gissen, 2009
□ AUGMENTED ATMOSPHERES - Diller-Scofidio, 2014
■ L'ARBRE BLA
E BLUE ECONOMY - Gunter Pauli, 2014
× DYNAMO - Chris Georgiev, 2015
TERRITORIAL ATMOSPHERES □ BIG LEAKS - Jeffrey Inaba
● FUKUSHIMA ACCIDENT, 2011
□ VATNSMYRI URBAN PLAN - Sean Sally
▲ MANHATTAN ATMOSPHERES - David Gissen, 2014
■ INSTITUTO LIBRE ENSEÑANZA - Amid.cero9, 2014

tmospheres

□ TAICHUNG GATEWAY - Philippe Rahm, 2012
▲ LANDSCAP
▲ MORPHO ECOLOGIES - Achim Menges, 2006
▲ ECOLOGICAL URBANISM - Mostafavi, Doherty (eds), 2010
▲ THE SELF-SUFFICIENT CITY - Vicente Guallart, 2014
▲ DECOLONIZING NATURE - T.J.Demos, 2016
AOLLIER HOUSES - Philip Rahm, 2005
▲ CITIES PROTOCOL - IAAC, 2011
● PARIS AGREEMENT - UNFCCC, 2016
● GRETA THUNBERG COP25, 2
OREST HOTEL - Enric Ruiz Geli, 2009
▲ ARCHITECTURAL CLIMATES - Philippe Rahm, 2018
AR FROM EQUILIBRIUM - Samford Kwinter, 2008
▲ NATURALEZA Y ARTIFICIO - Iñaki Ábalos, 2009
+ BIO TALLIN - Poletto-Pasquer
IES - Gilles Clement, 2007
▲ ADAPTIVE ECOLOGIES - Theodore Spyropoulous (ed), 2013
■ ROBOTIC HABITATS - Noume
IGITAL PAVILION - ONL
◆ THE MARTIAN - Ridley Scott, 2015
▲ MEETING NATURE HALFWAY - Marjan Colletti (ed), 2018
▲ LANDSCAPE AS URBANISM - Charles Waldhei
VIRTUAL MOVEMENT
▲ ENSAYOS SO
■ URBANEER - Terreform, 2009
× KINECT XBOX - Microsoft, 2010
■ H.CERAMIC - IaaC, 2016
× CREATION ARTIFICIAL DNA, 2016
□ THOUSAND ECOLOGIES - Eric Hörl, 2009
× PLAYSTATION MOVE - Sony, 2010
■ MAT-AERIAL - IaaC, 2015
× SIXTHSENSE (dev) - Pranav Mistry 2009
▲ ACTIVE MATTER - Skylar Tibbits, 2017
MIXED REALITY
■ LIGHT CEMENT - UMSNH, 2015
◆ BIOPLASTIC
▲ HYLOZOIC GROUND - Philip Beesley, 2010
▲ VIBRANT ARCHITECTURE - Rachel Armstrong, 2015
■ SELFREPAIR CONCRETE - TU Delft, 2014
▲ SYSTEMIC ARCHITECTURE - Claudia Pasquero; Marco Poletto, 2012
ALGAE MACHINES
▲ THE SILENCE OF SLIM MOULDS - Andrew Adamatzky, 2014
■ JARDINS DE METIS - Bitonti, Zientek, 2019
◆ ALGA(E)ZEBO - Cruz, Colletti, 2012
▲ BLACK ECOLOGIES - IAAC, 2019
■ THE LONG NOW - Sean Sally, 2018
◆ THE THIRD G
■ HYLOZOIC GROUND - Philip Beesley, 2010
× THE GARDEN WORLD - Damjan Jovanovic, 2020
WATCH - Apple, 2015
■ BRAGA PAVILION - Poletto-Pasquero, 2015
▲ SCREEN WORLD - Liam Young, 2019
■ STEAMPUNK
AILE GLOVE - Ryan Patterson, 2002
■ INHUMAN GARDENING - Poletto-Pasquero, 2015
◆ LIVE CYCLES - IAAC, 2018
× HTC VIVE - Vive, 2016
OOGLE GLASSES - Google, 2013
■ BIQ HOUSE - ARUP, 2013
▲ SYNTHETIC BIOLOGY - D. Nestbeth, 2016
× MICROSOFT HOLOLENS - Microsoft, 2016
BIT STEP COUNTER - Fitbit, 2010
+ ALIVE: NEW DESIGN FRONTIERS - Carole Collet, 2013
▲ VIRTUAL REALITY AND THE BUILT ENVIRONMENT - Jennifer Whyte, 2002
▲ DIGITAL POETICS - Marjan Colletti, 2013

Performing Matter

× GOOGLE GLASS - Google, 2013
× FREEMO VR
ANDERERS - Neri Oxman, 2014
ECOLOGICAL THOUGHT ▲ GREY ECOLOGY - Paul Virilio, 2009
× OCULUS RIFT - Oculus, 2012
as de Monchaux, 2011
▲ GENERAL ECOLOGY - Hörl, Burton (eds) 2009
× TRIMBLE CONNECT - Trimble, 2017
itz, Mavrommati, Kameas, 2007
▲ TOWARD AN ECOLOGY OF MATERIALS - Timothy Ingold, 2012
▲ THE VIRTUAL STATE AND THE FALL OF EMPIRES - Mychilo Cline,
ERIAL COMPLEXITY - Manuel Delanda, 2004
▲ DARK ECOLOGIES - Timothy Morton, 2016
▲ DOWN TO EARTH - Bruno Latour, 2018
▲ THE ANTHROBSCENE - Jussi Parikka, 2015
TER MATTERS - Manuel Delanda, 2005
▲ VIBRANT MATTER - Jane Bennett, 2009
NOTES TOWARD A PERFORMATIVE THEORY OF ASSEMBLY - Judith Butler, 2015
▲ THE QUESTION CONCERNING
ERIAL ELEGANCE - Manuel Delanda, 2007
▲ NEW MATERIALISM - Dolphin, Tuin (eds), 2012
▲ PRINTED PHYSICS - Bühlmann, Hovestadt (eds); 2013
▲ MEETING THE UNIVERSE HALFWAY - Karen Barad, 2007
Urban Future ▲ BARBA - The Why Factory, 2015
Trans-Inclusivity ▲ XENOFEMINIS
▲ NEW MATERIALISMS: ONTOLOGY, AGENCY, AND POLITICS - Coole, Frost (eds), 2010
▲ PHYSARUM MACHINES - Andrew Adamatzky, 2010
NEW MATERIALISMS
▲ WHAT IS POSTHUMANISM? - Cary Wolf, 2010
▲ ARE WE HUMAN? - Colomina, Wigley, 2016
EPMIND - Hasabis, Legg, Suleyman, 2010
RES - Marc Burry, 2011
▲ THE POSTHUMAN - Rosi Braidotti, 2013

EXPANSIVE PROTOCOLS

▲ L'HUMANITE AUGMENTEE - E
ODE - Daniel Shiffman, 2012
▲ POSTHUMANISM - Pramod K.Nayar, 2013
ARTIFICIAL INTELLIGENCE
POSTHUMAN AGENDA
COUNTRYSIDE AGENTS
▲ MALIGN VELOCITIES - Benjamin Noys, 2014
▲ L'INTELLIGEN
× WALL-E FOR COWS - ACFR, 2013
▲ INVENTING THE FUTURE - Snicek, Williams, 2016
▲ LA VIE ALGO
HE QUADRUPLE OBJECT - Graham Harman, 2011
× SWAGBOT - Salah Sukkarieh, 2016
▲ PLATFORM CAPITALISM - Srnicek, Williams, 2016
▲ LA SILICOLO
HE DEMOCRACY OF OBJECTS - Levi Bryant, 2011
ROBO-ARCHITECTURE
▲ ROBOTIC BUILDING - Claypool, Jiménez García, Soler (eds), 2019

DISTRIBUTIVE PROTOCOLS
2000-2010

THE ECOLOGICAL CONDITION: CONNECTING NETWORKS AND PROPAGATING ENVIRONMENTS
Manuel Gausa

1. CONNECTING NETWORKS

1.1. From Infrastructure to Network

1.2. Internet 2.0 and the Second Digital Revolution

2. ECOLOGICAL CONDITION

2.1. Braided Territories, Interwoven Territories

2.2.. Urban Systoles and Interurban Diastoles.
Connecting Discontinuity, Working with Mixture

2.3. Territorial Matrices (or Mosaics)

2.4. Links and Proto-Sensors

Physical Eco-Networks and Urban Re-Naturalisation

3. OTHER NETWORKS

3.1 Web 3.0 Internet of Things and Mobile Phones
Connective Ubiquity.

3.2. The G-Phone generations. Exponential Evolutions

4. PROPAGATING ENVIRONMENTS

4.1. Reactive Ambient-Architectures

4.2. Global Interaction

4.3. Experimentation and Prototyping

4.4. Interconnected (Interactive) Self-Sufficiency

4.5 Collaboration:

From Distributive Models to Distributed Models

THE ECOLOGICAL CONDITION: CONNECTING NETWORKS AND PROPAGATING ENVIRONMENTS
Jordi Vivaldi

1. THE ECOLOGICAL CONDITION

1.1. Open Networks

1.2. Information Age, Information Societies

1.3. Reactive Environments: Emergence and Self-Sufficiency

2. CONNECTING NETWORKS

2.1. Transitions, Reevaluations

2.2.. Net-Buildings

2.3.Digital Crafts:
Re-production, Mass-production, Co-production

2.3. Global Cities and Hyper-Connected Neighbourhoods

3. PROPAGATING ATMOSPHERES

3.1 Diffusive Gardens: From Prolongation to Propagation

3.2. Climatic Structures

3.3 Hydro-Thermal Landscapes

3.4 "Guerrilla" Activism and Public Space

4. TRANSFERENCES

MANUEL GAUSA

DISTRIBUTIVE PROTOCOLS

The Ecological Condition: Connecting Networks and Propagating Atmospheres

I- CONNECTING NETWORKS

I.I From Infrastructure to Network

In the final third of the 20th century an experimental, embryonic project (associated with what was called DARPA – Defense Advanced Research Projects Agency), aimed at favoring direct communications between remote computers, resulted, in the 1970s, in the ARPANET network, formed by 23 interconnected academic institutions.[1] In the 1980s, it underwent a considerable scalar leap with the development of the computer industry and technology, in general, and with the advent of personal computers, in particular.

The first "Web", with growing interconnections, was definitively catapulted in the early 1990s with the launch of the World Wide Web in 1991, a series of linked portals or "sites" that could be located and displayed using http (the Hypertext Transfer Protocol).[2]

_1. The interconnection of a first network data-exchange system, promoted by DARPA (Defense Advanced Research Project Agency) for military and rapidly scientific-academic purposes, began with a first link between the University of California-Los Angeles (UCLA) and the Stanford Research Institute, at 10:30 p.m. on October 29, 1969. As Leonard Cleinrock (MIT) related:
"We initiated a telephone connection between the colleagues of the SRI. We dial an L and ask by phone:
Do you see the L?
Yes, we see the L, they responded.
We mark an O and ask Do you see the O?
Yes, we see the O, they responded.
Then we marked the G and the system fell.
But a real revolution had begun."
See: https://en.wikipedia.org/wiki/History_of_the_Internet

_2. The concept of WWW, World Wide Web, a network of "sites" interconnected and visualized using the HyperText Transfer Protocol (HTTP), was designed by Tim Berners-Lee and some CERN scientists (Conseil Européen pour la Recherche Nucléaire) in Genêve, interested in easily searching and viewing documentation through the Internet. In 1991 this technology was presented to the public and began to be used in various academic and institutional fields.
On the history and evolution of Internet see: http://www.fib.upc.edu/retro-informatica/historia/internet.html

WWW technology revolutionized the very concept of "network", shifting from a physical and infrastructural conception (network as a connective "mesh") to a much more global, physical and immaterial conception (network as an inter-connective link).

In spite of an initial lackluster reception, its growth was spectacular in a short time: at the end of 1992 the network had 50 sites; in 1993 there were 150; and at the beginning of 2000 the growth was already exponential.

In the early 20th century, everyday use of the Internet (now entirely consolidated) represented a spectacular breakthrough in the spatial conception associated with the encounter of "information + interaction" and in the interpretation of socio-urban environments, increasingly understood as complex systems (linked to constant processes of readjustment between, more or less thematic, layers of information and, more or less accorded, networks of relationships), multiplying the complex equations between "networked" relational (economic, cultural, commercial and, unexpectedly, social) scenarios.

E-mail, browsers (Explorer, Mozilla, etc.), chats, search engines, on-line encyclopedias and electronic commerce demonstrated the emergence of a new type of territory for (virtual, immaterial) exchanges, which overlapped with the traditional types. The concept of "data communication" (i.e., the transmission and interconnected distribution of data between Wide-Area-Networks), beyond the initial research of the 90s dealing with the instrumentalization of simultaneous informational layers, or windows, (combinatorial systems of exchange between variable information, initially understood as processed or combined requests, programs or messages, and later as parameterized algorithmic data) implicitly led to a renewed focus on efficiently communicated and integrated matrix systems.

The digital irruption that had made it possible to address complex and differential processes through the refinement of new numerical operating systems and a fundamentally "multi-layer" (multi-level and multi-scale) approach to the (physical and virtual) environment, also paved the way for a greater inter-connective potential between scenarios, uses and users; means and media.

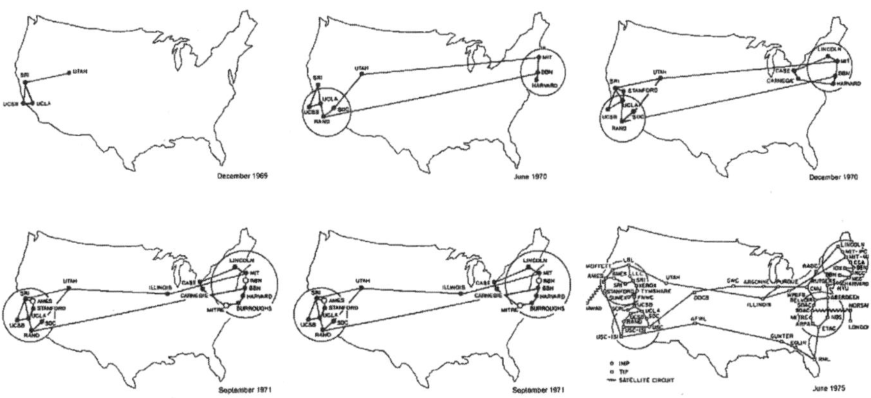

Increasing evolution of *ARPANET*, the precursor of the Internet system (1965-1975)

1.2 Internet 2.0 and the Second Digital Revolution

During the first decade of the 21st century Internet access spread in parallel with the development of mobile telephones (smartphones and other cellular devices) and computational portability, providing universal access to work-related and domestic routines.

Although, at the beginning of this century, digital recording/reproduction was still dependent on optical discs (floppies, CDs, DVDs), since the early 2000s the rise of software programs like Java Script, AJAX, HTML4-CSS and other programming frameworks has fostered the rapid development of network communications.

The first designs of Web 1.0, before 2000 (the *Internet of Institutions*) with static websites, limited text navigators and little capacity for interaction) saw spectacular early development from 1997 to 2001 with the appearance of "dotcom" companies and a first unexpected economic bubble.

However, the launch of Web 2.0 (the *Internet of People*), and the associated digital and computational developments, accelerated the adoption of the Internet in the domestic sphere, in many cases with software programs that were already incorporated into the hardware.

The acceleration of storage technologies, data access, speed and connectivity, Memo and RAM, etc. also favored (based on an increasing computational capacity) new approaches to communication between users, and especially the emergence of the first exchange platforms with databases like Wikipedia - 2001, and/or search engines like Yahoo - 1996-2000 and Google - 2000-2002, etc. 3[3] On the other hand, the 2000s saw the consolidation of a new type of thought that was more sensitive to a holistic integration between anthropic systems and ecological systems, physical (mobility, accessibility) networks, informational (social and cultural) networks, and natural (eco-systemic) networks.

The 92 Earth Summit in Rio helped to mobilize a certain holistic awareness, attuned to the need to foster more responsible agendas associated with more sustainable development. The Rio Agenda left its mark on many other agendas and subsequent lines of action (both global and local) developed during the first decade of the new century and reinforced by other meetings (2000 UN Millennium Development Goals / 2005 Kyoto Protocol / 2007 Climate Change Panels, etc.).

Curiously, what for many would be an opposition or confrontation between the technological and the ecological world was nothing more than the expression of a multiple common phenomenon generated through a new processing capacity, able to calculate and simulate in a more and more precise way the devastating effects themselves of the increasing anthropization of our environment (climate change, land-use, pollution, greenhouse effect, etc.); but also through a new sensibility more aware (from the exponential growth of social networks and global communication itself) of the threats and responsibilities faced to these conflictive realities).

And, finally, directly related with this "new logic" associated with the potential "information + interaction + integration" that was marking our new era and where the same notion of integrated informational interaction, beyond types, programs, spaces, requests or contexts, it was still the authentic emerging theoretical and operational framework associated with the own social and environmental challenges and responsiveness.

_3. See also: http://www.fib.upc.edu/retro-informatica/historia/internet.html, Op. cit.

Global map of internet world hyper-connexions (2005 – 2015)

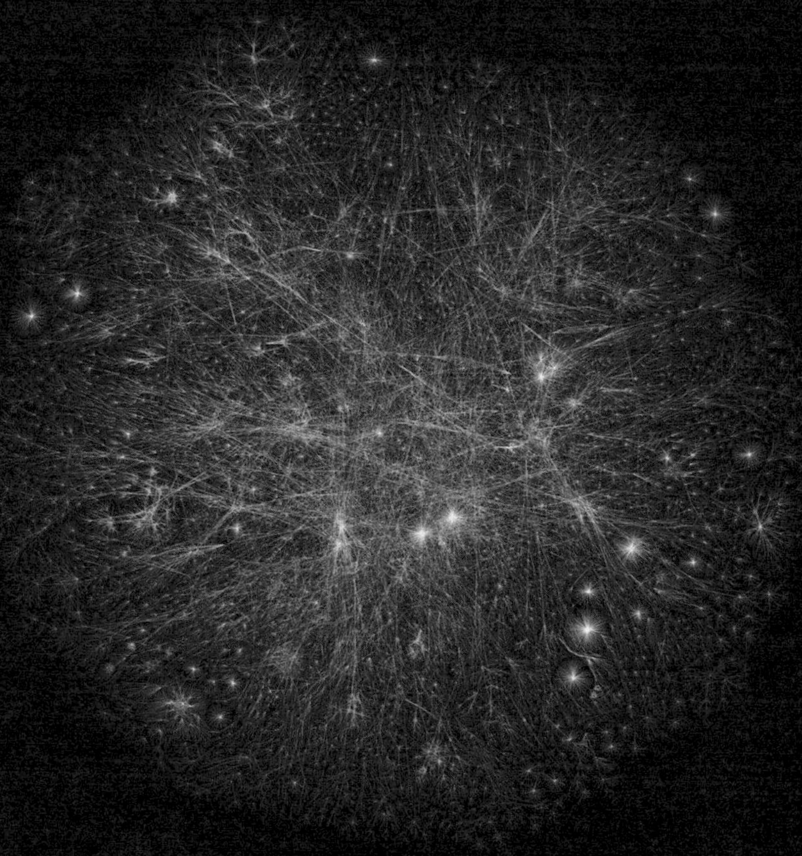

Stephan Perella: Haptic Horizon, 1995 ("Hyper-surfaces, *socius fluxus*" in *The Virtual Dimension*, Princeton Architectural Press, New York, 1995)

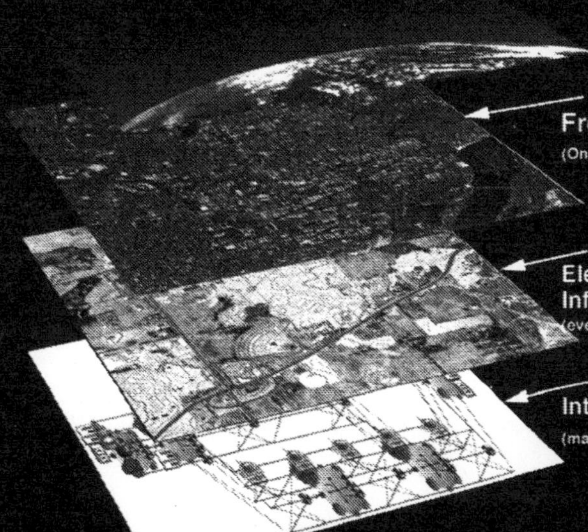

2- ECOLOGICAL CONDITION

1.3 Braided Territories, Interwoven Territories

The growing urban dynamics of the turn of the century led to the emergence of a two-fold equation based, on the one hand, on the competitive positioning of cities and territories within a global economic framework, associated with the networked distribution of exchanges and the growing internationalization of the real estate market, and, on the other, on the emergence of a new cultural and environmental sensitivity that highlighted the need to promote more systematic reflections on urban development, recycling and reactivation processes, while promoting operations of integration and articulation, consolidation, preservation and identification that could be significant, innovative and qualitative within the global "circuits" of flow and exchange.[4]

The growth of mobility and interconnection also demonstrated, in an increasingly explicit way, the dynamic nature of urban systems and their new "geo-urban" dimension.[5]

The new city-territory emerged as a complex "poly-territory" of relations, apparently intended – as asserted by Salvador Rueda – to favor the dispersed implementation of uses and functions, generally pursuing the highest economic return between activity and location.[6]

The first familiarities with the popular use of Internet (web 2.0, Internet of People) from the mid to late 90s, also favored a logic associated with the expansion of the notion of network, beyond the mobility meshes; a notion coordinated with ecological, landscape, environmental matrices, etc.

The qualitative – and not speculative – approach of this new networked urban-territorial organism, contemplated in these terms, brought up the need to design more territorial coordination and interconnection, on a large scale, promoting frameworks for action (and relationships) with the ability to generate not only new economic approaches but authentic systems of relationship involving territorial places and "in-between-places".

Faced with the mechanistic dynamics of the diffuse city, as well as the paradigm of the large compact and homogenizing city, a third avenue emerged, advocating for a networked urban distribution that would be preferably polycentric, meshed and coordinated.

It would be based on the existence of medium-sized (urban) cores with varying densities and large intermediate (green) spaces as (in-between) "intermediaries" in a dis-dense systematics of multi-urban settlements, with sizes adapted to the natural and geographical conditions of the region where they would be located.[7]

The reading and articulation of a new networked, diversified and integrated condition (like the paradigm of the neo-modern metropolitan city once was) emerged as a possible focus for research, associated with the progressive implementation of the notion of "network" as a connective/distributive device. This led to the exploration of a new type of territorial organization – and urban redefinition – where the notions of *Multi-city* or *Poly-polis*, as well as that of *Re-Citying*, alluded to an interpretation of the city-region as a new geo-urbanity, both articulated and reinforced.

_4. Manuel Gausa, *Multi-Barcelona, Hiper-Catalunya. Estrategias para una nueva Geo-Urbanidad* (Roma-Trento, List Laboratorio Editoriale Internazionale, 2009), 1 - 280.
_5. Michael Batty, "Sobre el crecimiento de la ciudad", *Fisuras,* no 5 (1997), 6.
_6. Salvador Rueda, "Models d'ordenació del territori més sostenibles (o un nou urbanisme per a abordar els reptes de la societat actual)" in Manuel Gausa (ed), *Cap a un habitat(ge) sostenible* (Barcelona, Ed. CADS, 2011).
_7. Francesc Muñoz:, "Territoris i hàbitats sostenibles, estratègies d'ocupació, sinèrgies d'urbanització" in Manuel Gausa (ed), *Cap a un habitat(ge) sostenible* (Barcelona, Ed. CADS, 2011).

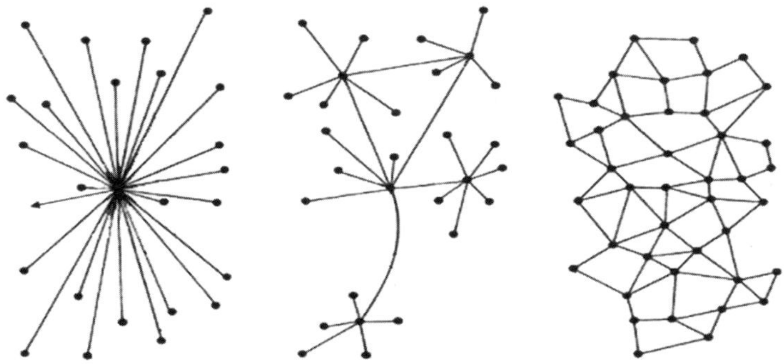

Successive urban structures: radial mononuclear (centripetal), semi-articulate sub-nuclear (satellital), networked poli-nuclear (multi-relational).

Territory, landscape, city: the exploration of new interwoven matrices (*Land-links, Land-grids, Meshed Networks, Nets & Sets, MixedAbbes,* etc.) suggested strategic actions of inter-connection and eco-interlacement, beyond the old network-infrastructure associations. Strategies in which infrastructures networks would be of such importance as landscape networks, those of a meshed nature and those of an urban density in discontinuous sequences.[8] The debate regarding the benefits of the traditional "compact" city (density, proximity, mixed-uses, concentration of resources, etc.) versus the conflicts of the "diffuse" and/or "poly-disperse" modern and post-modern city (fragmentation, dissolution of relationships, disconnection, specialization, consumption of resources) also gave way to a new paradigm, that of the plural – polycentric and pluri-compact – "intertwined" city and its interwoven, networked articulation.[9]

A new dimension that was global and local at the same time (associated with a possible flexible networked structure of knots/nodes – or focal and dense centers, articulated circuits, and characterized landscapes) which called for a diversified polycentric – infra-structural and inter-structural, intra-structural and eco-structural, but also informational – configuration. This also tied in with a new dynamic sensorization of spaces and an integrated (intelligent) management of flows, transportation, energy, water, relational circuits and circulations, etc.: a new smart logic connected with a new sustainable sensibility, in an eco- and bio- smart approach, essential to the future of the city and the territory.[10]

The new urban-territorial city thus appealed to a new, more capable and imaginative re-programming systematics, associated with a new (more strategic, dynamic and informational) conceptual logic that favored the meshed orientation of its areas of development (and the associated points of intersection and transfer). But also an effective relationship with the landscape and between landscapes (in other words, a reflection on the boundaries between the natural and the artificial); and, in any case, a qualitative (re)definition of the large central and nodal fabrics and, therefore, the reuse and specific recycling of pre-existing urban conditions (but also the large-scale territorial nodes of intersection) rooted in a commitment to a new spatial, programmatic and social mixture.[11]

_8. Manuel Gausa (ed), *Cap a un habitat(ge) sostenible* (Barcelona, Ed. CADS, 2011).

_9. Manuel Gausa, "Canvi climàtic: territori, urbanisme i edificació. nous models (més) sostenibles" in *A.A.V.V.(2011), Segón Informe sobre el canvi climàtic a Catalunya (*Barcelona, IEC, CADS, Generalitat de Catalunya, 2011)

_10. Ibid.

_11. Manuel Gausa, "Rinaturalizzare la multi-città. Verso una nuova centralità eco-a(tra)ttiva" in Mosé Ricci, *Nuovi Paradigmi,* (Trento: List Laboratorio Editoriale Internazionale, 2012), 50-57.

2.2 Urban Systoles and Interurban Diastoles. Connecting Discontinuity, Working with Mixture

This framework for reflection and investigation served to articulate some of the emergent research and territorial prospection focused on addressing this dis-dense condition of the new *geo-urban* structures and the potential they provided for generating braided territories and possible serial (and rhythmic) matrices based on sequences of "colonization-landscape-infrastructure" or "fullness-emptiness-links".

Rather than hypothetical planning and planimetric maps to be reproduced (master-plans) the idea was to generate possible "strategic scenarios" (diagrammatic maps) to serve as frameworks-devices for synthesized cities, expressed and designed through possible "evolving diagrams" (*diagrammatic-cities* or *diagrammaticities*) as criteria for action, oriented and with a focus on the territory, with the potential to be manipulated, altered and tactically adapted according to specific dynamics of evolution.

"Strategic scenarios", in any case (models, outlines – diagrams, in short) harnessed to combine areas of occupation and areas of preservation, spaces for densification and spaces for expansion, into possible frameworks that could be environmental and infrastructural at the same time.[12]

– From an "extra-urban" territory, we moved to an "interurban" (*geo-urban)* territory.

– From a "ground" territory to a "mesh" territory.

– From a passive territory to an active territory.

– From an enclosed city – and a dispersed city – to a networked city.

Conceiving the city "outward and inward" at the same time; promoting operations of interurban "linking" but, also, of urban "reinforcement" – consolidation, containment or coagulation, concentration, restructuring and/or recycling – while also instrumentalizing the idea of landscape not only as an interstitial void but as an authentic "operating system" open to use and activity.

These dynamics required, in effect, new governance criteria (not always well received) capable of addressing the plural dimension of the city and/or the territory, promoting the combination (confederation) and reactivation (re-information) of its multiple centers or multi-nodal nuclei.

Criteria capable, at the same time, of reformulating the power of negative space (void) not as a remainder – or a residual reserve – "between things" but as a structuring mechanism on a territorial scale (and, therefore, as a "catalyst" for new supra-municipal strategies).

Strategies in which the landscape – as meaningful void – did not break up but rather interlaced. In which the landscape was no longer a passive element – the leftovers of occupied space – but an active system: a new actor that was no longer secondary but clearly a central player on an urban and territorial level.

_12. See "Lan-Links" in Gausa-Guallart-Müller, *The Metapolis Dictionary of Advanced Architecture* (Barcelona: Actar Publishers, 2003).

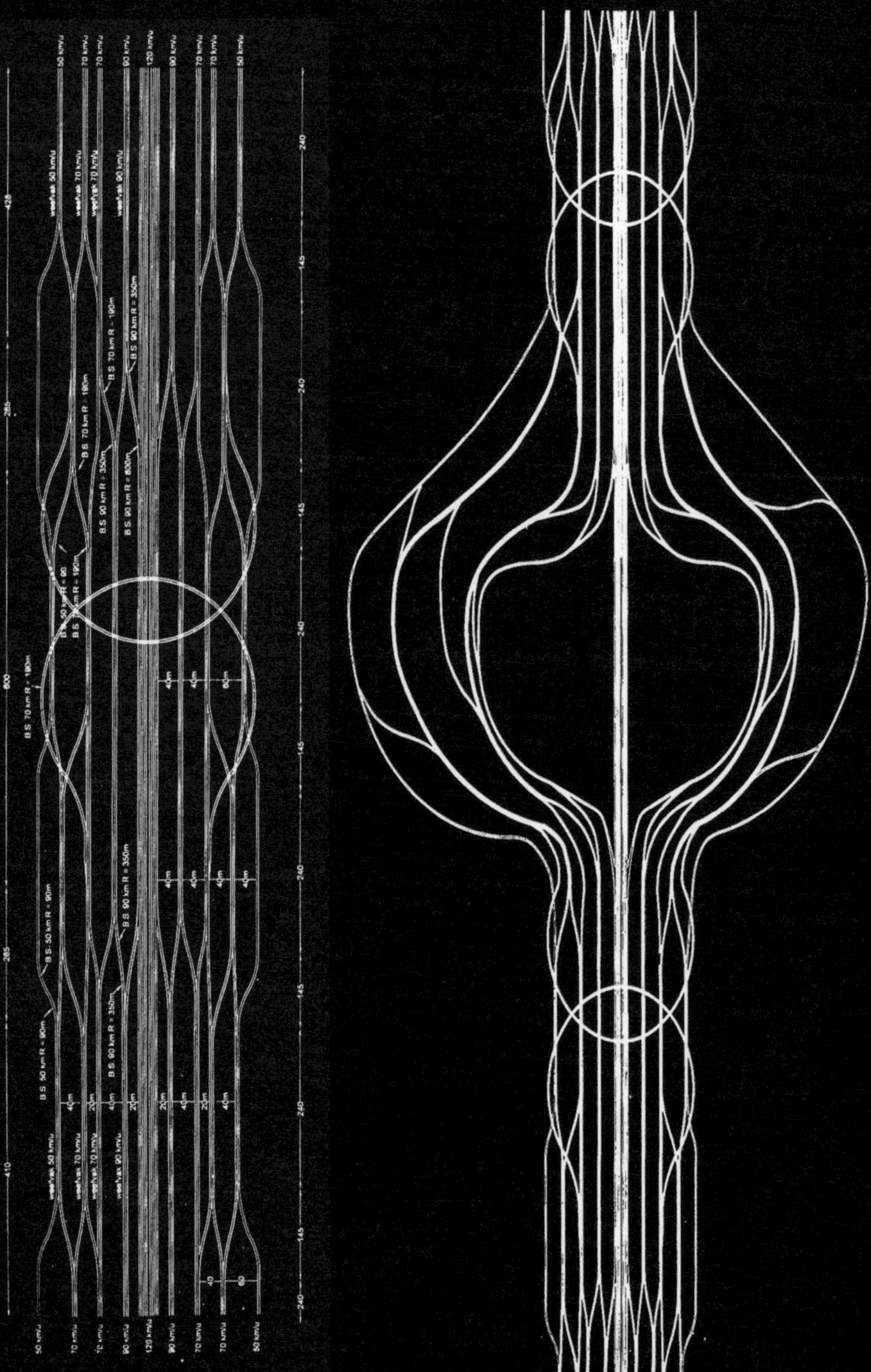

MVRDV: Diagrams according to speeds of a road skein (in "Living along the Highway", *Quaderns* n. 218, 1997)

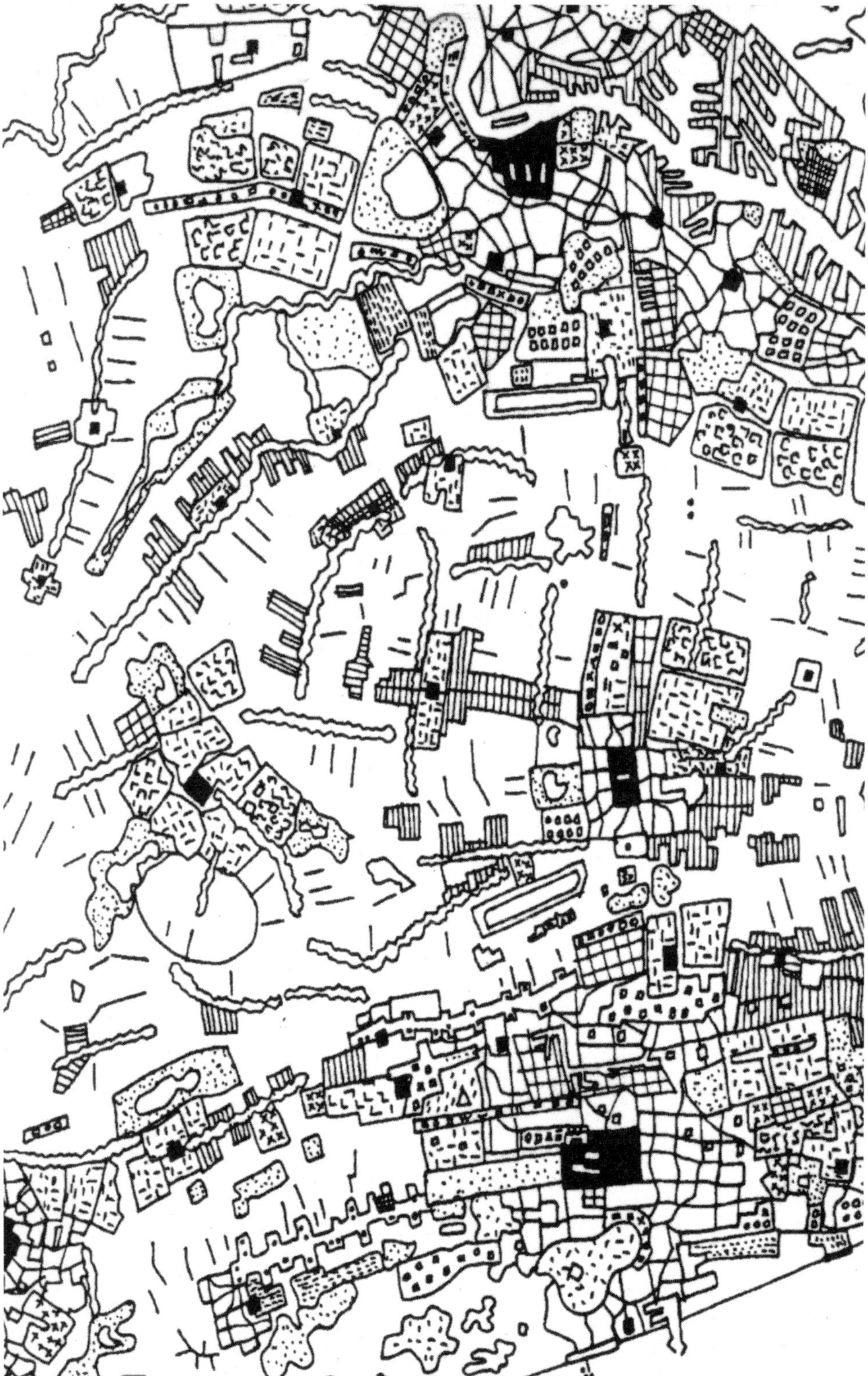

Previous page: W.J. Neutelings. Patchwork City, 1994-2000: The integration of mesh systems and interweaved models of the 90s was parallel in the early 2000s to the explosion of the internet and networks.

Willem Jan NEUTELINGS (1992): "Patchwork City" and "Mesh (or Interlaced) Networked City" in *Patchwork City*, ed.010 Publishers, Rotterdam, 1992.

2.3 Territorial Mosaic-Matrices: Land-Links, Land-Grids.

A pioneering project like O.M.A.'s Mélun-Sénart (1990), with its infrastructural intermingling of city and landscape (suggested by the expressive interlocking matrices ofYves Brunier[13]), had a decisive influence on many later proposals that were more intentionally linked to the notion of a network, particularly the interesting research by "ex-OMA" figures (Kees Kristiansee, Willem Jan Neutelings, Max, etc.).

Mélun-Sénart was one of the first projects that formulated a design using the void as an active tool, capable of providing a "flexible horizon" for urban complexity and uncertainty through a basic, inductive "landscape-infrastructural" framework: a "comprehensive formal scheme – a K of linear and infrastructural landscapes – beyond the form of the building itself". Later on, in the essay *The Ring Cultuur* (1993), and in his "Patchwork City" project (1998)[14] for the new development of The Hague, Willem Jan Neutelings delved further into these poly-matrix dynamics in which the urban system itself – in this case, The Hague – appeared as a "scattered collage of fragments" adapted through flexible articulation operations with the capacity to "systematize disorder" through a "striping" or "weaving" of the territory, forming parallel strips of development (a flexible bar code that can be altered and distorted according to needs).

The MVRDV project for the South of Almere (1997-98) explicitly investigated this type of potential16 by looking into the possible "unraveling" of infrastructures converted into "strings" of varying speeds (with their corresponding definitions regarding access and minimum radii of curvature), intended to reformulate the road layout as a virtual mosaic associated with a flexible and tactical "lacework" (dentelle). This possible flexible mesh, interconnected and de-localized at the same time, allowed for incorporating existing landscape elements and/or large-scale metropolitan and real estate projects into the system – joining them into several interconnected "bags" – as well as establishing links between the new sites and existing ones, thus transforming unqualified voids into unexpected poles of development.

Associated with this type of research different multi-urban experiences were conceived in those first years of exploration with the notion of "network" not only infra or info but also intra, echo and trans structural, such as those developed by the Villard d´Hallencourt group in Italy, Metápolis in Spain or the early experiences from the Landscape Urbanism Office at Harvard.

The territorial redefinition project Barcelona Land-Grid,[15] presented by Actar Arquitectura for the exhibitions *1856-1999: Barcelona Contemporània* (Centre de Cultura Contemporània, Barcelona, 1996) and *Barcelona Metápolis* (RAS Gallery, Barcelona 1998).

The project proposed, a new "operative map" for the diffuse poly-nuclear reality of the new meta-city[16] based on the promotion of a possible flexible and balanced grid: a flexible "guide" of strips and tracks for movement rooted in a balanced sequence of old and new areas for growth, along with landscape reserves (semi-natural grounds and possible operative "topographies"), to ensure an effective alternation of "colonization/landscape", responding to local demands but drawing on a global matrix.

_13. The MELUN-SENART project has appeared in various publications. It should be noted the following one: Jaques Lucan, *OMA-Rem Koolhaas* (Paris, Electa - Le Moniteur 1990).

_14. Willem Jan Neutelings (1994): "Patchwork City" in *Architectual Design* no. 3/4, vol. 64 (1994).

_15. For a complete definition see: MVRDV, "Living along the highway", *Quaderns,* no. 218 (1997), 54.

_16. François Asher, *Métapoles ou l'Avenir des villes* (Paris, Odile Jacob, 1995).

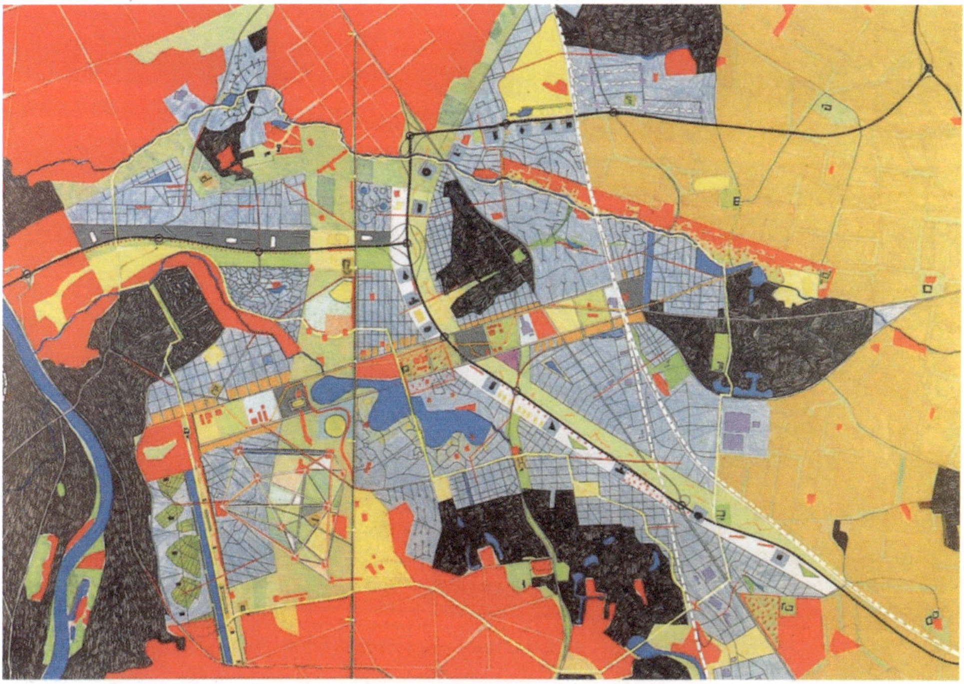

OMA. Project for a new urban development in Mélun-Sénart - Paris (1990)

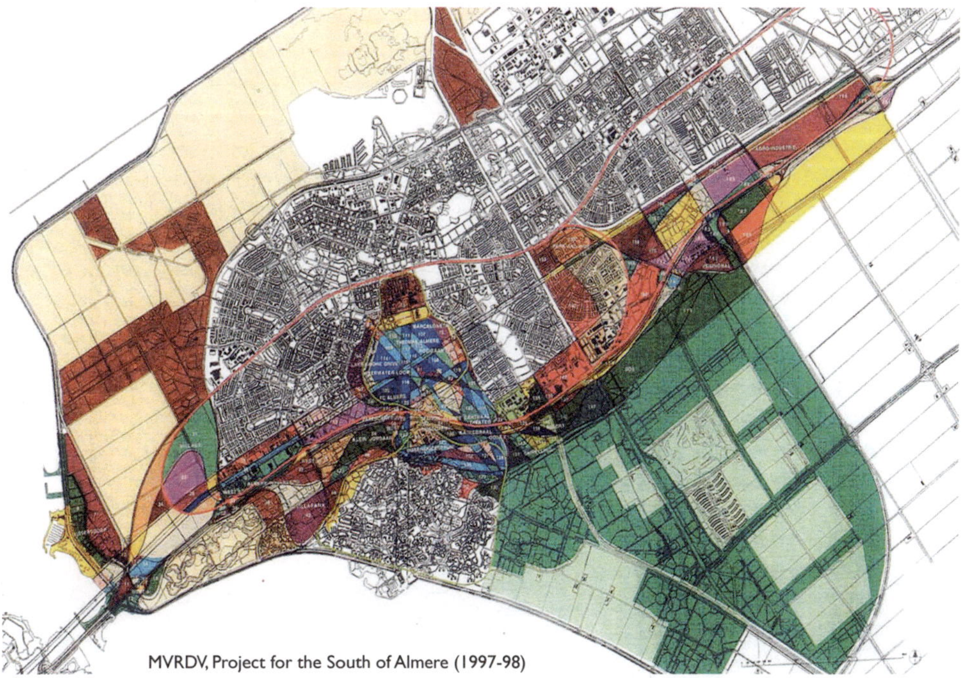

MVRDV, Project for the South of Almere (1997-98)

Links, keys, nodes and connections; Douglas R.Hofstadter, 1996.

Mosé RICCI University of Genoa and University of Salento. "EccoLecce", New strategic eco-plan for the city of Lecce (curated by Mosè Ricci with Federica Alcozer, Sara Favargiotti, Luca Mazzari, Clarissa Sabeto, Emanuele Sommariva, Jeannette Sordi, 2012)

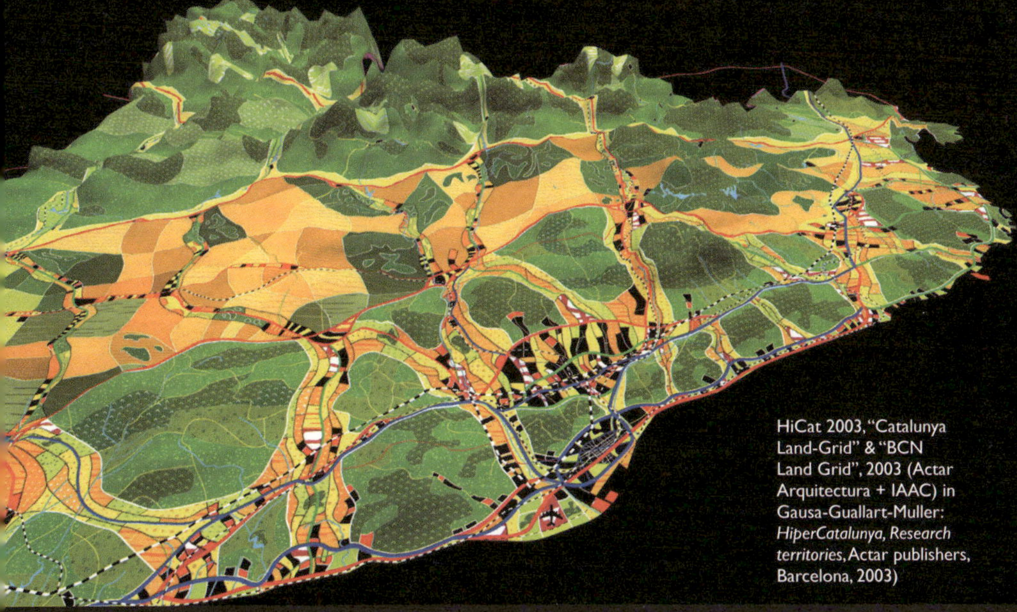

HiCat 2003, "Catalunya Land-Grid" & "BCN Land Grid", 2003 (Actar Arquitectura + IAAC) in Gausa-Guallart-Muller: *HiperCatalunya, Research territories*, Actar publishers, Barcelona, 2003)

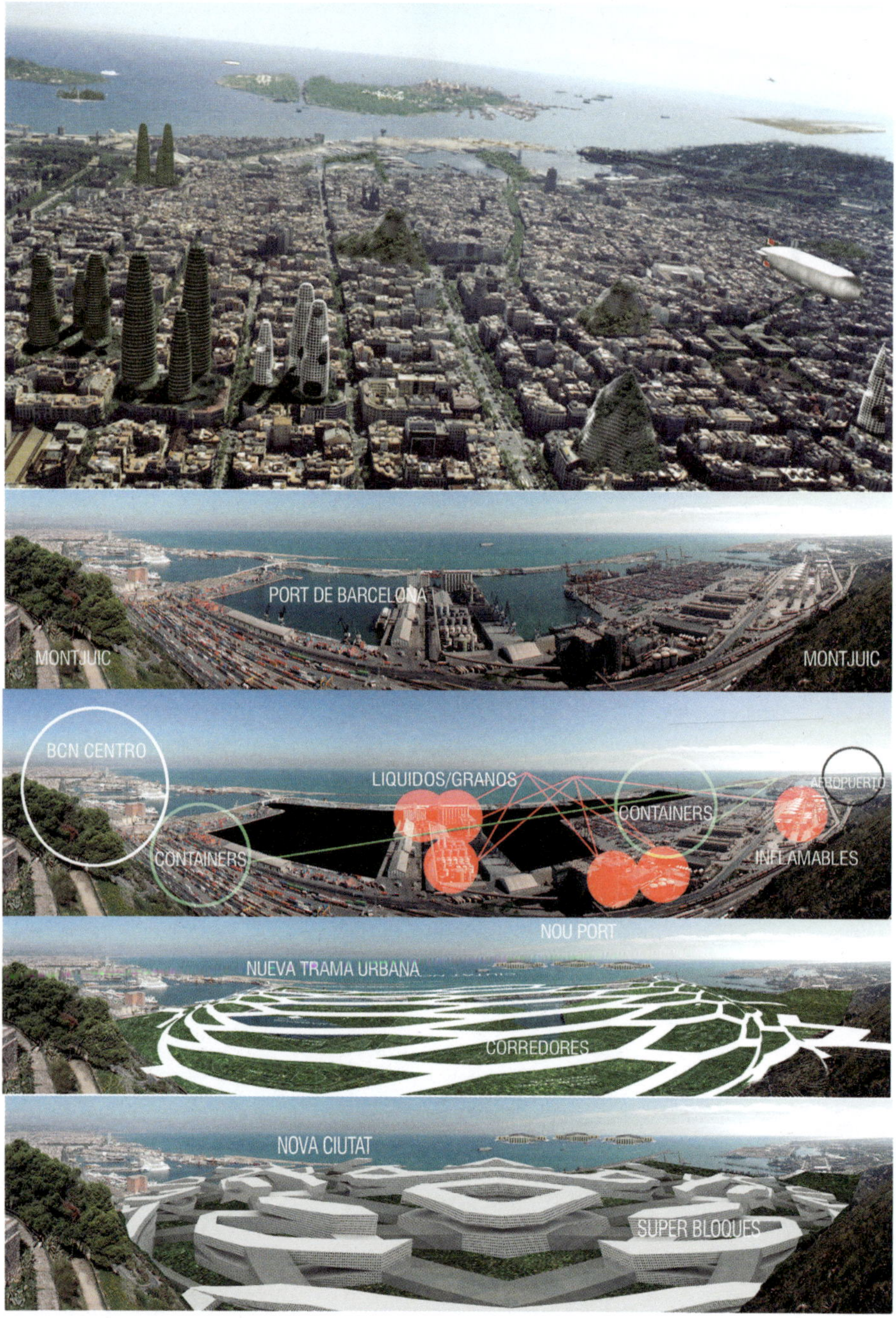

HiCat 2003, Vicente GUALLART, "Re-informed cities, natures & environments" and Willy MULLER, "Barcelona, New Harbour, new city" in Gausa-Guallart-Muller: *HiperCatalunya, Research territories,* Actar publishers, Barcelona, 2003)

This framework of prospective and urban action was the context for the project *HiperCatalunya, Territories of Research* (Gausa-Guallart-Müller, 2001-2003), one of the first research projects developed at IaaC (still IAAM at the time) and practically coinciding with the Media-House Project (2001-2002). The complexity of an ambitious project like HiCat, aimed at proposing a possible series of evolutionary scenarios for the territorial future of a multi-territory (Catalonia), associated with a flexible multi-layer and multi-format taxonomy (intended to combine operative scenarios and new networked matrices based on an eminently strategic approach to design) responded paradigmatically to those premises. However, it was also a response to some incipient research linked to the new network concepts, caught between the anti-typological research of the 1990s and the new importance of linking systems at the beginning of the 2000s.

Launched in 2003 by the Catalan government, the *HiperCatalunya* prospective proposal was developed with the aim of engaging in advanced prospecting focused on the Catalan territory: 25 international teams and more than 30 researchers investigated the territory to reveal its capabilities and latencies.[17] Beyond the traditional mechanisms of territorial definition, this action – analytical and projective at the same time – aimed to recognize and express a multidisciplinary way of approaching the milieu. It promoted an open investigation of a possible interaction between what existed and what could be imagined, generating potential "operative frameworks" but, also, "strategic layers" of action intended to anticipate, and also to visualize, key issues for the development of an open territory: new logics – and new aesthetics – for new scenarios of progress.

A multiple dimension that demonstrated the importance of a growing interaction between scales, scenarios and categories – but also between disciplines, cultures and fields of knowledge, which showed a desire to recode physical and virtual territories into hyper-territories of connection. This growing networked geostrategic dimension of the territorial systems and the new social realities (produced by the different population flows, the establishment of new markets – and new global circuits, the development of the future telecommunication nodes linked to a new information society, and the construction of high-speed, physical and virtual, networks) underlay the *poly-phasic* and *multipolar* foundation for the *HiperCatalunya* project and was ultimately formulated through multiple areas of analysis and design ("00-borders and relations", "01-geographies and logistics", "02-networks and systems", "03-habitats and cultures"), understood as frameworks (and layers) of action intended to articulate both real situations and virtual situations, assets and potentials.[18]

In some way *HiperCatalunya* represents an important moment of confidence in an urban-territorial prospective connected largely with the Netherlands (but also with a certain Barcelonian tradition related to the Laboratories of Urbanism and Large Scale of Manuel Solà-Morales, Joan Busquets or Eduard Bru); but it was also going to constitute a transitional stage between the ability to "strategically formulate and guide" the city and the new emerging potentials of an open logic that allowed to take, sometimes provocatively (to the limit of the system), situations and operations understood as driving or catalyzing vectors for the future, with the possibility of varying, altering, adapting and changing, without losing criteria of action. A dynamic action that was soon to be combined with the increasing computational capacity to manage and optimize data, indicators and variables and to simulate them in interconnected and diverse scenarios at the same time.

_17. Gausa, Manuel – Guallart, Vicente y Müller, Willy (2003): HiperCatalunya, Territories of Research, Barcelona, Actar.
_18. Ibid.

2.4. Links and Proto-Sensors: Physical Eco-networks and Urban Re-naturalisation

We have already pointed out how the proposals developed in the second period of research associated with a new advanced logic delved into the exploration of the new capacities linked to the new digital universe of (real and virtual) Networks and Environments. On the one hand, this was based on an attention to the supra-structural condition of the new hyperlinks and/or connective matrices (hyperlinks and matrices) – as paradigms directly associated with a new integrated and integrative system – and, on the other, on the investigation of a new environmental sensitivity (sense-contexts) as a complementary paradigm associated with the new responsive (and/or reactive) systems.

The emergence of a new inter-connective (multi-link) definition for inhabited environments, but also a new environmental interaction (associated with the new sustainable agendas and the interactive quality of a growing networked sensorization and sensitization) characterized many of the experiments produced during that period.

Nets, webs and matrices (Nets & Webs), but also adaptable topologies, parametric indicators and environmental sensors were combined to delve into aspects of Interconnectivity (and Real-Time Simultaneity) based on distributive models of transfer, link and responsiveness (reactivity) with the environment (synergistic mediations). This resulted, on the one hand, in new connective (infra-, intra-, info- and eco-structural) nets and, on the other, in a new kind of environmentally sensitive approach (self-sufficiency, eco-efficiency, environmental optimization) based on new adaptable and adaptive structures.

Information understood as a message (or space-temporal demand) and/or as an (environmental) indicator gave rise to new parametric formulations progressively inclined toward the conception of new flexible and articulated structures or toward the exploration of new mediating and synergistic responses based on a preferably systemic – distributive, inter-connective and/or responsive – approach to architectural and spatial design and its preferably "(eco)logical" definition, not only as relationships "in" a system but also "between" systems.

Interconnection, sensorization and parameterization, data optimization, the design of intelligent interfaces and the design of responsive devices: in the early 21st century, the dispositives of a-scalar transfer that were characteristic of much of the research in the mid-1990s no longer seemed necessary; in their place was a new, more empathetic, more "natural" and spontaneous approach, intended to combine not just "sense and sensibility" but, also, "sensorization and sensory perception".

Stemming from a desire to resonate with the conditions of reality while, at the same time, qualifying them efficiently and propositionally.[19]

Specifying methodologies, investigating processes, generating and simulating scenarios, and, above, all producing optimized actions in a re-informed environmental reality, were the new challenges of this (still ongoing) research. On the other hand, some benchmark publications such as *Telepolis* (Javier Echevarría, 1999), *The Information Age* (Manuel Castells, 2002) or *Network Society* (Manuel Castells, 2006) and *The Rise of the Network Society* (Manuel Castells, 2009), *The Global City* (Saskia Sassen, 2001), *The Age of Access: The New Culture of Hyper-Capitalism* and *The Third Industrial Revolution* (Jeremy Rifkin, 2000) and *The*

_19. Manuel Gausa, "City Sense: Territorializing Information" in *A.A.V.V. : City Sense, 4th Advanced Architecture Contest*, (Barcelona, Iaac - Actar, 2012), 6-13.

Hydrogen Economy (Jeremy Rifkin, 2002), *Cradle to Cradle: Remaking the Way We Make Things* (Michael Braungarts, William Mac Donough, 2003), *HiperCatalunya: Territories of Research* (Manuel Gausa-Vicente Guallart-Willy Müller, 2003), *Media House Project* (Vicente Guallart, 2003), *Cities and the Creative Class* (Richard Florida, 2005), *Morpho-Ecologies* (Michael Hensel, Achim Menges, 2006), *Creative Cities* (Maurizio Carta, 2007), *Intelligent Cities and Globalization of Innovation Networks* (Nikos Komninos, 2008), *New Paradigms* (Mosé Ricci, 2012), *Self-sufficient City: Envisioning the Habitat of the Future* (Vicente Guallart, 2010/2012) helped to conceptualize those pursuits.

Twenty years after the Rio Summit (1992), the United Nations Conference on Sustainable Development in Rio de Janeiro (Rio+20) (June 2012) influenced this new understanding of networks from a more ecological but also a more eco-systemic perspective: networks were understood not only as inter-connective physical meshes but as intelligent links (processors) intended to combine holistic interconnection and environmental sensitivity, interpreting this term in all its meanings, as sensitive consciousness and as sensory (and sensorized) response. The subsequent reports issued since 1988 by the Intergovernmental Panel of Experts on Climate Change (IPCC) helped to assess (using verified scientific data) the effects of human activity on the global warming of the planet and its environmental, economic and social consequences. This brought to light the intensity of the changes that have taken place and the risk factors derived from them if we fail to modify the conditions of the most widespread development models, mostly associated with the construction of our principal habitats.[20]

Rethinking production systems toward the goal of sustainability involved designing new models aimed at "reinvesting" processes, feeding back entirely into the conflictive linear dysfunction of the cycles associated with materials, energy and water, based on processes similar to those taking place in the biosphere: establishing new criteria aimed at reformulating – or replacing – "open cycle" models (without final reuse) with "closed cycle" models with returns (based on reuse, recycling and regeneration) both in terms of construction and building, as well as in the city as a whole.[21]

The new models in the sustainable chain cycles – referred to as *Cradle to Cradle* and Interactive self-sufficiency[22] – fundamentally contemplated more rational metabolic relations with the environment, maximizing self-sufficiency and the use of local resources.

Aspects like urban recycling (*Re-Citying*), functional diversity and mixicity, distributive flexibility and polyvalence (associated with a possible reversibility of spaces), or typological coexistence and the growing structural capacity to promote complex sections (which combine types, programs and uses) were some responses capable of promoting new project models (pilot operations) – increasingly present in the field of research and disciplinary prospection but not always easily and fully developed in a field (architecture) that is too constrained by parameters of procedural routine.[23]

In this framework of info-environmental researches, the "Sociopolis Project", Valencia 2003 (Guallart architects / Main architects: Vicente Guallart, Maria Diaz) appeared – paraphrasing the authors – as a proactive essay to explore the possibility of creating a 'shared

_20. Joan Sabaté , "Construcció i habitatge: objectius i accions" in Manuel Gausa (ed), *Cap a un habitat(ge) sostenible* (Barcelona: Actar, 2011).
_21. Bruno Sauer, "Cap a una aproximació mès subtil al nostre habitat", in Manuel Gausa (ed), *Cap a un habitat(ge) sostenible* (Barcelona: Actar, 2011).
_22. William Mc Donough and Michael Braungart, *Cradle to Cradle*, (New York: North Point Press, 2002).
_23. Manuel Gausa (ed), *Cap a un habitat(ge) sostenible* (Barcelona: Actar, 2011).

and interactive habitat' to encourage a greater social interrelation between environment, types and its inhabitants, proposing new housing (anti)typologies in keeping with the new familial conditions of our time, in a setting of high environmental quality and a hybrid landscape-building condition. The combination between social and environmental mixed aspects, in a pioneering experience of holistic land interaction, was essential for this discussed project (criticized for main political reasons) that tried to propose one of the first real prototyping and experimental advanced neighbors in Spain and probably in Europe, combining social communities, new landscape interlacements between city and nature and a new kind of public multi-programmatic formats and repertories of dwelling-services buildings called to encourage social inter-relations and exchanges (an arts center, a kindergarten, a sports zone, a social center, a youth center and studios for artists, etc.).[24]

– The project had an eminently social impetus, impelled by agents that work with groups at risk of social exclusion, generating new forms of inclusive housing and social programs.

– At the same time the project, as a piece of generic city-landscape research, was located on a site on the edge of the city of Valencia, in the Huerta (the agricultural amazing surface of the city), in order to address a common situation of encounter and crossing.

– Identity took, in this way, a new dimension. In the face of globalization, the fact of having a landscape and a culture of the Huerta in the city could be a key differential factor, breaking out of the city-country dichotomy and generating new models of transition between the two, creating "rurban" and "re-naturalizing" recycled scenarios, guaranteeing certain values of the same are assumed as own of our culture and our time[25]:

"*In the post-industrial era a new techno-agricultural society is emerging, in which as citizens of the planet we participate in its culture and economy through the information technologies, we travel to distant places by high-speed transport systems, but at the same time we affirm the quality of the local, of the immediate habitable environment; of a new intelligent balance between what we generate and what we consume*".

Understanding the housing-habitat spaces (dwellings and public spaces) as new territories of research Sociopolis proposed an open-ended organization of residential units, facilitating multiple configurations within a single building and enabling each house to be as individual as the people who live in it. In Valencia the opportunity to launch the Biennial of the Arts permeated to generate this creative a d operational project that would provide a basis for this universal reflection. Sociopolis was presented at the Valencia Biennial in 2003, as a project in which 13 international architecture firms took part. [26]

Following the presentation of the project it was decided to construct a first neighbor of 2,500 homes in the La Torre district to the south of the city of Valencia, on a 350,000 m2 site on the banks of the new course of the diverted River Turia; the same principles would be followed, but on a larger scale.

In contrast to an urbanism of the peripheries we now propose an interactive, non-linear urbanism capable of interacting with its environment on an appropriate scale, in which the analysis of the functional and environmental conditions of the site serves to develop ad hoc responses.

_24. See the explanation of the Sociopolis Project in http://www.guallart.com/projects/sociopolis

_25. Ibid.

_26. The architects participating in the project include V. Guallart, Abalos & Herreros, Actar Arquitectura, E. Arroyo-NOMAD, J. M. Torres Nadal, Sogo Arquitectos, Willy Muller, A. Lleyda / E. de la Peña, Toyo Ito, MVRDV, Greg Lynn FORM, Duncan Lewis, J. L. Mateo, Kim Young-Joon, JM Lin, J.M. Lozano, M. Colomer. See GUALLART, Vicente (2005): *Sociópolis, Project for a City of the Future, Barcelona-Wien*, Actar Publishers and Wien Architektur Zentrum.

Top: Vicente GUALLART, General Curator: "Sociopolis Master Plan" (2005).
Center: Actar Arquitectura, "Social Housing Dwellings and Kindergarden"
Bottom: Willy Muller & Associates. "Dwellings and recycle centre".
In Vicente Guallart. (2005), *Sociópolis, Project for a City of the Future.* Barcelona-Wien, Actar Publishers–Wien Architektur Zentrum.

Actar Arquitectura + GICLab Genova: "Barcelona, Multistring Central Park" from the concept of Super-Blocks (Agencia de Ecología Urbana de Barcelona) in Manuel Gausa, BCN-GOA, *New Multistring Centralities*, (Trento: ListLab, 2013). Images of the model and general plan.

Political reasons and the economical crisis of 2008 interrupted the project, that remains yet as a referential unfinished proposal for the future advanced habitats.

The landscape, therefore, has become the new building of the new Multi-City but also of the complex Endo-City,: a structuring element of a possible integrated order – on multiples scales– more flexible and relational (and not more the "possibilistic" remnant of the old building or planning construction.

A scheduling order able to reset and to redirect the random and wild growths of our existing urban structures and to create more versatile connective systems – not imposed – resonating with the metropolitan dynamics triggered today.

Another substantial project was the Super-Blocks proposal for a new Barcelona eco-structure (Salvador Rueda with the Agencia de Ecología Urbana, since 2000), and the linked project BCN Multistring Central Park Schema designed by Actar Arquitectura and the Gic.Lab of Genova (2012): the limitation of the city road traffic to a new module of 3x3 urban blocks (taking up an old intuition of Le Corbusier in the Plà Macià, 1933, and reinterpreted by the City Urban Ecology Agency) was susceptible to permit the pacification of the city mobility and allows the recovery of some streets for pedestrian or combined use.

The old/new grid of the city was used to rethink and to re-cycle the urban structure itself valuing the landscape role in the urban life and the social dynamics (*Re-Citying*). Recuperating vertical lines to recreate a green infrastructure of linear landscapes in a virtual *Multistring Central Park* that permitted to re-naturalize the very dense existing urban fabric, crossing, interlacing and connecting Barcelona from the sea to the mountains.

The international collaboration in these consultation, study and re-search between the Agencia de Ecología Urbana, the GicLab of Genova and the Design Hub of Barcelona (Ajuntament de Barcelona), in the 150 years of the Plà Cerdà was a good example of interdisciplinary collaboration between entities.[27]

In a similar framework, the paradigmatic importance of the New York High Line reuse (2009), inspired in the "Coulée Verte" of Paris (1994-2004) and designed in collaboration between James Corner Field Operations (Project Lead), Diller Scofidio + Renfro, and Piet Oudolf showed the possibility to recycle networked infrastructures as new Green Meshes (in these case, a sinuous axe) along six acre of private-public partnership between The City of New York and Friends of the High Line. This synergy led the design and construction of this 23 city block-long elevated railway reclaimed as an extraordinary public space in the heart of Manhattan's West Side. [28]

Since it's opening in 2009, the High Line has become an icon for innovative *ReCitying* design, a defining feature in its neighborhood, a powerful catalyst for investment and an inspiration to cities worldwide. Distinctive paving, planting, furnishing, lighting and social spaces create an authentic and memorable experience, with a recognized huge success able to demonstrates the value in creating new and fresh public spaces in the City, replicated in other urban contexts as Seoul with the SEOULLO of MVRDV (2017), etc., incorporating also some elements of *Urbaneutica*, that is, sensor elements to manage the environmental indicators and experiences of the milieu and the holistic operation.

_27. Manuel Gausa: *BCN-GOA, New Multistring Centralities*, (Trento: ListLab, 2012).

_28. Joshua Daviews- Robert Hammond, *High Line: The Inside Story of New York City's Park in the Sky* (New York, Farrar, Straus & Giroux Inc, 2011).

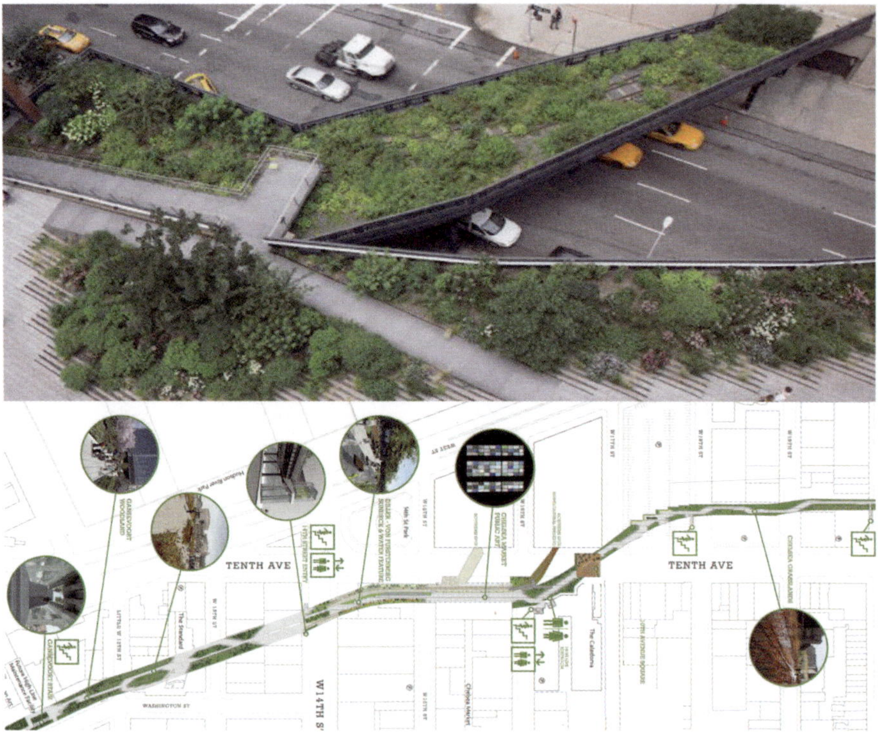

Left and right: James Corner Field Operations (Project Lead), Diller Scofidio + Renfro, and Piet Oudolf, New York High Line Green Reuse (2009)

3- OTHER NETWORKS

3.1. Web3.0. Internet of thinks and Mobile Phones. Connective Ubiquity.

Despite the growing development, at the end of the 90s, of the notion of network associated with the progressive popularization of the Internet (websites 1.0 and 2.0) the conception, at the end of the 1990s and early 2000s, of the so-called Web 3.0 (*Semantic Web or Internet of Things*) largely promoted by experiments at the Media-Lab/MIT, enriched the communion between users but also between devices and objects (things) with contents and stimuli that were not only treated syntactically but also semantically (not merely exchanging content but also messages and languages).[29]

Perfected between 1990 and 2000 with Web 1.0. (the *Internet of Structures*, or *Internet of Institutions*), beginning in 2001 and throughout the first decade of the 21st century, the "Web" underwent exponential development with Web 2.0, (the *Internet of People*), intended to standardize protocols in parallel to the development of the third-generation Web, or Web 3.0, (the *Internet of Things*), perfected at MIT's Media Lab.

_29. Manuel Gausa, "City Sense: Territorializing Information" in *A.A.V.V. : City Sense, 4th Advanced Architecture Contest*, (Barcelona, Iaac - Actar, 2012), 6.

Left: Guallart-Ruiz-Muller, Metápolis; "Media-House Project", 2001 (Media Lab-MIT of Boston and Barcelona Metápolis group with FPC, Fundació Politècnica de Catalunya, I2CAT Cluster and Elisava School of Design

It is worth recalling the approach, of the Metapolis group, demonstrated by a paradigmatic proposal like the Media House project, an exploration that coincided with the *Hiper-Catalunya* proposal, where the idea of a territorial network was replaced by the idea of a spatial, architectural network that was physical and virtual, performative and habitational, at the same time: an explicit collaboration with the Media Lab at MIT and its research into the new concept of the web 3.0, "Internet of Things", focused on the connections not only between people, but between objects and spaces.

Resulting from this strategic alliance between the *Things that Think* consortium at the Media Lab at MIT of Boston, the Metápolis group in Barcelona and the FPC, Fundació Politècnica de Catalunya, with the collaboration of the I2CAT Cluster and Elisava School of Design, the purpose of the Media-House (Metápolis, Guallart-Ruiz-Muller, with N. Gershenfeld 2001) was to combine these potentials to build an experimental prototype to test out the new Information Technologies by incorporating them into domestic life.

The technologies were incorporated into the constructive logic itself through small micro servers called on to "question" each other intelligently, drastically reducing costs by integrating – and interconnecting – physical structure, electrical network and data network in a dynamic and configurable combination between all the entities (people, objects, spaces, limits, networks and content) implicated in creating the habitable environment.

As the architects would say, "*The house is the computer; the structure is the network.*"[30]

From the middle of the first decade of the 20th century (2005-2008) the *mobile revolution* accelerated Internet access by emphasizing the new potential of more ubiquitous networked connectivity – social, environmental and material.

Behind that immersed, immersive and integral interconnectivity lay the desire for a more negotiated (material and social) environment and space – more responsive and adaptive but, also, more reactive, precisely because it would be fundamentally interactive.

At the beginning of the 21st century, the advances seen in the new technologies seemed effectively to respond to these principles. The progress in the evolution of computing devices (the release of the i-Mac-G3 in 2002 and the i-Mac G5 in 2005, as well as the iBook G4 in 2003 and the MacBook PRO in 2006), new interfaces that combined technological efficiency – and aesthetics – with new multi-level features, was rounded out by the launch of new operating systems, essential in multiplying the capabilities of interaction between means and medium. In that sense, the consolidation of the FAB-LABs, beginning in 2000, as a consequence of the evolution of new technologies (especially 3D-printing devices) fit entirely into this type of dynamics, in which conceptual production and digital production were assimilated into new distributive systems as the result of the parallel evolution of open source software. Fab-Labs (or Fabrication Laboratories) became new open spaces for physical and digital production, distributed throughout the city and dedicated to productive innovation and to knowledge.[31]

At the same time, the launch of ARDUINO in 2005 (an open source platform for electronic prototypes, based on a simple board with analog and digital inputs and outputs that revolutionized the language of programming) illustrated the growing implementation

_30. Manuel Gausa, "Theoretical framework" in Vicente Guallart, *Media House Project* (Barcelona: Actar Publishers, 2004).
_31. See https://es.wikipedia.org/wiki/Fab_lab
In 1980 Chuck Hull developed the first 3D printing that extended its performance in 1992 with the DTM (first selective laser sintering Machines) and was perfected in the late 90s. From 2001 to 2005 the development of Fab-labs is growing. The incorporation of the first European Fab-Lab in the IAAC dates from 2003/2004.

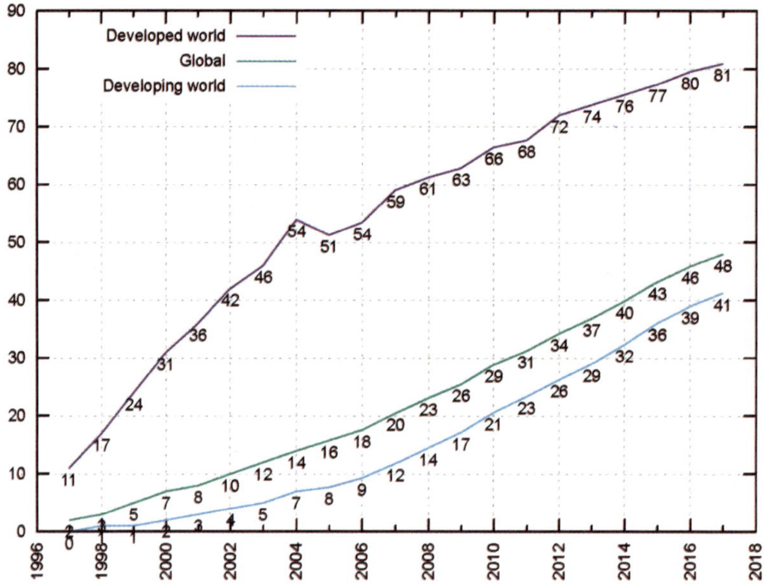

Increase of Internet Usage per 100 inhabitants (source: International Telecommunications Union).
In 2015 the usage was estimated about 3.2 billion people

of programs intended not only for editing or representing but for programming and simulating dynamic, variable and/or fluctuating processes duly parameterized by means of algorithmic formulations. The initial launch and subsequent development, from 2007 to 2010, of the GRASSHOPPER parametric management programs as an evolution of the RHINO 3D programs illustrated the dynamics associated with the improvement of OSS (open source software) from 2000 to 2010.

In fact, the research developed at IAAC (Institute for Advanced Architecture of Catalonia, founded in 2001 and launched in 2003 by Vicente Guallart, Willy Mûller and Manuel Gausa) in those early years was particularly coherent in the approach to the triad "architecture-housing-habitat" and its translation into experimental prototypes on a 1-to-1 scale, evolving from the investigation of the inhabited structure as an evolving informational mesh (*Media House* Project, 2001) or domestic space as a networked intelligent scenario (*Hyperhabitat*, Venice Architecture Biennale, 2008) to the distributive city (*Barcelona Energrid, Networked City*- GSS, 2010-2011).

3.2- The G phone-Generations. Exponential Evolutions

In this sense, a new substantial phenomenon occurred with the appearance – in early 2000 – of the first personal digital assistants (PDAs) and the spread, starting in 2007, of mobile applications, combined with the development of smartphones (2003 - first Blackberry, 2007 - iPhone, 2008 - Samsung Galaxy) with a direct involvement in the progressive and widespread access to the Internet.

"Hyperhabitat. Reprogramming the World" (2005). Research directed by Guallart Architects with the IaaC (Institute for Advanced Architecture of Catalonia) and the BCN Fab Lab with Bestiario. Biennale di Venezia 2008.

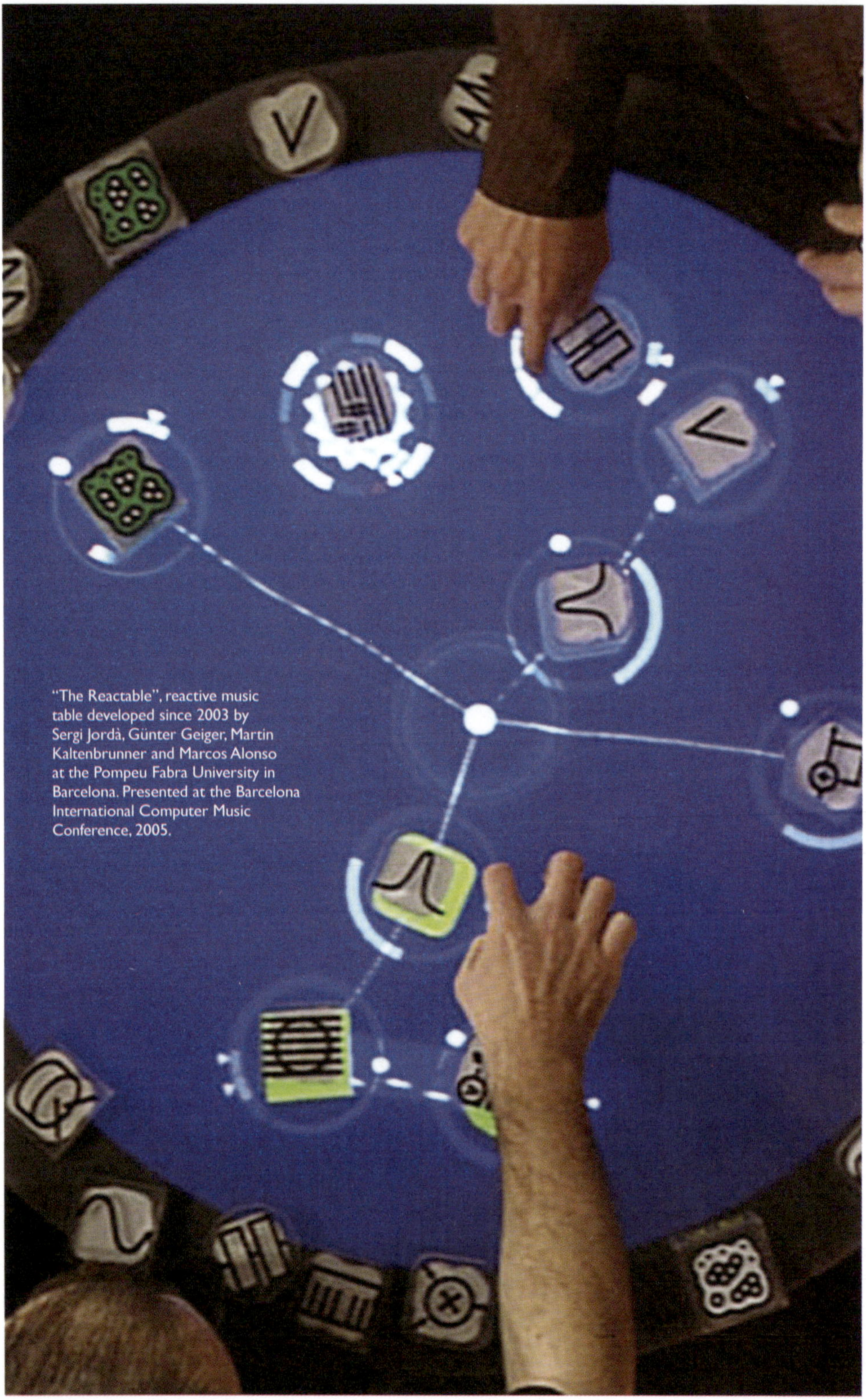

"The Reactable", reactive music table developed since 2003 by Sergi Jordà, Günter Geiger, Martin Kaltenbrunner and Marcos Alonso at the Pompeu Fabra University in Barcelona. Presented at the Barcelona International Computer Music Conference, 2005.

IAAC - BCN Fab Lab, founded in 2008, under the direction of Vicente Guallart and directed today by Tomas Díez.

Whereas first-generation mobile phones (1G) launched in the 80s had primitive and bulky structures, associated with radio transmission, the second-generation (2G) mobile phones typical of the 90s, despite their basic and rigid structures, incorporated new digital technologies, including the ability to send and receive some messages. Third-generation (3G) mobile phones, developed in 2000/2001, incorporated much more affordable and user-friendly browsing technologies, along with widespread access to the Internet, which revolutionized social interconnectivity.

Since 2007 (and especially since 2011), fourth-generation (4G) mobile phones began presenting themselves as intelligent interfaces (smart phones) with an increasing speed of access to communication and social networks and the very important development of the first interactive applications.[32]

The development of the digital/informational apparatus and its translation into new operative environments – quickly consolidated with the spread of networked research projects, digital production and manufacturing (distributive productive processes, or DPP) and the spectacular irruption of social networks (1996-2000, Yahoo; 2000-2002, Google; 2002, Linkedin; 2004-2007, Facebook; 2005-2006, Youtube, 2006, Twitter) – contributed to the advent of a new networked framework for relationships and exchanges that was not only "virtual" in its operative definition, but "real" in its (socio-economic, cultural and environmental) effects.

In fact, with the authorization (on May 16, 2006) of drone flights for civilian purposes (data collection) by the FAA (Federal Aviation Administration), the capacity for data recording, storage and management was exponentially accelerated (BIG-DATA), with close ties to the appearance of the *Smart Cities* concept.

The growing importance of networks for (inter)connection and (inter)change, but also the growing influence of real-time data processing and the potential of a new type of environmental sensorization to capture and manage information (quickly associated with

_32. On the history and evolution of mobile telephony see: https://en.wikipedia.org/wiki/History_of_mobile_phones

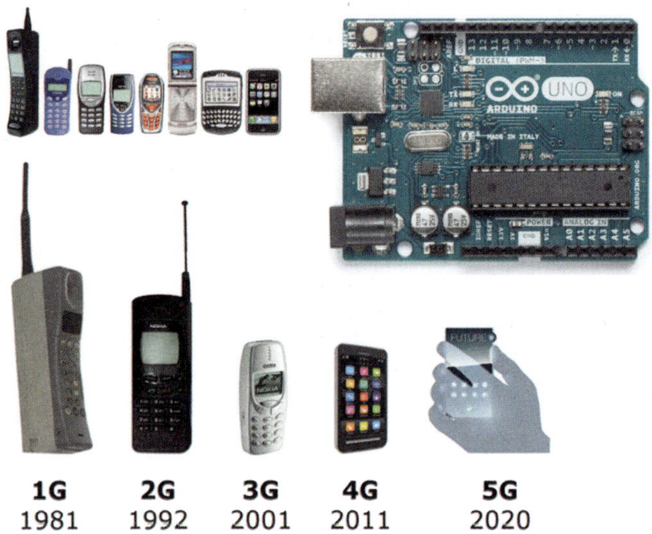

The G phone-generations exponential evolutions. From telephone transportability to interactive Smart Phones and future IA interfaces. Above: Arduino as a useful C++ device: defined constants don't take up any program memory space on the chip. The compiler can replace other references.

the concept of smart cities or smart contexts), multiplied the interactive capabilities of a new type of scenarios, which were more advanced and more reactive at the same time.

The concept of *Smart Cities*, fundamental at the beginning of the 21st century, called for a new type of urban management in which the city increasingly tended to be understood as an information system designed to integrate and process multiple information parameters using new networked communication technologies (ICT, IOT, etc.) in spaces that were (theoretically and tendentially) more secure, qualitative (and innovative), with the potential to address the new urban challenges related to comprehensive data management. Along with those new technologies, there were also new reactive and creative (responsive) strategies aimed at reinforcing the levels of quality, efficiency and interactivity in *Urban Services, Structures and Spaces* (or U.S.S.S.), reducing costs and the consumption of resources and promoting new positive interactions between citizens, habitats and local governance. A new – networked – management and design of traffic, energy, water, health, waste, more innovative agriculture, or urban planning, were involved with sectors of the community that participated in a new intelligence for cities, which:

"resides in the increasingly effective combination of digital telecommunication networks (the nerves), ubiquitously embedded intelligence (the brains), sensors and tags (the sensory organs), and software (the knowledge and cognitive competence), as well as the increase in specific (personalized, customized) reactions, that are necessarily more innovative and responsive, to the diverse (and diversified) social, cultural and spatial solicitations" (Mitchell, W., 2007).[33]

Beyond the initial explorations of the notion of a network as an eco-physical (environmental, spatial and landscape) structure, the geo-urban n-city, or multi-city, appeared, at the end of the first decade of the 21st century, as an increasingly holistic and interactive environment, more parametric and parametrizable, in which the very notion of informa-

_33. Wiliam J.T. Mitchell (with Borroni-Bird, Christopher; Burns, Lawrence D., 2010). *Reinventing the Automobile: Personal Urban Mobility for the 21st Century* (Cambridge, MA: MIT Press, 2010).

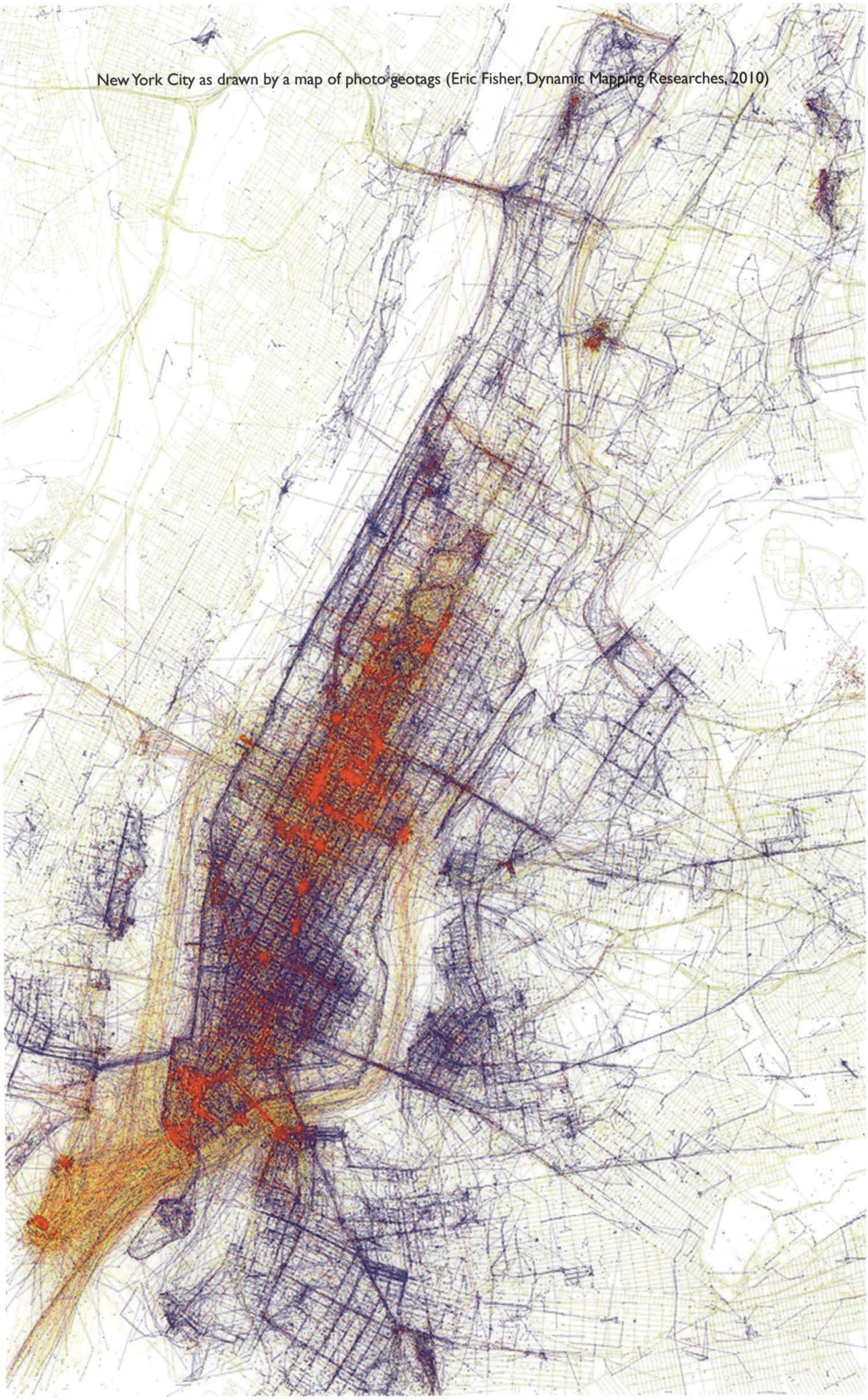

New York City as drawn by a map of photo geotags (Eric Fisher, Dynamic Mapping Researches, 2010)

Carlo Ratti and MIT Research Team: Senseable City Lab at MIT. Urban data on car movement to improve urban transport at Jersey (2014).

tion was increasingly understood as data or as an (economic, functional and environmental) indicator that was implicitly and explicitly optimizable. The notion of Smart Cities appealed to the potential for sensorization and real-time co-productivity (*Real-Time Data, Data Optimization, Ener-grids, Fab-labs & Fab-Citizens, Eco-Agendas*, etc.).

Info-city, e(co)-city, sense-city: these are, all of them, different terms to describe a city understood, in short, as a "reactive medium" from which to explore new (responsible and responsive) sustainable agendas and new eco-efficient (even self-sufficient) models. It is also a medium for exploring a new relationship with the urban environment capable of prioritizing the eco-systemic conditions of the new networked city and the sensorized optimization of its response to the environment as a new phase in research – beyond the initial approaches of the 90s, focused on the interest in addressing patterns of organization, articulation and or complex configuration – from which to prioritize a new environmental and social interaction.

It is evident that the importance of Carlo Ratti and its *Senseable City Lab* at MIT has been a fundamental contribution to this type of new urban approaches that require new "representations" and/or "expressions" to address *realities* and *capabilities/capaCities* (information potentials). Unlike the 1990s, a period in which digital computational spatial development seemed to be associated with morphogenetic parametric researches in the virtual world, the development of new Information Technologies - and their consequent translation into efficient, multidimensional digitization - brought each again the representation of the processes to a progressively "virtual and real" condition, at the same time; a mapped and recorded condition more precisely and rigorously, but also more dynamic, opening up an immense repertoire of possibilities in the field of *materiality-informationality-evolutionary* combination.

Digital production thus opened, from the beginning of the century, to the opportunity to combine interaction, registration, representation, expression and production in new, more (inter)active and dynamic models (and environments). This increased capacity, responsive and monitored, sensory and sensorized, (sensorization) of our material contexts confirmed the possible passage of the idea of "design" (and the old idea of representation) as a formal production (the object as a fundamentally subjective element, aesthetic-ecstatic) to a conception of design understood as a dynamic process, a multiple and multi-level exchange program ("design" as a n-strategic, multilayer and multi-relational interface).

Industrial products, buildings, urban habitats or networked contexts (ie "design", represented and (re)produced at all levels and at all scales) would thus combine the substantive complexity inherent in the processes with the ability to evolve and change according to data and solicitations, in a new, more dynamic, adaptive and differential condition; a "multiple" condition, open –even– to the expression of diversified scenarios, as optimal and optimized as variable and varied.

Scenarios that, in fact, referred to a triple operational quality:

1- A dynamic and evolutionary condition, related to a changing, tendential/intentional (sensory and sensitive) reactivity/responsiveness with an optimized vocation towards the surrounding conditions and the surrounding context.

2- A relational condition, associated with a new information-interconnection-interaction open to the exchange not only of the element with the environment, but also of the element with other co-participated (and co-participants) elements, in networks of connections and shared information (real time data, open source, operational apps).

3- A multiple condition referred to a production/simulation of "possible" scenarios – simulated and shown in "real" time, recorded and recordable, generated and generative - that would transcend the classical notion of project (re)production (formal, regulated, unitary, unique: centralized, "vertical" and more or less typified) and its replacement by a new type of multiple, evolutionary and differential (transversal) production, more variable, surprising and diversified in its own "beam" of open, specific and differential solutions.

In summary, a capacity for "open interaction": global and local, general and particular, systematized and differential, predictable and surprising, orientable and variable, related to the information exchange process itself but also with that progressive interconnection networked capacity of a whole heterogeneous and complex series of sources - distributed - of more horizontal registration, generation conception and production (open source technologies, fab-labs, 3D prints, energrids, etc.). In any case, they would be conditions (and qualities, these) associated with factors of greater eco-systemic, global and local efficiency: greater capacity for exchange, between efforts, stimuli and energies (reactivity), greater capacity for interaction and communication (interconnection) and greater capacity for distribution and variation (diversity).

4– PROPAGATING ENVIRONMENTS

4.1. Reactive Ambient-Architectures

After the pioneering approaches of the 1990s, the first decade of the 21st century was characterized by the implementation of new technological advances associated with the digital realm and, therefore, with new conceptual and procedural contributions.

It was also a decade of new sensibilities and of new generations that had already received an education that was open to the idea of complexity and the importance of interactivity as we are describing it here.

Pioneering projects in the 1990s, like the ones by Knox and Kaas Oosterhuis for the "Water Museum Pavilions" (H2O, 1997) proposed new fluctuating and reactive "enclaves" decoded from traditional space.

The project "Fresh H20 Expo Pavilion" responded to an ambitious exhibition program conceived from outside the classic static notion of "museum". The space did not "contain" an exhibition, in the classical sense, but rather "generated" it by merging images and sounds that depended on the visitors' activities and actions.

Like inside a wave, ground, wall and ceiling blended together in literally "interactive" environments, where the manifestation of the building as a device no longer responded only to visual experiences but also to real interactions between the environment and the individual[34].

Along this same line of action, we would highlight proposals such as the "Mediatic building" by Enric Ruiz-Cloud 9 (Barcelona 2007), a 14,000 m2 structure located in the 22@ district of Barcelona, designed to interact with new technologies in a lightweight, translucent and plastic structure made from EFTE foil that is flexible and sensitive to the environment (an iconic design in the author's career, complemented by other similar research, such as the aviary for Barcelona's marine zoo or the "Villa Bio", 2006).

_34. See the project in Quaderns n. 218 (Arquitectura Reactiva) 1996, pp.4 -19.

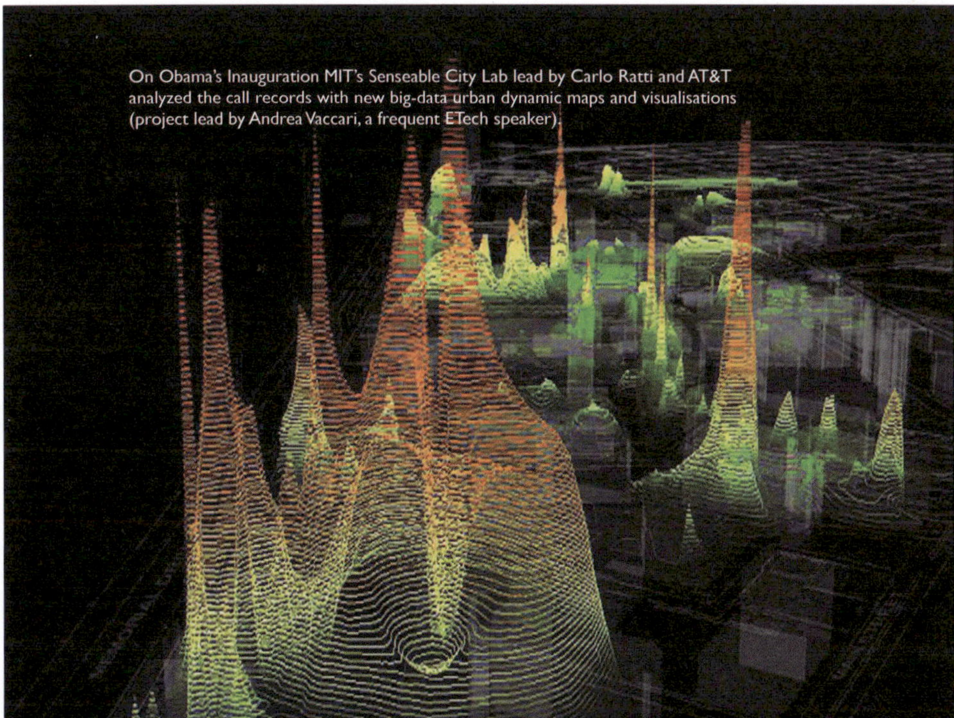

On Obama's Inauguration MIT's Senseable City Lab lead by Carlo Ratti and AT&T analyzed the call records with new big-data urban dynamic maps and visualisations (project lead by Andrea Vaccari, a frequent ETech speaker).

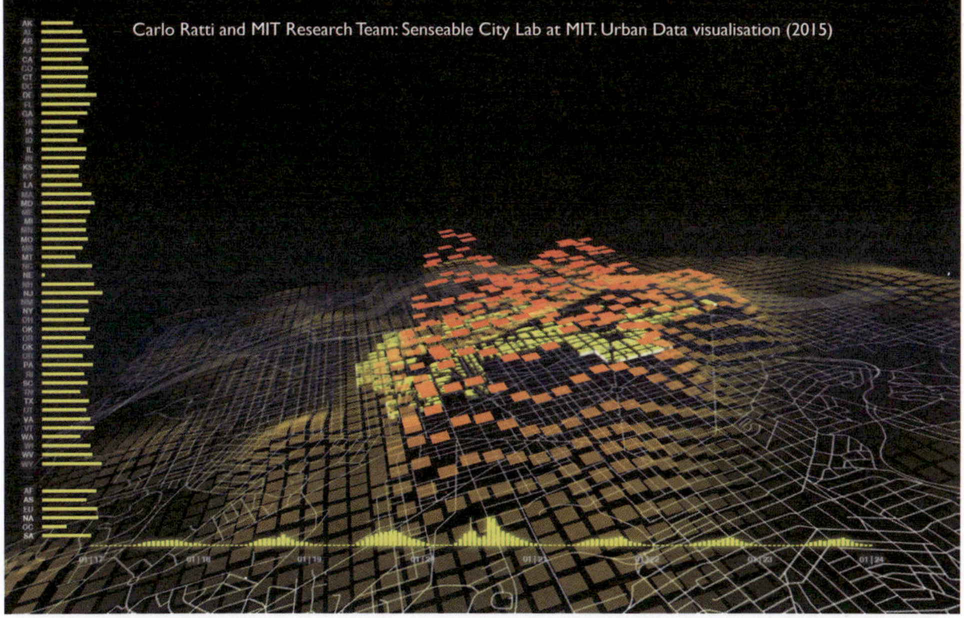

Carlo Ratti and MIT Research Team: Senseable City Lab at MIT. Urban Data visualisation (2015)

"NetworkedCITY": distributed energy research for BCN super-blocks (IAAC, Institute for Advanced Architecture of Catalonia in collaboration with Hangar, Global Summer School 2011). Faculty Areti Markopoulou, Tomás Diez with V. Guallart, W. Muller, M. Malé, E. Ruiz-Geli, M. Branzi).
Initially launched in 2001 as IAAM (Institute for Advanced Architecture Metapolis), the present IAAC, (Institute for Advanced Architecture of Catalonia), was officially founded by Vicente Guallart, Willy Müller and Manuel Gausa, and has today a new generation of personalities on the Board of Directors, including Areti Markopoulou (Academic Director) and Tomás Diez (Fab Lab).

Other examples include the "Blur Pavilion" by Diller and Scofidio, Swiss Expo, 2002 (a lightweight structure in which the architectural envelope appeared (un)defined by an artificial and foggy cloud of varying thickness and density, controlled by environmental sensors) and the "UNPlug Tower" by François Roche & DSV for Paris La Défense, 2001 (a sensitive skyscraper with a "furry" skin of interconnected sensors – one of the best known works from the designer's second period, consistent with his research into progressively complex and parametric hybrid organisms), as well as Philippe Rahm's research into variable and adaptable atmospheres, such as the emblematic "Jade Eco-Park" ("convective apartments", 2010; "Oranis Sport Hall", 2011, etc.).

The aforementioned designs are not dissimilar to later investigations using customized devices by Carlo Ratti for Arco Tietê (2013); in most of these proposals, there is a common interest in approaching scenarios capable of combining flexible and responsive – essentially dynamic – structures with open processes associated with a decidedly atmospheric definition of space, cementing the shift from the old figurative imago to the mediating ambiens.

Other designs, like the ones by Poletto-Pasquero (Eco-Logic Studio) or Marcos Cruz at the Bartlett School, which used bio-organic structures, or those of Achim Menges, with elastic structures, were particularly important in defining proposals with the potential to combine Networks and Environments in new spatial devices.

Environments, atmospheres, diffusion and interconnection, multi-nodality, glocal, eco-systems, ICTs, emerged as keywords for an era of truly networked research.

Throughout the 20th century, there was a shift from an architecture understood as typological-ritual figuration toward an architecture conceived as a functional machine (mechanical artifact and iconic object at the same time). Subsequently, in the neo-modern and post-modern stage, it was understood as a semantic calligraphy. Finally, with the advent of the digital revolution in the 21st century, architecture came to be generated as a (multi)relational environment (an interface space, a multi-layer system, and an interactive scenario all at once) that is synthetic and systematic (global) while, also, unique and non-transferable (local).

The idea of design as an "operating system" – a flexible device capable of processing received information and transforming in response to it, capable of evolving and changing according to general and particular demands – emerged in a paradigmatic way.

The challenge of contemporary design was to explore the operative and informational potential of architectural space, combining strategic decisions and synthetic data: simultaneous layers of processed information, intended to alter the primitive abstract definition of the "architectural object-box" to provide it with a new interactive purpose.

– The "compositive-object" was replaced by the "dispositive-environment".

– Geometric volume was replaced by the operating system.

– "Retroactive" movement was replaced by "reactive" capacity.

The ongoing research illustrates this shift from an eminently circumstantial action through architecture – a transformative intervention in the milieu (positivist) – towards an environmental (inter)action – a mediating (positive) relationship – in/with/from/through and for the milieu; a relationship that is supported by the processing (reactive, and reactivating) nature of architectural space, in an optimization of the information (data and demands from the surroundings) as an essentially qualitative (re)qualifying response.[35]

_35. Manuel Gausa, "City Sense: Territorializing Information" in *A.A.V.V. : City Sense, 4th Advanced Architecture Contest*, (Barcelona, Iaac - Actar, 2012), 6-13.

Enric Ruiz-Geli. Matter particles' environmental interaction; expressive map for The Bulli Project (2010-2014)

Enric Ruiz-Geli- Cloud 9. Barcelona's Marine Zoo, Winner Project, 2006

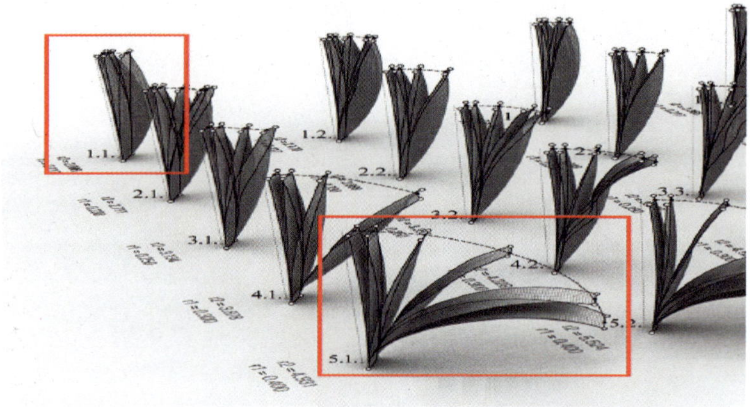

Jeff Knippers. "Kynematic structures" ("Moss Voltaic Prototype", IaaC Archive, 2014).

4.2. Global Interaction

Well into the first decade of the 21st century, the digital universe gave rise indisputably, to an "informational" space full of possibilities open to new spatial definitions capable of resonating with, tuning into, and "projecting" onto reality.[36]

A new period in architecture seemed to emerge, connected with different spheres of research and technological production: a period associated with new technical and formal, cultural and spatial concepts, capable of responding to the challenges inherent in the new informational environments that are still emerging today, and to the definition of their own technological developments and those of a more innovative construction and industry (supported by more variable and flexible systems of conception, production and manufacturing); but also the acceptance of a new eco-milieu and a new eco-mediation and its respective relationship with an approach to the landscape, to the environment, and to a (multi)city in balance with, in, and between, its(s) territory(ies); and, finally, to the exploration of the new possibilities of computational management, simulation, programming and animation translated into new digital conceptions of form and its possible concretion in more intelligent, sensitive and imaginative (private and collective) scenarios: both real and virtual.[37]

The exploration of these dynamics has driven ongoing processes of definition that are present in a whole generation of ideas and stimuli, rooted in this paradigm shift that overcame classical, modern and post-modern conceptions, pushing them toward a new, more advanced informational logic.[38]

The digital world and new information technologies (the *Internet of Things, smart cities* and *smart citizens,* etc.) have exponentially expanded this potential for exchange between situations and needs; but they have also increased the parametric capacity to design and (re)design, to program and reprogram, to process and reprocess our own relational

_36. Neil Gershenfeld, *When things start to think* (New York: Henry Holt & Co, 2000).
_37. Manuel Gausa, "Theoretical framework" in Vicente Guallart, *Media House Project* (Barcelona: Actar Publishers, 2004).
_38. Manuel Gausa; Guallart, Vicente; Müller, Willy, *The Metapolis Dictionary of Advanced Architecture* (Barcelona, Actar, Publishers 2003).

"UNPlug Tower", reactive environmental polluted air façade (François Roche & DSV, Paris La Défense, 2001)

"HygroSkin: Meteorosensitive Pavilion". Institute for Computational Design and Construction: ICD Research prototypes-University of Sttutgart, Prof. A. Menges, O. Krieg, S. Reichert, 2013 (Images courtesy of ICD, University of Sttutgart).

SOMA: "One Ocean Pavilion" in Yeosu - South Korea
Expo 2012 (a big surface with kinetic lamella)

Philippe Rahm & Catherine Mosbach, Jade Park, Taichung (2011-2016).
General views and different details of the athmosphere devices.

environments (in the form of precise, recordable, trackable and reeditable algorithms in multiple and variable formats, trajectories and contexts).[39]

Unlike the 1990s, when digital computational development seemed to be associated with the assumption of a new formal/procedural complexity, as well as the investigation of the physical/informational binomial, the second decade of the 21st century began with the development of new information technologies and their translation into an efficient, multidimensional – and often nano-dimensional – sensorization, associated with a reality that is not only multi-layer but also multi-network, which can be recorded in an increasingly precise and rigorous manner, opening up an immense range of possibilities in the field of real/virtual, material/digital combination.

The progressive development of digital manufacturing thus called for the use of old organic materials, living (bio-logical) materials, and new composite materials, combining sensorization and manufacturing in new productive developments and new intelligent, more (re)active and (inter)connective industrial systems – structures, constructions, products – sensitive to a more efficient and qualitative mutual collaboration (in and with the environment): recording data associated with energy and water consumption, CO2 emissions, air pollution, noise levels, urban mobility, the social economy, public space, collective self-organization, etc.[40]

The importance of the concept of interaction (as a processed – and programmed – exchange of information) was posited, in this new century, as fundamental in relation to a more intelligent and more sustainable development, understood not only as an ethical responsibility and a socio-economic necessity but also as a coherent consequence of the ongoing informational/relational revolution. The process alluded to a shift from a merely aestheticist (and/or functionalist) urbanism and architecture toward a more "*(inter)activist*" approach – more relational, in short – with the potential to promote a positive (global and local) interaction on all levels: with the environment and with the surroundings, with the landscape and with the context, with the individual and with the community, with technology and with the economy, with culture and society.[41]

These approaches were associated with a new increasingly widespread ecological awareness which, although it still displays a certain tendency toward accepted convention (technical-superficial solutions), demonstrated the potential of a new, more open and imaginative, sensitivity in traditional spatial disciplines. And, therefore, the need for clear innovation applied to a suitable articulation of "Housing-Habitat-Sustainability".[42]

4.3 Experimentation and Prototyping

Although the gradual assimilation of a certain ethics of responsibility associated with a new – politically and technologically accepted – awareness of sustainability became evident in many fields related to the current socio-cultural dynamics, it still tended to be lacking, at the beginning of the 21st century, from design initiatives – and experiments – in the field of large-scale urban-architectural interventions (ambitious projects, clearly referential built proposals, etc.).

_39. Neil Leach, "Adaptation", in *IAAC Bits*, no. 1.4.1 (2015), 1 - 2

_40. Jeremy Rifkin, *La nouvelle société du coût marginal zéro* (Paris: LLL Les Lines qui Libèrent, 2014), 26.

_41. Manuel Gausa, "City Sense: Territorializing Information" in *A.A.V.V. : City Sense, 4th Advanced Architecture Contest,* (Barcelona, Iaac - Actar, 2012), 6-13.

_42. Manuel Gausa (ed), *Cap a un habitat(ge) sostenible* (Barcelona: Actar, 2011).

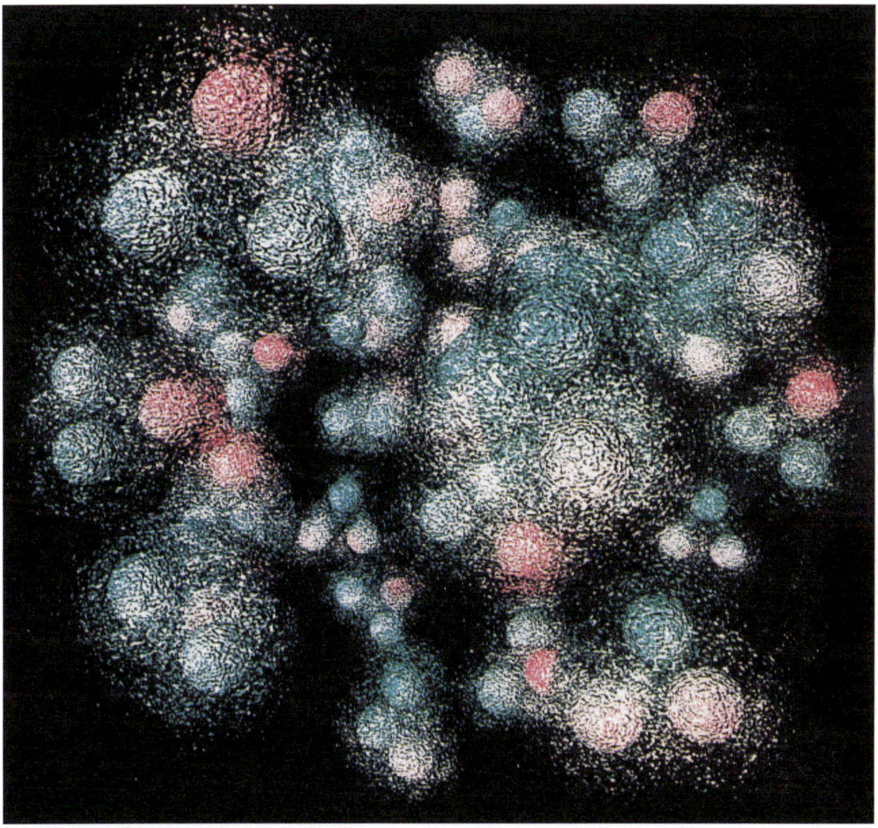

Nuclei of atoms and sets of particles. Computerized and digital simulations allow visualization of infinitesimal structures and point out interacting variable subsets using colored patterns(file)

Technology was presented, however, as one of the main allies in favoring a possible change of tack in architectural conception and construction.

In that sense, although the majority of real estate developments and public housing or facilities programs, commercial typologies or domestic spaces still relied on neo-analogical and late-modern architecture, based on "guaranteed" standards, it seemed clear that (given the new advances in intelligent industrialization, digital fabrication, constructive micro-robotics, and material and environmental sensorization, etc.) that in a short time the assimilation of this new, more experimental, more innovative operative logic (which has broken free from any pre-determined aprioristic and/or retro-aesthetic) would become the natural evolution of the ongoing technological, cultural and formal development.[43]

In this sense, and as we pointed out earlier, the trajectories of the research developed at various research centers (AA, Bartlett, CITA and specifically IAAC, in those years) was particularly coherent in approaching the triad "architecture-housing-habitat" and its

_43. Manuel Gausa, "City Sense: Territorializing Information" in *A.A.V.V. : City Sense, 4th Advanced Architecture Contest*, (Barcelona, Iaac - Actar, 2012), 6-13.

parametric transfer/translation/transposition. In the case of IAAC, experimentation with experimental prototypes at a 1-to-1 scale was particularly important in illustrating its own experimental progression, developing from the investigation of the inhabited structure as an evolving informational mesh ("Media House Project", 2001) or domestic space as a networked intelligent scenario ("Hyperhabitat", 2008) to the prototypes for efficient solar homes as optimized, active and/or passive topologies ("Fab Lab House", 2010, "Endesa Pavilion", 2012, "FAB-10 Condenser", 2014) and, finally, the prototype-environment for Torre Baró ("Torre Baró Project", 2015).

The creative and intellectual adventure of these projects, and their relation to the conceptual and instrumental developments in the nearly 20-year history of advanced architecture, served to illustrate the challenges of this cross-cutting thought, related to the complex processing of information and its dynamic and evolving projection.[44]

Whereas the "Media House Project" (2001) ("a structure as a network") was proposed – as the first major experimental project by IAAC – as an evolving (infra)structural mesh/matrix with a flexible configuration and interconnection[45] (coinciding with other research at the time focused on the exploration of complex space-temporal systems – anti-typological matrix models or a-escalar networked recursive patterns, in which connective mesh appeared as an essential device), the "Fab-Lab Solar House" (2010), was described as an active topology, an elastic surface, variable according to its location, conceived as a parametric and differential configuration system (coinciding with a new type of research, more focused on informational development programs and a new adaptable genetics of form and data processing associated with evolving topologies).[46] Similarly, whereas the "Endesa Pavilion" (2012) and the "Fab 10 Condenser" (2014) ("a capturing and generating matrix" and a "passive living space", respectively) were designed as energy optimization systems and informational and environmental management systems (coinciding with research exploring new parameters for efficient environmental sensorization) the proposal for "Torre Baró Prototype",(2015), was presented as an "(inter)active environment" – or, if you prefer, a "(re)active environment" – for eco-efficient management (self-sufficiency) and social awareness (co-participation), delving further into the phase of research focused on "bio"- and "socio-" active information, as well as the development of positive and responsible sensorization: a lightweight and artificial tree form and an operative topography were proposed as spaces for "nature" (energy, food, urban vegetable gardens) and "nurture" (play areas, residents' associations, water, etc.) conceived as catalysts for communal activities in an – (inter)active – hybrid support landscape.

One could compare the research lines promoted by IAAC since its foundation, at the beginning of the first decade of the 21st century (characterized by the acceptance of new networked holistic frameworks) with those that gained importance at the end of the same decade, progressively inclined toward the new capacities for a distributed, co-productive and reactive (smart, in other words) management of our environments.

_44. Areti Markopoulou and Manuel Gausa, (eds). *MAA 2012-2014, Prospectus & Projects* (Barcelona: IAAC, 2014).

_45. "In 2001, in the first academic year of the Master in Advanced Architecture we developed the Media House Project, together with the MIT Center for Bits and Atoms, in collaboration with Neil Gershenfield. The objective was to develop a housing prototype that integrated the technological potential of American culture with the spatial and environmental potential of Mediterranean culture. ".
(English paraphrase). In: Vicente Guallart, *La ciudad autosuficiente* (Barcelona, RBA, 2012), 101.

_46. "In the summer of 2010 the IAAC participated in the Solar Decathlon Contest with the Self-Sufficient Housing prototype. The design was based on an optimization of the architectural form from an ovoid topology, configurable, deformable and adaptable according to the location. The form no longer followed the function, the form followed the energy".
(English paraphrase). In: Vicente Guallart, *La ciudad autosuficiente* (Barcelona, RBA, 2012), 95.

Above and left: "Fab Lab House" (IAAC, Institute for Advanced Architecture of Catalonia and Center for Bit and Atoms of MIT for Solar Decathlon Europe, 2010). – Directors : Vicente Guallart (IaaC), Neil Gershenfeld (MIT-CBA). Research Co-Directors : Daniel Ibañez, Rodrigo Rubio (Photography © Adrià Goula)

ENDESA Pavilion, an energy self-sufficient solar prototype. (IAAC- Institute for Advanced Architecture of Catalonia / Archs. Rodrigo Rubio and Miguel Guerrero (Photography © Adrià Goula)

Certain keywords, understood as neologisms giving rise to investigation and intrigue (*Hyper-Territories, n-Habitats, e-constructions, matteriatures, dynamic designs or media architectures*) made way for others that were operative and evolving at the same time (*Smart and Productive Cities , Digital Fabrication, Self-sufficient buildings – and lands, Technological Eco-systems, Bio-Intelligent Matters, New City-Senses and new Sense-Civilities, Reactive Interfaces*, etc.). In all these proposals, the underlying concept of induced self-sufficiency (as the goal of a proactive interaction with the environment: energy efficiency, reduced consumption, local resource use, recycling, etc.) appeared as a central factor, more or less explicit or implicit in the design approach, and which gained more and more weight as a responsible option aimed at maximizing a project's interactive capacity and its role as a mediating and processing interface.[47]

4.4. Interconnected (Interactive) Self-Sufficiency

The launch of the different editions of the IAAC contest: "Self-Sufficient Housing" (2005), "Self-Fab House" (2007), "Self-Sufficient City" (2009), "City-Sense" (2011), "Self-Sufficient Habitat" (2013), and the lines of research "Self-Sufficient Buildings" and "Digital Responsive Matters" (MAA-IAAC) were instrumental in encouraging this kind of approach and in sharing with young professionals and students from around the world this new kind

_47. Areti Markopoulou and Manuel Gausa, (eds). *MAA 2012-2014, Prospectus & Projects* (Barcelona: IAAC, 2014).

of experimental, cultural and environmental exploration in which IAAC has emerged as benchmark.[48] It is true that the very concept of self-sufficiency can seem particularly broad, favoring interpretations with ambiguous autarchic resonances – endo-production, self-sufficiency, self-management, etc. – related to the pursuit of autonomy and local productive-energy efficiency, associated with a new optimized logic.[49] However, the concept of (total or partial) self-sufficiency would preferably imply a responsible, rational (optimized) management of resources (energy, but also, water and matter, i.e., the reduction of CO2 emissions, bio-construction, recycling, etc.) as well as a resilient minimization of risks and threats (contamination, pollution, environmental fragility).

With the new "mediating" and "processing" capacity of the informational era, the possibility of independently and autonomously managing resources does not imply isolation, but should be accompanied by a rational exchange between each of the elements in the system, in order to ensure an active distribution of the flows of knowledge and information and an adequate distribution of benefits and qualitative gains (positive interaction). Implicit in the new concept of self-sufficiency is, therefore, that of relationality and distributed connectivity (inter-action): with the environment, with the landscape, with history, with the user, but also with culture and technology, etc.

_48. Vicente Guallart, *Self Sufficient Housing* (Barcelona, IAAC-Actar, 2006).
_49. See the definition of self-sufficiency in http://www.definicionabc.com/general/autosuficiencia.php

This conjunction between independence and interdependence[50] ensures a balance between the desire for individual (unique, individualized, local) independence and freedom, and the need for collective (shared, generalized, global) responsibility and solidarity. The emergence of a new procedural and computational era allows for an increase in the level of global (and informational) connectivity, while also incrementing the local output of resources. A qualitative leap in our relationship with the environment seems to be favored, in which networked systems and sets of systems, smart conditions and slow conditions, globality and locality, can coexist at the same time, taking advantage of a dimension of both proximity and distribution, beyond the deterministic, economistic, consumerist, industrial models rooted in a maximum material concentration and the universalization of exchanges and consumption.

The evolution of networked information and systems had a twofold effect.

– Optimizing, on the one hand, the reading, management and specific (differential, personalized, customized) elaboration of data, capacities and stimuli in order to orient the different elements of the system (buildings, neighborhoods, groups, sectors, zones) toward increasingly self-sufficient (singularized) patterns of behavior and consumption.

– Integrating, on the other hand, these elements into an increasingly more global network, capable of favoring the collective distribution and management of needs and the cooperation among the elements that make up the network, reducing potential weaknesses and deficits and/or the risk of absolute (widespread) dependence.

4.5. Collaboration: From Distributive Models to Distributed Models

These are dynamics in which the elements (and processes) would no longer depend on a centralized and global system (centralized model); rather, the system itself would depend on the local efficiency of its own autonomous elements (distributed model). The elements within the system would resolve their own needs by optimizing their contextual (local) conditions, only demanding from the (global) network those services that they cannot generate in – and by – themselves.[51]

This type of "(inter)connected eco-sufficiency"[52]is what allows us to achieve a dynamic equilibrium model based on mutually supportive feedback and an interactive collaboration – and integration – resulting from the logic of natural processes and a new networked connectivity, which, at the end of the second decade of the 21st century seemed to drive many of the new fields of research associated with smarter cities.[53]

The fundamental importance of endogenous energy production factors (renewables) and of the principles of adaptation to local and specific conditions (climate, topography,

_50. The term interdependence derives from the definition used for the first time in 1929 by Gandhi: interdependence, understood as self-sufficiency in turn, allowed to combine individual independence and social interrelation.

_51. "The new model appeals to an area of hyper-local self-sufficiency that produces as many local resources as it can, thanks to the fact that it shares knowledge globally through information networks. This is affirmed from the access to a universal knowledge, used for their own good and for that of their community. ".
(English paraphrase). In: Vicente Guallart, *La ciudad autosuficiente* (Barcelona, RBA, 2012), 83.

_52. Juan Requejo : "Territorio y Energía: La autosuficiencia conectada" http://www.atclave.es/publicaciones/descargas/pub_energia/27_territorio_y_energia_la_autosuficiencia_conectada.pdf

_53. https://es.wikipedia.org/wiki/Ciudad_inteligente

Natural Environment and artificial Big Data environments. "Trope: From Natural to Directed", by Sofoklis Giannakopoulos, Stefanos Levidis, Niccolò Marini, Georgios Soutos (IAAC 2013-2014).

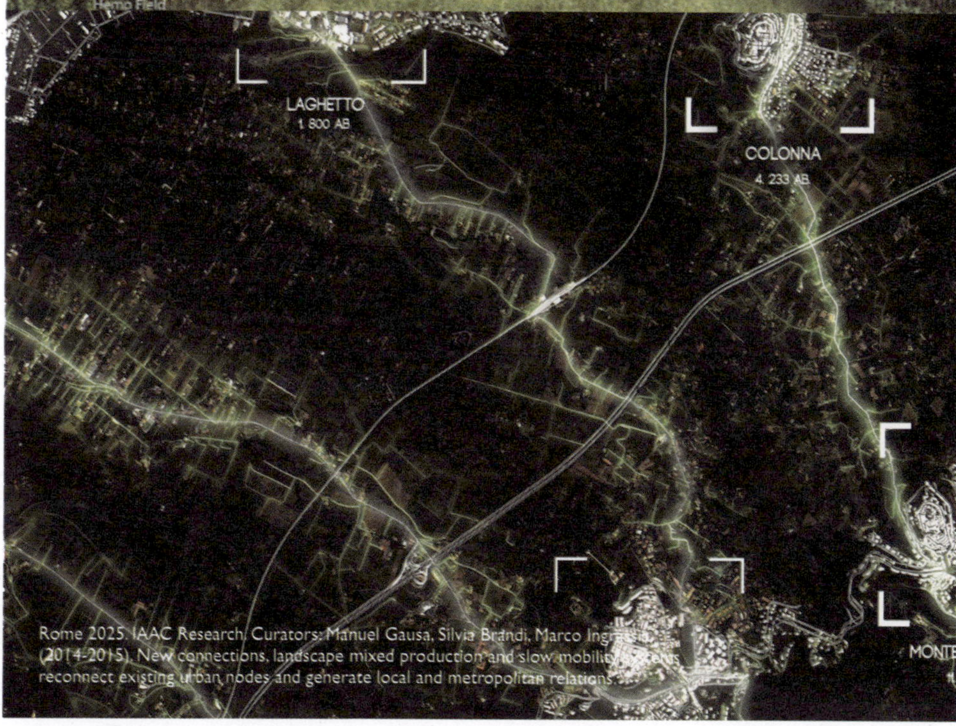

Rome 2025. IAAC Research. Curators: Manuel Gausa, Silvia Brandi, Marco Ingrassia (2014-2015). New connections, landscape mixed production and slow mobility systems reconnect existing urban nodes and generate local and metropolitan relations.

London Data-Table. Big Data Recording Device, 2012, in *IAAC-Bits* n.1 (1.2.3.)

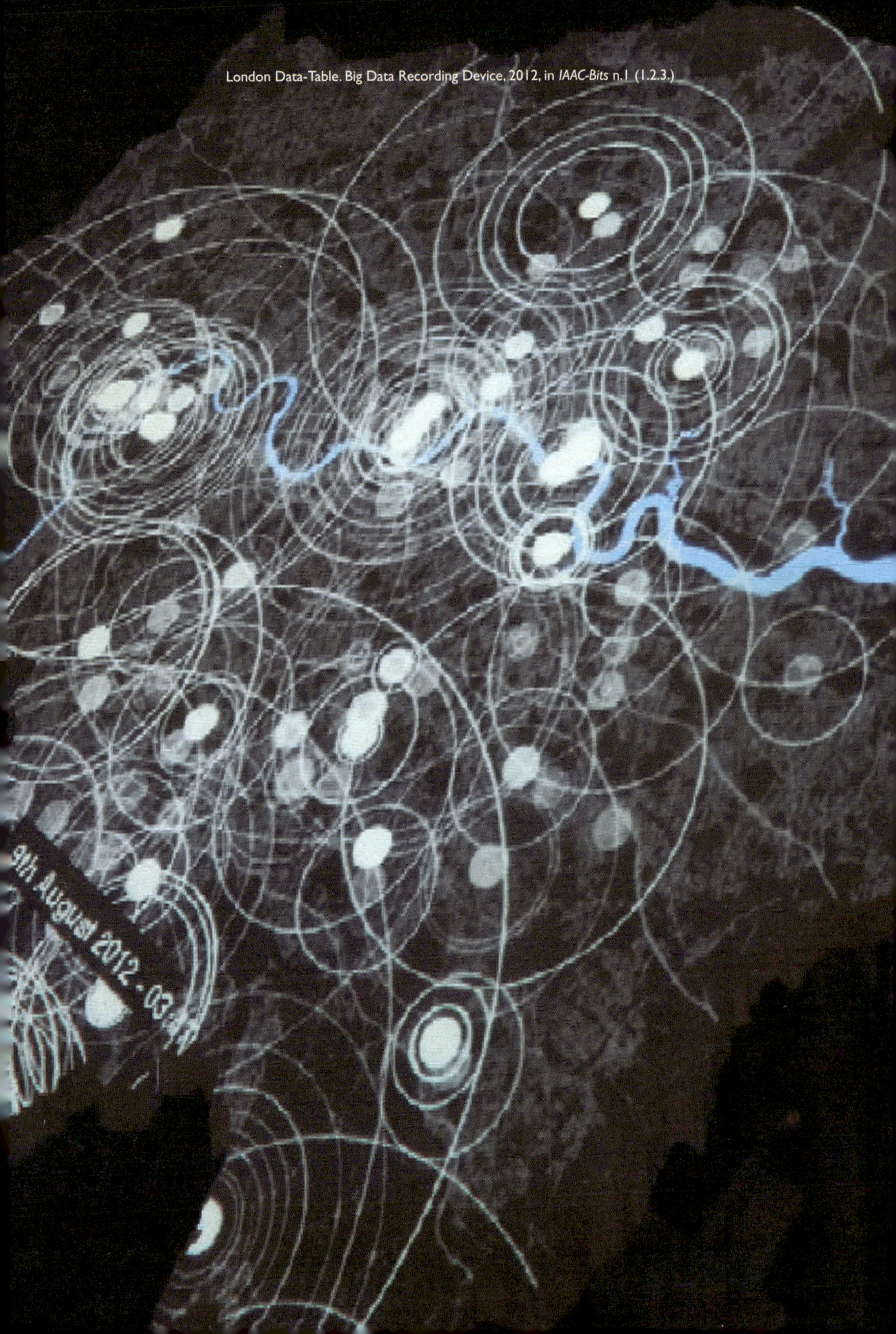

orientation, morphology, uses, etc.) combined with new forms of collective collaboration (integrated processes) favored the potentials characteristic of a new "info-, eco- and inter- connected" systematics, manifested as a paradigm for new glocal organization models capable of minimizing consumption and favoring a more optimized response to the environment.

This twofold eco-active and inter-active condition (characteristic of a new, more dynamic, mutable, variable and responsive informational era) seemed to demand not only the generation of new "co-productive and optimized environments" – and new "proactive scenarios" – but, also, new "imaginaries" and new collective "behaviors": co-productive visions, actions and strategies, capable of expressing, socially and qualitatively (orienting and inducing, representing and "designing") developments combining advanced technological models but, also, of favoring responsible ecological attitudes and more shared social actions with more expressive and unprejudiced morphological manifestations: rigorous, creative, imaginative and sustainable at the same time; capable of combining "sensory" and "sensitive" logics as translations of new technical and technological conditions, but also of new social, cultural and environmental capacities – and expectations.[54]

A new generation of investigations and proposals are intended to carry forward this fundamental digital revolution – associated with the acceptance of an informational interaction as a substantive part of a new space-time-information that is less linear in its behaviors – approaching it from parameters not only of synergy with the context, the landscape, the place or the city (or between structures, types and programs) but based on a positive and reactive exchange with the environment, with society, with uses and users; with (and between) the city and citizens; the polis ... and, why not?, the politics (or *polis-tics*), understood as a horizon of collective action.

_54. Manuel Gausa, "City Sense: Territorializing Information" in *A.A.V.V. : City Sense, 4th Advanced Architecture Contest*, (Barcelona, Iaac - Actar, 2012), 6-13

JORDI VIVALDI

DISTRIBUTIVE PROTOCOLS

The Ecological Condition: Connecting Networks and Propagating Atmospheres

I- THE ECOLOGICAL CONDITION

The experimental architecture of this decade has doubled down on many of the features that characterized it in the 1990s. Although some of them are still relevant in the early 21st century, the discipline has not been untouched by the cultural, scientific and technological developments that have taken place throughout this decade.

Whereas in the 1990s advanced architecture based the search for new formulative models on a set of "conformative" protocols, in this second decade, and coexisting to a large extent with the latter, other types of generative protocols have taken center stage under a logic that we define as "distributive". Under this new framework, the type of interaction that occurs between its elements takes place through a flat hierarchy based on "bottom-up" processes. Where conformative protocols emphasized morphological dispositions articulated under a "topological" condition -a system of relationships-, distributive protocols emphasize collaborative aspects under an "ecological"[1] condition -a relationship of systems-.

The concept of ecology is fundamental in order to approach the distributive architecture of this period. Traditionally the ecological integrity of an architectural object is judged by means of a technical and extra-disciplinary set of artifacts. Under this framework, the idea of architectural ecology is associated above all with a series of gadgets such as solar panels, algae systems, rainwater cisterns, geothermal installations, etc.

However, the notion of ecology should be interpreted here in keeping with the etymology of the Greek term *oikos* and its meaning of "house", understood as the set of people and objects that form a domestic space, which is regulated by the eco-nomy. When other

_1. Daniel Kohler, *The Mereological City,* (London: Transcript, 2016), 8.

disciplines make use of the term 'political ecology' today, they are not using it in the sustainable sense of the term, but in the ontological sense. The philosophical approaches of Bruno Latour, Timothy Morton or Levy Bryant, respond precisely to a crisis in the oppositions between nature-culture, human-nonhuman and subject-object. In a flat ontology such as the one proposed by these contemporary authors, there are no hierarchies or totalities, only collections. The term ecology, implies the resonance of these different collections: a set of objects and processes of all different kinds, comprehended within other sets, which establish certain relationships to one another that are not mediated by a single system. It is precisely in this sense that the term ecology should be interpreted here: it consists in a set of relations in between different systems and not in a single system of relations, as would be the case of conformative protocols. The difference is crucial: on the one side an ecology implies the co-existence of qualitatively distinct systems that interact among them, and on the other side an ecology precludes the presence of a super-system that determines all its constituents. Because of this reason, distributive protocols are much more extroverted than conformative protocols: the informational nature of the former refer to external indicators related to social, environmental, economical or demographical fields, while latter's information refers to internal geometrical parameters.

The term *oikos* represents with precision this extroverted actitude through a twofold distinction. First, it differs from the modern articulation of the platonic term *chora*: the space produced by distributive protocols is not an abstract receptacle in which any event can take place. Second, it differs as well from the aristotelian notion of *topos* articulated under the conformative protocols: the ecological space characteristic of distributive protocols does not refer to a singularized and singularizing substratum. Instead, an ecology deals with a collection of differentiated systems and elements that enter in resonance while generating a set of clusters and interlacements as a result.

However, the term *oikos* has traditionally been associated with another very similar one: *oikia*. Both have been translated as "house", in the most general sense of the word. Nonetheless, Xenophon[2] outlines a distinction that, although it was not entirely accepted by all Greek authors, it is very useful in approaching the question at hand. The Greek philosopher asserts that the expression *oikos* refers to a house in the strict sense of a place of residence, whereas the expression *oikia* denotes not only the house but also the property it contains and its inhabitants. Based on this distinction, the word *oikia* would refer to a collection of elements of different natures and sizes whose coexistence and eventual interlacement would give rise to a specific spatial conception. It is formed not only by the house itself, but also by the property it contains (animals, instruments, jewelry, furniture, etc.) and by its inhabitants (free men or slaves). It would therefore be a large composite of objects whose eventual interlacements over time would form what Xenophon defines as domestic space. However, there is something else that adds even more interest to the expression. Beginning in the 5th century BC several authors gave a new orientation to this term, relating the nature of *oikos* with that of the polis. Pier Vitorio Aureli[3] explains each of them by referring to different concepts: *oikos*, understood as an agglomeration of houses, and *agora*, understood as a political space where decisions were made publicly. Later, the Roman city, or *urbs*, substituted the political dimension of the polis with the economic dimension of the *oikos*, thus coming to understand the city as pure *oikos* without *agora* – in other words, a mere agglomeration of houses. In addition,

_2. Keimpe Algra, *Concepts of Space in Greek Thought,* (London: Brill, 1995). 32.
_3. Pier Vitorio Aureli, *The Possibility of an Absolute Architecture*, (London: MIT Press, 2011), 4.

while the Greek polis was encircled by its perimeter walls to emphasize its unity, the Roman urbs was not designed to be enclosed; rather, it tended to expand as a way of organizing the territory.

In that sense, the expression *oikia* refers simultaneously to a domestic space and an urban space, both unfolding like a set of Russian nesting dolls. These spaces not only contain and are contained by other spaces simultaneously, they also never appear as completely closed elements, despite remaining identifiable and extractable. *Oikia* is then not produced from a passive receptacle (*chora*) or an active substrate (*topos*); it is constructed from the multi-scalar co-existence of various groups and subgroups of systems.

Distributive protocols are based in this ecological framework, that is, in the insrumentalization of a set of interconnected objects of different natures and scales operating under the same target. These different multi-scalar clusters produce networks or atmospheres, forming what we define here as the ecological condition.

1.1 Open Networks

In 2010, Julius Popp presented his piece "Macro-spheres" in Vienna. A hasty reading might lead us to the conclusion that it is a representation of our planet, with no other interest than its singular open formalization. However, this giant sculpture contains the story of a true Copernican Revolution: in the 21st century, an observer in need of information is no longer situated on the earth's surface, the scope of his vision limited by the horizon; now, s/he is in the center of the sphere, that is, in a position that provides immediate access to any point on the planet. There could not be a more precise metaphor to evoke the informational explosion of the first decade of the 21st century, whose multidisciplinary nature has had a profound impact on the contemporary cultural and technological landscape.

It is impossible to understand the experimental architecture characteristic of distributive protocols without the generalisation of the Internet at the very start of the XXI century. In this sense, the dotcom explosion in 2001 brought a shift from the Web 1.0 system to the Web 2.0 system, a qualitative change that exponentially increased the Internet's operativity as a broadly accessible network of links and communications.

From that moment forward and together with the generalisation of Big Data, users not only took on an active role in the networks using various interaction channels (in the form of blogs or social networks), the traditional PC was also no longer the only means of connecting to the Internet, leading to a growing variety of devices specifically designed for the web. In that sense, connections were no longer limited to communications between one human and another; they extended to other types: between humans and objects or between objects.

Throughout the first decade of the 21st century, a series of unprecedented devices began appearing: the first "Blackberry" smartphone, Apple's "iPhone" and "iPad", the "Amazon Kindle", the first PDAs, etc. They all emerged in response to the need to expand the Internet's communication possibilities and, above all, to foster a type of communication that was increasingly less unidirectional, making way for an interaction in which the user plays a more active and less contemplative role. This was also the period in which, spurred by Web 2.0 and in close connection with the aforementioned devices, platforms like "YouTube", "Facebook", "Wikipedia", "LinkedIn", "Twitter", "Gmail", "Google Earth", "Android" and the first applications for mobile devices came to light. In the case

of mobile apps, it is essential to highlight the passage from 1G mobile phones to the recent 3G and 4G devices, capable of managing much more information in real time, generating a much more fluid interaction.

In contrast with the technological determinism that has taken root in our days, this research posits technology as a material culture. In other words, technology is read as a socio-cultural production that evolves under the auspices of an institutional environment based on the ideas, values, interests and knowledge of its creators and developers. In that sense, we are in agreement with Manuel Castells that, at any given moment, we have the technology that we have wanted, as opposed to being what technology has wanted us to be.[4] The concepts of "freedom" and "uncontrollability" are intrinsic to the very structure of a technology like the Internet; such is the case because it was designed, and especially developed, by people who understood it as a tool for open communication. Technologies are produced through historical processes, not simply by their "original designers". In that sense, the case of the Internet is symptomatic: although it was initially developed with funds from military organizations, scientific institu-

_4. Manuel Castells, *La era de la información. Vol. 1: La sociedad red* (Barcelona: Alianza, 2000).

tions were the first to use it, and the radical libertarian counterculture of the 1970s and 80s promoted its open development. The fact that the Pentagon tried, unsuccessfully, to sell the technology suggests that it was not initially a project with an economic underpinning. On the contrary, from the outset it was an open project, since the TCP/IP protocols created in 1973 were fully accessible. As such, the interchangeability of roles was high: the producers of the Internet were, in turn, its users, proposing constant updates in a completely open and comprehensive production process that has persisted into the present.

However, the exaltation of the network concept during this first decade was not at all exclusive to the world of technology, but deeply multidisciplinar. With the same "distributive" drive, but from an ontological perspective, Bruno Latour published his essay *Reassembling the Social* in 2005.[5] The network concept had already been theorized at the end of the 19th century in the sociology of associations posited by Gabriel Tarde, whose contributions were fundamental to the theses Latour began developing in the early 1990s. However, it was not until in the first decade of the 21st century that Latour generalized the concept of Network as an ontological construct. According to his Actor Network Theory, the world is made up of a set of hybrid realities that cannot be reduced either to Alan Sokal's Naturalism, Pierre Bourdieu's Constructivism, or Jacques Derrida's Language. All of them operate as methods of purifying reality, which is characteristic of Modernity. In Latour's terms, however, the world is composed of a network of actors, both animate and inanimate, that form a flat ontology in which human beings are not given any ontological priority over other objects: All entities are "actors", regardless of whether their essence is human, social, technological or natural. What defines an actor, in fact, is not its nature/essence, but its position and its role in the network: in other words, its action and its relevance in the hybrid reality in which it moves, encounters and relates.

Bruno Latour skillfully avoids falling into the traditional nature/culture or human/non-human dichotomy, placing emphasis instead on the fabric of relationships that occur between the two. As a consequence, objects are no longer understood independently, but based on relationships – in other words, not because of what they are, but because of what they do. Although this point is debatable from an ontological point of view[6], it accurately reflects the relational voracity that permeated the cultural landscape of the first decade of the 21st century. Moreover, Latour takes a step forward in the process of decentralizing the human being: his flat ontology does not offer privileges of any kind. Consequently, any object, whether human or not, is treated on an ontologically equal basis. This is a fundamental principle for distributive protocols, given that it promotes non-hierarchical interactions within all kinds of elements, regardless of their specific nature.

In this context, the widespread growth of the Internet and, particularly, the development of the "Internet of Things"[7] seemed to illustrate effectively what Latour was signaling from a different sphere. However, the characteristics of distributive protocols are not exhausted in the philosophy of Bruno Latour or in the technological contributions of the first decade of the 21st century. On the contrary, distributive protocols transcend these disciplines to penetrate into other contexts tied to large-scale sociological phenomena. This has led some sociologists to associate them with a new form of Society defined with the expresion "Information Society."

_5. Bruno Latour, *Reassembling the Social: An Introduction to Actor-Network-Theory* (London: Edición: New Ed, 2007).
_6. Graham Harman discusses this point in: Graham Harman, *Immaterialism: Objects and Social Theory* (London: Polity, 2016).
_7. The expression "Internet of things" has been coined by Kevin Ashton.

1.2 Information Age, Information Societies

In his trilogy *The Information Age*[8], published at the end of the 20th century, Manuel Castells points to the appearance of a new socio-cultural era. It came in the wake of two previous stages, based on two different modes of production, respectively: in an initial agrarian phase, production was rooted in the relationship between labor and natural resources; while in a second industrial phase, it was based on the relationship between new energy sources and the ability to distribute energy to feed the production and circulation processes. In this new informational phase, in contrast, the modes of production are based on the technology necessary to produce knowledge for the purpose of producing more knowledge. Information – understood as the communication of knowledge – was crucial in all three stages, but the information age implies the following unique characteristic: information is no longer a tool for the accumulation of products; rather its value resides in its capacity to generate even more information. As a result, information becomes a recursive value. In that sense, the Networked Society emerges as a social structure constituted by distributive systems of information networks and promoted by those new information technologies. The technologies do not determine it, since Castells' Networked Society is the result of a broader sociocultural pattern, but their participation is necessary for two reasons. In the first place, they are fundamental to its development, since they must be integrated into the day-to-day lives of users, who are forced to adopt new social behaviors. Second, and following Castells again, it is true that social networks are as old as humanity, but the new technologies are particularly suited to promoting them because they emphasize their inherent flexibility and resolve their needs for coordination, which was their main problem compared to more hierarchical structures. This is the case for new social movements[9] like the Umbrella Revolution, the Arab Spring, 15-M, or the Icelandic Constitution debated on Facebook, phenomena that took place at the beginning of the 21st century, revealing another form characteristic of the social application of distributive logics.

The cultural impact of the notion of link encompasses not only the technology, ontology and sociology of the period; it also articulates a third generation of human rights. The first was focused on individual "freedom", in the bourgeois revolutions against the ancien régime of the 18th century, and the second on the concept of "equality", manifested, for example, in the Keynesian Welfare State. Today, however, social movements are, above all, movements of connection, with the particularity that the agents involved are not necessarily only human agents, but, as we will see in the next chapter, multispecie agents. The 15-M movement, pacifism, environmentalism, animalism, indigenismo or the recognition of groups that have been discriminated against are good examples of this. As we will see shortly, they share a series of conceptual specificities that resonate with most part of the experimental architecture of this decade: they attend to local conditions, have a global impact, are relational in nature, lack centrality, etc.

This particular cultural scenario gives rise to an evanescent present, which, far from resting on the traditional pillars of the State, the Church or the Family, is supported by a fleeting reality built on the basis of information flows. In such an evanescent stage, the generalization of new distributed education and creation practices has led to the emergence of Open Source systems with an impact on the way culture its being displayed; its free and hyper-connected methods have called into question the role of a series of

_8. Manuel Castells, *La era de la información. Vol. 1-2-3: La sociedad red* (Barcelona: Alianza, 2000).
_9. Manuel Castells, *Redes de indignación y esperanza: Los movimientos sociales en la era de internet* (Barcelona: Alianza, 2012).

_"The Artist is Present", Marina Abramovic, 2010.

_"Confessions", Marina Abramovic, 2010.

"container institutions" that have traditionally based their effectiveness on their ability to accumulate information. [10]This is the case of institutions like the university, a traditional archive of knowledge, or the museum, a quintessential space of preservation.

The artistic domain is a good representative of this evanescent moment and its impact on the understanding of certain institutions, particularly the museum. At the beginning of the century, several artistic avant-garde currents questioned its role. Duchamp's ready-mades are emblematic of this subversive attitude. And yet, paradoxically, by the end of the 20th century, the number of contemporary museums had grown considerably. They are not just home to permanent collections, however. They also host temporary events such as screenings, conferences, performances, debates, etc. Their content has become fluid, escaping from the present not by attempting to resist the passage of time, but by aligning with its unceasing progression. While it is true that the art produced by Dada or the Futurists displayed a clear projection towards the future to the detriment of an increasingly decadent present, essentially it continued to produce artistic "objects". The contemporary art of the 21st century, in contrast, produces artistic "events": they dissolve with the passage of time and, as such, they cannot be preserved and presented as traditional artistic objects. However, "they can be documented, narrated and commented"[11]. This assertion is particularly relevant to our analysis, because where "traditional art produces objets d'art, contemporary art produces information about art events".[12]

The logics associated with distributive protocols– and particularly the use of the Internet – are, then, fundamental to an artistic circuit that has literally become "flow", rather than an object representing the idea of flow. The consequences of this phenomenon are significant: whereas Walter Benjamin announced that mechanically reproduced art objects would lose their aura of originality[13] if they lost their "here and now", the exact opposite is the case for digital reproduction. A digital file has no knowledge of the object, which is absent; instead it tirelessly reproduces the "here and now" through photographs, videos, texts, etc.[14] One of the clearest examples of this phenomenon is the performance by Marina Abramovic called "The Artist Is Present" (2010), in which spectators were invited to take turns sitting in front of the artist for a minute to share in her "presence". There is no closed-off artistic object: the action is concentrated within the development of the performance over time and expires with it. In 2013 the documentary *The Artist is Present* was premiered, directed by Matthew Akers. Together with an illustrated catalog, the film documented the performance. Every time we reproduce the document, it is not a mechanical reproduction of the "objectuality" of the work. Rather, we are digitally reproducing its "here and now", its inscription in time, its originality. We are re-actualizing it. Depending on the format, the software and the device that we use for the digital reproduction, we will obtain a particular "staging" or another, meaning that the digitized image or text will always appear in a different form. The image here would be operating like "a piece of music whose score is never identical to the piece" and requires our participation for its realization: digital reproduction is ultimately performative in itself.

_10. Boris Groys, *In the flow* (London: Ed. Verso, 2016).
_11. Ibid.
_12. Ibid.
_13. Walter Benjamin, *The Work of Art in the Age of Mechanical Reproduction* (London: Penguin Publishers 2008), 46.
_14. Boris Groys, *In the flow* (London: Ed. Verso, 2016).

I.3 Reactive Environments: Emergence and Selfsufficiency

Beside the socio-political impact produced by the new technologies, during the first decade of the XXI century there have been a consolidation of the climatic concerns emerged at the end of the XX century. Indeed, the inclusion of the environment as a performative element is part of a larger line of thought. In that vein, the concern for climate change – with precursors in the Club of Rome in 1968 and the 1992 Earth Summit in Rio – began to gather strength.

During this time – and evidencing a new desire for respectful and positive interaction with the environment – the "Aqua satellite" (2002) was launched with the intention of studying terrestrial water cycles and rising sea levels. Two years later, in 2004, concerns about the climate grew significantly as evidence of some environmental threats began to be confirmed: the town of Lataw, in Vanuatu, was forced to relocate its settlement due to the rise in sea levels. Its inhabitants were considered the first "climate refugees" in history.

Several important publications from the end of the first decade of the 21st century, such as *Blue Economy* (Gunter Pauli, 2011) and *Cradle to Cradle* (M. Braungart, W. Mcdonough, 2009), sent a similar message. In 2010, the Global Cities Covenant on Climate was signed in Mexico City. It recognizes the relevance of cities in a global panorama where the system of Nation-States, present since the Peace of Westphalia in 1648, has been called into question in the face of the rise of megacities and "corporate states".

These contributions show that the environmental reflections during the first decade of the 21st century began to move toward understanding the environment as a reactive field of demands with which a sustainable interaction needs to be maintained. The Rio+20 summit (2012) and the Sustainable Development Agendas developed during those years by a number of governments consolidated an ecological awareness that took root as an ethical model. Promoted by the establishment and often used in a reactionary fashion, its architectural materialization often resulted in banal constructions with little disciplinary interest. The naive optimism associated with the armies of solar panels inhabiting those projects confused the notion of "advanced" with what was merely technical. In any case, most of the research projects at the time shared the need to develop a positive interaction with the environment.

This was one of the main messages put forward by social networks and other phenomena characteristic of the decade, including the Anonymous collective, Bitcoin or crowdfunding platforms: networked synergies add collaborative value to the system. In this context, the statement "the whole is more than the sum of its parts" was the driving tenet that lead all these investigations. This conviction is based on emergentist postulates defended from ontological positions by authors like Manuel Delanda, whose interpretation of the Deleuzian concept of assemblage has been widely used in architecture since the end of the XX century[15].

However, the concept of emergence has also resulted in publications from other disciplines, such as the books *Emergence* (S. Johnson, 2000) and *Wikinomics* (D. Tapscott, 2006). Neil Leach and Philip Beesley also made relevant contributions to the debate with their *Swarm Cities* (2009) and *Responsive Architectures* (2006), respectively. In general, these publi-

_15. Manuel Delanda, "Deleuze and the use of the Genetic Algorithm in Architecture", Architectural Design, Vol. 1, No. 72 (1999).

cations emphasize the relevance of bottom-up processes, whose role in spontaneous and collaborative urban phenomena like informal growth (slums) is compared to biological phenomena, such as the organizations seen among ants and wasps.

However, despite the sympathy these processes inspire, a careful reading cannot but reveal their proximity to certain liberal tenets: when we exalt the emergentist processes of flocks of birds, herds of sheep or schools of fish, the underlying idea is that a society, and in particular a market, can be organized based on the total freedom of its individuals. Kevin Kelly highlights this phenomenon in his article *The Bottom Is Not Enough* (2008), even suggesting the need for a minimum of centralization not only to avoid monopolies and abuses, but also to optimize processes.

In any case, this is not only a question with immediate political consequences; it is also a debate that architecture began to make its own beginning in the 1960s and 1970s. Up until then, the role of the modern architect had been that of an authentic Promethean hero. As an ideological leader, builder of the Welfare State and champion of positivist progress, the top-down nature of his exercise was inspired by the centrality of the Cartesian subject. Then, his enlightened rationalism, founded on a narrative with epic, positivist and deeply optimistic overtones, crumpled in the face of the widespread brutality of the Second World War.

Alternative values emerged that called into question the centralized figure of the architect: architects like Cedric Price, Yona Friedman, Arata Isozaki and Nicholas Negroponte proposed a type of architecture in which users participated actively in the design process, displacing the architect's monopoly over it.

Projects like Cedric Price's "Fun Palace" (1961) and the "Generator" (1976) or Yona Friedman's "Ville Spatiale" (1959) embodied this collaborative intent, which was also present in the dynamism of radical proposals by Archigram and Superstudio.

The fact that they were never built did not detract from their suggestive and subversive power.

However, most of these proposals had a weak point. One of the biggest drawbacks of the flat hierarchy systems has to do with the difficulty of coordination and the joint definition of goals, which seriously hinders their operativity or, at least, delays it significantly.[16] After several false starts and clearly unsuccessful attempts, like Christopher Alexander's "Oregon Experiment" (1975), this type of project ended up serving as an explicit illustration of the well-known NIMBY mentality: "Not in my backyard".[17]

It is clear that the cultural interest in the radicality of this type of proposal never quite managed to instill confidence in users. In any collaborative project, the difficulty lies in maximizing participation while, simultaneously, maintaining a shared objective, which is very difficult to control using analogical means.

The current development of new informational technologies has made it easier to manage this kind of open processes in search for reactive environments. As we will see in what follows, the activities of connecting networks and propagating atmospheres are particularly well indicated to unfold these collective behaviours.

_16. Carlo Ratti, *Open Source Architecture* (London: Ed. Thames & Hudson, 2015), 43.

_17. The expression "Not in my backyard" (NIMBY) refers to the need to implement new and powerful infrastructures or innovative processes in the city, while ensuring they are far removed from personal property and interests.

2- CONNECTING NETWORKS

2.1 Transitions, Reevaluations

The transition between conformative protocols and distributive protocols is not immediate but gradual. In this sense, there is a number of advanced architectural designs that, due to their ambiguous nature, navigate between the logics associated with both protocols.

At the end of the final decade of the 20th century, the NOX group led by Lars Spuybroek and Kas Oosterhuis built the "Fresh Water Pavilion" (1997), a permanent structure that accurately illustrates the new type of museum we described before; instead of displaying a series of objects independent of the observer contemplating them, the Water Pavilion exhibits interactive, temporary and mutable content.

The pavilion creates and communicates. It produces an aquatic architectural environment where light, sound and projected images form a complete experience which adapts to the movements of observers through the use of sensors. Visitors will never have the same experience more than once, because the circumstances will always be different, depending on the number of other observers present and the paths they take through the architectural project.

Although a quick reading of its morphological dynamism might lead us to conclude that the project is framed by the topological research of conformative protocols, its interactive intent with the user reveals the networked interactive logics characteristic of distributive systems. However, the project should not be considered a full distributive work for two reasons: first, the relationship that takes place between visitor and building is more symbolic than performative because there is not an operative exchange; and, second, the relationships do not involve other ecologies outside the pavilion but take place only inside it.

Around the same time, MVRDV's "Data Town", the "Virtual NYSE" (New York Stock Exchange) by Asymptote, and the "Graz Museum" by Space Lab all transcended the informational understanding characteristic of conformative protocols; as opposed to looking at information as an abstract formal parameter, these three proposals celebrate it as an environmental indicator relating to one or more external factors. Although this "data exhibitionism" brings the projects nearer to the idea of networked information characteristic of distributive protocols, their function still does not achieve a true operative interaction between different systems, since the information does not play a performative role but merely an expository one. In general, these projects are more similar to the conformative logics of the 1990s than to the distributive logics we are describing here. There are two reasons for this.

First, there is no interaction between systems (ecology) but the interaction is established within one single system (topology).

Second, information is understood as a parameter tied to internal formal factors rather than as an external environmental indicator. In these projects, the concept of a network has been interpreted as a flexible and open spatial mechanism, but not as an interactive informational device.

2.2 Net-Buildings

Although the concept of a network is fundamental in all the contributions we have analyzed thus far, the information revolution has allowed for operating with networks based on an interactive – or performative – condition, rather than a merely structural, symbolic, material or formal understanding. In this sense, the notion of Net-Building can be summarized in two main points: (1) cooperativity with other buildings and (2) interaction with the environment. This aspects are essential when it comes to the experimental architecture characteristic of distributive protocols. Precisely for this reason, iconic architectural designs such as Toyo Ito's "Sendai Mediatheque" (1997) cannot be explained from a distributive perspective, despite their repeated allusions to the network concept. Specifically, on the one hand, Ito's project presents a program that is particularly dedicated to the world of information and, on the other, its immaterial appearance alludes to the evanescence of data flows. However, both attributes function allegorically: on the one hand, their understanding of information is not performative but programmatic; and, on the other hand, there is no operative interactivity either with the user, with the immediate surroundings, or with the environment. These characteristics in no way detract from its disciplinary contribution to architecture, but they do set it apart from an advanced understanding of architecture or, at least, a distributive interpretation. Something similar is the case with projects such as "14 billions" by Tomas Saraceno (2009) and "Floating Landscapes" by Numen (2011). In both cases, the networks do not serve as operative resources but rather as material structures, removed from any informational condition. The same can be said of projects such as the "Serpentine Gallery" (2004) or the "Omotesando Building" (2004), both by Toyo Ito: they also apply the idea of a network but, again, it is not from an informational point of view but a structural one.

In opposition to these projects, the "MediaTIC" building (2010) by Cloud 9 represents an emblematic example of a Net-Building. Although a "layered" reading of the project is possible, which means it can be described in terms of conformative complexity, approaching the design from a distributive perspective reveals issues that resonate with Jeremy Rifkin's "The Third Industrial Revolution" (2011): buildings as power plants, renewable energy sources, connection to smart grids, etc. However, beyond the building's networked operativity, the project has a reactive capacity that combines two characteristics. On the one hand, it operates through performative interactions: the building adapts its façade depending on the climate conditions. On the other hand, this interaction takes place between different ecologies: the project interacts first with the surrounding environment, second, with its own interior climate requirements and, third, with the other buildings around it (the 22@ district). The cubic building's formal simplicity further emphasizes its function as a distributive node, while it adopts the typical technological solutions used in such systems, including Arduino devices in the sensors or a program dedicated to ICT. In that sense, the design's objectual function distances it from the topological formulation characteristic of conformative protocols: the idea of a continuum is not understood in formal terms, but in collaborative terms. On the other hand, the use of a lightweight tensile structure emphasizes the immaterial dominance of a reality in constant flux, where connections are more important than the weight of materials, which seems to illustrate some of Latour's assertions regarding the inconsequence of actors when compared with the relevance of their role as participants in an exchange network. The New York Aquarium designed by the same author follows similar distributive patterns, although here it draws on the formal fluidity associ-

"MediaTIC", Cloud 9, 2010

ated with water. Slightly earlier works like Nicholas Grimshaw's "Eden Project" (2000) or the PTW Architects's "Water Cube" (2007) also display distributive characteristics. Both projects contribute to the production of a collaborative multidisciplinary cluster, which is the hub for dozens of technologies, publications and projects. However, although the "MediaTIC" building and the "Eden Project" share a distributed approach, both projects are traversed by completely opposite understandings of nature's notion.

Geli's nature is what Zizek would define as a techno-nature[18]: a manipulable entity that can and should be altered by humans in order to achieve their goals, sustainability and self-sufficiency among others. In the case of Geli, this approach is based on the concept of "particle", understood as the ultimate element of reality and therefore a powerful tool to manipulate it. Instead, the Eden Garden operates with a deeply conservative approach to nature: as its name suggests, nature is seen as a harmonious and divine origin that needs to be preserved rather than altered, which is the main role of the domes.

_18. ""Trash Nature" by Slavoj Zizek", YouTube video, 23:30, lecture on May 6, 2015, posted by "Top Documentary", https://www.youtube.com/watch?v=j_K_79O21hk&t=4s.

"Eden Project", Nicholas Grimshaw, 2000

Besides, and opposing the faustic desire for extroversion characteristic of propagative projects such as Diller-Scofidio's "Blur Pavilion" (2003), the domes are rather introspective, constituting an unidirectional relation in which there is almost no hygrothermal impact on project's surroundings.

However, as we will see soon in detail, this decade has witnessed a way more radical notion of environmental interaction that the one offered by "Eden Garden". The emergence of design softwares like "Grasshopper" (2007) incremented – both quantitatively and qualitatively – users' ability to interact with their surrounding by making it easier to manage external data. This extroverted attitude is precisely what makes it possible for projects like the ones we have just mentioned to be constituted through their interactions with other nodes – in this case environmental ones – and not only with themselves, as was the case with NOX's "Water Pavilion". Contrasting with the earlier "conformative protocols", the designed environment functions here as an operational context rather than as an inert container.

2.3 Digital Crafts: Reproduction, Massproduction, Coproduction

One of the main contributions related to networked distributive protocols has been made by Fab Labs. The Third Industrial Revolution has shed light on new and revolutionary production possibilities, suggesting the appearance of a new productive model that brings back several of the attributes of traditional handicrafts through a kind of craftsmanship 2.0.

In Book X of *The Republic* (380ac), Plato exposes his well-known theory of ideas by using several examples. Among them, Plato describes how the idea of a bed, the absolute reality of the corresponding entity, is first reproduced by the craftsman in the form of an object. Then, it is reproduced again by the artist in the form of a painting, losing ontological value in each iteration. This Platonic understanding of the craftsman as "copying" an ideal and pre-existing "model" remained in force until the First Industrial Revolution. A talented traditional craftsman, unlike what excessive romanticism might lead us to believe, was not someone who would customize each piece. On the contrary, the artisan would seek to eliminate any differences between objects in the same series. For him, the mastery and satisfaction of a job well done would lie in the exact similarity of the pieces' size and appearance: repetition was a virtue; whereas originality, especially in the Middle Ages, was associated with the figure of the artist. The craftsman has a "model", which he takes as an ideal and attempts to "reproduce" as many times as necessary with maximum accuracy. In that sense, for the traditional craftsman, producing consists, above all, in re-producing.

With the advent of industry, the understanding of craftsmanship changed entirely, and society's tastes shifted toward the pleasure of abundance and the precision of machines. The market for crafts also changed: it moved from the domestic world into the world of souvenirs. Small-scale handicraft productions began to be distinguished from industrial production by evoking an idyllic world, far removed from the bustle of the city, contrasting with the mechanicism of factories, and imbued with a deliberate, and often forced, picturesque quality. In parallel, the number of artisans fell drastically, and while a small percentage of them opted to maintain their traditional processes, supported by a romantic narrative inspired by authors like John Ruskin, the majority embraced mass industrial re-production. This phenomenon was consolidated after the Second World War with the arrival of the Welfare State and its promise to supply not just the wealthy few but the ordinary masses, which Post-Fordism had trained to be consumers.

The advent of the Information Society, however, has recovered some of the old ideas associated with craftsmanship through the concept of co-production. Working teams should no longer be understood as a proletariat distributed across a production chain, or according to a pyramid system articulated through the triad "master-journeyman-apprentice". Rather, they are to be understood based on the complexity of a variable group of networked "entrepreneurs", who are constantly producing and exchanging information under five main aspects: multiscalarity, singularity, permutability, extroversion and autonomy. Fab labs create an international network of laboratories in constant connection, which also allows for a high interchangeability of roles: a designer can simultaneously be a client and producer, contributing to the collaborative propensity of the whole. This kind of craftsmanship 2.0 shares several features with traditional craftsmanship – above all, the aforementioned interchangeability of roles and autonomous production, but it distances itself by contrasting its extroverted attitude with the guild secretism typical of the Middle Ages.

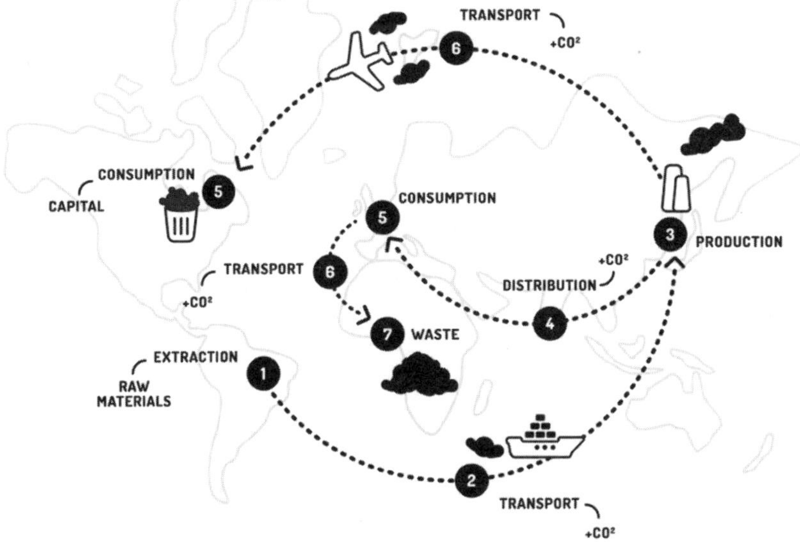

↳ PITO - Product in / Trash out

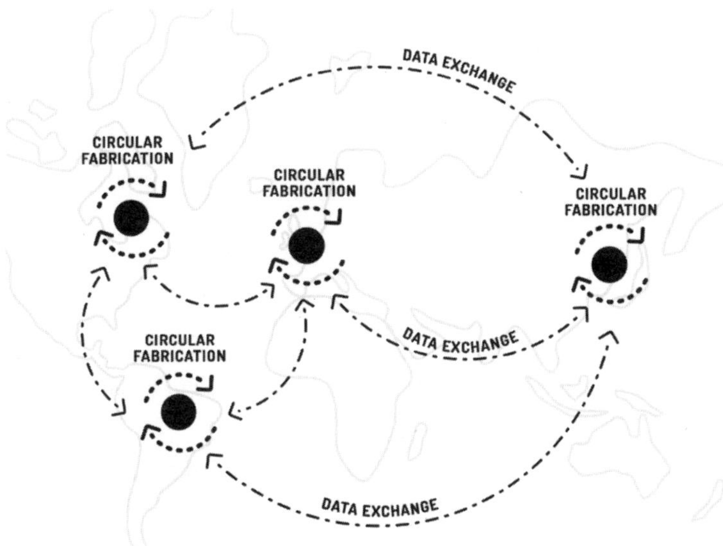

↳ DIDO - Data in / Data out

_"Productive systems"; FabCity, 2016.

Along with his experiments at the "Center for Bits and Atoms" (2001), Neil Gershenfeld's essay "How to Make Almost Anything" (2012) was fundamental for craftsmanship 2.0. On the one hand, it takes advantage of all the facilities offered by the Internet and multiple social platforms to operate as a network and, on the other hand, it benefits from the latest advances in digital manufacturing (3D printers, milling machines, lasers, etc.).

These dynamics have been translated into the field of architecture beginning with paradigmatic projects like the "Wikihouse" (2011). Setting aside the variability of results and their relative architectural quality, what seems undeniable is that this type of proposal breaks new ground in the design/production/user equation and allows the user to take on new autonomy and prominence. Other proposals to highlight with a clear bottom-up approach, although they are not associated with digital manufacturing processes, are some of Terreform's projects like "Urbaneer" (2010) and Carlo Ratti's designs, such as "Smart Home" (2010), "Earth Screening" (2013) and "Digital Water Pavilion" (2014).

In any case, the ensemble of this type of architectural production, together with new information technologies, social networks, Arduino, and the focus on social empowerment and democratization processes, form another great "multidisciplinary cluster", which includes several books, like the ones by Steven Johnson, Manuel Delanda, and Don Tapscott, discussed earlier, and other initiatives such as BitCoin or the Anonymous collective.

Other designs such as IaaC's "Fab Lab House" (2005) or the "Endesa Pavilion" (2012) fall midway between the approaches with more marked environmental concerns and the proposals with a greater sensitivity towards the phenomena of social participation more typical of this second cluster seen in our research. A derivative of the FabLab movement, which translated distributive systems onto the scale of urban design, was the "Fab City" concept, an international initiative developed in a collaboration between MIT, IaaC, the Fab Foundation and the Barcelona City Council. The project, connected to the global network of Fab Labs, was defined as an operative Think Tank for cities, bringing together urban leaders, makers, urban planners and innovative citizens into new interactive networks, replacing the old linear consumerist models ("import products to produce waste") with new circular models that can help cities to become structurally productive and progressively self-sufficient. Another project on an urban scale in the orbit of the aforementioned clusters is Carlo Ratti's proposal for Arco Tiété (2012), based on harnessing ICTs. The project focused on developing an efficient interface between the physical and the digital world, incrementing the interaction between public space, tourists and local inhabitants: its main technological tool (sensors on the one hand and smartphones on the other) allowed for a dynamic and constant communication between the city and its inhabitants.

The relationship between distributive protocols and the urban phenomenon is, in this sense, substantially different from the others: following Willy Müller[19], whereas the industrial era worked with information ratios developed through sedimentation, over the years, the technologies available to us in the information age have led to a shift from logics based on the accumulation of data to logics based on the substitution (or fluctuation) of data. Every few seconds, a distributed network of sensors in the city is capable of sending all kinds of data regarding its status. Given this type of framework, which is capable of maintaining real-time interaction processes with urban data, it seems evident that the design of the city cannot continue to be approached using the same 20th-century urban planning mechanisms.

_19. Willy Müller, "From urban planning to urbanetics", in *IaaC Bits*, no. 1 (2014), 2.

2.4 Global Cities and Hyper-Connected Neighbourhoods

If the 19th century was the century the Empires and the 20th century was the century of the States, the 21st century will probably be the century of cities. During the first decade of this century there was a turning point: for the first time in history there was more people living in urban areas than in rural ones. Moreover, cities as Hong Kong, Mexico City, Rio de Janeiro or London bear a demographic, technological and cultural complexity that the twentieth century had hardly experienced. Far from being reduced to a mere increase of urban population, the rise of cities also proposes a transformation of social habitats that impacts nearly all dimensions of the metropolis. The disembarkation of information technologies, the intensification of environmental concerns, the arrival of artificial intelligence or the generalisation of the Internet, have drawn an urban scenario that can hardly be managed with the industrial logic of the twentieth century.

Against this context, during this decade new distributive urban models are emerging in order to meet the demands of our days, illustrating what Thomas Kuhn would call a paradigm shift. To approach any problem necessarily means to confront it through a model that not only provides solutions, but also raises questions. That model is precisely what is meant by the term paradigm. In this sense, and following Thomas Kuhn's thesis, a paradigm defines practically all aspects that concern the approach of a problem: it stipulates what should be observed, defines what questions must be formulated, organises the results of the research, and lays out how they should be interpreted, suggesting what experiments should be conducted and even defining what kind of predictions can be valid. In this sense, the world of science has not always advanced on the basis of what Kuhn calls "Normal Science", at certain points occur "Scientific Revolutions." In the first case we see accumulative developments, which main feature is the linearity of its evolution. In the second one, on the contrary, we no longer face a merely quantitative change but a qualitative one. Indeed, a scientific revolution is a completely new approach towards the same subject.

The shift from the Ptolemaic to the Copernican scheme is a good example of this, as well as the shift from Newtonian to Einsteinian physics. In both cases, what happens is not a step forward in the same direction, but what actually occurs is rather a change of direction advocated by a paradigm accumulating recursive anomalies that it is incapable of explaining. This means that the model can't provide a satisfactory response against a growing number of incidents, and as a consequence, it requires a major number of ad-hoc explanations in order to keep its primacy.

This is precisely the situation that is generalised during the first decade of the XXI century in the field of urban design: The urban industrial models of the twentieth century are beginning to collapse in the face of an unprecedented demographic, cultural and technological context. In this sense, it is becoming more and more commonplace for main cities of the globe to have to face recursive anomalies of all kinds: public transport has severe operational shortcomings, private mobility systems generate more urban traffic jams than ever before, infrastructures become obsolete every time faster, housing stock is insufficient, ecological disasters are becoming more usual and sea-level rise threatens to be irreversible.

Given this renewed economical, social and climatic landscape, in the first decade of the XXI century advanced architecture is reconsidering public space design under distributive protocols by identifying one crucial fact: whereas, traditionally, public space has been the only place for interaction and encounters among citizens, in recent years social networks have generated a new digital public space – a sort of virtual big brother that has taken over a large part of this interaction and has forced us to rethink the design criteria for 21st-century public space. In this context, the urban environments of the 21st century have seen the emergence of a new actor: the hyperconnected citizen. Hyperconnected citizens differ from their traditional 20th-century counterparts in that they can establish and maintain a fluid, constant, global, personalized, instantaneous and, most importantly, geo-localized connection with other people, objects and institutions. However, the scope of their capabilities is not limited only to receiving, processing and transmitting information of all kinds; they can also experience it through the multiple augmented reality resources at their disposal. Hyperconnected citizens are thus immersed in a network of viral connections with agents of different natures. They are determined by and from a multiplicity which does not award them a privileged position; they operate on the same ontological level. This means that hyperconnected citizens no longer fit in with the Promethean narrative characteristic of the modern movement. Instead, they must accept a plural and shared reality, which forces them to operate as a multidisciplinary mediator rather than as a modern hero. We find a 21st-century individual who, through his socio-technological peculiarities, questions the established role of public space. Whereas, traditionally, public space was constituted as the setting for expression, where citizens celebrated their belonging to a certain urban collective, today social networks have taken over a large part of that representation, forcing 21st-century public space to reinvent itself.

There is a deeper underlying debate here: Can advanced architecture – and distributive protocols in particular – rethink how we manage cities? More than 40 years ago, Buckminster Fuller used to say that humanity was acquiring the best technology for the worst purposes. In our case, we have the technology to promote more participatory, more productive, more decentralized, and more sustainable cities. Paradoxically, however, the same companies that could supply the technology to make this happen are also the main suppliers of the technology that has the power to turn so-called "smart cities" into repressive, authoritarian and alienating places. Technology that has entered the market during the decade in question at the hands of companies like Cisco and has been essential in making the smart city a reality: real-time sensorization, smartphones, apps, etc.

And yet, in 2015, in the face of the wave of technological optimism associated with smart cities, Koolhaas was much more critical: "As a substitute for the French Revolution's liberté, égalité, fraternité, a new universal trinity has been adopted: comfort, security, sustainability".[20]

Strangely enough, the cities that are showing the fastest technological development are not the most democratically advanced. Of the 10 most populated cities, all display high levels of poverty or conflict (except Tokyo), and none of them are located in the West, although the technology used to develop their smart capacities is Western in origin. In that sense, distributive systems do not necessarily lead to a higher quality of democracy. In his book *If Mayors Ruled the World* (2013), Benjamin Barber pointed out how large corporations and technology companies – with an economic power and political influence far superior to that of certain states and cities – have tended to take over the role of public institutions in addressing new urban and socio-political challenges.

_20. Rem Koolhaas: "The Smart Landscape: Intelligent Architecture," Artforum, April 2015.

Despite the growing critical awareness of a new hyper-technological reality, we cannot fail to recognize the important subversive power also inherent in the potential of distributive protocols. This is evident in the emergence of another type of organizations like "Bitcoin" (2009) or "Anonymous" (2003), in the growth of different crowdfunding initiatives and even the implementation of applications like Fix My Street (2007), aimed at bringing urban decision-making closer to citizens. This latent subversive power inherent in the definition of new networked distributive protocols does not necessarily have to be revealed through computational phenomena or ICTs, but through a new operative intelligence that is in synthesis with the environment, and its informational optimization.

The clearest example of this, both on an urban level and in relation to the new advanced logics that we have been describing, is the "Floating School" (2013) by Kunlé Adeyemi. Despite its apparent formal, technological and material simplicity, the floating school interiorizes and responds to climate change by avoiding the problem of rising sea levels. In addition, its constant mobility and dynamic purpose give it the power to develop an operative interaction with its environment. Viewed on a territorial level, in the context of Lagos, the project offers images (similar to other settings like the Mae Klong Market in Thailand or the favelas in Rio de Janeiro) that could serve as perfect illustrations of some of Steven Johnson's postulates, and which confirm the ability of distributive protocols to operate, sometimes, beyond the scope of available technological resources.

3- PROPAGATING ATMOSPHERES

Distributive protocols are not exhausted in the use of the informational network concept. On the contrary, several distributive projects from the first decade of the 20th century replaced discrete connections with continuous propagations as a conceptual and operative tool: whereas the former act through links and networks, the latter do so through gradients and atmospheres.

3.1 Diffusive Gardens: From Prolongation to Propagation

Beside opposing the discreteness of the term "connection", the diffusive nature of the term "propagation" contrasts as well with the directionality associated with the term "prolongation": whereas "propagation" involves a form of growth that is not subject to pre-existing structures and is relatively unconditioned, the notion of "prolongation" assumes a type of extension that is subject to pre-established lines, which determine its development. A gas is propagated, not prolonged, whereas train tracks are prolonged, not propagated.

The architectural action of "propagating atmospheres" should be read under the light of three concepts proposed by Gilles Clement: the third landscape, the garden in motion and the planetary garden. The first one is particularly relevant to understand the nature of most of the architecture projects comprehended in this section: the notion of "third landscape" points to the fruitfulness and variety characteristic of all those spaces located on the margins of culture and nature which, despite occupying a space in our visual field, are forgotten and in disuse. Scattered across the planet in the form of roadsides, shores and embankments, the third landscape acts as the last refuge of diversity and vaguely refers to the "corrupted biotopes" of François Roche or the "anxious landscapes" of Antoine Picon.

Its emergence on the intellectual panorama of the first decade of the 21st century was fundamental to advanced architecture for a specific reason: it offers an understanding of the term "landscape" that sets aside the romantic symbology that traditionally accompanies the term. With Clement, the garden takes an operational relevance: far from the contemplative vocation of the rennaisance italian garden and its french and british derivatives in the 17th and 18th century, Clement's garden is understood as an unexpected and subversive source of diversity that spreads across the planet in an irregular way.

The concepts of "garden in motion" and "planetary garden" are thus of great interest to advanced architecture, not only for their holistic and "continuous" approach to the planet, but also, and above all, because of their performative condition: both concepts describe how nature diffuses across the space through material processes like windstorms, marine currents or animal movements. The uniqueness of these processes is that they know no borders or interruptions, highlighting the need to understand the planet as a single continuum rather than as a sectorized map. Under Clement's approach to the notion of "landscape", human beings become "gardeners" for the entire planet and not just for a part of it: the limits of human action transcend political borders, proposing a new type of diffusive -scattered and active- spatialities.

_"Le Jardin du Tiers Paysage"; Gilles Clementr, 1996.

3.2 Hydro-Thermal Buildings

This holistic vocation resonates with many of the environmental concerns we have cited here. In that sense, the notion of atmosphere is particularly relevant to approach an architecture of propagations because it encapsulates many of the characteristics that we have observed in Clement's notion of the "Third Landscape". However, the meaning of atmosphere considered here is completely different from the one used in other architectural contexts, notably among the swiss architecture of the last decades. The phenomenological architectures designed by architects like Peter Zumthor or Herzog & de Meuron instrumentalize the notion of atmosphere in order to establish an intimate, material and historical continuity in between the project and its locus. In this sense, there is a strong attention to the phenomenological interest on "how things appear to us" that is very patent in two dimensions: first, in its modes of architectural representation used, and second, in the utilisation of concepts such as Merleau Ponty's "flesh", which suggests that human bodies share basic attributes with the rest of the material universe. This fundamental interdependence between human life and the surrounding environment, so often evoked by architects such as Steven Holl, has been widely used in order to establish symbolic entanglements in between the user, the building and the site. Under this framework, buildings are understood to have a history of their own encounters with the world, and like Merleau-Ponty's ever-rolling snowball, its presence contain traces of their use accumulated gradually over their lifetime.

Projects like Holl's "Kiasma Museum" (1998) symbolically emphasize this "archive of encounters" through their unpolished materiality, which shows the different marks left during its process of construction and posterior use. In this case, the notion of atmosphere is conceptually used in order to evoke the underlying connection in between user, building and site: it operates as a sort of foggy patina that metaphorically unifies all actors. Well-known projects like Zumthor's "Therme Vals" (1996) illustrate the exaltation of these poetic, sensory and metaphorical intertwinings, particularly well described in Zumthor's book *Atmospheres* (2006).

Misty environments and nebulous spaces are also attributes that can be found in many works of art such as Olafur Eliasson's atmospheres. Space, for Eliasson, is not a container, but a material, and precisely for this reason his tangible atmospheres are deeply immersive and physically engaging. A similar effect occurs with architectural designs associated with distributive protocols, such as the "Blur Pavilion" (2003) by Diller & Scofidio, the "Augmented Atmospheres" (2014) project by the same authors, or the "Cloud Cast" (2015) project by Carlo Ratti. However, there is a crucial difference between the two types of projects: whereas the first two highlight phenomenological aspects through symbolic and metaphoric resources, the latter present an operative interaction with the milieu based on real-time information processing. Although they offer "misty" experiences that, in sensory terms, may be similar to phenomenological projects as Zumthor's "Therme Vals" (1996) or , they are not just contemplative, but substantially performative: their materialization deliberately alters measurable climatic values for the purpose of generating artificial sub-environments. This phenomena is particularly evident in Phillippe Rahm "Convective Apartments" (2010), described by the architect as "a thermal landscape with its different altitude of heat, temperatures, where the inhabitant could freely wander inside around like in a natural landscape, looking for specific thermal qualities related to the seasons or

_"Therme Vals", Peter Zumthor, 1996.

the moment of the day".[21] The operative vocation of Rahm's atmospheres is evident as well in its mode of representation. Rather than the models, sketches or watercolors used in the phenomenological atmospheres of Kerez, Zumthor or Herzog & de Meuron, Rahm represents his projects through data diagrams that permit the rigorous management of indicators. In this sense, the architect classifies his work through the concepts of radiation, conduction, convection, pressure, evaporation and digestion, that is, notions that are associated with the atmospheric quality of the space and to the human's body activity in it, rather than in the formal attributes that historically have been used to establish typologies.[22]

However and beside its operative capacities, the atmospheres proposed by these projects offer as well a subversive meaning. In this sense, the case of "Blur Pavilion" is particularly representative: contrary to the contemporaneous "transparence" denounced by Byung Chul Han[23], the "Blur Pavilion" is intentionally a low-definition and anti-spectacle device whose fog proposes an environment that is presented as "out of focus". By reducing the clarity of vision, the user experience becomes not just multi-sensorial, but also critical: the lack of visual evidence defies the well established current appetite for high definition visual media, immersive installations and hyper realistic simulations. Instead, it introduces Han's

_21. http://www.philipperahm.com/data/projects/convectiveapartments/

_22. Angélica Fernandez-Morales, "Evocar atmósferas. Arquitectura suiza contemporánea y su expresión visual del proyecto". *Boletín Académico. Revista de investigación y arquitectura contemporánea.* No. 4 (2014), 59.

_23. Byung-Chul Han, *The Transparency Society* (London: Stanford Briefs, 2010), 10.

_"Convective Apartments"; Phillippe Rahm, 2010.

negativity by presenting a rugous reality in which the repressive and hygienic transparency celebrated by modernism has been replaced by a thick and effervescent nebula: its dense atmosphere avoids transparent's tautologic immediacy, producing instead a mysterious, strange and sedate uncertainty. Under this framework and although its highly technological nature, the project of Diller Scofidio becomes the anti-modern device par excellence.

3.3 Climatic Landscapes

Far from manifesting as introverted bubbles isolated from the outside, this type of propagative environment is strongly entangled in its climatic landscape. However, these contextual complicities are not articulated through symbolic formal gestures, but through active hydro-termic intertwinings. This line of research is articulated through a series of multidisciplinary clusters, including several architectural designs that emerged during the first decade of the 21st century in association with different types of propagative actors. First, there are a number of notable publications, including the one we have already mentioned by Gilles Clement or the books by Phillip Ball *Self-Made Tapestry* (2009) and David Gissen *Subnature: Architecture's Other Environments* (2009). Second, there is also a more generalised and profound awareness of the environment that is complemented, third, with the use of new hardware (Arduino) or software technologies (Ecotect, Geco) to develop climate-related simulations. All these elements operate in conjunction, forming a large field of distributive forces whose "attractor points" are shaped over the course of the years.

Most propagative projects emphasize with clarity what Walter Benjamin calls "distracted perception"[24]: "Buildings can be received in two ways: through use and through contemplation. Or rather: tactilely and optically." As Eugenio Pandolfini reminds us,[25] this distracted perception does not represent the reduction of a hypothetical "attentive" perception: for Benjamin, distracted perception in the realm of architecture does not allude to a reduced perception; rather, it is inherent in the intimate and original relationship between architecture and human beings. Under this framework, the visual culture of the early 20th century differentiated between two modes of vision: the first is solely visual and refers to a view from a distance, an all-encompassing singular vision, a far-off image; the second is tactile, dynamic, and refers to close-range vision and a nearby image. Through this opposition, the omnipotence of the visual realm is questioned, expanding the aesthetic experience through the inclusion of the other senses, more intimate and linked by a synesthetic relationship. Walter Benjamin translates these concepts into the domain of architecture: for the German philosopher, in modernity the perception of architecture and art is distracted. In other words, it is more tactile than optical and, above all, it can easily become a habit. It is a mode of perception that does not necessarily set aside the sense of sight but incorporates it as a "haptic vision" – that is, a nearby, moving vision, associated with a more intimate and profound perception.

This distinction runs parallel to Deleuze's comparison between striated space and smooth space: while the first is associated with a fixed and far-off vision, the second implies a close-up and tactile perspective, or, as Deleuze calls it, a "haptic" vision: "Several notions, both practical and theoretical, are suitable for defining nomad art and its successors. First, "close-range" vision, as distinguished from long-distance vision; second "tactile" or rather "haptic" space, as distinguished from optical space. "Haptic" is a better word than "tactile" since it does not establish an opposition between two sense organs but rather invites the assumption that the eye itself may fulfill this non-optical function. [...] It seems to us that the Smooth is both the object of a close vision par excellence and the element of a haptic space (which may be as much visual or auditory as tactile). The Striated, on the contrary, relates to a more distant vision, and a more optical space – although the eye in turn is not the only organ to have this capacity."[26]

In that sense, and as we will see below, propagative designs are perceived through a variety of our senses – in other words, their aesthetic experience goes beyond the visual to include auditory and tactile phenomena. This kind of perception literalise Benjamin's distracted perception, where the reception of the project is integrated with the user in such a way that is no longer constituted as a visual experiential singularity and instead becomes a multisensory habit.

Citing some of the theses posited by David Gissen,[27] we could establish an initial group of propagative designs developed in close relation with water and its derivatives.[28]

The concept of humidity has generally been approached by architecture as a functional and symbolic inconvenience. Philippe Rahm rebelled against this when he presented

_24. Walter Benjamin, *The Work of Art in the Age of Mechanical Reproduction* (London: Penguin Publishers 2008), 112.
_25. Eugenio Pandolfini: "DustyRelief/BMU" in *Sobre Arquitectura moderna y contemporánea* (Madrid: Ed. Diseño, 2016), 256.

_26. Gilles Deleuze and Felix Guattari, *A Thousand Plateaus* (Minnesota: Ed. University of Minnesota Press, 1987) 492-3. Eugenio Pandolfini: "DustyRelief/BMU" in *Sobre Arquitectura moderna y contemporánea* (Madrid: Ed. Diseño, 2016), 260.
_27. David Gissen, *Subnature: Architecture's Other Environments*, (New Jersey: Princeton Architectural Press, 2009).
_28. The concept of humidity is closely linked to the idea of a "cave", which has given rise to all kinds of projects throughout the history of architecture, from Palladian "grottos" to Eisenman's excavations in Cannaregio.

_“Taichung Gateway Park”; Phillippe Rahm, 2008.

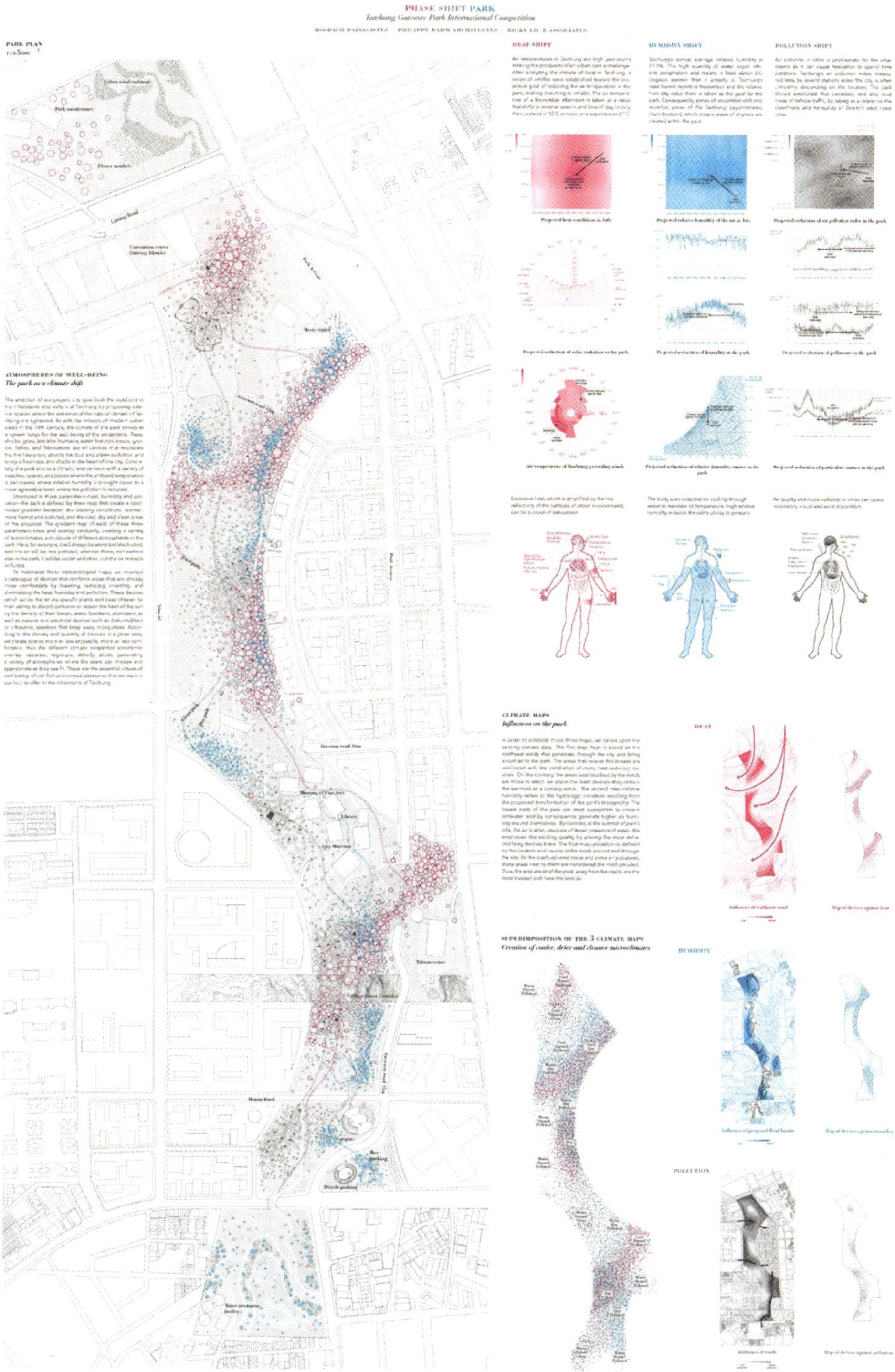

his "Underground Houses" project in 2005. In this work, the French architect proposes a series of semi-subterranean spaces which, depending on their depth, harness the underground environment in different ways, establishing a symbiotic relationship in which the design aims to take advantage of its situation for both heating and cooling. The architect proposes something similar in his "Mollier Houses" (2005): the residential complex is partially submerged in an aquatic medium, allowing the humidity gradually to take over each different unit of the residence and defining the uses for the spaces according to their individual humidity ranges. The humidity takes on a prominence that is not just perceived visually but also inevitably includes a tactile dimension.

Designs like the "Omnisports Hall" (1999) by Jean Gilles Décosterd can also be situated within the same line of research. The project consists of a sports center capable of condensing the H2O from the athletes' sweat and absorbing the CO2 from their breathing. Both are used to feed the plants that grow on the building's façade, which are also harvested as food for the athletes. Aside from the circular operativity of the project, there are notable symbiotic possibilities offered by the ensemble, for the mutual benefit of all participants.

During the same decade, a series of projects emphasized the use of water as the central propagative element, albeit in a liquid state. Traditionally, the presence of water in the built environment has been synonymous with disaster: particularly explicit in this respect are antique engravings by Piranesi and Robert Adam, as well as recent images of rivers overflowing their banks into cites. However, with their Super Galaxy (2009) project, Future Cities Lab's attitude is exactly the opposite. The project intentionally brings water into the building to interact with the environment through contamination or through the local flora and fauna, in order to generate a series of microclimates and unique light and sound conditions. The mechanism centers on leaving one floor open, where the levels above and below it are given an adjustable topography that can create different-sized puddles below and a series of aquatic bubbles above. This semi-aquatic environment fosters interaction with a variety of birds that benefit from these conditions, creating a true "interconnected environment" inside the building in keeping with the concept of planetary garden we described earlier.

Along the same propagative lines and following Gissen, another element that has also been a leitmotif in a number of designs is gas. As in the previous cases, the very idea of gas (and above all its derivatives in the form of pollution) has been read as problematic in architecture rather than as an opportunity. The effluvia characteristic of British industrial cities in the mid-19th century are a good example of this: the problem became so pronounced that maps were made of their spread through the cities of Manchester, London and Liverpool. The master plan for Reykjavic developed by Weather Architects (2007) inverts this logic. It maps the main pockets of steam distributed across the areas to be urbanized in order to organize the master plan based on their positions, promoting the generation of climatically unique spaces.

Similar concerns – in terms of scale and climatic questions – run through the project for "Jade Eco Park", by Phillip Rahm (2009). As the architect explains in his web page, "our design strategy is based on three major techniques: to spectralize the whole into single particles, to design the background rather than the foreground, and to compose by gradation rather than by lines."

The project manages to temper the warm climate of Taichung to achieve a series of microclimates, which reduce temperature, humidity and pollution. To that end, a series of dynamic flow simulations map the main currents of warm and cold winds, as well as pollution, to define the preexisting conditions in certain areas.

From there – and in keeping with a catalog of specific climatic devices – the most desirable conditions are emphasized. First, a series of natural mechanisms are applied: certain species are introduced to create heavy shade or to foster intense evaporation that can reduce the temperature of an area; or certain flowers are used, which reflect the sun's rays because of their size and color, to produce the same effect. Second, a series of artificial devices are installed, which emphasize the desirable existing conditions, adding mist, stimulating evaporation processes, reflecting sunlight, etc. This type of project can only be carried out with the implication of a certain environmental sensitivity, the pursuit of a performative integration of the environment, and a technological development which, both on the level of software (fluid simulation) and hardware (sensorization), makes it possible to optimize this type of dynamics. Here again, Benjamin's distracted perception is fundamental: the reception of the project is intimate and profound, taking hold more as a habit than as a singularity.

In addition to the concepts of humidity and gas, pollution (which is actually another type of gaseous manifestation) has also been the focus of architectural designs characteristic of distributive systems. In general, pollution has been and still is a serious problem for cities, which architecture has traditionally tried to isolate (or combat) in a hygienic vein, but without articulating the possibility of an operative symbiosis.

Yet that is precisely what François Roche proposed during the first decade of the 21st century, drawing on one of the most attentive architectural readings of Deleuze and Guattari. In his "B-mu Tower" (2002) a façade with an electrostatic envelope attracts the pollution produced by vehicles, which gradually accumulates on the façade, making citizens very aware of it. Unlike most of the propagative projects we have described here, in this project Roche does not promote an integration between the interior and exterior environment, but rather a contrast between them through an exercise in schizophrenia. While the interior is formalized through a Cartesian geometry – a stack of boxes that enclose an aseptic, deterritorialized, and timeless interior – the exterior façade follows a more irregular, non-Euclidean trajectory, as it is completed over time through the accumulation of pollution on its surface. In this case, the project combines the two perceptive types: while the interior space defined by Roche as "white cubes" is received as a strictly optical phenomenon, the exterior incorporates a tactile dimension that makes it more similar to Benjamin's distracted perception. Far from offering an image of salvation or redemption, the project exaggerates the danger of the external environment through the concentration of smog on the façades, isolating the museum's interior and depriving it of any relationship with the surroundings. By exacerbating this duality, the architect emphasizes the serious problem pollution represents for cities, in this case generating an interaction which, more than performative, (as in other projects by the same author like Acqua Alta or the Glass Museum) is communicative and/or provocative (in the sense of provoking, of eliciting a reaction). In the "Mosquito" project, also by Roche, the façade is given a thickness that lets a population of mosquitoes live inside it, coexisting with the inhabitant of the residence, separated

"Magic Mountain"; Amid.cero.9, 2004.

by a transparent surface. Again, the exercise experiments with a "living" material and with the unique human reaction resulting from such a domestic challenge, but there is never a true symbiosis between the two species. In this case and in the previous one, Roche addresses dangers – pollution in the first case, mosquitoes in the second – not through total exclusion, but through filters that mitigate fear: on the one hand, the danger is prevented from getting inside; on the other, users are allowed to accept the problem and become familiar with the sensations of it.[29]

In the "Magic Mountain" (2004) by Amid.cero.9 the entire building is covered with foliage, using a selection of species that have three functions: pollinate the environment, provide an animal habitat, and keep temperatures cool. The whole is structured through a system of "living" panels, alternating with a series of pots installed just inside the façade, which makes it possible to cover the building with the necessary flora to attract all kinds of small animals, like insects, butterflies and birds. With its propagative purpose, the project generates an environment that enters into a relationship of continuity with the surroundings, materializing the concept of the planetary garden and its motion.

3.4 "Guerrilla" Activism and Public Space

Simultaneous to this type of propagation typical of distributive protocols and its primary concern with establishing operative relationships with its social and ecological environment, in the first decade of the 21st century there is another type of propagation process associated with activism and social self-organization: processes with the potential to destabilize the social and political logics established by the dominant power.

Similar to the "Floating School" we mentioned earlier, this type of initiative does not necessarily use computer technology to carry out its proposals but bases its action on a "guerilla" strategy not all that far removed from sophistry and/or stratagem. A clear case of this phenomenon is the work by Santiago Cirujeda. By systematically detecting legal gaps in Spanish urban planning regulations, the architect implements several social proposals in neighborhoods around Sevilla and Madrid. The interventions show a high degree of community sensitivity: they are explicitly subversive, although most of them are rooted in urban planning legislation, where the regulations permit the temporary installation of urban furniture or scaffolding for construction. The architect takes advantage of some terminological ambiguity to manipulate these elements with the aim of improving public space, creating roof terraces or enlarging apartments. In most cases, these "urban recipes", developed with the participation and collaboration of networked collectives (including hackers, activists, up-and-coming urban planners, etc.), achieve broad functional and living improvements in urban spaces that would otherwise be residual.

Other projects along the same lines include those of "Ecosistema Urbano" in Madrid, or the mobile structures present in some of Andrés Jaque's designs. With limited means, both architectural studios produce results that are deeply collective, respectful with the environment and socially inclusive.

_29. Eugenio Pandolfini: "DustyRelief/BMU" in *Sobre Arquitectura moderna y contemporánea* (Madrid: Ed. Diseño, 2016), 264.

4- TRANSFERENCES

The projects mentioned throughout this text share fundamentally distributive protocols. Either by connecting networks or propagating environments, they operate based on the establishment of operative relationships between systems as opposed to their formal manipulation. As we have seen, these projects form a broad multidisciplinary cluster that is not limited to architectural design. On the contrary, it incorporates the technological, theoretical and socio-cultural elements that characterize the beginning of the 21st century. However, we can also recognize various elements of these "distributive protocols" both in the 1990s as well as in the second decade of the 21st century.

The former would include the early work on "www" protocols, the publication of *Global City* (1991) by Saskia Sassen, the contributions from Javier Echevarría with *Telepolis* (1994) and François Ascher *Métapolis or l'avenir des villes* (1995), as well as the initial developments of mobile phones or the birth of such important initiatives as "Google", "Amazon" or "Hotmail". Examples of the latter range from social phenomena like the refugee crisis or Islamic terrorism, to the emergence of products and proposals like "Smart Citizen" (2012) and applications deeply rooted in the network concept, such as "WhatsApp" (2011) or "Wallapop", (2012) as well as technologies that we find essential today, such as "Google Drive" (2011).

These elements are part of a series of multidisciplinary clusters whose focal points lie, as we have seen, in the first decade of the 21st century, despite the fact that several of its components may be found at other moments in time. That decade witnessed the emergence and consolidation of a new type of "advanced" – or "informational", more "distributed" architecture, in which the priority of the formal and topological resources characteristic of the conformative systems of the 1990s gave way to an architecture that was more concerned with interacting operatively with its environment through sensorized information, processed in a network and in real time.

It is a more performative and synergetic kind of architecture, less self-absorbed by its own formulations and with a much more explicit collaborative purpose. It is important here to make special mention of its independence from tendencies with a foundation that is more formal than truly responsive, such as parametricism – a movement that experienced intense growth in the first decade of the 20th century due both to access to new technologies like "Grasshopper" (2007) and to publications such as *The Autopoiesis of Architecture* (2010) by Patrick Schumacher or *Parametric Architecture* (2011) by Arturo Tedeschi.

Beyond a mere fascination with figurative metaphors associated with networks or atmospheres, distributive protocols construct a series of symbiotic complicities between ecologies, either through the interconnection of networks or the propagation of atmospheres. In any case, these are concepts and attitudes characteristic of the advanced architecture of 2000-10, which, as we will see next, the expansive protocols typical of the the next decade profoundly transformed in order to amplify their operativity.

"Cosmo"; Andrés Jaque, 2015.

EXPANSIVE PROTOCOLS 2010-2020

The Xenological Condition:
Mediating Agents and Performing Matter

THE XENOLOGICAL CONDITION

MEDIATING AGENTS

PERFORMING MATTER

XENO-SURREALISM

COLORARIUM

Expansive protocols operate through symbiotic entanglements. Their Xenological Condition consists in favouring intimate relations in between strangers; rather than autopoietic identities, expansive architecture aims for simpoeitic multitudes, that is, operative tunings in between ecological, biological, geological and algorithmic others. In resonance with the rise of artificial intelligence, Donna Haraway's multispecies and Eric Sadin's antrobology, expansive architecture assumes Rosi Braidotti's post-human subject: the human being becomes a moveable assemblage within a common life-space that s/he never masters nor possesses but merely inhabits together with a non-human community. Rather than unfolding a design framework based on geometric transformations or environmental transferences, expansive architecture produces multispecie enrichments, that is, symbiotic associations whose impact reverberates at multi-scalar distances.

Expansion implies thus miscegenation; it establishes bastard interlacements that doesn't constitute an additive and exceptional event, but an impure and tentacular regime that participates in a number of sequences every time more extensive of our quotidianity. In this scenario, expansive architecture operates by mediating agents and performing matter, that is, by crossing discrete species and synthesizing continuous substances.

These symbiotic articulations can be found in Philip Beesley's "Hylozoic Ground" (2010), Neri Oxman's "Silk Pavilion" (2013) and François Roche's "MMYST" (2015), but also in other disciplines during the same years: Neil Harbisson's cyborg constitution, Spela Petric's vegetal otherness or IBM's neuro-processors exemplify the desire for "operative miscegenations" characteristic of expansive protocols. These symbiotic intertwinings are constituted themselves as interactive platforms where the carnal co-habitation of (in)organic and evanescent bodies takes place.

1. Information as "Experience"
Information becomes experiential in a twofold sense. First, the recent carnal familiarity established with technology promotes a haptic informational interaction with humans that is no longer distant and visual, but intimate and multisensorial. Second, hyper-computational processes re-construct reality with a level of precision that positions the perception of this reconstruction as another experience in itself rather than as an abstraction of an experience.

2. Interaction in between "Species"
Interaction is multispecie: expansive architecture is "made out of" and "interacts with" sympoietic multitudes, independently of their algorithmic, biologic, geological or ecological nature. Rather than a human extension, interaction results in a multispecie expansion, an operative miscegenation that no longer fits into the classificatory epistemic categories characteristic of Modernity.

3. Transversality based on "Agents" & "Matter"
"Agents" and "Matter" are the result of a dense entanglement in between (in)organic bodies and digital codes. Its double ontology - physiological and evanescent - populates the planet with symbiotic aggregates that operate with and against us. In spite of their common triple condition - quotidian, nomadic and autonomous -, both differ in their formal constitution: while agents are discrete entities with an ubiquitous individuality, matter is a continuous substance with a synthetic structure.

4. Integration by "Mediating" & "Performing"
"Mediating" and "Performing" are two expansive processes of integration that produce multispecies entanglements. In spite of their common operative vocation, both processes differ in their mode of action: While "Mediating" promotes intimate and fruitful encounters in between physiological or/and evanescent creatures without compromising their agency, "Performing" is an artificial production that synthetises crossbreed aggregates.

5. Evolution as "Symbiosis"
Symbiosis occurs in the framework of punctuated equilibrium: It is not the result of a constant and gradualist trajectory of optimisation, but it is a set of sudden leaps interspersed with longer periods of relative stability. Symbiosis produces irreversible turning points: flashes of evolutionary lightning that generate novelty by bringing together individuals whose alterity fuels the complementarity of their capacities.

6. Openness based on "Platforms"
A platform operates as a digital/physical infrastructure that mediates in between heterogeneous groups of behaviours. It is not an empty and neutral space exterior to its agents, but a behaviour in itself with a double purpose: on the one hand, platforms provide assistance by supplying specific tools, products and services, and on the other hand, platforms regulate activity by structuring development processes under a specific ideological regime.

7. Heterogeneity as "Xenology"
Xenology consists in the full consideration of the radical "other" as an operative and self-governing being. It forms part of a moveable assemblage within a common life-space that is never under its complete possession. Independently of its geological, biological, algorithmic or ecological nature, its world's inhabitation is always in a community, a pack, a group or a cluster. Xenology therefore doesn't refer to a system of relations (topology) or to relations in between systems (ecology), but to systematic entanglements in between others.

AT IT MEANS TO LIVE IN THE NETWORK SOCIETY - S. Shaviro, 2003
MULTI STRING - Manuel Gausa, 2012
THE ZERO MARGINA
COPENHAGUEN WHEEL - Carlo Ratti
SMART HOME - Carlo Ratti, 2012
WORK SOCIETY - Manuel Castells, 2000
REASSEMBLING THE SOCIAL - Bruno Latour, 2005
SUPERMARKET OF THE FUTURE - Carlo Ratti, 2017
A NEW PHILOSOPHY OF SOCIETY - Manuel Delanda, 2006
WATER PAVILION - Carlo Ratti, 2008
PETITE POUCETTE - Michel Serres, 2013
EMERGENCE - Steven Johnson, 2001
BITFALL - Julius Popp, 2006
THE THIRD INDUSTRIAL REVOLUTION - Jeremy Rifkin
THE BOTTOM IS NOT ENOUGH - Kevin Kelly, 2008
4G, 2008
OBAMA VICTORY, 2008
FACEBOOK - Mark Zuckerberg, 2004
THE TRANSPARENCY SOCIETY - Byung Chul-Han, 2012
FACEBOOK ICELAND CONSTITUTION, 2011
OPEN SOURCE ARCH
YOUTUBE - Chad Hurley, Seteve Chen, Jawed Karim, 2005
WHATSAPP - Jan Kuom, 2009
NET - Terrorism
ISLAMIC STATE, 2014 (prominence)
NYU CUSP - Amand
WIKIPEDIA (WP) - Jimmy Wales, Larry Sanger 2001
INSTAGRAM - Systrom, 2010
NET SPACES - Kathrine Willis, 2017
SMART CITIES - Anto
LE EARTH - Google, 2001
WIKIHOUSE - 00, 2011
DROPBOX - Houston, Ferdowsi, 2007
REDES DE INDIGNACIÓN Y ESPERANZA - Manuel Castells, 2012
LAB - Carlo Ratti, 2004
WATER CUBE - PTW Architects, 2008
NET-SOCIAL MOVEMENTS
IF MAYORS RULED THE WORLD - Ben
TOMS - Neil Gershenfield, 2001
MEDIA TIC - Enric Ruiz Geli, 2009
ANONYMOUS, 2003
ARAB SPRING, 2010-12
GLOBAL COVENANT OF MAYORS FO
Guallart, Müller, Gausa, 2001
FAB LAB, Neil Gershenfield, 2001
15M SPAIN, 2011-15
SEVILLA SPIDER - Santiago Cirugeda,
N DESIGN LAB - Laura Kurgan, 2004
SMART CITIZEN, IaaC, 2013
FINANCIAL CRISIS, 2008
UMBRELLA MOVEMENT, 2014
John Palmesino, 2007
HOW TO MAKE ALMOST ANYTHING - Neil Gershenfield, 2005
MAKOKO FLOATING SCHOOL - Kunlé
ARDUINO TECHNOLOGIES - IVREA, 2005
CUPULA MILENIO - Enric Ruiz Geli, 2011
NET-BUILDINGS
DIGITAL CRAFTS
GUERRILLA ACTIVISM
IPAD - Apple, 2010
SUPE
HURRICANE, 2005

DISTRIBUTIVE PROTOCOLS

KINDLE- Amazon, 2007
JARD
POB
TUVALU CLIMATIC REFUGEES, 2009
NYC AQUARIUM - Enric Ruiz Geli, 2006
CONNECTED - Christakis, Fowler, 2009
COS
MAGIC MOUNTAIN - Amid.cero.9, 2002
BEC
, 2002
CITY TOWER - Ken Yeng, 2005
EARTH SUMMIT RIO II, 2012
SCA
TIGE, 2001
GEOLOGICS - Vicente Guallart, 2009
ECO
OPEN LANDSCAPES
SOCIAL URB-NATURES
G ISLAND GREEN DOME ,2005
ECO BOULEVARD - E. Urbano, 2007
SUPER BLOCK - Salvador Rueda, 2004
Braungart, McDnough, 2002
UNEXPECTED GARDEN - Carlo Ratti, 2008
TECH-ATMOSPHERES
PROJECT - Nicholas Grimshaw, 2001
VERTICAL GARDENS - Patrick Blanc, 2004
HEROUS FOREST- Amid.cero.9, 2011
VERTICAL FOREST - Stephano Boeri, 2015
GECO PLUG-IN - Uto
SPORT PLAZA - Venhoeven, 2006
ECOTECT - Autodesk, 2008
Combination of narrative atmospheres
HISTORIA DE LA MEVA MORT - Albert
HIGH LINE - Diller-Scofidio, 2009
CONVECTIVE APARTMENTS - Philippe Rahm, 2010
THE THIRD LANDSCAPE - Gilles Clement, 2003
JADE ECO PARK - Philippe Rahm, 2016
CLOUD CAST - Carlo Ratti, 2015
UNPLUG TOWER - François Roche, 2002
SUBNATURE - David Gissen, 2009
AUGMENTED ATMOSPHERES - Diller-Scofidio, 2014
DUSTYRELIEF/BMU - François Roche, 2002
THE BLUE ECONOMY - Gunter Pauli, 2014
OMNIS PORTS HALL - J.G.Décosterd, Rahm, 1998
TERRITORIAL ATMOSPHERES
BIG LEAKS - Jeffrey Inaba
FUKUSHIMA ACCIDENT, 2011
CTURE - Philip Beesley, 2006

Propagating Atmospheres

VATNSMYRI URBAN PLAN - Sean Sally
MANHATTAN ATMOSPHERES - David Gissen, 2014
ge, 2006
TAICHUNG GATEWAY - Philippe Rahm, 2012
N PROJECT - Aranda, Lasch, 2004
MORPHO ECOLOGIES - Achim Menges, 2006
ATMOSPHERIC COLOUR ATLAS - Olafur Eliasson, 2009
ECOLOGICAL URBANISM - Mostafavi, Doherty (eds), 2010
THE SELF-SUFFICIENT CITY - Vicente Guallart, 2014
MOLLIER HOUSES - Philip Rahm, 2005
CITIES PROTOCOL - IAAC, 2011
PAI
FOREST HOTEL - Enric Ruiz Geli, 2009
ARC
, MacCannell, 2001
FAR FROM EQUILIBRIUM - Samford Kwinter, 2008
NATURALEZA Y ARTIFICIO - Iñaki Ábalos, 2009
alakis, Young (ed), 2001
JARDIN D'EAU/ORTIES - Gilles Clement, 2007
ADAPTIVE ECOLOGIES - Theodore Spyropoulous (ed), 2013
ENED OUT - Jean Baudrillard, 2002
DIGITAL PAVILION - ONL
THE MARTIAN - Ridley Scott, 2015
MEETING NATURE H
VIRTUAL MOVEMENT
KINECT XBOX - Microsoft, 2010
H.CERAMIC - IaaC, 2
URBANEER - Terreform, 2009
PLAYSTATION MOVE - Sony, 2010
MAT-AERIAL - IaaC,
PARADIGMS - Mosé Ricci, 2012
THOUSAND ECOLOGIES - Eric Hörl, 2009
SIXTHSENSE (dev) - Pranav Mistry 2009
HYLOZOIC GROUND - Philip Beesley, 2010
VIBRANT ARCHITECTURE - Rachel Armstrong, 2015
SYSTEMIC ARCHITECTURE - Claudia Pasquero; Marco Poletto, 2012
WEARABLES ARRIVAL
ALGAE MACHINES
THE SILENCE OF SLIM MOULDS - Andrew Adamatzky, 2014
ALGA(E)ZEBO - Cruz, Colletti, 2012
BLACK ECOLOGIES - IAAC, 2019
HYLOZOIC GROUND - Philip Beesley, 2010
BRAGA PAVILION - Poletto-Pasquero, 2015
A. WATCH - Apple, 2015
INHUMAN GARDENING - Poletto-Pasquero, 2015
LIVE CYCLES - IAAC,
BRAILE GLOVE - Ryan Patterson, 2002
BIQ HOUSE - ARUP, 2013
SYNTHETIC BIOLOGY - D. Nestbeth, 2016
GOOGLE GLASSES - Google, 2013
ALIVE: NEW DESIGN FRONTIERS - Carole Collet, 2013
VIRT
FITBIT STEP COUNTER - Fitbit, 2010
DIGITAL POETICS - Marjan Colletti, 2013

Performing Mat

WANDERERS - Neri Oxman, 2014
ECOLOGICAL THOUGHT
GREY ECOLOGY - Paul Virilio, 2009
SPACESUIT - Nicholas de Monchaux, 2011
GENERAL ECOLOGY - Hörl, Burton (eds) 2009
THE DISAPPEARING COMPUTER - Streitz, Mavrommati, Kameas, 2007
TOWARD AN ECOLOGY OF MATERIALS - Timothy Ingold, 2012
SLOW FURL - Mette Thomsen, 2008
MATERIAL COMPLEXITY - Manuel Delanda, 2004
DARK ECOLOGIES - Timothy Morton, 2016
DOWN TO EARTH -
MATTER MATTERS - Manuel Delanda, 2005
VIBRANT MATTER - Jane Bennett, 2009
NOTES TOWARD A PERFORMATIVE TH
MATERIAL ELEGANCE - Manuel Delanda, 2007
NEW MATERIALISM - Dolphin, Tuin (eds), 2012
PRINTED PHYSICS -
DELANDA & MATERIALITY
Urban Future
BAF
MEETING THE UNIVERSE HALFWAY - Karen Barad, 2007
ABSTRACT SEX - Luciana Parisi, 2004
NEW MATERIALISMS: ONTOLOGY, AGENCY, AND POLITICS - Coole, Frost (eds), 2010
NEW MATERIALISMS
WHAT IS POSTHUMANISM? - Cary Wolf, 2010
WAY - Dean Kamen, 2001
DEEPMIND - Hasabis, Legg, Suleyman, 2010
SCRIPTING CULTURES - Marc Burry, 2011
THE POSTHUMAN - Rosi Braidotti, 2013

EXPANSI

THE NATURE OF CODE - Daniel Shiffman, 2012
POSTHUMANISM - Pramod K.Nayar, 2013
POSTHUMAN AGENDA
M
COUNTRYSIDE AGENTS
S - Gilberto Esparza, 2008-13
OBJECT-ORIENTED ONTOLOGY
WALL-E FOR COWS - ACFR, 2013
IN
her, 2012
THE QUADRUPLE OBJECT - Graham Harman, 2011
SWAGBOT - Salah Sukkarieh, 2016
PL
ROBO-ARCHITECTURE
N SAGA, 2000-2019
THE DEMOCRACY OF OBJECTS - Levi Bryant, 2011
ROBOTIC BUILDIN
HYPEROBJECTS - Timothy Morton, 2013
URBAN AGENTS
ECHO - Amazon, 2014
ROBOLOG - Log, 2
WATSON JEOPARDY - IBM, 2011
TRUENORTH - IBM, 2014
THE SECOND DIGI
GENESIS REDUX - Jessica Riskin, 2007
HOW TO CREATE A MIND - R.Kyrzweil, 2012
ON-SITE ROBOTICS
OGAMES - David Calkins, 2005
ACCELERANDO - Charles Stross, 2005
TESLA ROADSTER - Tesla, 2009
SCALED ROBOTICS
THE COMPANION SPECIES MANIFESTO - Donna Haraway, 2003
AUDI URBAN FUTURE - BIG, 2010
ADVANCED ROBO
G - Ben Fry, Casey Reas, 2001
EMPIRICISM AND OBJECTIVITY - Philippe Morel, 2004
GOOGLE CAR - Goggle, 2012
THE SHED - Diller-
MULTISPECIES
ELYTRA FILAMENT
TAIPEI PERFORMING ARTS CENTER - Kokkugia, 2010
HOW WILL WE LIVE TOGETHER? - Ve
onemberg, 1999
ANEMONE 0.4, 2014
HOMAGE TO LYNN MARGULIS - Sho
FAÇADE - Mateas, Stern, 2005
EMOTIVEWALL - Mark David Hosale, Chris Kievid, 2009
WHEN SPECIES MEET- D. Haraway 2
1997
INFLUX AND EFFLUX - Jane Bennet
ZOO-AGENTS
THE EYE OF THE OTHER - MAEID, 2020
MANIFESTO CONTRASEXUAL - Paul Beatriz Preciado, 2000
TESTO YONQUI - Paul Beatriz Preciado, 2008
SILK PAVILION - Neri Oxman, 2013
MMYST - François Roche, 2015
MOSQUITO HOUSE - François Roche, 2003
STRELKA, 2009
BIOTIC PLANET Lynn Margulis, 1998
COMPANION SPECIES MANIFESTO - Donna Haraway, 2003
ANIMAL ETHOS - Lesly Sharp, 2018
CONFESSIONS - Marina Abramovic, 2010
MIN
HYBRID WEBS - Tomás Saraceno, 2010
FREEMO VR - Straw Lab, 2017
Figurative Agent
PITCH BLACK - Hernan Díaz Alonso,

2000 - 2010

SOCIETY - Jeremy Rifkin, 2014

▲ THE GLOBAL TRANSFORMATION OF TIME - Vanessa Ogle, 2015
× ZOOM VIDEO, 2020 (generalisation)
× TEAMS, Microsoft 2017
× MIRO, Andrey Khusid, 2020

RE - Carlo Ratti, 2014
2013
n, 2015
□ FAB CITY - IAAC, 2014
arber, 2013
TE & ENERGY, 2016

CONNECTING NETWORKS

■ EDIBLE PARK - Nils Norman, 2010
ni, 2013
PARK - Topotek + Big, 2012
BILES - Coloco, 2017
S. BLOCK - IAAC, Serra, 2017
drés Jaque, 2015
Atxu Amann, 2018
Andrés Jaque, 2012
RD - ECOSISTEMA URBANO, 2007

● GILLETS JAUNES, 2018

FIGURATIVE FOG
◆ FOG ASSEMBLY - Olafur Eliasson, 2016
◆ LONDON FOG - Fujiko Nakaya, 2017
◆ BLIND LIGHT - Antony Gormley, 2007

LANDSCAPE PILING

013
□ THE VERTICAL VILLAGE - MVRDV, 2012
□ THE 5TH CITY - Peter Trummer, 2012
□ DONGGUAN MASTERPLAN - Steven Holl, 2012
■ L'ARBRE BLANC - Sou Fujimoto, 2019
▲ WASTE TIDE - Chen Qiufan, 2019
× DYNAMO - Chris Georgiev, 2015
■ QIYI CITY FOREST GARDEN - 2018
■ INSTITUTO LIBRE ENSEÑANZA - Amid.cero9, 2014
□ LIUZHOU FOREST CITY - Stefano Boeri, 2017
▲ LANDSCAPE AS URBANISM - Charles Waldheim, 2016
■ ASI Reisen Headquarters - Snohetta, 2019

PROPAGATING ATMOSPHERES

▲ DECOLONIZING NATURE - T.J.Demos, 2016
EMENT - UNFCCC, 2016
● GRETA THUNBERG COP25, 2019
URAL CLIMATES - Philippe Rahm, 2018
+ BIO TALLIN - Poletto-Pasquero, 2017
■ ROBOTIC HABITATS - Noumena, 2017
- Marjan Colletti (ed), 2018
▲ THE ARCHITECTURE OF CLOSED WORLDS - Lydia Kallipoliti, 2018
▲ LANDSCAPE AS URBANISM - Charles Waldheim, 2016
▲ ENSAYOS SOBRE TERMODINÁMICA - Iñaki Abalos, 2016
× CREATION ARTIFICIAL DNA, 2016
▲ ACTIVE MATTER - Skylar Tibbits, 2017
■ LIGHT CEMENT - UMSNH, 2015
◆ BIOPLASTIC CHAIR - Terreform 1, Genspace, 2014
■ SELFREPAIR CONCRETE - TU Delft, 2014

MIXED REALITY

■ JARDINS DE METIS - Bitonti, Zientek, 2019
◆ DATALAND: THE LINQ - Refik Anadol, 2019
■ THE LONG NOW - Sean Sally, 2018
◆ THE THIRD GLASS - Damjan Jovanovic, 2017
× THE GARDEN WORLD - Damjan Jovanovic, 2020
▲ SCREEN WORLD - Liam Young, 2019
■ STEAMPUNK PAVILION - Jahn, Newnham, Hahm, Pantic, 2020
× HTC VIVE - Vive, 2016
◆ MARIO KART HOME - Nintendo, 2020
× MICROSOFT HOLOLENS - Microsoft, 2016
× APPLE LIDAR - Apple, 2020
LITY AND THE BUILT ENVIRONMENT - Jennifer Whyte, 2002
× GOOGLE GLASS - Google, 2013
× FREEMO VR - Straw Lab, 2017
× OCULUS RIFT - Oculus, 2012
× TRIMBLE CONNECT - Trimble, 2017
▲ THE VIRTUAL STATE AND THE FALL OF EMPIRES - Mychilo Cline, 2013

PERFORMING MATTER

tour, 2018
▲ THE ANTHROBSCENE - Jussi Parikka, 2015
Guests & Hosts ◆ WESTWORLD - Nolan, Joy, 2016
ASSEMBLY - Judith Butler, 2015
▲ THE QUESTION CONCERNING TECHNOLOGY IN CHINA - Yuk Hui, 2016
n, Hovestadt (eds); 2013
Why Factory, 2015
Trans-inclusivity ▲ XENOFEMINISM - Helen Hester, 2018
▲ CLOSE UPT AT A DISTANCE - Laura Kurgan, 2013
▲ PHYSARUM MACHINES - Andrew Adamatzky, 2010
◆ IRIDESCENCE - Behnaz Farahi, 2019
◆ APOPHENIA - Ruy, Klein, 2018
▲ ARE WE HUMAN? - Colomina, Wigley, 2016
◆ ASTROCYTE - Philip Beesley, 2017
● COVID PANDEMIC, 2020

PROTOCOLS

▲ L'HUMANITÉ AUGMENTÉE - Eric Sadin, 2013
◆ PAHOEHOE BEAUTY - MAEID, 2018
◆ TERRESTRIAL REEF - MAEID, 2019

ARTIFICIAL INTELLIGENCE

ELOCITIES - Benjamin Noys, 2014
▲ L'INTELLIGENCE ARTIFICIELLE, OU, L'ENJEU DU SIÈCLE - Eric Sadin, 2018
THE FUTURE - Snicek, Williams, 2016
▲ LA VIE ALGORITHMIQUE - Eric Sadin, 2015
+ THE ARCHITECTURAL BEAST - Hernan Díaz Alonso, 2019
CAPITALISM - Srnicek, Williams, 2016
▲ LA SILICOLONISATION DU MONDE - Eric Sadin, 2015
◆ DEEP MEDITATIONS - Memo Akten, 2018
ool, Jiménez, Retsin, Soler (eds), 2019
▲ TARSS - RC3 Unit Bartlett B-PRO, 2017
◆ MEMORIES OF PASSERSBY I - Mario Klingemann, 2018
THE SOUL AT WORK - Williams Srnicek, 2009
■ THE SOUND AND THE FUTURE, ALEX SCHWEDER, 2015
- Mario Carpo, 2017
▲ FULLY AUTOMATED LUXURY COMMUNISM - A. Bastani, 2019
+ CITY INTELLIGENCE LAB - Angelos Chronis, 2019
Tecnalia, 2017
+ CODER LE MONDE - Pompidou, 2018
▲ CONTAGIOUS ARCHITECTURE - Luciana Parisi, 2013
× 5G, 2020
Maggs, 2018
◆ AUTO-MÀTIC - Edouard Cabbay, 2018-20
□ WANDER YARDS - Daniel Koehler, 2017
× INTEL LOIHI - Intel, 2017
ISTRUCTION - ACT, 2016
□ BLOCKERTIES - Daniel Koehler, 2018
2019

Mediating Agents

◆ CONTROL - Casey Rehm, 2016
N - Achim Menges, 2016
◆ HER - Spike Jonze, 2013
× HOUDINI, 2015
nnale, 2020 (2021)
▲ STAYING WITH THE TROUBLE - Donna Haraway, 2017
▲ HOW TO SPEAK MACHINE - John Maeda, 2019
Dubiner, 2012
▲ THE MULTISPECIES SALON - Eben Kirksey, 2014
▲ ESPECIES DEL CHTHULUCENO - Maria PTKQ (ed), 2019

MEDIATING AGENTS

GAMING

■ CHANGING ADAPTIVE STRUCTURE - Areti Markopoulou, 2017
◆ CTRL - Michael Sedbon, 2018
■ BLOOM - Alisa Andrasek, Jose Sánchez, 2013
NG
■ CITY GAMING - Play the City, 2016
□ FULFILLMENT CENTER - Greg Lynn, 2016
■ REDESIRE - Rezone, We are Muesli, 2016
◆ POKEMON GO - Nintendo, 2016
□ BLOCK'HOOD - José Sánchez, 2017
■ POBLEJOC - IAAC, 2020
- Markus Persson, 2011
▲ ARCHITECTURE FOR THE COMMONS - José Sánchez, 2020
▲ PERVASIVE GAMES - Ian Bogost, 2010
▲ THE GAME - Alessandro Baricco, 2019
Limits as vincles ▲ PLAY ANYTHING - Ian Bogost, 2016

- 2020

EXPANSIVE PROTOCOLS
2010-2020

THE XENOLOGICAL CONDITION: MEDIATING AGENTS AND PERFORMING MATTER

Jordi Vivaldi

1. THE XENOLOGICAL CONDITION

1.1. Black Gaia: The End of the Great Outside

1.2. Carnal Technologies: Algorithms and Promiscuity

1.3. Plastic Corporalities

2. MEDIATING AGENCIES

2.1. Allonomy, Autonomy, Automation

2.2. Animality: Symbiotic Constructions

2.3. Urban Supercomputation: A City of Quantities

2.4. Neighbourhood and Gaming: Re-presentation versus Re-presentification

2.5. Frontier Geologies

3. PERFORMING MATTER

3.1. Matterlessness

3.2. Synthetic Materiality

3.3. Organic Machines: From Artefacts to Artifices

3.4. Mixed Reality and the Inhabitation of its Pictorial Multiverse

4. XENO-SURREALISM

4.1 Presentation and Re-presentation

4.2 Automatism as a Device of Displacement

4.3. The Conjunction of Opposites: Closeness and Distance

COLORARIUM AUTOM-ACTING AGENTS & PERFORMING MATTERS UNDER AN ACTANT XENOLOGICAL CONDITION

Manuel Gausa

1. PERFORMING MATTERS

2. AUTOM-ACTING(ACTIVE/ACTIVATORS AS NEW MEDIATORS)

3. ACTANT XENOLOGICAL CONDITION

JORDI VIVALDI

EXPANSIVE PROTOCOLS 2010-2020

The Xenological Condition: Mediating Agents and Performing Matter

I- THE XENOLOGICAL CONDITION

Earthing with organic and inorganic beings that are no longer subordinated to the humans, but attuned to a vast litany of species. This is the purpose of the cultural condition alluded to here with the term *xenology*. In spite of its wide speculative vocation, the concept is rooted in the immediacy of our here and now: the hole in the ozone layer, frozen seed banks, global pandemics, xenobots, ocean garbage patches or transgenic animals[1] constitute some of those strange objects invading our world while circumventing the epistemic categories characteristic of Modernity. Bastard creatures conforming a vast litany of multispecie entanglements, eclectic composites and hybrid processes resulting from intimate relations between strangers, between "others", between xenos.

The xenological condition thus accounts for a new sensibility towards the biological, ecological, algorithmic and geological other: intelligent robots, planetary viruses, digital boots, human-made earthquakes, transgenic plants, etc. The otherness evoked by these creatures is no longer that of a "Galilean object" and its perpetual human subjugation, but that of an emancipated active being, a "Lovelockian agent"[2] that mutates and evolves in community with different forms of life: human and nonhuman, organic and machinic, cultural and natural. Thus, far from the invariably vampirized mark of alterity of classical

_1. Maria Ptqk, *Especies del Chthuluceno* (Bilbao: Gabinete Sycorax, 2019), 29.
_2. "With Galilean objects as the model, we can indeed take nature as a "resource to exploit," but with Lovelockian agents, it is useless to nurture il.lusions. Lovelock's objects have agency, they are going to react [...] and it would be naïve to believe that they are going to remain inert no matter how much pressure is put on them."
Bruno Latour, *Down to Earth* (Madrid: Gedisa Editorial, 2013), 229.

philosophy or the fetishized and necessarily othered other of deconstruction, the other is understood here as "a moving horizon of exchanges and becoming, towards which the non-unitary subjects of postmodernity move, and by which they are moved in return"[3].

As such, the vocation characteristic of this set of protocols is not constituted through a system of relations (topology) or through a set of relations between systems (ecology), but through systemic relations between self-governing "others" (xenology). In this context, the human being is no longer a privileged creature, but a moveable assemblage; it inhabits a common life-space that is never under its complete possession, but rather shared with a collective of human and nonhuman others. [4]

These multispecie entanglements are modulated in experimental architecture as a set of expansive protocols. The term "expansion" should not be read here in opposition to that of "reduction"; under the xenological condition, to expand does not mean to grow, to increase, or to add. It also does not mean to generalize or to spread. Instead, expansive processes are processes of deviation; they operate through recursive compressions that are not necessarily spatial but performative: the miscegenation of different species results in multi-dimensional "inclinations" based on qualitative variations rather than on quantitative extensions.

The notion of simpoeisis is pivotal in expansive processes. Following Donna Haraway and in opposition to what autopoiesis suggests, agency is not something that is made by itself but rather mutates and evolves together with others.[5] It is rooted in symbiotic interactions, capable of producing novelty through the intimate nesting of different agents. As argued by Lynn Margulis, "Symbiogenesis brings together unlike individuals to make large, more complex entities [...] that become multiunit symbiotic new individuals."[6] This reflection, as we will see in what follows, reverberates with most of the experimental architecture produced through expansive protocols.

Expansive Protocols presents one of the most difficult tasks for critical analysis, because we are a part of it and lack perspective. Besides, the experimental nature of advanced architecture is particularly present in this period; most of the projects presented here are closer to the format of the installation or the performance rather than to the solidity and large scale characteristic of architecture that remains outside the experimental realm.

Besides a number of exceptions, expansive architecture has been operating so far through pavilions, prototypes, houses, wearables, apps or light structures. Contrary to what it might seem, the small scale of these formats does not diminish its operativity: its light and agile constitution promotes its quick implementation in a series of real scenarios where its effects have been tested with a wide variety of results.

The impact on experimental architecture produced by the xenological condition occurs through a threefold influence: it affects our relation to nature, our relation to technology, and our relation to the body. As we will see next, the figure of Black Gaia and its desire for *earthing*, the carnal technologies associated with an algorithmic promiscuity, and the plastic corporalities related to human's subjectlessness, constitute a relevant part of the cultural background in which expansive architecture is inscribed.

_3. Rosi Braidotti, interview by Rick Dolphijn and Iris van der Tuin, "Interview with Rosi Braidotti" in *New Materialism: Interviews and Cartographies* (Open Humanity Press, 2012), 23.
_4. Rosi Braidotti, *Lo Posthumano* (Madrid: Gedisa Editorial, 2013), 229.
_5. *Donna Haraway, Staying with the Trouble: Making Kin in the Chthulucene* (Durham: Duke University Press Books, 2016), 126.
_6. Lynn Margulis, *Symbiotic Planet* (London: Basic Books, 1998), 9.

1.1 Black Gaia: The End of the "Great Outside"

Under the xenological condition, the tender and benevolent notion of mother nature becomes obsolete. Its idyllic, pristine and indulgent vocation is questioned by the emergence of Black Gaia, a narrative mode of *earthing with others*, a terrestrial sensibility, a logic of otherness. In resonance with thinkers such us Timothy Morton, Slavoj Žižek or Bruno Latour, the figure of Black Gaia not only challenges the boundaries between life and non-life, organic and inorganic, human and inhuman, but offers, above all, an alternative narrative.

Leaving behind a contemplative, harmonic, cyclical, patriarcal and normative mother nature, a techno-natural continuum emerges in its place: performative, chaotic, unpredictable and manipulable, it reveals itself as artifice rather than as artifact; it does not operate solely as a hyper-technological gadget but constructs a collective fiction: it renounces to a secularized version of the Eden Garden and its Adamian conception of the human in order to speculate instead about a subject that has become "a nomad assembly in a shared life space that it does not control or own. S/he just occupies it, always in community with biological, technological and cultural others."[7]

Black Gaia negates nature. Or better, it ignores it, it renders it obsolete: nature is no longer an exterior framework, a transcendent source of vitality to which we should establish any sort of connection. There is no longer a "Great Ouside": once Modernity's classifications have been blurred, nature becomes everything, that is, nothing: an empty term, a placeholder. Nature is irrelevant. Black Gaia's focus points instead to the Earth; *Gea, Terra, Tellus*. The Earth as a compost, as a conglomerate participated by humans. Participating: partaking, forming part; rather than inhabiting the Earth, humans are Earth, or better, humans *Earth* (verb). Humans are no longer driving Buckminster Fuller's Spaceship Earth as adventurous pilots scrutinizing Universe's corners with a wandering rocket. Humans are not the pilots of a spaceship. Humans are spaceship, together with a vast letany of organic and inorganic species.

Black Gaia is a de-mothering force. Ah, physis and maternity! An intimate and ancient union, a marriage sanctified by one of those totemic figures that underpins the western culture: *Gea*, *Ge*, also known with the terms *Gaya or Gaia*. As an invisible force or as an animate being, *Gaia* is the ancient mother, the roman *Tellus Mater* and the miscenic *Ma-ka,* the greek mythological and "universal mother who nourishes everything there is both on this holy land and in the sea and all that flies"[8]. As *naturata naturata* or as *natura naturans*, Gaia, the "wide-bosomed" Gaia, brings all to fruition; Gaia spreads vitality, Gaia favours abundance. Gaia is maternal protection. But, how to explain Dolly 's clonation under Gaia's immaculate mantle? How Gaia's pristine warmth could embrace something as dark and corrupt as a Xenobot? Transgenic plants, living machines, ocean garbage patches: dark bastardizations and perverse recombinations conjuring up multispecie compounds that oppose the pure and maternal spirit of Gaia. Mestizo and clandestine, Black Gaia negates Gaia. It brandishes an anti-maternal and anti-natural narrative; it presents a chaotic, immanent and finite Earth earthing, a myriad of organic and inorganic beings navigating across the universe under the sole light of their own free associations.

_7. Rosi Braidotti, *Lo Posthumano* (Madrid: Gedisa Editorial, 2013), 229.
_8. Homer, *The Homeric Hymns*. Translated by Thelma Sargent. (London: Norton Library, 1975), 213.

Black Gaia provides darkness. Darkness; the field of the unknown and the kingdom of the possible. Darkness; question and mystery, fear and fascination. Darkness; astonishment, surprise, tension. Vertigo. Gaia's ideological basis is subverted; Black Gaia perturbs Gaia's white, eurocentric, heterosexual and patriarchal modulation of Gaia by opposing its reactionary Christian appropriation. Associated with a virginal and secularized Eden Garden, the figure of Gaia is presented as a harmonic, cyclical and tender Mother Nature. Under the neoliberal notion of Green Ecology, Gaia is revealed as a new opium for the masses: a reactionary force that imposes an unquestionable authority, obstructs alternatives, identifies sins, applies punishments and, above all, defines moral values. In return, it offers a "promised land": the return to an immaculate nature, purified through the domestication of a modern man whose excessive artificiality has transformed the planet into a denatured place. The logic orchestrated by Black Gaia is exactly the opposite. Faced with a hyper-technified world, it offers more technology. Faced with an inhuman world, it offers more otherness. Faced with an alienated world, it offers more alienation. And, above all, faced with an adulterated world, it offers more artifice. Biological agents, ecological agents, technological agents and cultural agents cooperate in a reality that is no longer constructed based on Promethean epics, relativist ironies or primitivist nostalgia, but accelerated hybrids: poly-plural constructs blurring the borders between modern epistemic taxonomies.

Black Gaia does not redeem the excesses of the modern man. In opposition to the Prometeic pretensions of Gaya's green ecology, Black Gaia does not respond to a natural crisis. It is not meant to offer salvation from an apocalyptic dystopia, nor does it offer the nostalgic protection of a virgin nature: it does not yearn for a green planet; it does not exalt sustainability as a technocratic elixir. Black Gaia represents the accelerated reaction to an ontological crisis: that of naturalism, of positivism, of relativism. It stages resistance to a hierarchical understanding of the world, a world that still operates based on a 1000-year-old dichotomy: the confrontation between nature and artifice as irreconcilable opposites rather than as promiscuous reverberations. *Promiscuus*; the favouring (pro) of mixtures (miscere); the promotion of mutual exchange, the end of maternal protection, the replacement of domination by deviation, the desire for inclination, the viscous and permeable presence of an Earth no longer objectualized in front of us but enmeshed and intertwined; an Earth earthed by us and earthing through us.

Black Gaia is tactile. Where distance was what once broadened the mythical reach of Gaia's sacred nature, Black Gaia exalts intense contiguity; it embraces carnal technologies based on a new mythology of digital artifacts favouring a relation with the algorithmical, biological or ecological other that is no longer rooted in the insurmountable physical separation characteristic of Modernity, but rather in a carnal familiarity whose experience is not just sensory but also sensual. Radically pagan, Black Gaia is decipherable and manipulable; the propagation of artificial intelligence and the multi-scalar robotization of the organic establishes, in addition to a change of medium, a change of condition: its algorithmic power does not merely offer itself as an automatic pilot for daily life, but it also triggers a radical manipulation of Gaia's Adamian corporality: it sets up a perennial and universal intertwining between bodies and information that opposes Gaia's unpenetrable nature. The multidisciplinary generalization of machine learning, the progress in genetic engineering or the robotization of the mundane no longer refer to a humanity that is merely extended, but to a humanity that is expanded, that is, inclined, or better,

_"Ectogenesis&Phytoteratology" Spela Petric, 2016

deviated: it is woven by algorithmic, biologic, and ecologic agents whose symbiosis is not only metaphorical or figurative, but performative.

Accelerated and accelerative hybrids; multispecie composts distanced in equal measure from the blind gears of Modernity and the lived flesh of Phenomenology. Symbiotic aggregates and narratives of bastardization; strange creatures deviating any pristine and ideal origine, impure and irregular bodies, algorithmic folds, bionic composites, saturated nestings, ecological miscegenations.

Cartographical rather than classificatory, and, above all, anti-maternal, anti-natural and anti-humanist, Black Gaia is nothing but the radical *earthing* of our planet; it prompts the deployment of architectures based not only on processes, bastardizations and performances, but also on specific and hyper-realistic artifices. They no longer take shelter in abstraction, historicity or language, but are constituted as an operative assemblage: corrupt, rugged, disturbed, mestizo and definitely dark, the mysterious and the strange do not adjectivize experimental architecture based on suggestive allegories or salvific narratives, but through a performance that is more disturbing than it is redeeming. It confirms that there is no longer a "Great Outside"[9], that there can no longer be life stripped bare, that there is no longer a pure and transcendent nature to which we can always return.

The promiscuous architectures unfolded under the shadows of Black Gaia resonate with an increasingly artificialized society which assumes that the future is a better guide for the present than the past.[10] Although distributive protocols reveal a much more operative approach to nature than that of conformative protocols, during this third period this tendency is accelerated by the recognition of a nature-culture continuum, that is, a bio-scientific compost in which it is increasingly difficult to establish distinctions.

One of the main symptoms of this phenomenon has to do with the progress of biotechnology: the cloning of Dolly the sheep in 1996, the complete mapping of the human genome in 2006 and the creation of artificial DNA in 2016 marked, in 10-year increments, decisive advances in the understanding – and above all in the manipulation – of phenomena that were once considered the exclusive domain of nature. Many socio-cultural contributions resonate with these three advances, some of which are particularly emblematic: the artwork by Stelarc, especially "ExtraEar" (2007), the "Eyeborg" of Neil Harbison (2005), Spela Petric's "Ectogenesis/Phytoteratology" (2016), Anabel Quincoces' "Transmutación 11. Abisal Spaces" (2017), the rise of self-made prostheses, the first bacterium synthetically produced by the biologist Craig Venter (2010), the multidisciplinary exhibition "Alive: New Design Frontiers" (2013), or the advances resulting from the combination of nanotechnology and neurology.

As we will see in what follows, advanced architecture resonates with these multidisciplinary contributions. However, it has not modulated them through the geometrical operations typical of conformative protocols or the environmental transfers characteristic of distributive protocols, but through intimate entanglements associated with symbiotic processes: on the one hand, expansive protocols mediate between the behavior of biological agents and that of ecological, geological or algorithmic agents – like in François Roche's "MMYST" (2015) or Neri Oxman's "Silk Pavilion" (2013); and, on the other hand, they perform matter through a mixture of natural and technological compounds, as is the case with IaaC's "Bioplastic" (2016) or "Graphene" (2017).

_9. Bruno Latour, *Down to Earth* (Cambridge: Polity Press, 2018), 68.
_10. Avanessian Reis, "Introducción" in *Aceleracionismo* (Buenos Aires: Editorial Caja Negra, 2017), 25.

_"Mirny Mine" Staselnik (Photographer), 2014

In this context, the expression "green ecology" is progressively being replaced by Paul Virilio's "Grey Ecology" (2010) or Timothy Morton's "Dark Ecology" (2016), expressions in which the meaning of the word "ecology" is expanded in order to include technological and human agents. One of the clearest examples of this phenomenon is the recent rise of unconventional computing. Andrew Adamatsky defines it as "not just uncovering mechanisms of information processing in natural systems and using these mechanisms to develop novel architectures of computers but also in uncovering other ways, similar to alternative states of mind, to compute."[11] In this scenario, the term nature is understood as computing matter: "Brain is a computer, neuron is a computer, cytoskeleton of neuron

_11. Andrew Adamatsky, "Nature as Computing Matter", *IaaC Bits*, no. 9 (2019), 96.

is a computer, lipid vesicles along cytoskeleton filaments are computers, DNA molecules inside neuron's nucleus are computers."[12] In that sense, "man-made computers, as we use them, are part of natural computers, they are just extensions of our building computing abilities, in the same way as spiders outsource their intelligence to their web."[13] However, the intertwining of human artificiality and nature is not limited to the molecular level. It also takes place on large territorial scales in which the city is becoming a new infrastructural ground for the production of a new city, as part of the work of Peter Trummer in the Institute of Advanced Architecture of Catalonia suggests. The "Manufacturated Landscapes" (2018) of Edward Burtynsky are also a good examples of this phenomena.

_12. Ibid.
_13. Ibid.

Moreover, and aside from particular phenomena such as the ocean garbage patches, the slow but inexorable warming of the globe and the consequent rise in sea level, human beings are capable of producing large-scale natural disasters much faster and without realizing it.

The earthquake produced in Yunnan in 2014 as a consequence of the dam built by the Chinese government close to the city is not just a good example of this phenomena, but it also illustrates the need for a new approach to the Earth in order to understand its entanglement with the human being. The controversial term "Anthropocene" represents one of the most ambitious attempts in this direction. Defined by Bruno Latour as "the most decisive philosophical, religious, antropologic and political concept ever produced as an alternative to Modernity's ideas"[14], the notion of Anthropocene opposes the confrontation between our inherited idea of the world and its geologic and evolutionary reality; under its gravitational field, the *anthropos* is no longer the delirium of a species who believes itself alien to its own environment, observing it from afar as though it were a spaceship under its command.[15] Conversely, the Anthropocene aims to counter this deterritorialized planetary consciousness. However, even if it efficiently accounts for the human being as a geological force that has an impact on the planet, it still "centers its answer on the same techno-scientific and epistemological tools that have provoked it".[16] Thus, the Anthropocene orchestrates a narrative that still operates through a human-centered approach: it conjures up a mother-planet that paradoxically needs to be protected from the humans by the humans. According to Haraway, this approach seems to ignore the fact that change and evolution are always defined by narratives in which organisms adapt, mutate, mix, compete and collaborate in order to survive in environments that are always unstable. In this sense, Haraway's proposal of the Chthulucene, inspired by Lovecraft's tentacular character, emerges from the desire to orchestrate other modes of naming the world – that is, other *wordlings* that rather than orbiting around the human being, fluctuate through the vast myriad of species that populate the Earth.

Within this framework, expansive protocols do not insist on the ecologism that emerged at the end of the 60s and still widely present today. Prompted by documents such as Stewart Brand's *Whole Earth Catalogue* (1968-1972), William Ander's *Earthrise* (1968) or Buckminster Fuller's *Operating Manual for Spaceship Earth* (1969), this ecologism is emblematic of a human-centered narrative driven by a human that is literally positioned as exterior to its environment.

Expansive architecture will instead understand nature as a technologized territory of dissens in which the human being is no longer approached as an exterior entity observing the planet from outside, but as a terrestrial creature in coexistence with a litany of species. Among them, there is not a relation of natural harmony, but a relation of political tension that implies the presence of an ecological approach in which nothing is so sacred that cannot be reenginered and transformed. Opposing thus the naivety represented by the puritan greenery characteristic of green ecology, technology, often understood as a heteropatriarchal construct, no longer operates as a mechanical gear opposed to nature; it becomes instead a potential sphere of activist intervention whose carnal vocation replaces its industrial desire for optimisation by xenological processes of deviation and inclination.

_14. Bruno Latour, *Facing Gaia: Six Lectures on the Political Theology of Nature*, Edinburgh, University of Edinburgh, 2013
_15. Maria Ptqk, *Especies del Chthuluceno* (Bilbao: Gabinete Sycorax, 2019), 26.
_16. Ibid.,27.

"Adumbrate" Faculty: Peter Trummer / Student: Kavya Jose , 2019.

1.2 Carnal Technologies: Algorithms and Promiscuity

In one of his most famous reflections on the figure of the craftsman, Richard Sennett wrote that humans are "programmed to make things with their hands".[17] This statement is founded on a very particular conception of the human being: we are not satisfied with the mere external or intellectual perception and execution of the activities in which we participate; we need them to condense into an experience with direct ties to our particular psychomotor nature. Far from suggesting a neo-Luddite attitude complicit with regressive thought, this affirmation posits a serious cross-disciplinary challenge: so far, informational technologies cannot fulfill that requirement, since their tasks consist of storing, transmitting and processing data, which does not necessarily favor an interaction with human beings that is aligned with our multi-sensitive psychomotor nature.

During the second decade of the 21st century, the information age – essential to distributive protocols – has been supplanted by the experience age. One highly emblematic indication of this development is the shift from "Facebook" (2004) to "Snapchat" (2012). "Facebook" is characterized above all by generating an identity based on the accumulation of information: a priori, the first act a "Facebook" user must do is update his or her personal status bar – information that is then stored permanently in the system and which any authorized user can access simply by scrolling down. These features are characteristic of the information age. In contrast, "Snapchat" prioritizes the immediacy of the experience: users generate an identity that is no longer based on the intermittent stockpiling of written information but rather on the continuous broadcast of a bodily expression. In this context, information is no longer presented as a parameter or an indicator, but as an experience in itself – in other words, as a life event. This shift has involved a concerted effort from the world of technology to integrate ICT not only into our everyday habits and routines, but literally into the materiality and dynamics of our bodies.

Indeed, the transmission of information is no longer a discontinuous singular event but becomes a multi-sensory habit that is not just part of our daily lives, but it also participates in the constitution of our carnal corporality. In this way, the digital processing of information is no longer thematized as such, dissolving instead into the flow of our daily experience. Under this umbrella, humans's relationship with technology is not just customized or personalized, but intimate: technology does no longer operate through isolated objects distanced from us, but it is constituted as a promiscuous layer intertwined with our corporality. As we have previously stated, the term "promiscuous" should be read in its latin etymological register: promiscuus, the favouring (*pro*) of mixtures (*miscere*), that is, the promotion of mutual exchange. Thus, we are no longer under the modern understanding of technology as a physical apparatus of domination; technology operates here as a distributed dispositif of deviations, a viscous and permeable strata whose presence is no longer identified and thematized, but diffused and confused through the intimacy of its enmeshment with us.

The case of the sense of touch is probably the most representative. Whereas in the 1950s touch was still associated with the dazzled humility of the populace as, with intimidated ingenuity, they ran their fingers over the surfaces of their technological totems, the generalization of tactile interfaces in our times has reversed the roles: where distance was what once broadened the mythical reach of the technological object, now it is exalted by

_17. Richard Sennett, *The Craftsman* (New Haven: Yale University Press, 2009).

increasingly intense contiguity. As a result, a vast letany of digital artifacts emerges based on a carnal understanding of technology: the relation with the technological other is no longer rooted in the sacred distance characteristic of Modernity, but rather in a carnal familiarity whose experience is sensory, sensitive and sensual. Tactile interfaces, voice commands, facial recognition, the identification of gestures, etc., emerge as ergonomic principles rooted in the fluidity and immediacy of the most primitive of experiences, thus naturalizing the algorithmic management of information. Despite the wide variety of technological innovations that illustrate this phenomena, one point remains invariable: the desktop PC era is over. One of the most emblematic examples is wearables – that is, technologies that are no longer set out on a table like a computer but are connected to the morphology and mechanics of our bodies: smart watches and bracelets, shoes and clothing with microprocessors embedded in them, smartphones with augmented reality, computerized glasses, etc. One of the most emblematic cases is that of Neil Harbisson, whose antenna, which he had implanted in 2004, allows him to hear frequencies generated by the light spectrum, including invisible colors such as infrared or ultraviolet.

That is just the beginning, however: the idea is not simply to accompany human beings in their experiences, but to play an active role in the production of human experience. With that idea in mind, in 2015 Nintendo launched its smartphone game "Pokemon Go". Through the use of the phone's camera, the video game intersects our physical reality with elements of virtual reality, thus forming a third reality we might call "augmented". In that sense, the expression "augmented reality" not only refers to the informational strata that overlap with our immediate apprehension of things, but confirms a hybrid condition:[18] it represents an intimate blending of the body and the deductive power of processors.

This marks the end of the digital revolution, because the digital no longer operates within the framework of exceptional events, but rather in the context of domestic habits; a dual regime is thus constituted, operating as an expansion of our day-to-day life. In this new ontological scenario, computational power not only adheres to our bodies but "acts as body", altering how we perceive the world, like in the case of "Google Glasses" (2012). The latter are a very clear example of the progressive technological condition embedded in the expansive systems we referred to earlier: our physical reality is qualitatively deviated -expanded- through the different layers of information it merges with in order to produce a unified reality.

However, this integration is not merely general and symbolic but singular and operative: on the one hand, it is extremely specific in that it responds with precision to a particular spatio-temporal situation; on the other, it generates a complete fusion between its components, which goes beyond the mere programmatic or environmental interaction of earlier conformative or distributive protocols.

Other contemporary technological developments, in this case by Microsoft, have taken a similar direction. First, the company's "Hololens" glasses (2014) respond to a design experience that incorporates the use of physical gestures in a very natural way, letting the user mold shapes directly in space. Second, the "Kinect" device lets the system interpret body movements very precisely, giving rise to a series of applications that are activated through our physical gestures, as opposed to an aseptic communication of orders. However, perhaps the most eloquent technological example of expansion is the contact lens patented by Sony in 2017: a seemingly conventional device that, once

_18. Eric Sadin, *L'humanité augmentée. L'administration numérique du monde* (Paris: Ed. Éditions L' échappée, 2013), 32.

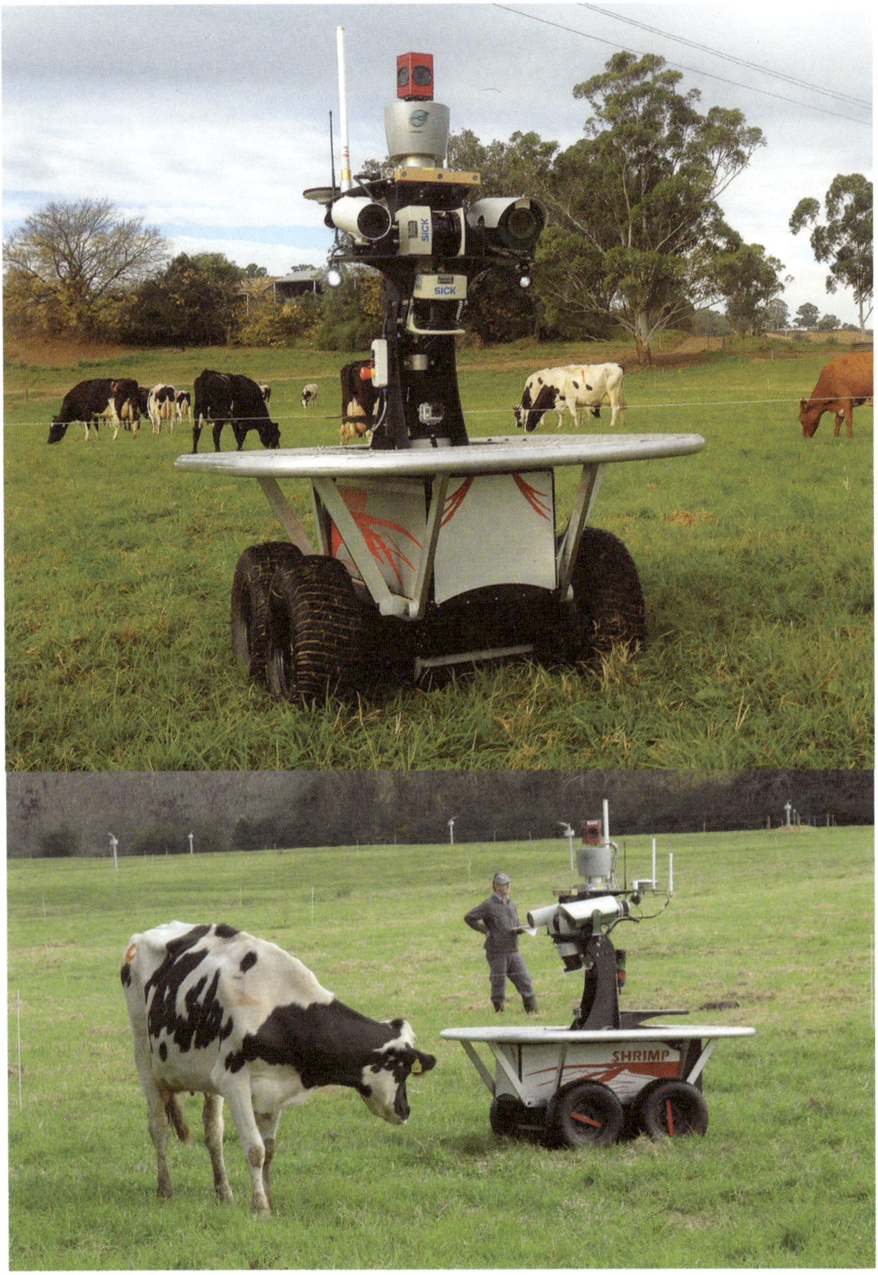

_"Wall-E for cows", Australian Center for Field Robotics, 2013.

attached to the cornea, lets users record everything they see, while also adding new layers of information. In this scenario, sight is no longer a human instrument meant to receive light from outside, but instead becomes a hybrid device aimed at superimposing new dimensions onto our reality.

Faced with a dual ontology that is no longer alluding to Heideggerian human nudity but to a planet inhabited by algorithmic beings that live with and against us, Eric Sadin defines this technological scenario as antrobological. This notion expresses the "increasingly dense intertwining between organic bodies and "immaterial elfs" (digital codes)"[19]. The propagation of artificial intelligence and the multi-scalar robotization of the organic establishes, in addition to a change of medium, a change of condition: its algorithmic power does not merely offer itself as an automatic pilot for daily life, but it also triggers a radical transformation of our human nature, setting up a perennial and universal intertwining between bodies and information; if in the 90s bits were associated with atoms, bits are now associated with cells such as neurons, myocytes or keratinocytes. In this sense, the multidisciplinary generalization of machine learning, the progress in genetic engineering or the robotization of the mundane no longer refer to a humanity that is merely extended, but to a humanity that is expanded, that is, inclined, deviated: it is woven by algorithmic, biologic, and ecologic agents whose symbiosis is not only metaphorical or narrative, but performative. Under this scenario, "artificial extelligence" becomes "artificial intelligence" through a process of in-corporation: intelligence, the *eidos*, what has traditionally been understood as form, is no longer an external entity that articulates (in)organic bodies from outside, but it is carnally embedded in them. However, rather than as a legendary form of alien cognition *in silico*, it is more reasonable to consider machine learning as an instrument of knowledge magnification that performs pattern recognition[20]. This epistemological demystification is foundamental in order to secularize Artificial Intelligence from the auratic narrative of autonomy that underpins a neoliberal practice worldwide: the growth of a geopolitical regime of high-tech companies invisibilizing workers' autonomy through a corporate apparatus of knowledge extractivism and epistemic colonialism. In this sense, the age of experience and the intimate relation established with the technological other amplifies one of the main dangers associated with the information society: the loss of critical perspective. As argued by Byung-Chul Han, "the negativity of the 'other' or the 'strange' has been eliminated: it perturbates the flat and smooth communication of the transparent society"[21]. According to Han, the exhibition society, the evident society, the porn society, the accelerated society, the immediate society, etc. are all expressions emphasizing a type of society in which mystery, strangeness and secrecy have been set aside for the sake of an "easy" and, above all, "superaccesible" society.

What Han does not mention is to what extent this decade's age of experience increments that danger. Indeed, in a society based on continuous informational immediacy, any possibility of generating critical distance is discounted, because it obstructs the compulsive consumption established by the markets. In that sense, the era of experience does not tend to mitigate this danger, since, as we have seen, it suggests precisely the opposite; it aims to further reduce the distance between action and reaction, that is, to reduce the

_19. Eric Sadin, *L'humanité augmentée. L'administration numérique du monde* (Paris: Ed. Éditions L'échappée, 2013), 46.
_20. "As an instrument of knowldege, machine learning is composed of an object to be observed (training dataset), and instrument of observation (learning algorithm) and a final representation (statitical model)." See: https://www.skynettoday.com/editorials/nooscope?fbclid=IwAR0c2YwJmn6utSwp-YQSyBcaAKe0oiQgVPMmS4VyY_mehy4SYoA5WkhlkNQ
_21. Byung-Chul Han, *The Transparency Society* (London: Stanford Briefs, 2010), 10.

lapse between input and output in order to favour communication. This phenomenon suggests the advent of a new type of control over human beings. Whereas in the 1970s Foucault differentiated between the public, celebratory and exhibitory punishment to which medieval prisoners were subject and the private, secret and enclosed punishment characteristic of Bentham's Panopticon, today we are experiencing what might be called an Omnipresent Panopticon. As is well known, in the medieval punitive system prisoners occupied the center of the public square. In the modern punitive system, the jailer takes position in the center of the panopticon, and in this case he is surrounded by the inmates. In the age of experience, at a time when computer and information systems are no longer used discreetly but continuously in both time and space, control is no longer perspectivistic and executed by isolation; instead, it is dissolved in each of these devices and executed by hypercommunication. In other words, control is digitally integrated into our own experience. A number of science fiction series, like "Westworld" (2016), have been based on an Orwellian-like technological dystopia, inspired by this type of omnipresent control promoted by a particular instrumentalisation of Sadin's algorithmic otherness. In this context, phenomena like "post-truth" or "hyper-normalization" foster an extremely stable and uniform political scenario that, following Fischer, makes it easier to imagine the end of the world than the end of capitalism.[22]

As such, and as we will see in detail later, the experimental architecture of these years has partly abandoned the Promethean epic characteristic of Modernity: salvific tales such as "green ecology" or "social emancipation" have been mitigated in favour of other aesthetic and performative narratives. Mark Fisher alludes to this political scepticism when he affirms that "capitalism seamlessly occupies the horizons of the thinkable"[23], including concepts such as "alternative" or "subversive". Under this umbrella, and faced with a technological scenario that seems to be orchestrated by the political right, some accelerationist strategies such as those defended by Benjamin Noys in *Malign Velocities* (2014) claim that, although technological innovation may have been prompted by capitalism, its instrumentalisation is not necessarily limited to the frameworks of the established system.

On the contrary, accelerating their development may be the only way to push the system beyond its limits. Accelerationism argues the need to re-articulate and promote the productive forces engendered by neoliberal ideology to make them into a jumping off point for a post-capitalist future: an alternative to capitalism can only be imagined from the advent of a post-industrial world. From that standpoint, we can interpret part of this decade's advanced architecture as a subversive architecture: although the technological otherness articulated by robotization, artificial intelligence, synthetic materials, etc. comes from the broad corporative powers of the establishment, its entanglement with expansive architecture is not necessarily derived from an intent to celebrate the capitalist system that engendered it, but rather from a desire to overcome it. Rather than reducing the potential offered by these technologies to the speculative realm, the establishment of a political agenda is crucial in order to approach social inequalities and the associated lack of affordable housing. As we will see in detail later, most expansive designs during this decade offer their users greater levels of autonomy and preparation, drastically reducing their dependence on large corporations.

_22. Mark Fisher, *Capitalist Realism: Is There No Alternative?* (London:Ed. Zero Books, 2009), 8.
_23. Ibid., 14.

1.3 Plastic Corporalities

The emergence of the xenological condition has also modified our understanding of the human body, positioning it as a potential site for feminist technopolitical intervention. If Deleuze and Guattari stated that they wrote *Anti-Oedipus* together and since each of them was several, there was already quite a crowd[24], the plastic corporalities characteristic of the xenological condition should be read as multispecie crowds; the "I" is now possessed by a plethora of others, it is a body touched and infused by absolute *arrivants,* autonomous agents not necessarily posited as invaders or occupiers, but as alien creatures whose most immediate circumstance is that of *arriving from abroad.* "L'homme-type", the modulor muscleman characteristic of modernity, has mutated: it has been reshaped under a combination of prosthetic devices that perverts the clean and pristine harmony traditionally associated with the Adamian body, replacing it with what we define with the expression "plastic corporalities" and its twofold instrumentalization of the term "plastic".

First, plastic corporalities are "plastic" in the sense of opposing any naturalisation of the human body: under this scheme, the body operates as a moveable and impure assemblage, an organic device in constant exchange and symbiosis with a myriad of algorithmic and biological others. Far from being impenetrable castles with defined and rigid contours, plastic corporalities are porous and permeable, absorbent sponges contrasting with the sliding hardness of marbles. The poliplur alities constructing them are no longer reducible to the organic realm, but expanded through a series of algorithmic and robotic folds that deviate its strictly "natural" constitution.

Second, plastic corporalities are "plastic" in the sense of being able to assume, without collapsing, permanent deformations, that is, deformations that cancel its original condition once the deviating forces are no longer operating. Thus, plastic corporalities oppose resilience; they are not preceded by any initial point where to return in case of collapse. They are instead in constant variation, in constant movement and vibration, animated by a set of transformations that are not accumulative as a set of compiled layers, but reformulative in its permanent fluctuation. Following Catharine Malabou, plasticity, in opposition to resilience, implies indeed the emergence of a new form, but it also entails the permanent destruction of the previous one. In spite of keeping it as an imprint, it becomes increasingly difficult to recognize the past in its new identity.

The decentralization of the human being proposed by post-humanism has been crucial in this process of de-naturalization. Although tentatively manifested at the end of last century, post-humanism has been consolidated and radicalized during the past decade by a series of thinkers who explicitly define themselves as post-human. Publications such as Rosi Braidotti's *The Post-Human* (2012), Cary Wolfe's *What Is Post-Humanism* (2010), and Pramod K. Nayar's *Post-Humanism* (2014) account for a philosophical current whose decentralization of humanity resonates with a series of technological developments belonging to our times. Raymond Kurzweil's *The Singularity Is Near* (2005) or Stuart Armstrong's contributions to the "Singularity Summit" (2012) emphasize the adherent presence of an algorithmic otherness whose self-governance is increasingly palpable. Contemporary science fiction has also devoted a lot of attention to the subject, both in literature, with works like Charles Cross' *Accelerando* (2015), and in cinema, through commercial films such as Spike Jonze's *Her* (2013) or Alex Gandarld's *Ex_Machina* (2015). In this sense, some advances in artificial intelligence have literally decentralized the human being: the

_24. Deleuze and Guattari, *A Thousand Plateaus* (Minnesota: University of Minnesota Press, 1987), 3.

"Google Car" (2012) and Tesla vehicles (2015) provide a driving experience in which the human driver is secondary, as it is also the case with drones or driverless submarines. Likewise, the technification of agriculture has not been free from this type of technology: several prototypes for robotic "farmers" and "ranchers" are able to maneuver through mountainous areas in order to control and herd livestock. IBM has also made decisive advances in the ability to replace human beings with its Watson computer; the computer's victory in 2011 on Jeopardy showed its ability to handle metaphors and wordplay, representing one of the most celebrated technological successes involving artificial intelligence. Computational agents develop, in this context, a certain taste for sociality, becoming thus a sort of conversational beings whose evanescent presence permeates the traditional epistemic categories of modernity. Human's de-centralization suggested by post-humanist thinkers and by the self-governing capacities of the algorithmic other reorient the approaches to the body characteristic of modernity and phenomenology. While the former approached the body as a mechanic machinery and the latter as a holistic lived experience, expansive protocols understand it as a multispecie device, an aggregate made up of a wide variety of biological and algorithmic processes.

Modernity's conception of the body is Cartesian: the body is a mechanic artefact whose operativity is strictly reduced to the physical realm. The understanding of the body as a machine is at the core of the modern practice of medicine: under its umbrella, the body is, above all, a *divisible* body. The possibility of a body's zonification allows for treating its dysfunctions as local and limited, ignoring those parts that are not explicitly affected.

Instead, rather than conceiving the body as a *res extensa* whose parts are juxtaposed like in any mechanism, phenomenology emphasizes the holistic lived experience of it. Merleau-Ponty's differentiation between the body as object (Korper) and the body as subject (Leib) is revealing: while the former is subject to the forces of reality like any other object, the latter is not known as something external, but is experienced in the first person. This second aspect is what Merleau-Ponty defines as "flesh", and it encompasses – in addition to the materiality characteristic of any body – all kinds of impulses, desires, appetites and fears. The body belongs to the order of the subject, but also to the order of the object: both are constituted by "flesh", that what allows a reciprocal insertion and intertwining in between body and world. The body is thus not a divisible body, but a lived body: a body that is experienced from within, in its entirety, and, above all, *as* world rather than *in* the world.

The plastic corporalities characteristic of expansive protocols adopt the holistic conception of the body associated with the phenomenology of Merleau-Ponty and its Heideggerian reformulation. However, the bareness of the Heideggerian body is expanded by intersecting it with a dense tissue of algorithmic and biological processes; the question is not just that of creating cyborgs augmented by artificial organs, but of intertwining them with data that is individually adapted to each of our particular situations. These devices are not only in contact with or attached to the body; they are integrated with it to the point of constituting an algorithmic fold rather than a robotic addition. This dual regime – biological and algorithmic – recognizes the uniqueness of each being, offering each individual an enriched -expanded- present based on an affective computing that is not limited to logistical aspects but incorporates an emotional dimension.

Expansive protocols constitute thus plastic corporalities, heterogeneous composts distanced in equal measure from the blind gears of Modernity and the lived flesh of Phenomenology; symbiotic aggregates deviating the pristine and ideal conception of

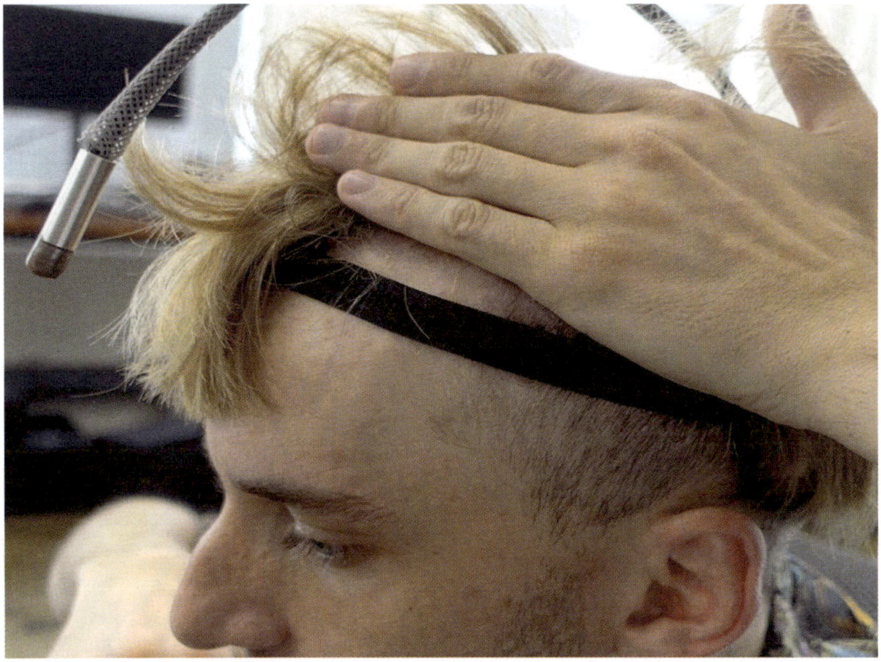

_"Eyeborg", Neil Harbisson, 2014.

the Adamian body: impure and irregular, plastic corporalities are intimately intertwined with a series of algorithmic and biologic agents, producing a miscegenation in which it is increasingly difficult to differentiate the original components. Under this umbrella, the body can no longer be understood as a starting point for our human nature, but rather as a multispecie process, a set of rhythmic relations through which the divine origin of the Christian body is inclinated: the artistic work by Stelarc, Orlan or Harbisson, and the investigations of Nery Oxman, with "Wanderers" (2015), or that of Behnaz Farahi, with "Bodyscape" (2017), illustrate the extent to which part of the experimental architecture of this period will no longer respond to a strictly biological or biographical corporality. Instead, it recognizes its algorithmic dimension as intrinsic, that is, as an inner fold of its constitution rather than as a mechanical appendix. The fact that an increasing number of the body's surfaces are being covered and traversed by digital flows represents a form of inseparable interlacement between biological and robotized organisms: it constitutes a physiological interweaving that opposes the naturalized vision of the body in its modern divisibility or in its phenomenological liveability. Its aggregated constitution inevitably evokes fictional figures such as Golem or Frankenstein; hybridized corporalities whose menacing monstrosity emanates from their ability to surprise and exceed the expectations of their multiple anonymous designers. The xenological condition characteristic of this third period should be read as the multidisciplinary background in which advanced architecture deploys two expansive strategies: first, the mediation of agents, and, second, the performance of matter. Both cases qualitatively amplify its conventional constitution through bio-technological symbiotic processes in which the simultaneous participation of human and non-human species is decisive.

2.0 MEDIATING AGENTS

The mediation of agents consists in the facilitation of symbiotic scenarios without compromising individual agency, independently of the agent's human, biological, algorithmic or ecological nature. It does not necessarily aim at harmony and it does not preclude conflict; it does not look for consensus, but for the emergence of mutualist processes through the perennial modulation of different interests.

The symbiotic requirement characteristic of this decade resonates with the question posed by the curators of the Venice Biennale 2020: "How will we live together?". Under this scenario, architects are no longer bringing multitudes together just as human beings, who, despite their increasing individuality, need to inhabit communities that demand equity and inclusion, but also as species that coexist with other species across digital and real space.

A great part of the experimental architecture of this decade deploys this mediation through expansive strategies, that is, processes of deviation consisting in the recognition and amplification of the autonomy deployed by each agent in relation to multispecie communities.

2.1 Allonomy, Autonomy, Automation

The notion of "Alllonomy"[25] refers to a transdisciplinar condition that builds on the kantian concepts of heteronomy and autonomy. It consists in the recognizement of the capacity of all surrounding objects -and not just the object in its selfness, as would be the case of autonomy- to produce its own *nomos*, that is, it's own "form", independently of their human, ecologic, zoologic or algorithmic nature. In this sense, it is crucial to differentiate it from the notions of automation and autonomy, whose etymology is particularly revealing: while the former involves elements that "move" on their own (*auto matos*), the latter involves elements that "govern" on their own (*auto + nomos*). Automated elements are deterministic artifacts located outside the system that governs them. We consider them to be *first-order cybernetic systems*: their main function consist in executing patterns that have been established previously by other entities. This group would include architectural designs in which behaviors have been pre-established. The vast majority of digital manufacturing projects involving robots fall into this category.

The ICD/ITKE "Research Pavilion 2012" (2012) or Gramazio and Kohler "Flight Assembled Architecture" (2012) are good examples of it; Kuka robots or drones execute orders based on a minimum degree of autonomy. This fact does not detract from the value of those projects, but it does limit their interest as expansive architectural designs: automated processes applied to manufacturing are tantamount to the assembly line, characteristic of modern 20th-century industry, although their applications in architecture began at a later date. Something similar can be identified in projects like Diller & Scofidio's "The Shed" (2019). As the New York-based architects proclaim, the building contracts and expands by rolling a large telescopic roof on rails, in what seems, finally, to be the construction of the famous Archigram sketches. However, there is no autonomy in this movement; in spite of being metaphorically suggested by the animal-like form of the drawings produced by the British group, the movement is nothing but the automated execution of a pre-established pattern.

_25. Jordi Vivaldi, *The Allonomous Condition* (Lecture in University of Trento on 04-04-2019).

How exactly is autonomous behavior different, then? What is derived from the fact that a system is behaving intelligently? In parallel to the definition above, we propose the following: autonomous elements are intelligent artifacts located within the system that governs them. We consider them to be *second-order cybernetic systems*:[26] their main function is to create and eventually execute patterns. In that sense, allonomous systems are those which, unlike automated systems, are capable of handling stochastic events – that is, events in which a prior state does not necessarily determine the following one. But, unlike autonomous systems, allonomous systems refer to systems that are not just autonomous in themselves, but that identify that they operate in an environment where the alien, that is, the other, is also autonomous. Traditionally, only humans have been part of this group. However, the post-humanist theses of recent years have emphasized the ontological relevance of non-human agents in this type of tasks, operating not only under Maturana and Varela's autopoiesis –the ability of a system to reproduce and maintain itself-, but also in what we have previously defined as sympoeisis. In this sense, an allonomous being is constantly negotiating its agency in relation to other agencies: it understands its surroundings as composed of several different autonomies, opening to them for the exchange of matter and energy.

During this period, experimental architecture has modulated the notion of allonomy through a twofold register.

On the one hand, the technological contributions of the 21st century have allowed for the development and generalization of the phenomenon of artificial intelligence, giving rise to computational beings that are no longer fixed on cloud servers or networks, but deployed through physiological materialities. Eric Sadin defines this computational intelligence based on five main points: (1) initiative in making decisions, (2) reasoning ability thanks to the power of data triangulation, (3) the capacity of learning by itself, (4) multi-platform flexibility that provides free circulation through all kinds of formats and finally (5) the tendency to communicate and cooperate[27]. This develops in an environment where, as the volume of data exchanged between agents increases, more and more mutual cognitive growth takes place.

On the other hand, and in resonance with Latour's flat ontology, the current ethical, political and cultural sensitivities of our days have recovered a certain animist understanding of the world; the planet is now inhabited by a series of species whose agents are cemented as autonomous beings with the potential to roll out their own logics of action in the world.

Given this scenario, a large part of the advanced architecture of this decade will be approached as an exercise of mediation whose purpose is to coordinate sets of intelligences for the co-production of multi-scalar habitats. As such, the main question we must address is as follows: How does the advanced architecture of this decade operate based on the mediation of behaviours among human, technological, ecological and zoological agencies? And, above all, in what sense can this mediation be read as an expansion? If we understand the word "mediation" as the act of arbitrating among intelligences, we can assert that, during this decade, a great part of experimental architecture has exercised this ability through a set of projects that have several features in common: their results tend to be open, that is, difficult to foresee and inconclusive, their algorithmic logics can be applied to all phases of the architectural project, including analysis, design, manufacturing and management, and their development remains, to this day, in an incipient and embryonic state.

_26. Güvenç Özel, "Toward a Post-Architecture", *Log*, no.36 (2016), 101.
_27. Eric Sadin, *La humanidad aumentada* (Buenos Aires: La Caja Negra, 2017), 112-113.

This final feature is a consequence of the fact that there has not been enough time to translate and mature the aforementioned expansive developments, which are practically contemporary to the production of this text. In addition to being small scale, temporary, and generally lightweight, they also depend on applications of the expansive protocols we have just described that are, although not metaphorical, limited and partial in comparison with the potential that those systems hold. Ozel Office's unbuilt "LiveF0rms" (2014) is a good example of this phenomena. It consists in an installation designed for a British electronic music festival. The music that is being played guides the robotic manufacturing processes, generating complicities between sound, materiality, feeling and human emotion. Although robots' role is not merely automated, since their movements are unpredictable and open-ended, their autonomy is relatively limited, since the movements are a response to a prior musical pattern. The "Bionic Bar" (2014) by Carlo Ratti follows a similar line: the two robotic arms take the place of the bartenders respond to a given prior situation, although it cannot have been foreseen in the initial programming. Neither of these cases works from a logic that lets us intuit correlations between series of events that would have otherwise been undetectable by human perception. In other words, there is no algorithmic deduction. As Andrew Witt suggests[28], artificial intelligence and machine learning are transforming the role of robots from being mere productive automatas to being heuristic agents, *in-silico* creatures capable of actively operating in the territories of design and form, something that does not occur in any of the aforementioned projects.

The installation by Diller Scofidio at the Whitney Museum of American Art in 2003 comes closer to the robotic autonomy characteristic of this decade, although it takes a different position. In this case, the project is posited as a dissident robot, placed on rails attached to the interior partitions on the fourth floor of the Whitney Museum, as part of the designers' "Aberrant Architectures" (2003) exhibition. During the exhibition's three-months duration, the robot moves arbitrarily around the museum with a specific task: using its drill to make half-inch holes in the partitions. At first, the holes are only scattered dots in the blank walls. Then they begin to generate recognizable clusters. Finally, sightlines begin to emerge between the different rooms, as the same hole is made on both sides of the wall. The sensation is that of an autonomous element that operates "on its own", uncontrollable and unpredictable; above all, it redirects the viewers' attention, traditionally focused on the work hanging on the walls, toward the wall where the work is hanging. However, there is no intelligence in the exercise because the ensemble doesn't react to stochastic phenomena, and in this sense, there is no operative interaction. Its autonomy consists in the arbitrariness of its behaviour– which is nevertheless limited to the framework designed by the architects, in this case the rails. There is a similar effect in part of the work developed by Edouard Cabay, although the process and the result are also well known by its strong aesthetic impact, which particularly resonates with the surrealist work of André Masson and its automatic drawings. Cabay's mediation of an outer and robotic otherness neglects the desire to represent in favour of the physical and temporal translation of unrelenting gestures produced by a set of mechanical devices; a swarm of artefacts that wander and float on the canvas through a logics that is absolutely external to ours. Based on these drawings, Cabay explores the aesthetic possibilities suggested by this type of methodology, although placing more emphasis so far on the indetermination of the robotic behaviour than on its autonomy as a non-human intelligence.

_28. Andrew Witt, " Cartogramic Metamorphologies; or, Enter the RoweBot", *Log*, no.36 (2016).

_Collage of projects lead by Edouard Cabay, 2018-2020.

_"The Sound and the Future", Alex Schweder, 2015.

The installation "The Sound and the Future" (2015) by Alex Schweder delves in this line of thought. However, the bigger scale of this installation in relation to the previous ones produces a decisive impact in the use and understanding of spatial interiorities. With a daring aesthetic and a definitively apocalyptic mise-en-scène, the installation involves a giant octopus sitting in the center of the room, whose long tentacles twist around constantly, powered by a pneumatic system. The design responds to stochastic events, such as users' locations and the rhythm of the music in the venue, offering a continuum of different formal responses that change the spatial arrangement of the whole. The project celebrates the shift from the idea of function-machine characteristic of the industrial age toward the idea of the objective-system inherent in designs like those of Cedric Price, moving away from the misinterpretations of the British architect's ideas produced, in their day, by works such as the "Pompidou Center" (1977) in Paris. Alex Schweder conceives his installation as a system that does not have a specific task to undertake; its main argument is its coexistence with users. In addition, the animal aesthetic and, above all, the unpredictability of the tentacular movements, give the whole an autonomy that lets us understand it as an emancipated "other" rather than as a complementary "addition" to an inert architecture. In this sense, the project aims to elicit disquiet and fascination in the user, feelings that arise when detecting a giant, heavy, slow and suffocating presence in the space – a gigantic sea monster constantly writhing in what seems like an apocalyptic dance.

However, the richness of the spaces that are generated and, above all, the temporary nature of the configurations make the project one of the clearest examples of what the age of experience represents. The reason lies not only in its strong visual and haptic presence, but above all in its continuous expressiveness through a series of unique configurations that are neither stored nor accumulated, and are therefore neither repeatable nor recoverable. In turn, the slowness of the movements and the unusual gravity of the ensemble elicit a profound sensation of the uncanny in its users, a few moments of mys-

_"Center for Fulfillment, Knowledge and Innovation", Gregg Lynn, 2016.

tery that, for a while, seems to emancipate us from the accelerated world denounced by Han's transparent society.

The mediation of a set of technological agents whose presence expand the possibilities of architectural structures has involved as well the use of aerial robotics. Beside being used as data-collection tools for environmental mapping, as is the case of Noumena's "NERO" (2015), its operativity has been implemented in the field of architectural design through a set of experimental proposals. Gregg Lynn has been particularly interested in this through his "Center for Fulfillment, Knowledge and Innovation" (2016). In expansive terms, the most remarkable aspect of the project is the mile-and-a-half-long "drones highway" folded over itself like a small intestine and designed to connect the different programmatic nuclei, providing for the movement of goods, equipment and materials. Lynn is interested in designing spaces simultaneously shared by drones and researchers, recognizing the particular autonomy of each type of agent. However, despite the project takes into account the autonomous presence of drones, the building in itself does not constitute an "otherness"; it indeed permits a multi-species existence, but it is not constituted by it. Although the construction seems to be built based on the metaphor of the body, with its differentiated organs and flows, its programmatic and formal approach lacks the viscosity, flexibility and malleability of a natural body, which actually runs counter to the main capability of a drone: its freedom of movement.

In this sense, Ozel Office's "Morphogram" (2014) approaches the presence of drones in an architectural scenario in a completely different way: rather than producing spaces for drones, the space is defined by the movement of the drones themselves. The project consists in a hyper-technified device in which a swarm of drones support the vertices of a triangulated flexible mesh that hangs below them, creating an inhabitable space underneath. The position of the drones is determined by a processor capable of responding to users' position, movement and emotions through a network of sensors; it can also overlap direct top-down orders to measure users' reactions and adapting their position. However, the adaptation is not always in the interest of optimizing a process; in many cases it operates like Price's "Generator Project" (1976-79): it activates new dynamics rather than merely responding to them. The project does not aim to harmonize the coexistence of both algorithmic and biologic species, but to produce some friction for the purpose of introducing conflict as a disruption of routine and apathy. The result is literally an "expanded" marionette, a character that dances above our heads and that emerges as a technological agent capable of shaking us through strange gestures and contortions executed in real time. A subversive tendency which, in parallel to the installation by Alex Scheweder, is based on a fundamental requirement: it is not meant to be read as just another chapter of the "polite architecture" so characteristic of contemporary smart cities. Instead, in its ability to unbalance, disturb and even "bother", there is the possibility of escaping the technological optimism so firmly established in our times and based on what Koolhaas would highlight as the new values of the 21st century: comfort, security and self-sufficiency, substitutes for the already obsolete revolutionary values of *liberté*, *egalité* and *fraternité*. The intelligence acquired by our current processors makes them not only able to interpret and act according to our gestures, but also to present themselves as rational, non-anthropomorphic beings, suited to living out their existence more and more freely.

One of the most radical interpretations of the notion of algorithmic autonomy in experimental architecture is the work of Bartlett RC3's Unit, lead by Tyson Hosmer, Octavian Gheorghiu, David Reeves and Panagiotis Tigas. The systematic implementation of artificial intelligence and machine learning processes into architecture permits to expand the discipline into what the RC3 's Unit has defined as "Living Architecture". Under this umbrella, the studio develops a series of projects whose computational intelligence permits to deeply rethink the notion of housing. From its environmental implementation to its understanding of property, the work questions a series of assumptions related to the 20th century through projects as "TARSS" (2018). The assemblage consist in a fully automated series of tensegrity structures that are self-assembled through machine learning protocols in order to produce extra-terrestrial dwellings. These robotic structures are in constant self-arrangement and should be read as individuals which do not exactly reproduce human taks, but they mainly operate new type of actions under an algorithmic logic which not necessarily can be deduced from ours. In this sense, each structural module has an autonomous life, recursively wandering in artificial environments and constantly taking decisions in relation to its "lived" events. Its indetermination and volatility permits them to constantly be "in the right position in the right moment", in the sense of being systematically facing not just events in course of formation, but also the allonomous condition produced by the autonomy of each one of the rest of the modules and of its inhabitants. Through a dense intertwining in between organic and non-organic agents, "TARSS" establishes unprecedented forms of co-inhabitation with a humanity that has been expanded under cognitive algorithmic processes that transcend human's natural capacity. Notions as "property" or "typology" are re-evaluated under a hypermobile and interconnected system that converts housing into a fluid modular service whose flexibility and constant adaptation permits to face some of the specific nomadic lifestyles produced by the 21st century. "TARSS" does not aim at the production of consumer goods to facilitate our inhabitation, but it is conceived to subvert the latter through three key shifts: from housing as a property

_"TARSS", Faculty: Tyson Hosmer, Octavian Gheorghiu, David Reeves and Panagiotis Tigas.
/ Students: Linlin Cao, Ziming He, Shi Ren, Ning Wang, UCL Bartlett BPRO, 2018.

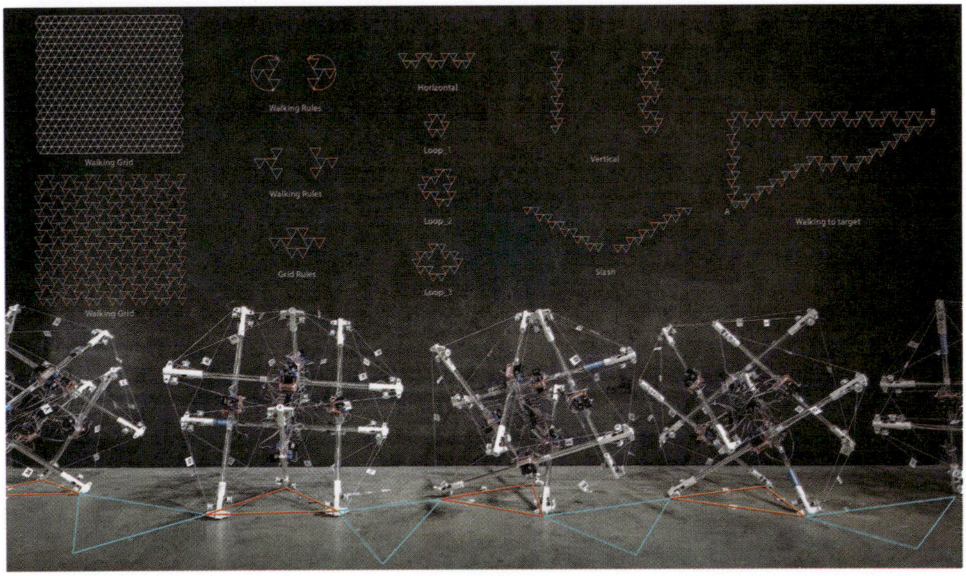

to housing as a service, from spatial standardisation to spatial specification, and from architecture as a container to architecture as a companion species.

The introduction of Artificial Intelligence and Machine Learning in architecture has an impact as well in the way it is perceived; as Mario Carpo suggests, "the emergence of artificial intelligence in technology and in the arts already warrants a more than robust amount of natural discomfort and the feeling of 'alienation'"[29], which is the result of the ongoing post-industrial separation of the minds of the thinkers from the tools of computation. From an aesthetic point of view, machine learning can be interpreted as the "strangement device" defined by Viktor Shklovsky in relation to poetic language; it acts as a distancing apparatus that prolongs the process of perception: "The goal of art is to create the sensation of seeing, and not merely recognizing, things; the device of art is the "enstrangement" of things and the complication of the form, which increases the duration and complexity of perception, as the process of perception is, in art, an end in itself and must be prolonged."[30] This method was frequently used by Leon Tolstoi, particularly in his book *Strider* (1886), in which the entire story is narrated from the perception of a horse. Bertold Brecht has also alluded to this phenomena through his notion of "alienation effect", defining it as "playing in such a way that the audience was hindered from simply identifying itself with the characters in the play. Acceptance or rejection of their actions and utterances was meant to take place on a conscious plane, instead of, as hitherto, in the audience's subconscious"[31]. With this distancing effect Brecht eludes the Aristotelian catharsis: by alienating his audience from characters and action, Brecht obtains distanced observers who don't become involved emotionally with his theater, but intellectually, that is, critically.

The algorithmic otherness of machine learning produces a similar distancing effect. It precludes a full empathization with the user because there is always a remainder of otherness that cannot be fully comprehended. In opposition to vintage artificial intelligence, current machine learning processes applied to architectural proposals as "TARSS" are no longer trying to imitate the logic of the human mind; conversely, they develop its own logic, a mode of action whose algorithmic nautre is capable to manage big data processes far too vast for our human mind. This brutal data-processing capacity produces designs and behaviours that are radically different from what we can conceive.

It is precisely this strangement process what precludes Walter Benjamin's complete absorption and the "distracted perception" described in the previous chapter. The "natural discomfort" and "alienation feeling" that Carpo relates to the use of artificial intelligence in the arts produces, in *Second-Order Cybernetic Architecture,* a remainder of alterity that opposes "distracted perception" by the demand of focus, attention and caution.

Özel's "LivefOrms" and RC3's "TARSS" are good examples of this: robot's coordinated movement follows a logic that is closer to that of a machine than to our own. The strangeness and apparent arbitrarity of its gestures and forms are nothing but a symptom of a "technical logic that we may master and unleash, but that we can neither replicate, emulate, nor even simply comprehend with our mind". [32]

_29. Mario Carpo, *The second digital turn.* (Cambridge: MIT Press, 2017), 80.
_30. Viktor Shklovsky. "Art, as Device." *Poetics Today* 36, no. 3 (2015): 162.
_31. Bertolt Brecht. "On Chinese Acting", translated by Eric Bentley. *The Tulane Drama Review* 6.1 (1961), 130–136.
_32. Mario Carpo, *The second digital turn.* (Cambridge: MIT Press, 2017), 81.

In this sense, the set of modular tensegrity units of "TARSS" operate as artificial life forces, and the more they are freed from us, the more they direct the course of the world in their own way. Antoine Picon summarizes this requirement in a very expressive way with the exclamation "Free the robots!"[33], alluding to the fact that in order to obtain the best performance from each agent its autonomy has to be respected and emphasized to the maximum. The Luddites of the 18th century complained about something similar, when they exclaimed that it was useless to use intelligent creatures as though they were mere mechanical tools, because it was a great waste of their potential. Antoine Picon seems to mean something similar, but in our case it would not only apply to robots but would extend to all the agents – ecological, technological and human – that make up the nomadic assemblage of the 21st-century subject. However, this desire for algorithmic freedom is politically problematic: in many cases it leads to the legitimation and even reinforcement of the established political power. The construction of a political agenda capable to orient these contributions not just in a speculative way, but also under a socio-political register is crucial in order to denounce and subvert the inequalities produced by the established power. In resonance with some political authors related to the notions of *accelerationism* and *xenofeminism,* the emphasis on automation applied by the Design Computation Lab UCL[34] delves in this direction: its work "revives a socio-political discourse on the role of technology in architectural production", particularly in relation to the production and management of a democratic and equitable spatiality.

2.2 Animality: Symbiotic Constructions

The mediation of agents in the advanced architecture of this period does not involve only robotic or algorithmic "others". The discipline has recently witnessed the operative involvement of zoological agents, whose symbiotic entanglements with human and robotic beings is established through a non-hierarchical framework. There has recently been a number of proposals coming from different disciplines aiming at empowering animal's recognizement without falling in reactionary anthropomorphisms. Donna Haraway's "Companion Species" is a good example of it: Although Haraway's use of this expression is not reduced to animals, she considers animal writing a branch of feminist theory, or vice versa. In this sense, the co-existence in between animals and humans is approached as a flat cooperation in which animals do not play a surrogate role. As Haraway writes, "they are not here just to think with. They are here to live with".[35]

The "Silk Pavilion" (2013) by Neri Oxman resonates with this statement. In this case, the protagonist is not constituted by any technological agent, but the silk worms that "weave" the pavilion. Needless to say, this is not the first time that animals are the main players in an architectural exercise; one of the most emblematic project in that regard is Lubetkin's penguin pool for the "London Zoo" (1934). In recent years, BIG has designed a project in the same vein, in this case for the pandas at the "Copenhagen Zoo" (2017). The difference between those two projects and Neri Oxman's pavilion consists in that the latter approaches animals as performative agents capable of building a pavilion through the architect's mediation of their zoological activity. In the first two cases, the animals are understood as agents for contemplation, around which there orbits an architecture whose materiality has not been produced *by* them but *for* them. There is, however, anoth-

_33. Antoine Picon, " Free the robots!", *Log*, no. 36 (2016).
_34. The Design Computation Lab UCL is lead by Mollie Claypool, Manuel Jimenez Garcia, Gilles Retsin and Vicente Soler.
_35. Donna Haraway, *The Companion Species Manifesto: Dogs, People, and significant Otherness* (London: Prickly, 2003), 3.

er relevant comparison with the previously mentioned "Flight Assembled Architecture". In it, a swarm of drones constructs a small pavilion using a series of blocks. The exercise not only demonstrates possible uses for drones beyond the habitual military and analytical exercises, but it also highlights the abilities of this type of technology when it is democratized. In this case, however, the technological agents behave like perfect automatons: these have been programmed just like an industrial robotic arm, although their greater freedom of movement allows them to build higher and more complex structures. Ultimately, however, as the research team explains, the drones operate exclusively in response to the instructions they have received from humans. Therefore, the result is closed, predictable and conclusive, although it can easily be repeated or edited.

On the contrary, the Silk Pavilion project is entirely aligned with the expansive logic that underlies this decade, framed by the aforementioned notion of Black Gaia, for two main reasons. First, because of the variety of agents that participate operatively in the project: a human programs a CNC technological agent to produce a structure in an automated way. Then, a series of biological agents – silkworms – are added, which act autonomously as biological printers. Second, because of the silkworms' autonomy, which implies that the result is open, unpredictable and without a specific endpoint. In fact, it is the silkworms' activity that generates the final density variations; affected by the lighting and spatial conditions in their tendency to migrate towards the darkest and densest areas, they generate a series of patterns that reflect the particular lighting conditions of the space.

As a result of the technological advances in the miniaturization of the sensors in the 21st century, each worm is equipped with the necessary technology to monitor and understand its behavior, since the role of the architect will be to mediate between the behavior of the different silkworms used for the purpose of producing an architectural space. This mediation takes place in the generation of the necessary conditions to execute a specific task – in this case, building the pavilion. This includes erecting the primary structure and arranging the necessary lighting conditions to "direct" the worms' behavior as the pavilion takes shape. However, and despite the activity of the warms builds the pavilion, there is not a symbiotic relationship between species; the result of its coexistence does not transcend the mere construction of the pavilion. In this sense, François Roche's "MMYST" (2015), located in Krabi, Thailand, is particularly revealing. Besides not conjuring up a preconceived homogeneous formal structure with the anthropocentric and Renaissance reminiscences characteristic of Silk Pavilion's dome, Roche's project transcends the mere co-existence between the two types of autonomous agents that populate its space: human beings on the one hand and birds of the Collocaliini species on the other. Aside from being designed through several digital fabrication mechanisms using local material (petrified lava), the design's main virtue draws on the desire to exalt what Roche defines as an exercise in "mutualism" – in other words, how two organisms from different species can exist in a relationship where each individual benefits from the activity of the other. The project establishes an operative continuity between human beings and zoological beings without privileging one over the other. The construction is built using a metal structure, with transparent, well-lit areas for humans (about 70 m2) as well as much more opaque and dark zones, where the birds build their nests (about 70 m2). One of the peculiarities of the Collocaliini species is that it cannot be domesticated: the birds usually die after only a short time if they are caged. Thus, the only possible strategy is to attract them without taking away their freedom, a necessary condition for them to build their nests. The nests are highly prized because the birds only use their saliva when making them – instead of twigs or leaves – and the result is not only edible for human beings but has been proven to possess a series of nutritional and psychological virtues that have promoted its consumption by man since time immemorial.

In this way, the birds obtain a habitat that is perfectly adapted to their needs, and the humans receive ingredients on which to base part of their diet. The exchange evokes Guattari's three ecologies in its desire to join together "environmental ecology with social ecology and mental ecology". Roches's building promotes a productive economy, it preserves and increases the ecological wealth of the area, it is financed by a collaborative Kickstarter campaign and in 10 years it is demolished and returned to the land as a commitment to the idea of architecture that can be reabsorbed by nature. They are, without a doubt, characteristics that lay bare the zeitgeist of our era, through, above all, a deeply post-human penchant in its desire to bring about an operative coexistence between different natures instead of insisting on the centrality of the figure of the human being. In fact, most of the projects we have seen so far pursue exactly that: generating value by arbitrating between autonomous agents, regardless of their nature. Each one of them is expanded through its integration with the other, and in that sense it is important for each agent to be able to act with a maximum of independence, since precisely that is the challenge of "mediating intelligences". As such, with more or less success, these designs pursue a two-fold autonomy. In the first place, they recognize the extension of the capacity for interpretation and initiative acquired by the technique, whose algorithmic power allows acting not only as a delegate of human beings, but also as an autonomous agent. In these projects, we see a desire to generate an animated architecture – not in the

_"Silk Pavilion", Neri Oxman, 2013.

merely locomotive sense of the term, but in the full sympoietic sense. Second, autonomy is established based on the expanded subjectivity with which the contemporary individual has been endowed – i.e., an autonomy that has been expanded thanks to the physiological mechanisms established by agents of different natures. This establishes a revised cartography of powers among human, zoological, ecological and computational agents, where the latter have generously increased their interpretative and decision-making capacities.

2.3 Urban Supercomputation: A City of Quantities

In conjunction with the agency provided by artificial intelligence and machine learning, today's computational power, in its brute force of computing, represents in itself a "technical logic that we may master and unleash, but that we can neither replicate, emulate, nor even simply comprehend with our mind"[36]. Many ambits related to Economy or Industry have been impacted by the generalisation of big data processes in which massive peer-to-peer relations have replaced hierarchical structures of distribution. Blockchain protocols, with its massive management of data doesn't rely on an ultimate and given whole, but they are built on sheer quantities: millions of juxtaposed participatory individuals whose multiple interrelations expand by far our human capacity of comprehension. And quantities, indeed, begin with individuals, that is, with discreteness, something that as we will see next impacts the way cities can be designed.

However, the notion of "discreteness" needs differentiation: not all the interpretations of this term understands individuals in the same manner. In this sense, it is crucial to note the type of discreteness articulated by pre-Socratic philosophy: beside the continuity emphasized by Anaximandrus' Apeiron, Democritus' atomic model is the most popular representative of this discrete approach to matter. For the greek philosopher, atoms are not just eternal and indivisible, but also homogeneous, that is, generic. Although atoms differ in form and size, its internal qualities are constant in all of them, producing difference only through its grouping modes. Atoms are then particles: generic individuals whose variable conglomerates produce the difference that we observe in the world.

As Graham Harman affirms, this form of materialism is "based in ultimate material elements that are the root of everything and higher-level entities are merely secondary mystifications that partake of the real only insofar as they emerge from the ultimate material substrate".[37] Indeed, the atomic model is overall a reductionist model: the different specificities that conform the world are mere composts of a privilege and ultimate physical element. In opposition with the continuous form of materialism, the discrete atomic type is easily misunderstandable due to a frequent confusion: that in between "part" and "particle". This association is specially present nowadays in architectural experimental design, particularly in the field of urbanism and under the notion of "digital" and its inherent discrete nature. Computation's power of today, and particularly blockchain processes, has been aligned with this position through the recognition that "designers use the power of today's computation to notate reality as it appears at any chosen scale, without converting it into simplified and scalable mathematical formulas or laws".[38] It assumes the inherent discreteness of nature, where the abstract continuity of the spline doesn't exist. However, this process of architectural discretisation can be differentiated in between a set of elements which are countable (mathematically discrete) from a set

_36. Mario Carpo, *The Second Digital Turn* (Cambridge: MIT Press, 2017), 82
_37. Graham Harman, "Materialism is Not the Solution", *The Nordic Journal of Aesthetics,* no.47 (2014), 100.
_38. Mario Carpo, *The Second Digital Turn* (Cambridge: MIT Press, 2017), 71.

of elements that are also distinct (ontologically discrete). In this context, the notion of part becomes fundamental: rather than being reduced to particle's countability, a part is defined here as an interactive and autonomous element whose discreteness is not only based in countability but also in distinction.

In this sense, the work of Daniel Koehler and Rasa Navasaityte consists in an exercise of urban part-thinking that resonates with the mediation of agents described in this chapter: each part is not absorbed by an hypothetic whole, but it retains its autonomy in spite of simultaneously establishing relations with other parts. As the german architect suggests, "departing from parts a preconceived whole or any kind of structure does not exist. Parts do not establish wholes, but measure quantities"[39]. From this point of departure, Kohler and Navasaityte elaborate a methodology based in quantities of architectural parts that operate in an urban scale and whose immanent mediation aims to confront classical urban problems as the case of urban poché. The notion of poché has repeatedly been wielded from various formalist theoreticians, among which stands out the historical analysis of Colin Rowe. The British architect "used this approach being convinced of the efficacy of an immediate visual analysis that was essential for the perception and for any iconographic or historical formulation"[40]. In its most basic sense, poché literally means 'blackened parts of plan or section filled with black to indicate the parts of a structure that are cut, as could be done by stippling'[41]. Emmanuel Petit connects[42] the verb *pocher* with *la poche*, the pocket, and then *pocher* would mean *mettre en poché*. Hence, by *poché* we should understand literally pocketed or "bagged", an ideal shape put into a bag, surrounded with tissue. Koehler and Navasaityte re-interpret this classical notion through their project "NPoché" (2017), showing how classification algorithms based in Big Data can be used in interplay with architectural form. According to both architects, multi-dimensional classification is used to sort simulations consisting of self-aggregating housing parts, in which certain agglomerations were selected to formulate specific local conditions, namely access, light, open space, and ventilation, but also a three-dimensional circulation that questions the epistemic borders in between architecture and urbanism.

The computational Poché-Space developed here and based in processes of big data in general and Block-Chain in particular, requires an exercise of mediation given the agency possessed by each part. In this sense, we are confronting a type of mediation that is local, ephemeral and developed by the parts themselves: there is no transcendental entity that from an exterior dimension unfolds a coordinational action. However, and although parts constitute quantities rather than totalities, in the composition of the "Npoché" project there is still a vague remainder of a general background that vectorises part's distribution, although in a blur and definitely weakened version.

Emphasizing the countability and distinction characteristic of discreteness requires instead to avoid any ultimate condition in order to understand form as spatio-temporal ephemeral structures that, beside establishing local and ephemeral relations, possesses one particularity that singularise them: they operate at every level of scale. It demands the assumption that there is always a form beyond any given form, avoiding any continuous (field) or discrete (particle) ultimate background in which parts could be reduced. In this sense and as Graham Harman affirms, "although what is admirable in materialism is its

_39. Daniel Koehler. *Large City Architecture: The Fourth Part* (London: 2018), 19.
_40. Anthony Vidler, *Histories of the Immediate Present.* (London: MIT press, 2008), 80.
_41. Emmanuel Petit, "Rowe after Colin Rowe". *In: Reckoning with Colin Rowe*, ed. Emmanuel Petit, (London: Routledge, 2015), 145.
_42. Ibid, 146

sense that any visible situation contains a deeper surplus able to subvert or surprise it, the kind of formalism approached here does not deny this surplus, it merely states that this surplus is also formed"[43]. Block-chain technologies and Big Data systems are particularly well suited for it, as soon as peer-to-peer paired with data-richness fosters decentralized decision making, which permits the emancipation of any type of reductionism. Beside the theoretical and highly speculative approach of Koehler and Navasaityte, the combination of big data and super computation have crystallised in other design methods whose vocation is more pragmatic: the KPF's use of urban data analytics for informed decision making in the design of buildings and cities (2019) or the work developed at the City Intelligence Lab at the Austrian Institute of Technology (2019) are good examples of interactive digital platforms whose digital urban planning workflows imply a change of design method: rather than involving a team of professionals that conceive a limited number of design schemes, computational design techniques permit to simulate and test a massive number of designs while simultaneously quantifying their performance. However, the challenge of these procedures is not just scientific-technical, but also socio-political; otherwise, it risks becoming a mere accelerator of the logics and inertias characteristic of the established power and of most of the enterprises that provide the required technology. The algorithmic intelligence can be used to propose new urban models, based in bottom-up processes of mass-collaboration, with the potential of providing a certain level of emancipation in relation to the big corporations.

For this purpose, it is crucial to democratize the access and understanding of urban data. The use of expansive technologies in the urban realm does not necessarily crystallise in design processes, but it can also systematize analytical processes by using swarms of epistemic bots. The bots are constituted as computational beings; immaterial and super-informed agents whose activity does not consist in replicating human tasks, but in carrying out new kinds of activities. They are individuals with autonomous lives, destined to wander indefinitely through artificial environments. The latest advances in machine learning provide these beings with the necessary autonomy to make decisions based on "experienced" events and acting as true informational agents, that is, evanescent, imperceptible and unplaceable individuals that are affected by a sensitivity that is computational in nature. However, this does not prevent them from establishing operational interlacements with entities of a different nature, whether human, ecological or animal.

The emergence and generalization of this type of beings has led to the incorporation of several computational instruments into the field of experimental urbanism. Tools like "Anemone", "Nursery" or "Quelea" simulate the simultaneous behavior of sets of agents, whose trajectories and attributes can be adjusted by the user or optimized by genetic algorithms. These types of tools have many applications in the field of advanced design: simulation of urban flows, formal modeling, process optimization, data management, environmental analysis, etc. The case of "Neighbourlytics" (2017) is illustrative: it provides users with on-demand data on how people use and experience the places where they live and work, rising holistic understanding of resident's needs. Something similar occurs with the work of 300.000kms: from demographic and employment to transport and health, the catalan office provides data to urban stakeholders in order to take better data-driven decisions. However, one of the most emblematic applications,

_43. Graham Harman, "Materialism Is Not the Solution" in *The Nordic Journal of Aesthetics*, no.47, (2014), 100.

_"Npoché", Faculty: Rasa Navasaityte and Daniel Kohler with Silu Meng, Ruohan Xu, Qianying Zhou. UCL Bartlett BPRO, 2018.

due to the theoretical connection it establishes with architecture, involves the urban analysis of voids and built volumes. Andrew Witt presents the case of "RoweBot" (2016), a computational being that, to an extent, aims to contribute disciplinary novelty to the realm of architectural theory – in this case, the formal associations and affinities that occur within the corpus of a city's buildings. This issue has been addressed extensively in earlier eras using manual means, including the famous Nolli Map, the drawings by Colin Rowe, or the rationalistic Enlightenment reflections by Durand.

RoweBot aims for a similar goal but operates in a completely different way, following four basic steps: first, it detects and measures each urban figure from a database; second, it calibrates the differences for each pair of figures; third, it constructs a network of relationships; and finally, fourth, it establishes a hierarchy of relationships based on tree structures. This definitively linear approach uses different bots as form-focused search engines, as the equivalent to a search engine that targets text or images.

The goal is to find hidden relationships and patterns in the urban forms that surround us. The bots are autonomous, in the sense that they not only deal with unexpected figures but are also expected to make certain decisions in order to establish relationships among hundreds of thousands of figures. This method of analysis is radically different from the usual method, in that it is capable of offering results that are again open, unpredictable and indefinite. The procedure is something like an extractor/revealer of links between phenomena, and its virtue lies in the deductive power of algorithms, capable of deciphering the secret affinities between phenomena that were thought to be unconnected. As such, the processors are presented as external sublayers intended to broaden or deepen our general intuitions about things: it does not involve analytical thought but rather reveals the complex nature of some of our actions, perceiving certain decisive, and often unsuspected, aspects of our realities with a higher level of precision. And, as in other applications that we have already discussed, the role of the architect is once again that of mediator: s/he is responsible for coordinating and adjusting autonomies – in other words, arbitrating between intents that are not always aligned with one another..

One of the most emblematic examples of this phenomena has to do to do with the introduction of driverless cars into cities. In recent years this has come very close to becoming reality, with vehicles like the ones created by Google, Tesla or Faraday Future, some of which are already circulating on our streets. Their range of action combined with their decision-making ability turns them into autonomous robots that need mediation with the other agents that inhabit the city in order to ensure peaceful coexistence.

A number of projects have been developed in recent years in line with this hypothesis. The coexistence of pedestrians, cyclists and cars has always been a subject of debate in the urban realm, and recently a lot of effort has been put into integrate all three elements. However, some simulations suggest that the introduction of smart cars will exponentially increase cars' presence, in the same way that widening roads results in the same levels of congestion but on a larger scale. In any case, the way smart cars circulate calls into question the usefulness of a particular urban tool with more than 150 years of history: the traffic light. Invented in the 19th century for railways and imported into urban areas in the early 20th, namely since the introduction of the Ford Model T, the traffic light is one element that has persisted throughout the 20th century virtually unchanged. Yet a simulation carried out by the Senseable City Lab at MIT in 2011 illustrates very convincingly

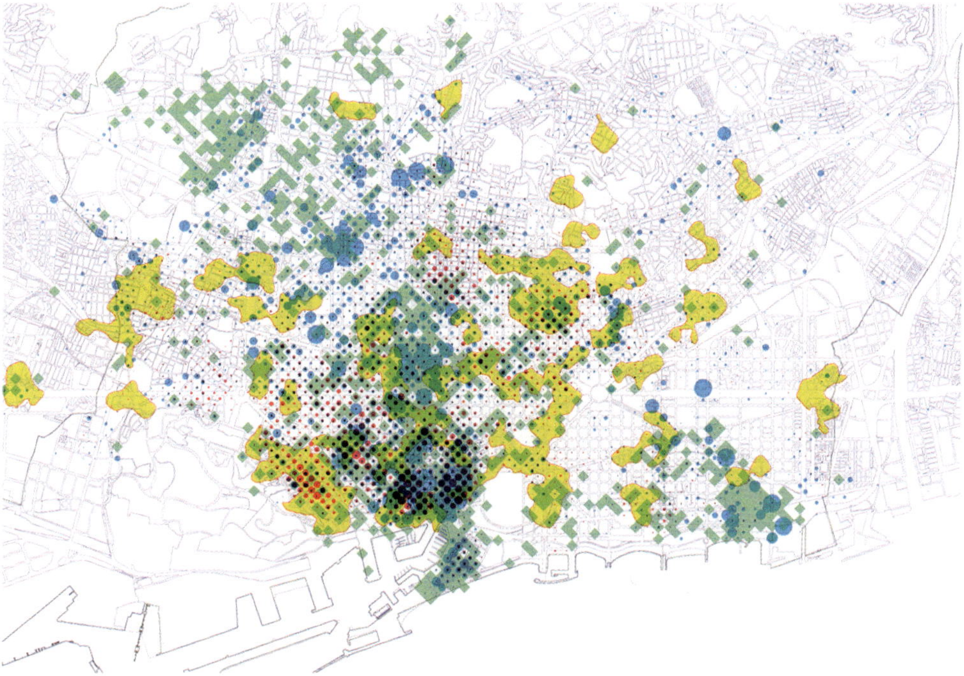

_"Urban Fabric Analysis", 300.000km/s, 2019.

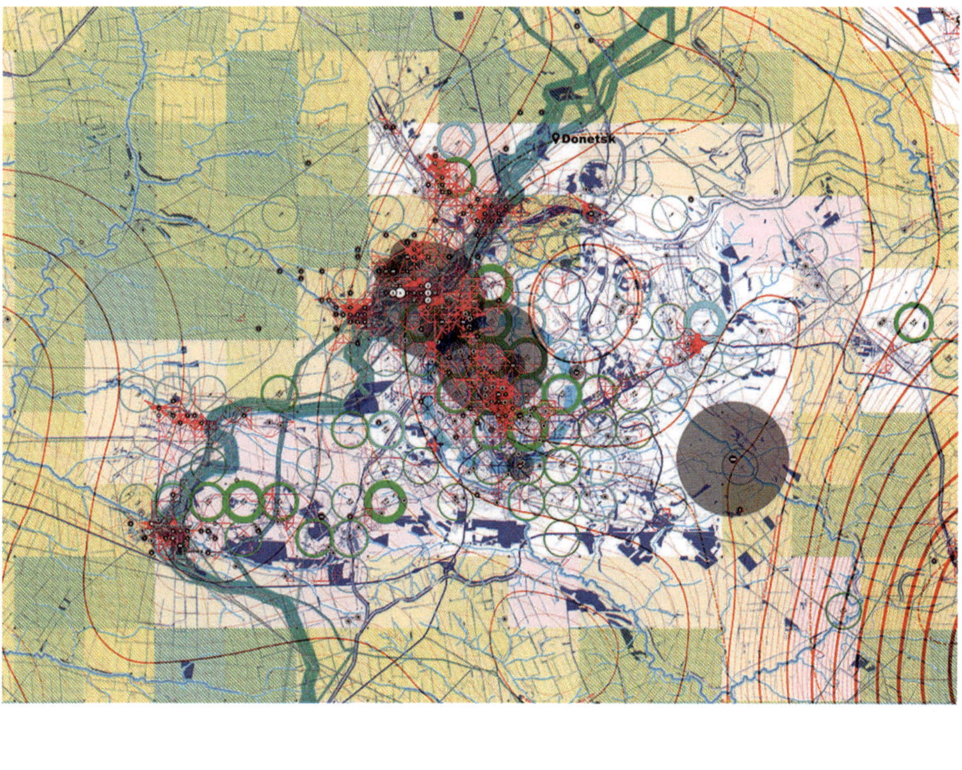

_"New York Transportation System", Harvey Wiley Corbett, 1923.

how multiple smart cars can travel in different directions and varying speeds through a busy urban intersection without colliding. There is a fundamental element missing from their simulation, however: pedestrians. The real challenge is not to mediate behavior within a group of smart cars, like the sorting robots in an Amazon distribution center, but to mediate the behavior between smart cars on the one hand and pedestrians on the other: i.e., between computational agents and human agents.

Given this requirement, some cities such as Minneapolis and Calgary have chosen to differentiate pedestrian traffic from vehicle traffic on different levels, a solution that recalls the drawings for New York by Harvey Wiley Corbett (1923).

In his design, the American architect aimed to decongest New York vehicle traffic by separating it from pedestrians in section. The result is just the opposite: it radically increases the urban congestion of Manhattan. The entire surface of the city becomes a single plane of traffic, a veritable ocean of cars in which the city blocks of Manhattan float like islands in an archipelago. This solution increases the road traffic potential by 700%, while the sidewalks are raised one level and pedestrians can reach any point of the city, through a network of bridges, without touching the ground.

The vision is more dystopian than utopian, the polar opposite of what BIG submitted in 2010 for the Audi Urban Future Award. In their project, Bjarke Ingels' team puts forward an urban vision in which smart cars, pedestrians and cyclists simultaneously occupy a public space that is outfitted with a network of sensors to provide vehicles with data in real time in order to avoid collisions. This solution – based in plan, unlike Corbett's emphasis in section – eliminates any separation between sidewalks, bike lanes and roadways, while

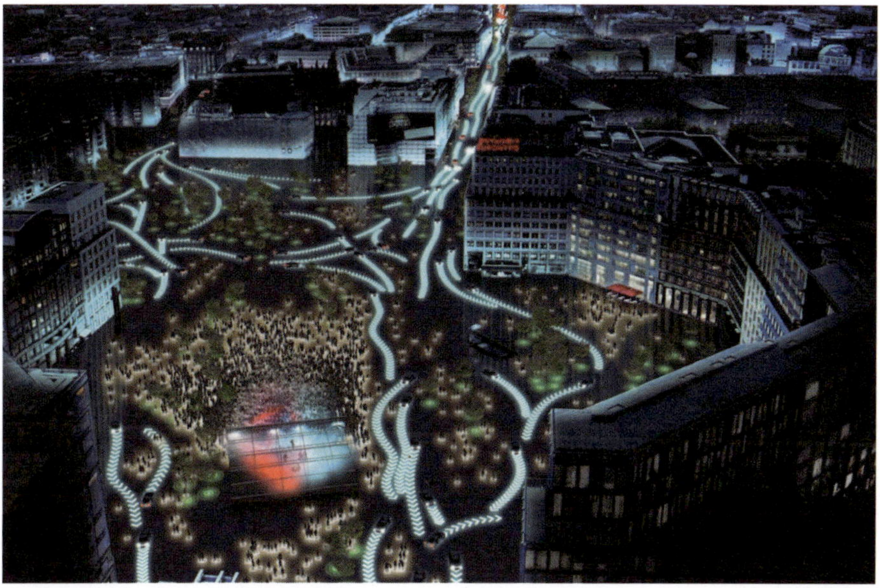

_"Entry for the Audi Urban Future Award",BIG, 2010.

simultaneously ensuring the safety of users, offering what is ultimately a flexible urban surface that can be adapted to the required uses at any given moment.

Like the majority of BIG's projects, the strategy it presents is based on an active, optimistic and extroverted vision. However, it errs on the side of excessive confidence in the pacifying power of technology. This aspect makes the proposal seem idealistic and somewhat naive, situating it in what Rosi Braidotti defines as analytical post-humanism, that is, a post-humanism in which the centrality of the human is replaced by that of technology. Besides, it is unclear what role public transportation plays in this scenario, or whether the proportion of cars to pedestrians will be the same as it is now. What is most alarming, however, is how public space is read as a mere space for circulation, dominated by the compulsive effervescence of contemporary finance capitalism and devoid of the political dimension that any public square should have as a site for expression.

At any rate, this speculative exercise offers a very clear example of an "expanded" city, where human agents are no longer the sole central figures in the urban terrain and must share it with other types of autonomous entities, in this case computational agents. Here, the smart car becomes a technological fetiche, similar to what the iPhone once was, presented as a deity shaped from a surface of metal and glass and animated by millions of lines of code that lend it a "power of spirit" that is posited as infinitely superior to our own. In parallel, smart cars are seen as a new kind of technological totem: no longer revered for their Promethean physical power, but for their silent, robotized urban omnipresence. Whereas the advent of the first automobiles were accompanied by an auratic stature, generated by their extraordinary singularity and the distance implied by their price, smart cars operate via an "emotional veneration" rooted not in any promised logistical efficiency but in the strangeness of their otherness.

Although as we have seen the experimental urban realm is not being impermeable to the cultural and technological contributions that we have previously described, its impact can be detected in other directions beside the implementation of artificial intelligence processes in the analysis and design of urban environments. The development on digital interfaces aiming at enhancing collaborative design and the production of gaming platforms not necessarily based on technology have impacted as well the local scale of the neighbourhood.

2.4. Neighbourhood and Gamification: Re-Presentation versus Re-Presentification

In recent years, the activity of arbitrating between behaviors in the field of urban design and advanced architecture has been expanded by the emergence of play as an alternative interface. Games have been discovered as a useful urban design tool for two main reasons associated with Hans-Georg Gadamer's notion of "representification".

First, games draw on the fact that reality contains a whole range of possibilities that can be executed. In that sense, games make "a deal with the possible" – in other words, they interpret the representation of a possibility "as though" it were reality. As such, in a game there is no representation, but rather representification: the game is not limited to merely representing a possibility, it presents it "as if" it were real – which has a lot in common with the act of designing.

Secondly, as Gadamer asserts[44], play exists in its own self-presentation – i.e., in a back-and-forth movement in which it is repeatedly renewed. It does not have a particular goal, nor is it significant who the subject playing is, because the game consists precisely in its being played. In that sense, play cannot be solitary: one always plays with someone and something – in other words, play implies leaving oneself behind and taking on a specific role that is different from the habitual one. It is, again, a representification, which in this case consists in acquiring a renewed role.

Play equals dynamism, interaction, process, involvement and imagination. It follows that play is a particular type of bottom-up process, in which collaborative teamwork takes place. Fun has a very significant role, which was already present in the Archigram imaginary and in the names of emblematic projects, like the "Fun Palace" (1972). However, as a design methodology, it has several limitations. These became evident in another emblematic project of the 1970s: "The Oregon Experiment" (1975), led by Christopher Alexander. The proposal failed for several reasons that can be reduced to one: the human difficulty of coordinating the simultaneous action of a large number of autonomous agents.

Today, this difficulty no longer exists, due to the algorithmic power of the available computational tools. Moreover, the gaming revolution that has taken place recent decades has emphasized one of the most distinctive characteristics of the immersive power video games: it encourages the performance, i.e., the experience of new definitions of oneself. One of the most emblematic examples of this phenomenon is "The Sims" (2000): players talk about the extent to which they begin to consider their own lives as a set of parameters to satisfy. Similarly, many designers have discovered the potential hidden in video game classics such as "Age of Empires" (1997) or "Minecraft"

_44. Diego Sanchez Meca, *Teoría del Conocimiento* (Madrid: Editorial Dykinson, S.L, 2012), 457.

(2009). They allow for a type of collaborative design in which, in the guise of play, a whole series of human relationships are generated. Through their coexistence they propose and, above all, manage a shared city, while also providing a collection of data that is significant in terms of both quantity and quality. No doubt, one of the most powerful contemporary examples of play as a mediating element between behaviors is "Block'hood" (2016), by José Sánchez. As its author explains, the video game can be used to design a building, to carry out participatory urban processes or even to raise awareness of ecology. This is because one of the main virtues of this type of mechanisms is that, on the one hand, it offers the possibility for citizens to make decisions about their urban environment and, on the other hand, it makes them aware of problems and the resources that are needed to keep our cities running.

However, perhaps the most interesting aspect of this phenomenon is found in the two tensions that frame it: first, the tension between what is real and what is fiction; and, second, the tension between what is physical and what is digital. In the first case, reality seems to become a true gaming platform, and what seemed like just a few imaginings co-produced by a network of "players", over time can become a productive crash-test to be put into actual practice. In the second case, examples like "Pokemon Go" illustrate the extent to which the digital and physical worlds can coexist in a kind of third world – in an allusion to Popper's three worlds – that connects both. In short, it is a type of activity that could be included among the type of actions that Paul Mason described as post-capitalist: several people, always collaboratively, produce value – without receiving money in return – that everyone can access for free, as would be the case of Wikipedia. On the other hand, the work is not understood as a burden, but as a pleasant activity connected with playful enjoyment.

In this sense, most of advanced architecture contemporary productions cannot longer be reduced to Promethean artefacts with salvational pretensions; rather, they are presented as playful devices in which the instrumental aspect is no longer the only focus.

_"Block'hood", José Sánchez, 2016.

_"City Gaming",Play the City, 2016.

This phenomenon takes place in two dimensions. First, the rise of design methods based on gaming not only points to a significant increase in participatory processes; these methods also introduce fun as a distinctive element in the design process. Projects like "Play the City" (2015), "Block'hood" (2016) or "Redesire" (2016) follow this logic, where computational power helps overcome the inconveniences of coordination that plagued C. Alexander's Oregon Experiment in the 1970s. Second, projects like the "Braga Pavilion" (2015), "Cloud Cast" (2015) or the "Silk Pavilion" (2017) are not based on "problem-solving" strategies; they are exploratory devices with a significant playful component. The images in the visual material used by the authors to present the projects almost always include situations of play, often involving children who seem to dance around these devices as though they were giant toys. This attitude is not exclusive to the advanced architecture of the 21st century: in the 1960s and 70s, the aforementioned "Fun Palace" (as its name suggests) was presented as a project whose leitmotiv consisted of its ability to spark fun through mechanisms of flexibility and adaptability. Yet, this point should not overshadow the fact that the project, along with others from the same period by Archigram or Archizoom, was drawing on a specific political and social agenda, despite the fact that its imaginary "gave the movement the appearance of a considerable lack of seriousness, because these elaborate perspectives increasingly offered some of the most attractive iconography of fun and leisure that architecture had ever produced."

In this sense, the "Play the City" platform hides under its ludic mask a radical political agenda. Developed by Ekim Tan, the platform is posited as a horizontal negotiation of the urban future in the places where the players live. The players contrast their interests in an accessible, playful and relatively simplified scenario, which offers the possibility of developing visions that are both compatible and shared. However, the simulated horizontality of this type of platforms contrasts with the power hierarchy that still structures Western society, often making this type of playful proposal into a naive approach to reality. As such, if they fail to engage productively with reality, they become just another attribute of the capitalist realism described by Mark Fisher that we discussed earlier: a tool with a subversive intent that has nevertheless been absorbed and even commercialized by capitalism through a soft, painless and almost imperceptible coercion. In this scenario, gamification runs the risk of becoming a just a playful simulation of reality, parameterized and analgesic, whose capacity for impact has been domesticated: we would no longer be dealing with the representification characteristic of play – i.e., the operative production of a new present – but a mere infantilized representation of it. This is compounded by the playful and pleasant aspect that video games, messaging or portable music lend to today's electronic devices: they are included in a regime of entertainment that, paradoxically – under the premise of making everyday things easier – have led to an almost continuous attachment to technology through a compulsive connection to mobile phones or an addictive relationship with the Internet.

In this sense, it is essential to understand games from the standpoint of representification: the subversive power of collaborative design resides in the ludic development of a possibility "as though" it were a reality. Contemporary gaming adds the necessary computation power to the virtues of play, so that the problems associated with coordination do not hamper its continuous renovation. It allows for creating and maintaining the playful connection necessary to establish a shared mediation between desires that are not always contradictory.

2.5. Frontier Geologies

The intimate entanglement in between biological and artificial agencies have also produced a form of environments that we define here with the expression "frontier geologies". Rather than the purified and idyllic nature that traditionally is associated with notions such as geology or landscape -particularly in its french or english registers-, the frontier environments characteristic of this decade emphasize a multispecie compost in movement, a territory of flows and interchanges involving natural and artificial agencies.

Under this umbrella, the notion of frontier should be read in the Roman sense of the term *Limes*: rather than being an infinitesimal line, in the Early Roman Empire the limit was a territory, a promiscuous and oscillant stripe that mediated in between the Roman Empire and the foreign tribes. Precisely because of its "in betweenness", the *Limes* was a land of radical miscegenation: its inhabitants, the *Limitanei*, were composed not just by roman soldiers and their families, but also by all sorts of merchants and german tribes. The *Limes* was therefore populated by vivacious and eclectic poles of activity, although its horizon was always threatened by the radical otherness of the barbarian tropes, whose incursions were recursively waving and resewing the "limits of the *Limes*".

Frontier geologies are thus liminal geologies, that is, inhabitable oxymorons, spaces of junction and disjunction, unstable territories of conflict whose effervescence and compressed diversity by no means could take place within the clinic abstraction of the euclidean line.

Under this umbrella, natural and artificial agencies are not isolated in specific mediums or ecosystems, but inserted into dynamic networks of "co-inhabitation, co-evolution and sociability". This tentacular multiplicity has been approached in the work of artists such as Shoshanah Dubiner, whose paintings like "Endosymbiosis: Homage to Lynn Margulis" (2012) represent microscopic saturated landscapes that celebrate the beauty of the microbial world described by Lynn Margulis.

However, the symbiotic relations characteristic of frontier geologies are not limited to its usual organic realm. Instead, they permeate its biologic borders in order to include other inorganic species such as algorithmic bots or robotic agents. Frontier geologies are thus expanded geologies; thick and dense territories occupied by different agencies whose co-activity establishes a sophisticated magma of symbiotic forms of intelligence. In close relation to the previously discussed notion of anthropocene, these mestizo territories permeate the epistemic conventional classifications of modernity in order to propose new geographies of association: swarms of interconnected "apparatuses" that co-produce irregular, hybrid and disturbing environments. The photographic work of Edward Burtynsky or Andreas Gursky identifies this phenomena at a large scale: wide areas of miscegenation in which the simultaneous activity of different species produce disquieting geological scenarios evoking both familiarity and alterity; oil bunkering, phosphor tailing ponds, saw mills, pivot irrigations… spaces of multitudes whose co-existence does not produce clean and pristine landscapes, but corrupted regions that break conventional epistemic dichotomies such as nature and culture, pure and impure, viable and dysfunctional or proper and improper. In this sense, the work developed at the Synthetic Landscape Lab at Innsbruck University (2017) is paradigmatic of an emerging interest from the realm of experimental architecture in mapping and simulating the impact of the human being on its geology. In spite of a certain over-aestheticization of phenomena like the retreating glaciers of Alp, the work of the lab succeeds in questioning the "material,

_"Endosymbiosis: Homage to Lynn Margulis", Shoshanah Dubiner, 2012.

_"Hylozoic Ground",Philip Beesley, 2010.

morphological, social and exo-systemic nature" of climate change without reducing it to an anthropocentric problem-solving perspective.

However, the notion of frontier geologies has been conjugated as well under other formats closely associated with the notion of landscape. In this sense, the exhibition "Alive: New Design Frontiers" (2013) stands as a foundational event, exploring – through its catalog of 34 projects – the possibility of a world in which synthetic biology redefines the possibilities of manufacturing. Namely, the exhibition shows how different emerging technologies related to genetic engineering and synthetic materials can re-program living matter, such as bacteria or algae, in order to manufacture products. Projects like Suzanne Lee's "Biocouture", EcoLogicStudio's "Hortus. Paris", or Collet's "Biolace" are key to understanding the extent to which the salvatory narrative of turn-of-the-century sustainability is in decline in some experimental spheres, having given way to a certain nihilism that celebrates the aesthetic and playful impact offered by these synthetic environments.

Under these conditions, the "Hylozoic Ground" (2010) by Philip Beesley stands out for its exuberance, complexity and ambition. The installation consists of an acrylic forest, set up inside the Canadian Pavilion at the 2010 Venice Architecture Biennale, covered with sensors, micro-processors, mechanical joints and filters. The structure moves in response to its surroundings, gradually producing a hybrid ground through hanging geotextiles that filter the air and collect particles from the environment.

The "Hylozoic Ground" is thus a bio-technological landscape shaped by chemical exchanges between living and synthetic materials, which behaves like a coral reef, following

_"Pahoehoe Beauty",Daniela Mitterberger and Tiziano Derme, 2018.

a series of cycles of opening, contracting, filtering and digesting. Again, on the one hand, in its variety of natural, human and technological agents, the project is framed by the critical post-humanism that we described at the beginning of the chapter, offering a conception of nature that is radically distanced from romantic, contemplative and idealized visions. On the other hand, however, our perception of it is not merely visual: it is a tactile, auditory and even olfactory experience, where perpetual movement and transformation make it unpredictable and surprising, entirely in line with the main features of the age of experience. Surprisingly, however, in its aesthetics there is still a certain subordination to the idyllic image of a lush forest. It is paradoxical that after an exercise of desacralizing nature in order to synthesize it using bio-technologies, the general and multi-sensorial appearance of the project replicates the usual figuration of a forest. In other words, as it is also the case with some of the projects that we will see further in this chapter, there is a very evident tension between a stance that has no problem in manipulating and disturbing a nature that has been taken off its pedestal, and another stance that idealizes it by formally replicating the aesthetic patterns and imagery of its western cultural conjugation. It is precisely in this sense that Maeid's projects such as "The eye of the Other - II" (2019) and "Pahoehoe Beauty - I" (2018) represent a step further. The multispecie entanglements that vertebrate their work do not attempt to constitute a staged and hyper-technological version of the Eden Garden. Rather than emulating a pristine mother nature through replicating the morphological, kinematic and chromatic characteristics of a virgin forest, "Pahoehoe Beauty" is presented as a dark multispecie geology, a compost of organic and inorganic agents which are not merely juxtaposed or overlapped, but mutually entangled. Under this umbrella, and together with projects such as Noumena's "Robotic Habitats" (2017), the green discourse and its neo-modern salvific rhetoric has been replaced by the radical assumption of one premise: to live "together" necessarily implies the emancipation from the Christian myths and its various modern secularizations attempting to separate nature and culture. In this sense, the techno-organic geology constituted by "Pahoehoe Beauty" opposes the plant figurativeness and the green fragrance that structure Beesley's artificial forest: Maeid's hybridisation of 3d printed soil and hi-tech robotic agents does not aim for domestication and familiarity, but for wildness and alterity, for a disturbing emancipation that is not constituted as a cause for fear, but as a horizon of possibilities.

3. PERFORMING MATTER

"Digital Matter"; "Intelligent Matter"; "Behavioural Matter"; "Informed Matter"; "Living Matter", "Feeling Matter"; "Vibrant Matter"; "Mediated Matter"; "Responsive Matter"; "Robotic Matter"; "Self-Organized Matter"; "Ecological Matter"; "Programmable Matter"; "Active Matter"; "Energetic Matter". There is indeed no term enjoying better reputation in today's experimental architectural discourse than "matter"; the previous expressions, gently provided by a myriad of studios hosted in pioneer universities around the world, illustrate the redemption of a notion that has traditionally been dazzled by form's radiance. Today, in spite of being a deeply problematic concept, as we will see in what follows, "matter" is an unavoidable term that illuminates not just the field of experimental architecture, but the whole spectrum of our cultural landscape: several streams in Philosophy, Science and Art have also vigorously embraced it by praising its vibrant fruitfulness and holistic constitution. In this context, the architect's role is not characterized by mediating a discrete set of agents, but by performing a continuum of matter, that is, by matter's artificial construction rather than by its natural extraction. The notion of performance should be read in opposition to the concept of metaphore and, above all, under the gravitational field of Deleuze's *abstract machine*. Manuel Delanda approaches this notion with enlightening clarity in the following text:

"When we say (as marxists used to say) that "class struggle is the motor of history", we are using the word "motor" in a purely metaphorical sense. However, when we say that "a hurricane is a steam motor" we are not simply making a linguistic analogy; rather, we are saying that hurricanes embody the same diagram used by engineers to *build* steam motors -that is, we are saying that a hurricane, like a steam engine, contains a reservoir of heat, operates via thermal differences, and circulates energy and materials through a (so-called) Carnot Cycle".[45]

Delanda suggests that Deleuze's *abstract machine* operates in different manners according to its tecnological or metereological context. Thus, with the expression "Performing Matter" we refer to those relational operators that articulate different natural and cultural fields through the same engineering diagram, rather than merely producing relations of allusion, as would be the case of the metaphore.

To perform matter implies a complete reformulation of the conventional understanding of the term; since the Ancient Greece and generally speaking, architecture has interpreted the notion of matter through the Aristotelian and heteropatriarchal *hylomorphic* scheme: traditionally, matter has been understood as a disordered, passive and homogenous mass (*mother*) in attendance for being vertebrate by a structured, active and heterogeneous

_45. Manuel Delanda, *A Thousand Years of Nonlinear History* (New York: Swerve Editions, 2010), 58.

pattern (*father*). According to this framework the architect is constituted as a *Platonic demiurge*: s/he operates from a transcendent plane in order to in-form matter, that is, in order to vertebrate its pre-assumed chaotic constitution through a defined pattern. Since the Enlightenment, matter has gradually replaced its attributes with those of form through three concatenated strategies: *Truthfulness*, *vitalism* and *antrobology*. However, as we will see in what follows, the current culmination of matter's revival process in experimental architecture is, paradoxically, nothing but the exaltation of form; under the same signifier, matter's signification has been replaced by form's signification: all attributes that in the hylomorphic model were associated with the latter, have now moved to the former, converting matter's signifier in just another term to conjure up the significance of form.

3.1. Matterlessness

The concept of *truthfulness* in architecture should be read in opposition to the idealism of authors like Alberti or Palladio. Alberti claimed that "architecture is not about artisan techniques but about "cose mentale""[46]; what concerned him were not material attributes such as color or texture, but the geometrical proportions of the forms that he produced with matter. This statement becomes evident in his façade for the "Palazzo Rucellai" in 1446. Conversely, some centuries later authors like John Ruskin, Viollet-le-Duc or Gottfried Semper defended the relevance of matter in architecture, asserting that the choice of a material should depend on the laws dictated by its nature, such that "brick should look like brick; wood, wood; iron, iron, each according to its own mechanical laws"[47]. Rondelet and Choissy also gave importance to the truth of the material, particularly throughout their exhaustive constructive drawings. However, this group of authors still remained idealistic. The use of materials always had unbreachable limits, determined by the idea that the architectural object was intended to express. In that sense, and although its internal structure was recognized, matter was still subordinate to an external idea, that is to say, to an external form. Some decades later, in his *Life of Forms in Art* (1881) Henri Focillon dignified matter through an strategy based on a different concept: *vitalism*.

Although arguing that the development of art is inextricably linked to external socio-politic and economic characteristics, Focillon associated an autonomous formal mutation to it through underlining matter's inherent capacity of movement and metamorphosis. Already present in the Baroque and empowered by the Enlightenment idea of "natura naturans", concepts like the "Bildungstriet", the "Thatkraft" or the "Urpflanze" articulated a vitalist approach to matter closely related to German Expressionism. Ruskin and Semper's seminal materialism based on material's truth gave way to a radical pragmatism in which architects used hybridized materials in order to relate to natural metamorphosis. Many glass-based projects from the early 20th century replicate these morphogenetic processes, an attitude already present in the gothic. In resonance with Henri's Bergson's "élan vital"[48], certain uses of concrete imitated the formal exuberance of some morphogenetic natural processes, as we can see in the "Goetheanum" from Rudolph Steiner in 1928 or the "Einstein Tower" from Erich Mendelsohn in 1921. Moreover, the use of concrete established a continuity between form and structure that is characteristic of the organic beings that were so greatly admired at that time. As a consequence, a progressive

_46. Leon Battista Alberti, *Re-Aedificatoria* (Madrid: Ediciones Asimétricas, 2012), 21.
_47. Gottfried Semper, *The Four Elements of Architecture and Other Writings* (Cambridge: Cambridge Press, 1969), 45-73.
_48. The concept of *Élan Vital* was introduced by Henri Bergson in his seminal work "Creative Evolution". It is a hypothetical force that fuels the evolution and development of organisms.

material vitalism was thus constituted through an hylozoic approach based on Einstein theories of matter and energy interconvertibility, which suggested a comprehension of matter as a set of energetical perturbations instead of mere inert mass. In this sense and according to Henry van de Velde, matter had not only a mechanical value, but an active dispositionality that was the consequence of its "formal vocation". However, vitalism had also its conservative reverse. Fueled by the phenomenological work of Rasmussen and Norberg-Schulz, architects as Herzog & Meuron, Steven Holl or Peter Zumthor propose a haptic approach to architecture that relies on materials as symbolic shapers of architectural space. Under this scenario and in close relation to Merleau-Ponty's notion of "flesh"[49], matter is still understood as a holistic repository of tactile and cultural memory.

In parallel to the general disdain that Modernism showed for materiality during the first half of the 20th century, according to Eduardo Prieto[50] *truthfulness* and *vitalism* have gradually contributed to the reconsideration of matter as a substance with a certain agency. This process was based not on the exaltation of the passivity, neutrality and homogeneity that originally characterized matter, but on the importation of attributes from the notion of form. Ruskin's truthfulness is based precisely on the understanding that matter has a specific inner "character" that makes it heterogeneous, while the vitalism of Steiner alludes to the metamorphic capacities of living beings. However, both cases remain idealistic. *Truthfulness* asserts the need for an external form to choose the matter that best suits to its purposes. *Vitalism* claims that matter should be seen as a material of organic expression that still needs an artist or architect to unveil its aesthetic The concept of *Élan Vital* was introduced by Henri Bergson in his seminal work "Creative Evolution". It is a hypothetical force that explains the evolution and development of organisms. potentialities of metamorphosis. In both cases, matter is still seen not just in opposition to an external form, but also under its control. In this sense, the vitalism defended by Bergson differs from the vitalism of Deleuze: for the former, matter is still a generic substance that needs an artist to particularize it, that is, needs an élan vital to form it. Conversely, for Deleuze, matter is an immanent reality: it provides form to itself and does not require any transcendental agent. This Deleuzian conception of matter has been emphasized today through New Materialism, whose statements in relation to the problem matter-form are based "on the idea that matter has morphogenetic capacities of its own and does not need to be commanded into generating form"[51]. In this sense, matter is not any more seen in opposition to form, that is, "it is not a substrate or a medium for the flow of desire, but it is always already a desiring dynamism, a reiterative reconfiguring, energized and energizing, enlivened and enlivening"[52]. This philosophical approach reverberates with our current technological condition. The historical and incremental process of matter legitimation, based initially on the truthfulness of Ruskin and the vitalism of Steiner, culminates today with the celebration of the notions of platform, information and performance that singularize Sadin's *antrobology*. Recent theorisations on concepts related to computation and design such as Keller Easterling's *Medium Design* (2018) or Benjamin Bratton's *The Stack* (2015) are as well deeply underpinned by these three expressions.

_49. The notion of "flesh" combines physical materiality with all kinds of impulses, desires, appetites, fears, etc.

_50. Eduardo Prieto, *La vida de la materia* (Madrid: Ediciones Asimétricas, 2018), 28-102.

_51. Manuel Delanda, "Interview with Manuel Delanda", in *New Materialism: Interviews and Cartographies*, ed. Rick Dolphijn & Iris van der Tuin, (London: Open Humanities Press, 2012), 43.

_52. Keren Barad, "Interview with Keren Barad", in Rick Dolphijn & Iris van der Tuin (ed), *New Materialism: Interviews and Cartographies* (London: Open Humanities Press, 2012), 59.

However, it is crucial to note that the term "form" is present in all of them, associating each expression to one of the three main form's attributes: structure (in-formation), activity (per-formance) and heterogeneity (plat-form) .While matter "is that which resist taking any definite contour"[53], form refers to the active presence of a distinguished and qualified structure that contain other forms at every level of scale and that can occasionally change and establish relationships. It is under this framework that the previous terms should be read in relation to experimental architecture. To provide a "platform" means to provide the conditions for an evolving "intertwining" in between forms that permits the coordinated co-existence of difference, that is, of heterogeneity. Is important to underline here that a platform is not a field, because the former doesn't permit any sort of reductionism, that is, its elements are not mere emergences of it, as occurs with fields. To "inform" means to provide "structure": it consists in preventing spatio-temporal messiness by establishing an order both in time and space. However, given that every entity has already a form and we cannot imagine a formless element, to inform means actually to transform. To "perform", in contrast, means to be radically present: it produces an operative impact on the set of conditions in which it is placed, instead of merely symbolizing a non-present entity.

Under Sadin's *antrobology*, the disorder, passivity and homogeneity that traditionally identified matter are replaced by those characteristics that qualified form in the hylomorphic model: structure (information), activity (performance) and heterogeneity (platform). However, if the process of legitimation of matter is rooted in replacing its attributes by those of form, it is increasingly more unsustainable to keep referring to it as "matter", when actually, especially in Sadin's *antrobology* and from a hylomorphic point of view, matter is empty of matter and full of form.

However, the rupture of the dichotomy caused by matter's absorption of form has implied the introduction of a pre-Socratic matter's condition: that of being ultimate. Matter is not understood anymore as one of the components of a dualistic model, but as a single holistic substance whose structure, activity and heterogeneity underlies the emergence of any specific entity. This model, technologically underpinned by Sadin's *antrobology*, has been articulated by contemporaneous experimental architecture according to one of the most popular representatives of pre-Socratic approaches to matter: Anaximandrus continuous field. For the greek philosopher, *apeiron* refers to the notions of indefinite and unlimited, alluding explicitly to the origin (arché) of all forms of reality. Precisely because *apeiron*, as suggested by its etymology, is that which cannot be limited, it doesn't have in itself any specific form, that is, it is not definible, being, according to its author, inengenerated and imperishable. It is therefore a continuous material sustrata, vague and boundaryless, capable of supporting the opposites from which all world's differentiation emerges. Besides Bruno Latour's "Plasma", described by its author as that unknown and material hinterland which is not yet formatted, measured or subjectified, one of the most popular contemporaneous elaborations of this *apeiron*'s holistic theory is Jane Bennett's "Throbbling Whole". For the American philosopher, objects would be "those swirls of matter, energy, and incipience that hold themselves together long enough to vie with the strivings of other objects, including the indeterminate momentum of the throbbing whole", something that according to Harman "we already encountered, in germ, in the pre-Socratic

_53. Graham Harman, "Materialism is Not the Solution", *The Nordic Journal of Aesthetics*, No.47 (2014), 100.

_"Allmannajuvet Zinc Mine Museum",Peter Zumthor 2016.

apeiron"[54]. Beside certain comformative continuities as Alejandro Zaera-Polo's "Yokohama Terminal" (2000) or François Roche's "Asphalt Spot" (2002) , we can find a similar holistic vocation in projects whose renovated notion of matter is usually referred to as behavioral matter, living matter, ecological matter, digital matter, expanded matter, data-driven matter or intelligent matter. Paradoxically, what is relevant in all these expressions is not the term matter, but its qualifier, which systematically refers to spatio-temporal formal arrangements rather than hylomorphic matter attributes. The different projects that we will see in the following pages are based in this antrobologic understanding of materiality. They unfold structural, energetic, thermal and, ultimately, operative capabilities that qualitatively expand their original capacities and that are analysed in the following groups of projects: Synthetic Materiality, Organic Machines and Mixed Reality.

3.2. Synthetic Materiality

One of the most obvious examples of the application of the hylomorphic framework to architecture is that of concrete. It behaves like an authentic Aristotelian "matter" – i.e., an amorphous, neutral and homogeneous mass capable of acquiring the most fanciful of forms through a formwork system. Its habitual white color demonstrates the desire to exalt the intelligible purity of forms as contrasted with raw material, something Le Corbusier celebrated when he affirmed that "whitewash is absolute; on it, everything stands out, inscribes itself absolutely; it is sincere and loyal"[55]. According to this framework and through geometry and proportion, the architect is constituted as a demiurge, that is, as a being capable of acting from a transcendent plane and endowing, as if it were a miracle, structuring way to plain matter. Concrete has been the quintessential 20th-century material. From the first buildings by Auguste Perret (Rue Franklin, 1904) to the latest structures by architects like Jean Nouvel (Agbar, 2005), authors working from diverse ideologies –

_54. Ibid., 98.
_55. Le Corbusier, *When The Cathedrals were White* (New York: Mc Graw-Hill Book Company, 1964).

_"Hydro Pavilion",Achim Menges, 2013.

from Le Corbusier to Peter Eisenman, Frank Lloyd Wright or Aldo Rossi – have all used concrete as a fundamental material in their designs. However, perhaps the architect who best illustrates its possibilities is Oscar Niemeyer. Eminent pursuant of Le Corbusier, the Brazilian architect honored his origins in Rio de Janeiro with a formal, exuberant and voluptuous approach, in which concrete allowed him to display a great formal richness, although a high price had to be paid: due to the poor performance of the material in the face of natural agents such as sun, rain or humidity, his buildings require constant maintenance, are difficult to recycle, and require all kinds of machinery merely to offer adequate climate conditions for their users. Other authors who have made extensive use of the formal advantages of concrete include such precursors of parametricism as Max Berg, Luigi Moretti, Pier Luigi Nervi or Vladimir Schukov, whose warped forms and double curvatures required the use of materials with high formal flexibility. It is also true, however, that architects like Eladio Dieste in his "Church of Christ the Worker" (1960) built similar structures, not through the exaltation of continuity, but using strategies of discretization drawing on brick construction.

The material approach put forward by advanced architecture during this decade is just the opposite. As expressed by Marco Poletto and Claudia Pasquero, when matter is freed from essentialist conceptualizations that see it as an amorphous entity, regulated by transcendental geometric laws, it becomes generative and self-organized. Henri Focillon alluded to this issue already more than a century ago in his *Vie des Formes* (1881), where he emphasized the formal prestructure that inhabits any material. Manuel Delanda has also written extensively on this subject in *Matter Matters* (2007), one of the texts that most clearly addresses the concept of matter from an expansive perspective. In this way, Ruskin and Semper's seminal materialism based on the idea of the truth of materials gives way to a radical pragmatic expansion in which architects have no objection to working with hybridized, heterogeneous or artificial materials, because what is relevant is not the figurativeness of the material, but its metamorphic capacity as a performative effect

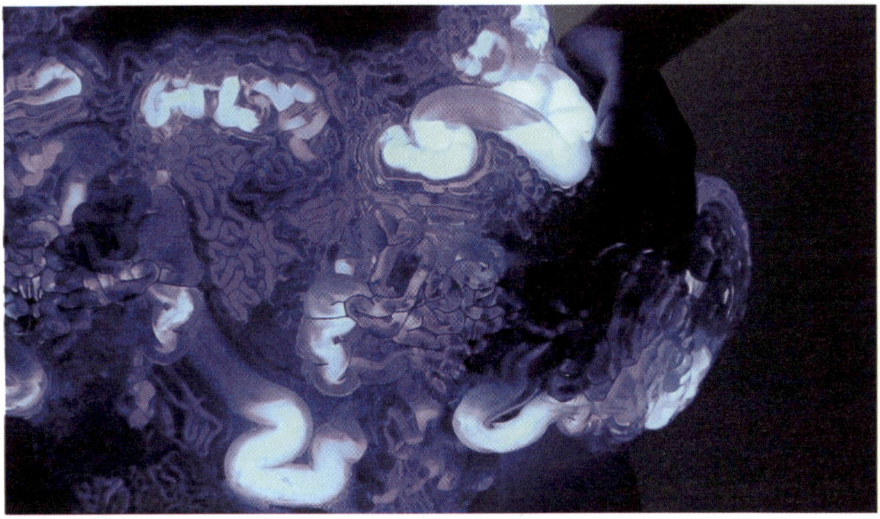

_"Wanderers", Neri Oxman, 2014.

and aesthetic affection. In this context, the idea of "event" replaces the idea of "true substance": the architect behaves more like an alchemist, that is, a chemist who is "less interested in materials (homogeneous, static, sincere) than in matter itself (heterogeneous, dynamic and equivocal). A material hylozoism is thus constituted, which, however, also has its conservative reverse, which is articulated through the phenomenology of the material anticipated by Steen Eiler Rasmussen and Christian Norberg-Schulz, based on the ideas of Martin Heidegger and championed by Juhani Pallasmaa. It proposes a haptic approach to architecture that relies on materials as symbolic shapers of architectural space, understanding them as the repositories of a tactile and cultural memory that stands in contrast to the supposed technical and ideological alienation of modernity. The idea has a certain Ruskinian slant and is diametrically opposed to the performative and operative character of advanced architecture. In this context, the concept of *biomimetics* is fundamental and, in general, widely misunderstood. Delanda defines the term as "a subfield of the science of materials that examines biological creatures in an attempt to derive design principles that may be utilized in an industrial context". Following to this approach, the goal of *biomimetics* is not to replicate a material that already exists in nature. Delanda illustrates this idea through industry's use of the spider's web: since arachnids cannot be domesticated, their proteins are extracted for insertion into a domesticated animal, in this case the goat, and the material is recovered from its milk. Through a series of processes, the material that is obtained can be used in structural designs, given the particular strengths of spider silk when it is under tension. However, this is not the case of a biomimetic process, since there is no extraction of an abstract principle to be applied to a different material. A much more appropriate illustration of the concept of *biomimetics* would be the architectural interpretation of the structural arrangement characteristic of vertebrates: its combination of elements capable of working in tension, i.e., muscles, along with elements capable of working in compression, i.e., bones, emerges as a logic that has often been applied in architecture, albeit with completely different materials.

_"In Vitro - Habitat", Terreform, 2013.

In this sense, throughout this second decade of the 21st century, advanced architecture not only attempts to reveal the "pattern" of each "matter" in order to act accordingly, it also concentrates on the processes of material expansion – in other words, on increasing the capabilities of a material by synthesizing it with other external elements. As such, the advanced architecture of those years engages in an in-depth exercise of bionic engineering, in which abstract principles from nature are developed using mechanical-chemical instruments. In that sense, designs like the "Hydro Pavilion" by Achim Menges (2013), despite their powerful disciplinary contribution, inhabit a line of work that is set apart from biomimetics and the most advanced expansiveness. After a thorough study of the patterns according to which wood contracts and dilates with variations in humidity, Menges built a wooden pavilion that benefits from this movement to open and close the holes in the main body. It is an architectural exercise in which materiality has taken on two new aspects in relation to the traditional material approach. In the first place, it is no longer a receptive and amorphous element but instead possesses a formal predetermination that conditions its use. Second, it is no longer a passive element mobilized by external artifacts but instead possesses its own movement that can be put into operation. In other words, materiality has become a performative agent.

Nevertheless, it is not an expanded system. It is not because, as we have seen, the aim of an expanded system is not to replicate the function of a material that already operates as such naturally. On the contrary, expanding a material requires understanding a series of abstract principles from nature, or other technological processes, in order to apply them to materials that do not work in that way a priori, but doing so increases their "performance" qualitatively. That is not the case with Menges's pavilion, since its approach consists in replicating a process that already exists in the behavior of wood, rather than in expanding its nature. Rachel Armstrong's insist in this point through her coordination of "Living Architecture" (2016), a project that couples the computational properties of the natural world with matter at far from equilibrium. Rather than mimicking biological outputs, Armstrong is interested in understanding the metabolic processes that shape these outputs. In this sense, the prototypes developed by her are a good example of the multispecie entanglements that characterize the xenological condition: under Armstrong's "Living Architecture" project, the relationship established in between spontaneous natural processes and humans may no longer be passive, but "we may begin to "speak" chemically, physically, biologically, mechanically and even digitally (through electricity) with the living world."[56]. These material systems are characterised by operating far from equilibrium states, possessing their own liveliness and agency, two points that resonate with Nery Oxman's "Wonderers" (2014). The project came to light during the exhibition "The Sixth Element: Exploring the Natural Beauty" of 3D Printing in Frankfurt and consists of a series of structures printed in 3D with Stratasys multimaterial 3D printing technology, in which biological material is inserted to increase the operational capabilities. Following this framework, each piece contains living and synthetically manipulated substances that are distributed through a series of cavities and internal capillaries arranged in the printed material, making it into an "expanded material" capable of transforming oxygen to breathe, photons to see, biomass to eat, bio-fuel to move and calcium to build. In short, it is a spongy 3D-printed material into which synthetically processed microorganisms are infiltrated, and through their biological processes they are able to provide oxygen, light, nutrients and energy to the users in hostile environments, such as other planets. The project is located at the intersection between multi-material 3D-printing and synthetic biology, under an entirely operative and manipulable understanding of nature and with the objective of generating self-sufficient human micro-habitats. In that sense, and in the words of Oxman, the future of this type of expanded materials lies precisely in designing augmented extensions of our bodies, emerging as artifacts that can blur the boundaries between our environments and our being, in resonances with what we have defined as plastic corporalities. As such, our bodies are no longer made up only of human processes. They are no longer the zero point of our human nature, because the notion of Adamian body has been shifted. It has been hybridized to incorporate other processes of a biological and computational nature. However, this expanded material, as presented by the Israeli architect, has not been set up in a particular architecture. Or, in any case, it has taken the form of a kind of space suit far removed from the typologies to which we are accustomed. This fact is more interesting than it may seem at first, since it shows that these "expanded fabrics" provide their users with all the functional conditions traditionally resolved by architecture, such as thermal comfort and protection from the elements. This fact undoubtedly rattles the foundations of the discipline and elicits the following question: What is does architecture's role become when its original functions of protection and basic comfort can be solved by other devices?

The "in vitro – habitat" project by Terreform One implements the opposite strategy: instead of expanding our bodies through the introduction of processes of a non-human nature, the US office expands architectural materiality through the introduction of biological processes. The design is based on the use of 3D-printed pig cells to create entirely organic dwellings. For now, there is only one prototype that is made up of a mixture of synthetic materials, pig cells and sodium benzoate to preserve fungi and bacteria. This experiment is interesting because of its provocative and subversive capacity, which highlights the extent to which sustainability requires a new radical vision of inhabitation, and not a mere strategy of resilience. Both projects resonate with Black Gaia's voca-

_56. Rachel Armstrong, interview by Richard Bright, "Living Architecture", *Interalia Magazine* (2017).

tion; nature is no longer a maternal entity, pure and incorruptible; it has ceased to be a secularized version of the Garden of Eden. On the contrary, Black Gaia emerges as a manipulable assemblage that we can alter on a molecular scale. In that sense, all these projects illustrate the extent to which the relationship between architecture and nature is moving in a new direction. At times, architecture has taken nature as its model: in some periods, such as Art Nouveau, it has stood as a formal point of reference, while at other times, like in the Middle Ages, nature has served as a structural reference. When Victor Horta used natural patterns as the foundation for ornamental motifs he was engaging in a highly complex cultural act, yet the relationship to nature was essentially visual *mimesis*. Beginning in the mid-18th century, nature was presented as an element of validation through two fundamental procedures. On the one hand, appealing to an ideal and perfect geometry (revealed by Newton through his Physics), to which the architectural elements were compared, as Laugier did with his "Primitive Hut". And, on the other hand, dividing and classifying buildings and their elements into complex taxonomies comparable to the classificatory systems developed Buffon and Linnaeus, later including Cuvier and his focus on function.[57] Throughout the 20th century, a series of projects have looked to nature as a structural point of reference through an in-depth understanding of its geometry, which is illustrated precisely in Darcy Thompson's book *On Growth and Form*. However, as Marcos Cruz states[58], the major change that has occurred in this decade has to do with the transition from a "nature-inspired" model to a "bio-integrated" model. In this sense, the concept of bio-integration goes beyond the idea that nature is a model or a stimulus: "Bio-integration tries to find new technological and material hybridities in a world where the 'natural-nature' is vanishing. Our influence is so profound that we are facing a 'supra-nature'."[59]. In that sense, the concept of bio-integration extends beyond the mere extrapolation of nature's principles: the idea is not just to take advantage of them, but to understand – as Delanda says when defining his concept of bio-mimesis – processes such as growth, mutation or evolution in order to approach them from completely new points of view. The materiality of architecture is no longer understood as tectonic performance, but rather as an integrated system of inert matter and organic matter, a constructive fabric with a cellular-based structure. Given this new conception of materiality, an aesthetics of the unpredictable emerges: i.e., an aesthetics based on the volatility of biological phenomena, which lends value to the concept of "impurity", leaving behind entirely the ideal perfection according to which nature was interpreted traditionally. Nature is no longer the mild and holistic harmony to which we return as a respite from the anxiety characteristic of urban effervescence: human beings do not inhabit that kind of divine garden. Rather, we "coexist anxiously in fragile, flawed clusters among other beings such as axes and horses, rain and specters, without a father sky god or god-king".[60]. In his project "Alga-Cellunoi" (2013), Marcos Cruz explores several of these reflections, setting aside nature as a mere source of inspiration, positing instead as one element integrated with other types of processes. The proposal centers on a wall with recesses that contains algae, a plant substance that can supply both nutrients and energy. In conjunction with the material that surrounds it, both function as an expanded material that, in this case, is arranged as a vertical partition, but which could have other uses depending on its configuration.

_57. Anthony Vidler: "The Third Typology", *Architecture Theory Since 1968* (New York: Ed. Columbia Books, 2000), 291.
_58. Marcos Cruz, interview by Jordi Vivaldi, "Bio-integrated Design", *IaaC Bits*, no. 9 (2019), 76-89.
_59. Ibid., 78.
_60. Timothy Morton, *Dark Ecology: For a Logic of Future Coexistence* (New York: Ed. Columbia University Press, 2016), 111.

This understanding of materiality is radically different from what we find in Steven Holl's Kiasma, where the "expansion" is not operative, but fundamentally metaphoric: it alludes to human's life, but the material in itself it is not "alive". In opposition to this phenomenological approach to materiality, noteworthy work has been done in the 2010s by the Digital Matter studio at the IaaC, directed by Areti Markopoulou. The Greek architect promotes built architecture in which materials can change their formal and performative conditions, thus precluding the reduction of the production to a mere inhabited space. In this context, the studio investigates how smart materials combined with responsive technologies can generate architecture that adapts and responds to the needs of the user and the environment. Projects such as "Translated Geometries" and "User-Driven Adaptive Structure" apply principles drawn from nature – such as contraction, withdrawal or evolution – but using industrial elements. This bionic application is extremely faithful to Delanda's concept of biomimicry, although its meccano-like character distances it from the synthetic and chemical processes that we find in other material developments from the same decade. Other projects by the same research group, such as the "Graphene Composite" study, set aside the idea of a "mechanism" to look at the possibilities offered by graphene as an expanded construction material. Something similar occurs in other projects that investigate new materials with the potential to mimic organic processes in order to create microclimates – as in the case of "Hydroceramics", "Breathing Skin" or "Hydromembrane" – creating constructive systems capable of breathing, sweating, and so forth.

All these projects incorporate the idea of a living materiality: in other words, the bionic crystallization of living systems. In the 1980s Maturana and Varela defined the logic of the living as follows: "The individual organization can be shown to be one of self-construction through recursive production of components, and it is this specific organization, autopoiesis, which is at the base of the autonomy of living systems."[61]. The term autopoiesis refers to a system that reproduces and maintains itself autonomously through an organization capable of recursively producing its own components. For that to be possible the system has to be able to evolve: i.e., it has to be able to change in a particular direction. It is in this context that the expression "living materiality" makes sense, even if – like in the case of the projects directed by Areti Markopoulou – the living system is not necessarily organic.

In recent years, Mette Thomsen from CITA has undertaken an extensive and in-depth investigation of the subject. Notable among the series of projects is "Slow Furl" (2012). It is a textile installation that engages with and reacts to human occupation. An "expanded fabric" retreats and contorts slowly as the user moves, continuously generating new and surprising spatial configurations. As opposed to acting as a mere flat receptacle, as would be the case with a conventional fabric, it generates a true cybernetic environment that contains its own patterns of action and reaction. This "expanded fabric" is outfitted with a system of sensors that activate a series of micro-controllers; the combination of its own activation mechanisms and the shared interaction mechanisms generates a new material that has a certain degree of indeterminacy.

The project sits halfway between augmented materials and the mediation of intelligences, since it generates an architecture that has its own behavior, as opposed to an architecture that can be reduced to a mere mechanical interaction. In that sense, the proposal fits in clearly with the expansive systems we have been describing, because it proposes an expanded fabric capable of producing architecture but, at the same time, it is not qual-

_61. Francisco Varela, "Describing the logic of the living. The adequacy and limitations of the idea of autopoiesis" in Milan Zeleny (ed), *Autopoiesis: a theory of living organization* (New York: North Holland, 1980), 36-48.

itatively reducible to the conventional and inert idea we have of fabric. In addition, it is interesting to highlight how several features characteristic of the age of experience are present in this exercise: the installation is visually striking, but what is most fascinating happens when a user touches the fabric and senses the pulse that supports it. Its sensory-mechanical system folds and twists into a series of different configurations that never repeat or accumulate, letting users sit, lean or lie down depending the formal layout. Finally, there is also a possible post-human reading of this "expanded fabric", since it is presented as an autonomous agent, with a certain capacity for interaction, but also with a certain indeterminism. It is an element with its own dynamics and sense of existence, with an autonomous behavior that makes it an intelligent agent and not a mere mechanism.

3.3. Organic Machines: From Artefacts to Artifices

Throughout the second decade of the 21st century, another way of performing matter has developed based on a new interpretation of the concept of machine. Here, it is essential to distinguish between the industrial machine characteristic of modernity and the desiring machine theorized by Deleuze and Guattari. The activity of the industrial machine is limited to the purpose for which it was designed: a thermostat, a washing machine or a telephone would be some good examples. In contrast, the process characteristic of a desiring machine is based on a force of appropriation – that is, on the tendency to incorporate what lies outside it. It is a device that adapts, evolves, dialogues and, ultimately, engages in an operative coexistence with its surroundings.

Deleuze and Guattari use the example of the orchid and the bee to describe this type of machinic phenomenon. Orchids from the Ophrys species need a pollinator in order to reproduce. Instead of attracting any type of visitor, they have specialized in attracting a certain group of insects, specifically bees and wasps. Their strategy is to mimic the shape and smell of the females of these insects, so that the plant is pollinated as the males try to mate with the flower, a phenomenon called pseudo-copulation. In this case, we conceptualize the flower-insect pair as an assemblage – in other words, a set of elements that need each other and that adapt and evolve according to their needs and the context of their interaction. Thus, "desiring machines" are inextricably embedded in the environment in which they operate, just as an animal is in its habitat.

These are precisely the type of devices that advanced architecture proposes during this decade: assemblages that involve, among other agents, an expanded material that interacts operatively with its surroundings. We could define these devices as organic machines, that is, machinic assemblages that perform living processes. This is not the case of the closed mechanics characteristic of the artifact, but rather the tentacular extroversion of the artifice: where the former acts blindly and is subject to given facts, the latter opens up to the future through its operative incorporation into the world. In that sense, we need to differentiate, on the one hand, between the operative relationships established between the environment and the propagative mechanisms from the decade 2000-2010 and, on the other hand, the relationships established between the environment and the augmentative mechanisms of the decade 2010-2020. In the first case, the interaction with the environment is established through the geometric propagation of certain behaviors characteristic of nature, increasing or reducing the parameters that determine it, such as in projects like Rahm's "Convective Apartment" (2010). In the second case, the interaction with the environment is established by per-

_"Alga(e)zebo", Marcos Cruz, 2010.

forming certain materials through biotechnological operations that substantially transform the nature of those materials. As a result, in this group the integration is much tighter, since the manipulation takes place in the very nature of the material (which is why we call it an expansive system) and not only in the relationship between materials that are "given" – which would be the case of distributive protocols.

The "Braga Pavilion" (2012) by Poletto-Pasquero is one of the clearest cases of organic machines. The project contains a series of remote sensors to detect temperature, pH, radiation and CO2, which inform the device so that it moves around a certain amount of living matter – algae in this case – through specific formal organizations such as branching tubes and surface folds. The goal is to generate a set of performative processes, such as evapotranspiration and photosynthesis, capable of generating a high amount of oxygen through the simple coexistence with the surrounding environment. The result is an artifice with a machinist, futurist and hyper-technological aesthetic – a device that seems to have dropped down from another planet but nevertheless maintains a performative and intimate connection with our own. Again, it recalls some of the animal-like artifacts by Archigram, but with capabilities that are not limited to mere mechanical movement, establishing a chemical synergy with the environment around them. However, there is a certain conceptual tension in the design. On the one hand, it seems like it is basically oriented by physiological processes conveniently calculated and optimized for the proper functioning of the algae. On the other hand, however, it transmits a certain aesthetic drive through a series of formal patterns that are operatively irrelevant but nevertheless play a big role in the visual effect of the whole. The project questions the established limits between architecture, engineering and art by managing an intense physical-chemical complexity that is formalised through an expressive aesthetical language. Although the project resonates with Black Gaia's narrative we mentioned earlier, its exuberant aesthetics surpasses

_"House Solvay", Victor Horta, 1895.

any other dimension of the design: it emerges as a true living being whose bio-chemical processes offer a futuristic spectacle that distances it from the sobriety characteristic of other disciplines. As such, the design cannot be reduced to the engineering explanation of how it operates, as has often been approached; rather, it has to be understood first and foremost as an aesthetic exercise.

The authors have completed several projects along similar lines, including "Algaetecture" (2014), in this case in collaboration with Carlo Ratti, which is capable of producing as much oxygen as four hectares of forest by harnessing the photosynthesis of micro-algae. In this case, the interaction between technology and biology also has certain functional architectural consequences: with more intense sunlight, the algae grows, reducing the transparency of the covering and increasing the density of the shade. In this sense, the transparency and color of the whole are a real-time result of the climate, the visitors, the micro-algae and the digital control of the systems. In any case, this type of project overcomes the traditional segregation between technology and nature characteristic of the industrial era to embrace what in the words of Poletto-Pasquero would be a "systemic architecture" – i.e., an architecture in which "the borders between material, spatial and technological aspects have been carefully articulated to achieve efficiency, resilience and beauty."[62]. The project represents a very clear example of work based on the ideas of systematicity and multi-scalarity, using an approach to the city based on a series of assemblies that range from the bacterial scale to the urban scale. It is also a non-anthropocentric urban perspective, in which, just as it is impossible to draw a boundary between nature and artifice, it is impossible to separate landscape and city. Although the approach begins with work rooted in materiality, the multi-scalarity of the designs often implies an urban

_62. Marco Poletto and Claudia Pasquero, *Systemic Architecture* (London: Ed. Routledge, 2012).

reading that is not developed based on a set of typologies but rather based on dynamic systems. In any case, and as the authors themselves assert, their machinic developments, unlike industrial machinery, do not have a specific purpose: they are simply systems that evolve based on a physical-chemical interaction with the environment.The devices are not presented from the standpoint of a salvific narrative; rather, they harness the ecological account to construct a compelling aesthetic phenomenon.

Another project that runs along similar lines is "Alga(e)zebo" (2010), by Marjan Colletti and Marcos Cruz. In this case, the exercise consists in an installation for the Euston Square Gardens made using a metallic structure that evokes the trees that surround it. A series of vertical bio-reactors made of transparent plastic are installed inside the metallic trunks.They incorporate different types of micro-organisms: from CO2-consuming micro-algae to bacteria native to the environment. However, despite the excellent work done in cutting the pattern into the metal surfaces to structurally and figuratively evoke tree branches, the result is closer to the Art Noveau's decorative gesticulations than to an expansive "apparatus": the algae introduced into the vertical columns grows and changes depending on the invasion of local species, but their productive capacity in relation to their environment is very limited. In conceptual terms, the apparatus does not operate as Deleuze's *abstract machine*, but, in spite of its biotechnological narrative, it ends up constructing a technological, chromatical and figurative replica of a tree rather than a performative implementation of an abstracted "tree diagram". Thus, its impact on the user unfolds primarely in the symbolic realm of those allusions and metaphores that celebrate the welfare provided by the archaic figure of the tree.

However, Colletti's and Cruz's "Alga(e)zebo" manages to establish as well a multiscalar bio-integration: on the largest scale, the perforated pattern of the corten steel obeys structural purposes, although on a figurative level it creates a relationship with the foliage of the surrounding trees. On a medium scale, the gazebo can be read as a scaffold to support the growth of a variety of plants. On a smaller scale, the algae is introduced into a series of tubular recipients, making it possible to observe its growth. The Alga(e) zebo project should be read thus as a set of decorative, performative and structural elements promoting the co-inhabitation of several kinds of biological agents. However, it does so through an aesthetical and conceptual narrative that still wants to evoke, through its figurative and chromatic gestures, the protection and welfare provided by a notion of nature that is still deeply maternal.

Most of the artifices presented at the bioTallinn exhibition (2017), curated by EcoLogicStudio, work along similar lines. The exhibition involved participation from a variety of architects, artists and engineers whose lightweight devices involved this type of evolving machinic phenomena. In this sense, IaaC's project "LiveCycles"[63] is emblematic of what we have defined here as an organic machine: by establishing symbiotic processes in between artificial and natural agents, the projects aims at creating a bioartificial system while generating and printing aggregated matter that has been digested -filtered- from Baltic sea water. However the scale of the project does not exceed that of the pavilion, and, thus, its translation to a medium-big scale architectural environment remains open. In this sense, the "BIQ House" (2015) in Hannover is representative: its "expanded façade", formed by a series of micro-algae panels that absorbs heat to cool the building, explores the possibilities of organic machines applied in a building scale. Its similarity in size, proportion and sustainable vocation resonates with Geli's Media-TIC building. However,

_63. LiveCycles has been developed in IaaC by a project team lead by Maria Kuptsova.

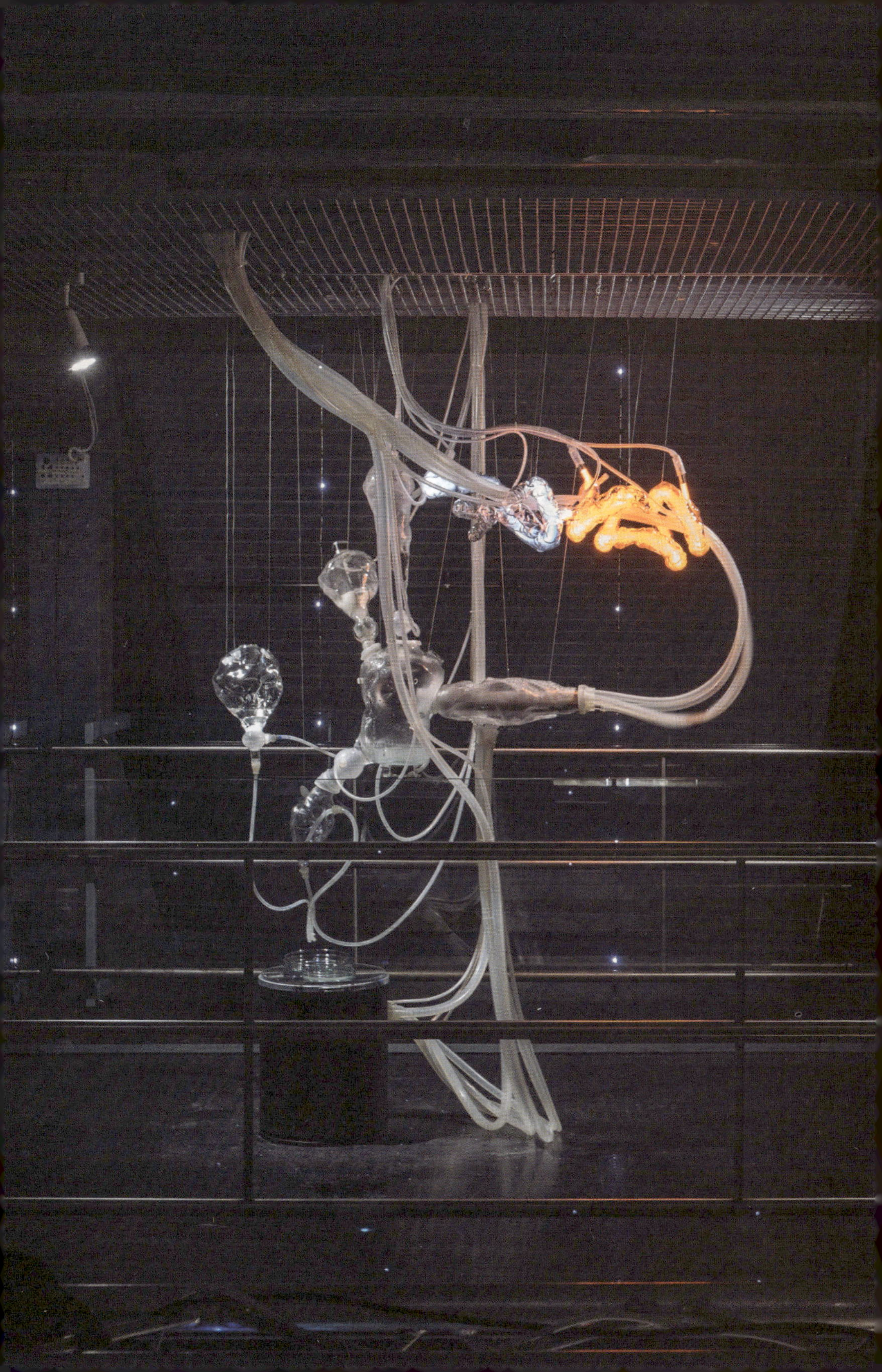

there is a fundamental difference, tied in with the *zeitgeist* characteristic of this second decade of the 21st century: whereas the façade of the Media-TIC building draws mainly on a geometric operativity, based on overlapping positive and negative patterns to let the sun in or protect against it, the building by BIQ harnesses a chemical operativity, with algae cladding that can literally breathe and digest, an essential characteristic of expansive systems. In opposition to Geli's Media-TIC, BIQ's project resonates with Armstrong's statements because it shares some of the attributes usually associated with living systems, such as cooperation, openness or synthesis. In this sense, the project can be understood in Armstrong's terms, that is, as a "soft, dynamic, hypercomplex, "mortal" configuration of matter with metabolisms and a potentially augmenting relationship with natural systems".[64] However, paradoxically the building combines green performative façades with green metaphoric façades: the first ones are green due to the algae, while the second ones are green due to its painting. The first ones operate by producing energy and cooling down the building, while the second ones operate mainly as a communication tool, that is, under the symbolic realm. Besides, the interior distribution responds to the commercial standards without offering any novelty related to its algae façade. In this sense, the experimental dimension of the building is limited to a set of algae panels hanging in two façades, contrasting thus with the holistic approach characteristic of Geli's "Media-TIC".

3.4. Mixed Reality and the Inhabitation of its Pictorial Multiverse.

At the end of the 1980s and throughout the 1990s, the realm of the virtual seemed to have plunged us into a trivialization of reality. It was understood as an approximation, or better, as a mimetic exercise that on the one hand offered much lower resolution and precision than what is captured by our senses, and, on the other hand, it did not add any kind of external data capable of producing a qualitatively different experience. This lack of precision reduced its uses in the field of architecture to the manipulation and basic representation of forms, without offering the possibility of a true paradigm shift in the design process. In the first decade of the 21st century, however, the virtual phenomenon evolved to the point of offering the exact opposite: a reading of reality whose precision largely expands our natural capacity, being capable of giving us an in-depth understanding of materiality and, as such, serving as an effective design tool. In this second decade, the virtual phenomenon, which includes not just new images but the whole cyberspace of geo-finance, the space of multimedia and the information superhighways, has begun to emerge not only as a more or less precise tool for contact with reality; it is constituted as a reality in itself that expands the physical realm by merging with it and performing a hybrid materiality. The clash at the planetary level between the real and the virtual has not implied Baudrillard's dissociation between a very high-frequency virtual space and a zero-frequency real space; the french philosopher presented both worlds as "no longer having anything in common, nor is there any communication between them"[65] because "the unconditional extension of the virtual [...] brings with it an unprecendented desertification of real space and all that surrounds us".[66] However, there is every time less discrepancy in between both: its intimacy no longer involves just visible information on a screen; rather, there is a simultaneous perception of signals that is tactile, textual, visual, auditory, etc. But the phenomenon of augmented reality not only consists of a series of

_64. https://www.interaliamag.org/interviews/rachel-armstrong-living-architecture/
_65. Jean Baudrillard, *Screened Out* (New York: Ed Verso, 2002), 65.
_66. Ibid., 66

_"BIQ House", Arup, 2015.

multisensory informational layers that give us an immediate understanding of things. It also emphasizes our own hybrid condition "by mixing, in an increasingly intimate way, bodies and the deductive power of processors[67]"; it constitutes a saturated pictorial multiverse: an overlap of multiple representational registers that define a kaleidoscopic aesthetical framework whose inhabitation challenges the conventional and lineal interpretative patterns associated with time-space's perception. As such, we are not dealing with a virtual reality, understood as a parallel reality, or an augmented reality, understood as the multisensory perception of a digital phenomenon, but a mixed reality – in other words, a reality that is simultaneously made up of physical elements and virtual elements that affect an increasingly broad number of sequences in our daily lives. This generates a dual regime of experience in which contemporary technology "intensely experiences" the present, offering each individual a hybrid present where is increasingly difficult to differentiate the digital or material nature of its parts. We are no longer facing a virtual world that inhabits screens and projections, but a digital realm that becomes occupiable due to its intimate intertwining with the physical world. In spite of this crazed technological optimism and its messianic incantation of the virtual, the intimate entanglement in between both realms has not created a new political situation or a genuine crisis: instead, it has so far solidified the techno-political establishment by favouring the monopoles associated with the big technological enterprises and by assuming that a big part of earth's population has no access to this double realm despite its capacity to impact the way we inhabit cities. Following Liam Young, the coming collapse of Artificial Intelligence and Mixed Reality will permit us to just dial up or down the levels of opacity with which we see the world: the physical materiality will start to be recursively expanded through the projection of various forms of digital and augmented content, converting architecture in the background in which the digital world is build. This means that the rules of the screen will become the rules of the space, and the physical makeup of the world will just be a very small part of our experience. The emergence of occupational virtualities, that is, digital simulations whose projection on the physical reality permit its inhabitation, suggests the need for a new urban infrastructural operativity that will structure and define cities in a different way: bandwidth and refresh dates will be as relevant as public systems of power and water networks are today. In this sense, graphic card power and processing speed will become primary forms of urban infrastructure.

Companies like Trimble are moving in this direction, opening up new business avenues through the production of software applications to manage mixed reality processes and holography, including "Oculus Rift" (2012), "HTC Vive" (2011) and "Hololens" (2016), notably. However, one of the most high-profile cases, with an impact most closely related to the sphere of urbanism, is the aforementioned case of "Pokemon Go" (2016). Its implementation shows that the collapsing of the logics of the screen on top of the logics of the physical world has the potential of qualitatively changing the meaning of inhabiting the world, and therefore, the meaning of designing the world. Under the framework of mixed reality and following Young, architects would operate more as game developers or as visual effect artists, rather than as makers and shapers of physical objects. However, this approach reduces the figure of the architect to a mere "effectist" or "scenographer", reviving some of the attributes that singularised the discipline during the Baroque. The fact that architects become experts in the spatialisation of conventional screen dimen-

_67. Eric Sadin, *La humanidad aumentada* (Buenos Aires: La Caja Negra, 2017), 119.

sions such as resolution or pixels animation is eclipsing the critical role of its figure: its productions seem often to be limited to mere evanescent spectacles, void of the critical, visionary and artistic intent that should singularize an architecture that claims to be experimental or speculative. There are some incursions into this field offering alternatives, although in most cases the instrumentalization of these technologies in the field of architectural design has been merely representational. One of the first actions in this direction was launched by a group of architects including prominent professionals like Greg Lynn, Neil Denari and Ooterhuis, who were dissatisfied with how Koolhaas' "Fundamentals" exhibition at the architecture Biennale (2014) ignored the digital phenomenon and decided to hack the exhibition. They developed an alternative floor plan of the exhibition that included locations where pointing with a smart phone camera loaded a 3D model of projects that were not included in the official exhibition catalogue. It is a rather anecdotal case of limited disciplinary value, but it nonetheless emphasizes some of the subversive possibilities of this type of technology.

The Ozel Office project called Liveforever (2014) represents a step forward. The project lets the user experience an augmented reality in Los Angeles, through the screen of a tablet or smart phone, specifically on the trail that leads to the Hollywood sign. Again, there is no architectural contribution; in this case, it is about establishing a communication that basically offers information about future narratives related to Hollywood and the urban culture of Los Angeles. The novelty begins to emerge in how we interact with nature: suddenly technology becomes an element that mediates between what is visible and what is invisible, what is real and what is it is virtual, generating a mixed reality that does not follow the rules of how we are used to interacting with nature. This same phenomenon is harnessed by the architects Andrew Zientek and Francisi Bitonti for the "Metis Garden" contest. In the project, a space is designed that, in the words of its authors, acts as a "latent landscape", waiting for operations of addition and subtraction. With a phone or tablet, users can operate in the virtual dimension of the garden, where they can choose what kinds of plants they want to see, what kind of paths they want to follow, and they can even leave messages to be read by future users. And so, the garden grows not only in the physical dimension, but also in its virtual informational dimension, establishing a mixed reality that constantly feeds on the relationships between its physical and virtual dimensions. In general, so far the architectural production based on mixed reality is brief and limited in scope. The main drawback is that mixed reality is still mediated by infrastructures that are not implanted into our corporality like an organ into our organism; they are still accessory artifacts rather than algorithmic folds. Plus, the results obtained through these type of processes are still incorporated at the end of the design process, focusing basically on issues of representation and not design. Only few projects suggest the possibility of making mixed reality a design augment, as is the cases of the "Metis Garden" we have just seen. In this sense, the project "Nina" (2019), developed at the "Da. Digital Art in FEFU" is representative of this designing vocation: the proposal, placed at the liminal space in between arts and architecture, aims at rethinking and radically amplifying the design possibilities of a hospital room by blending both realms under a poetic and narrative design experience. The project is also pretty representative of an aesthetical phenomena particularly related to the inhabitation of this dual regime: rather than coherent, predictable and passive animations, mixed reality unfolds a chaotic set of unpredictable and emancipated simulations that interact in real time with the physical world; simulations that, in opposition to animations, are no longer "about" anything in

_"Nina", Da. Digital Art. Tutor: Ildar Yakubov / Curators: Maria Kuptsova, Eduard Haiman, Vadim Smakhtin. / Students: Ekaterina Pryanichnikova and Alexander Serechenko, 2020.

particular in the classical sense[68] - much like "reality" is not about anything in particular-, but operate instead as a medium that bridges the two sides of the dual regime associated with mixed reality; they offer an open-endedness and chaotic pictorial time-space that opposes the traditional narrative structures based on the classical tropes of storytelling and its lineal and progressive assignation of meaning. Under this kaleidoscopic aesthetical framework, mixed reality orchestrates the "infinite blending and remix of multiple, traditionally separate or opposing aesthetic regimes"[69]: physical scenarios coexisting with the figurativity of cartoony characters, the abstraction of geometric solids, the effervescence of visual effects or the semantics of textual objects; multiple representational registers constituting one single world, that is, a fully saturated pictorial multiverse.

4. XENO-SURREALISM

Beside the arrival of new fabrication strategies, new design methods or new adaptive devices, the implementation of expansive protocols in experimental architecture sets the background for what we have defined here with the term Xeno-Surrealism. The expression alludes to an aesthetical re-interpretation of Surrealism and its original structural principles, as defined by Rosalind Krauss in *The originality of the avant-garde and other modernist myths* (1986). As we will see in what follows, rather than instrumentalizing an inner human unconscious, Xeno-Surrealism instrumentalizes an algorithmic outer otherness (*xenos*), resonating with XX's century Surrealist aesthetic principles while simultaneously demanding a profound renovation of Surrealism's theoretical apparatus.

In spite of some scattered references in Surrealist work – the empty streets inGiorgio de Chirico's paintings or the mysterious châteaux in André Breton's poetry, architecture does not immediately come to mind when Surrealism is evoked[70]. The Surrealists associated buildings with the heaviness, monumentality and order that they wanted to subvert. This relation seems even more tenuous when technology is also conjured up: Surrealism was not interested in the positivism associated with scientific methods, technical systems or new materials because its hyper-rationality seemed to shade the multivalent meaning that lies beneath reality. However, the generalisation of machine learning and bio-robotisation that we have witnessed in experimental architecture during the second decade of the 21st century has promoted a form of bio-computational intelligence that exceeds the 19th-century positivism despised by Surrealism. As we have previously mentioned, Eric Sadin has defined this new technological framework according to five points: autonomy, reasoning, learning, ubiquity and cooperation.[71] Most of the experimental architectural projects based on expansive protocols have integrated some of these advancements, receiving the name of Second-Order Cybernetic Architecture (SOCA) due to their capacity to act within the system they operate.

Although the Surrealists paid little attention to architecture, its relation is a long-overlooked topic that has mostly been articulated through notions such as "unconscious", "desire", "dream" or "impulse". Roth's analyses[72] of Rococo architecture, such as Cuvilliés's "Pavilion" in Amalienburgare (1739) or Bouffrand's "Salon Hotel" in Paris (1745), are

_68. Damjan Jovanovic, *The Garden World* (Los Angeles: Sci-Arc Seminar Visual Studies, 2020), 6.
_69. Ibid., 10.
_70. Dickran Tashjian, "Home Poor Heart" in *Surrealism and Architecture*, edited by T. Mical (London: Routledge, 2005), 41.
_71. Eric Sadin, *La humanidad aumentada* (Buenos Aires: La Caja Negra, 2017), 112-113.
_72. Leland Roth. *Entender la arquitectura* (Madrid: Gustavo Gili, 2016), 424.

_"Piazza", Giorgio de Chirico, 1950.

precursors in the use of these terms, and Surrealist approaches to Modern architecture (Tashjian 2005) like Corbusier's "Villa Savoye" (1929)[73] or Costa's "Brasilia" (1960) have also been based on them.[74] Even some studies on Surrealism and architecture in the context of the recent technological paradigm shift have appealed to these terms.[75]

However, as we have previously seen, the cultural scenario posed by the xenological condition is decisively different; the intimate interactivity in between organic and inorganic species questions the foundations that underpin the epistemic modern building: it opposes Modernity's obsession in compartmentalizing reality by categorically separating all ambits of our experience. Instead, the xenological condition assumes a chaotic scenario constructed by the superimposition of many worlds, abundant and polymorphic, with "different times, scales, senses and languages"[76]. In this context, Surrealist traditional focus on human's unconscious insists in an anthropological exceptionalism that is obsolete: it still retains the hierarchical separation in between the human species and the rest of the biosphere, as if the former would be a deterritorialized creature. The Surrealism promoted by Breton defied Modernism by unveiling and celebrating the unconscious structures that govern reason, that is, by questioning the validity of Descartes' "Cogito ergo sum". However, these unconscious structures are still human structures: the unconscious other is still a human other, and therefore the "antropos" still centralizes the Surrealist stage. Rather than relating to a specific figurative imagery or to anthropocentric concepts such us "unconscious", "desire", "impulse" or "dream", the relation in between Surrealism and the expanded architecture of this decade follows a different argumentative line. Its association is based in Rosalind Krauss's structural strategy applied at the end of the XX century by the American art critic in order to associate the Surrealism with Photography[77]: "beyond a specific imagery, it is possible to arrive to a structural common logic [...] in relation to the topics and form approached"[78].

In his lecture *What Is Surrealism?*, given in Brussels in 1934, Breton reminds us of his definition of Surrealism from 1924: "Surrealism, masculine noun. Psychic automatism in its pure state, by which one proposes to express [...] the actual functioning of thought [...] in the absence of any control exercised by reason, exempt from any aesthetic or moral concern ". However, he later redefines it by stating that automatic thought is not only removed from rational control but also from any conscious aesthetic or moral concern. Based on this definition, Krauss emphasises the centrality of photography in Surrealism by highlighting three of the movement's aesthetic structural principles: (1) the priority of presence over representation; (2) the centrality of the notion of automatism; and (3) the conjunction of opposites. These principles are crucial in order to understand in which sense the expansive protocols seen in this chapter suggest the emergence in advanced architecture of a new form of Surrealism that replaces human's inner unconscious otherness by an outer algorithmic or biologic one. This phenomena is particularly evident in three projects already mentioned: Özil's "Livef0rms" (2014), Bartlett RC3's Living Architecture[79] "TARSS" (2018), and Beesley's "Hylozoic Ground" (2010).

_73. Dickran Tashjian, "Home Poor Heart" in *Surrealism and Architecture*, edited by T. Mical (London: Routledge, 2005), 41.
_74. Gorlin, Alexander. "The ghost in the machine". In Surrealism and Architecture, edited T. Mical. London: Routledge. 105.
_75. Neil Spiller, *Architecture and Surrealism* (London: Thames and Hudson, 2016).
_76. Maria Ptqk, *Especies del Chthuluceno* (Bilbao: Gabinete Sycorax, 2019), 63.
_77. Rosalind Krauss, *La originalidad de la vanguardia y otros mitos modernos* (Madrid: Alianza Editorial, 2015), 126.
_78. Ibid.
_79. The RC3 unit is lead by Tyson Hosmer, Octavian Gheorghiu, David Reeves and Panagiotis Tigas

_"Automatic Drawing", André Masson, 1924.

4.1. Presentation and Re-Presentation

Contradictions between presence and representation are typical in Surrealism. On the one hand, Breton welcomes representation when he affirms that "it is irrelevant if there are noticeable differences in between evoked beings and real beings"[80] thereby rejecting these distinctions. On the other hand, Breton appreciates "automatism" because it promotes the emergence of the unconscious not as a representation, but as a presentation.[81] When Breton prefers automatic writing over images, he seems to invert the Platonic aversion for representation, while stating that the suspicions are on the pictoric image, and the truth is in the cursive trace.[82] However, according to Krauss, "this apparent inversion doesn't confront the Platonic aversion towards representation. It confronts the visual images of traditional paintings because they are representations of a dream rather than the dream itself."[83] In this sense the automatic drawings by Masson are not the representation of the author's unconscious through a symbol but the presence of this unconscious through a register – a similar phenomena to the lines traced on paper by a seismograph or a cardiograph. Rather than a representation of the artist's unconscious, Surrealism demands its radical presence.

Most of the projects that we have seen based on expansive protocols share this aesthetics of presence through its operative vocation. Indeed, to operate means to have a tangible impact on the set of conditions in which an artefact acts. Therefore, its effect cannot be ignored or postponed, which contrasts with the distance generated by symbols and metaphors. Özel's "Livef0rms" articulates this performance through the physical impact that "the accumulation and dispersion of matter without a final form"[84] has on the user. Its spatial consequences cannot be postponed, but require user's immediate reaction. This phenomenon produces a particular mode of perception, which, like Surrealism's relation to the unconscious "other", does not treat the algorithmic "other" as a subaltern but as an autonomous subject. As a consequence, experimental architecture's autonomy precludes it by always producing an inexhaustible remainder of alterity that cannot be fully integrated in the user. Something similar occurs in RC3's "TARSS", whose constant spatial re-configuration implies the radical presence of the other at play, and not its mere symbolic reference. Its indetermination, power and autonomy evoke the alterity produced by figures like the Golem or Frankenstein, but without the attributes of a menacing monstrosity. Beesley's "Hylozoic Ground" relation to nature shares this performativity: its chemical exchanges between living and synthetic materials and its constant production of sounds and movement affects people not just on an emotional or poetic level, but also on a hydrothermal and occupational level. As occurs with Surrealist works, what is at the center of these actuations is never a symbolic representation of the "other", but its radical presence. Expansive advanced architecture opposes Modernism's symbolic use of technology by wielding the operative presence of an algorithmic other and re-interpreting Surrealism's notion of automatism.

_80. André Breton. *Surrealism and Painting* (London: MFA Publications, 2002), 2.
_81. Ibid., 78.
_82. Ibid.
_83. Rosalind Krauss, *La originalidad de la vanguardia y otros mitos modernos* (Madrid: Alianza Editorial, 2015), 117.
_84. Güvenç Özel, "Toward a Post-Architecture", *Log* 36 (2014), 101.

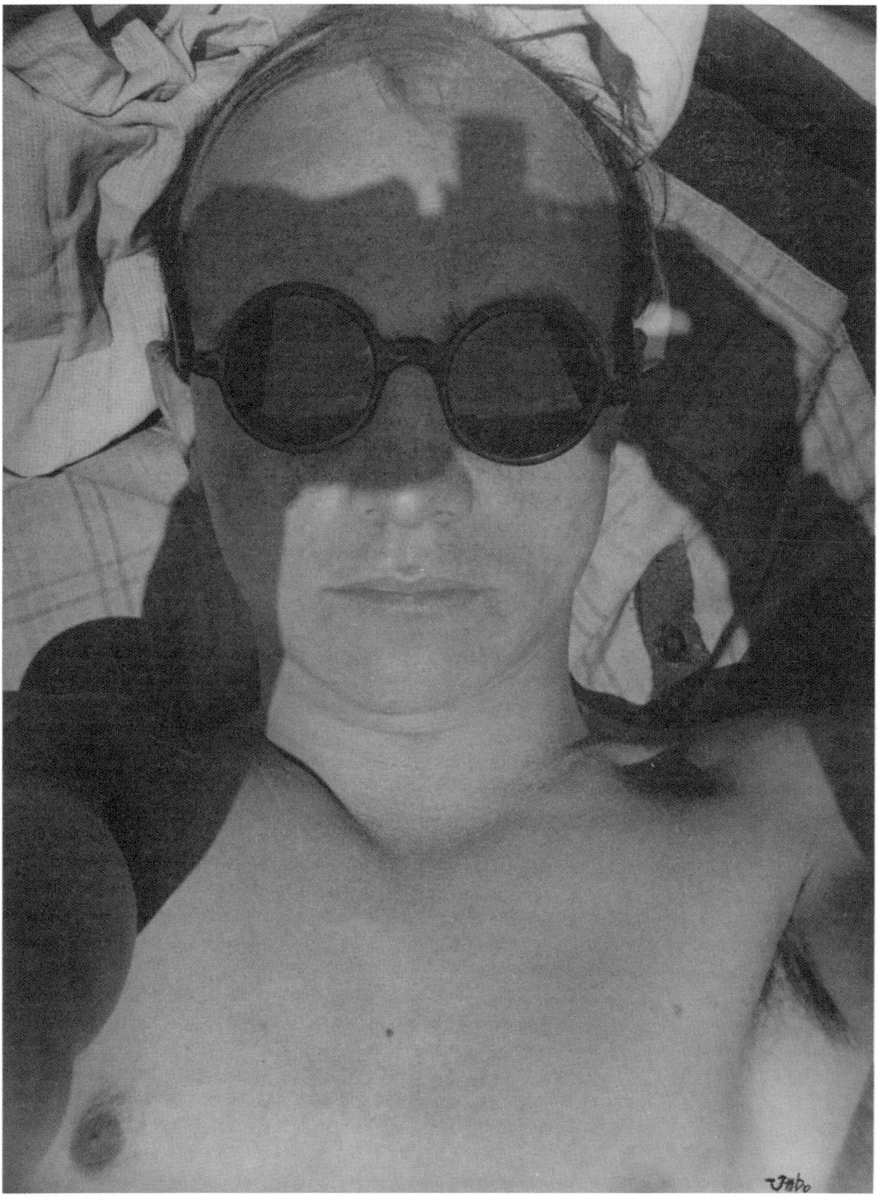

_"Self Portrait at the Beach", Otto Umbehr, 1930.

4.2. Automatism as a Device of Displacement

The centrality that "automatism" holds in both Surrealism and expansive advanced architecture is far from being accidental. "Automatism" means "movement by itself", thus distancing from human's rationality as it doesn't require its continuous presence. This distance is fundamental for Breton, for whom automatic protocols are a crucial creative tool: the alienation implied by its detachment avoids the aesthetic and moral filters of our consciousness. Automatic writing is a great example of it, but the photographic camera adds a second detachment, in this case towards outside, whose aesthetical effect is even closer to expansive advanced architecture. As stated by Krauss, the use of the camera is central to Surrealism. Contrary to pictorial representations (icon), photography operates as a register (index): it extends on a continuous surface the footprint of all what is perceived by our gaze, inextricably unifying impression and reality through a photomechanical transfer. The vision of the camera implies an extraordinary ampliation of our normal vision: it views faster, from stranger angles, from different distances, with several tonalities... Thereby it configures reality according to its own terms: the camera "supplants the spectator himself, it is an assistant that becomes an usurper"[85]. This is best represented in "Self-portrait" (1930) of Umbo, where the shadow of the camera on author's eyes unveils a crucial fact that applies as well to most of the projects of expansive architecture: any ampliation is, at the same time, a displacement.

Indeed, similar to what the camera did for Surrealism, robotised machine learning positions, "in front of the human, another being that is able to do everything the human was doing but faster, with more precision, etc"[86]. This is the case of Özel's "Lifef0rms": it amplifies the architect's capacities not just through automatic processes of "data collection from multiple sensors that measure structural stability, human proximity, and sonic composition"[87], but also through real time construction strategies and autonomous decision-making. The robots automatically re-assemble the pavilion according to an automatic feedback loop produced by an autonomous and ubiquitous algorithmic "other". However, as Surrealism's use of the camera, the ampliation offered by the automatism inevitably implies a displacement. By expanding the capacities of the architect, the algorithmic and robotic agents configure the pavilion according to its own form of mediating reality. As happens with RC3's "TARSS", the pavilion is articulated through a series of patterns that evoke Surrealist aesthetics due to the alienation effect that its logics produce in relation to human intelligence.

This process of displacement produced by an automatic technique that initially seems to merely amplify the architect's capacities produces a distance that emphasises the user's impossibility of completely absorbing the project through their perception. There is always an otherness that remains at a certain "distance" from the user, precluding its complete integration and therefore demanding a certain attention, while at the same permitting the project to act in the background, facilitating its integration into user's daily life. This phenomenon is present in the case of Beesley's "Hylozoic Ground". In particular, this effect is produced through a complex sensorisation and feedback system that offers an experience that Beesley himself has qualified as surreal[88] because of the immersive feeling produced by its automatisms. However, the architect is absolutely displaced by an oniric

_85. Rosalind Krauss, *La originalidad de la vanguardia y otros mitos modernos* (Madrid: Alianza Editorial, 2015), 126.
_86. Eric Sadin, *La humanidad aumentada* (Buenos Aires: La Caja Negra, 2017), 71.
_87. Güvenç Özel, "Toward a Post-Architecture", *Log* 36 (2014), 100
_88. Beesley, Philip. "Hylozoic Ground". Youtube video, 4:02. Posted by "Vernissage TV", September 19, 2010. https://www.youtube.com/watch?v=v86B9Nz_LVU

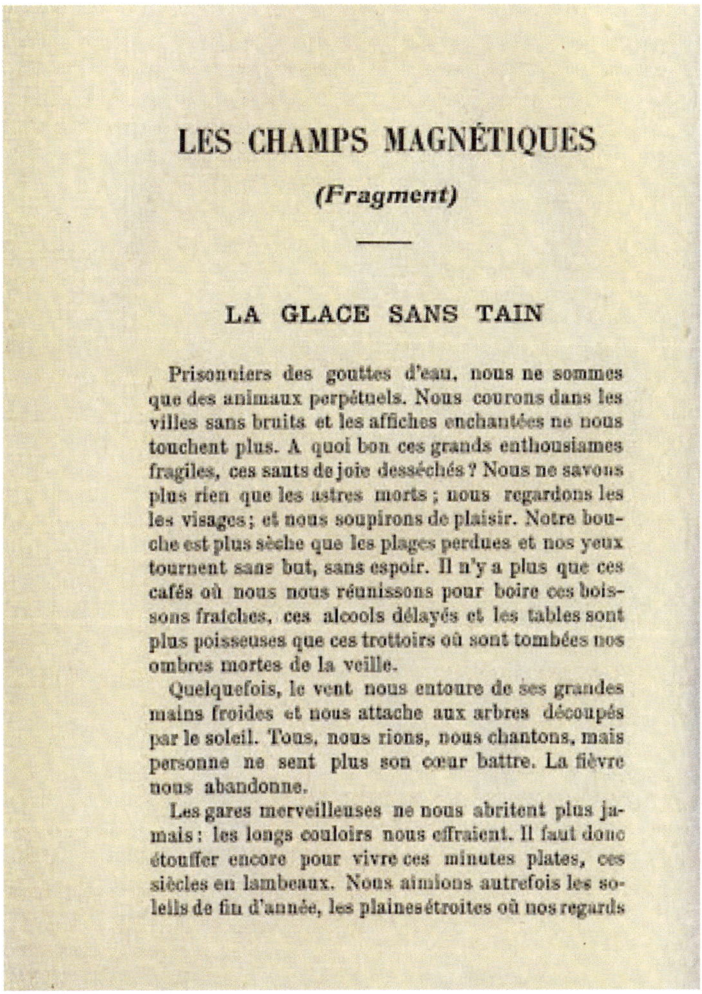

LES CHAMPS MAGNÉTIQUES

(Fragment)

LA GLACE SANS TAIN

Prisonniers des gouttes d'eau, nous ne sommes que des animaux perpétuels. Nous courons dans les villes sans bruits et les affiches enchantées ne nous touchent plus. A quoi bon ces grands enthousiames fragiles, ces sauts de joie desséchés ? Nous ne savons plus rien que les astres morts ; nous regardons les les visages ; et nous soupirons de plaisir. Notre bouche est plus sèche que les plages perdues et nos yeux tournent sans but, sans espoir. Il n'y a plus que ces cafés où nous nous réunissons pour boire ces boissons fraîches, ces alcools délayés et les tables sont plus poisseuses que ces trottoirs où sont tombées nos ombres mortes de la veille.

Quelquefois, le vent nous entoure de ses grandes mains froides et nous attache aux arbres découpés par le soleil. Tous, nous rions, nous chantons, mais personne ne sent plus son cœur battre. La fièvre nous abandonne.

Les gares merveilleuses ne nous abritent plus jamais : les longs couloirs nous effraient. Il faut donc étouffer encore pour vivre ces minutes plates, ces siècles en lambeaux. Nous aimions autrefois les soleils de fin d'année, les plaines étroites où nos regards

_"Les Champs Magnétiques", André Breton and Philippe Soupault, 1920.

and alienating experience provided by thousands of algorithmic and robotic agents. It shares with Surrealism the discovery that, without a particular preconceived intention, automatic production "exudes an infinitely precious substance"[89]. As Surrealism, automatism in expansive advanced architecture engages processes born from, yet indifferent to, human agency:[90] it produces a paradoxical perception that simultaneously articulates closeness and distance.

4.3. The conjunction of opposites: Closeness and Distance

Soupault's *Les Champs Magnétiques* (1920) exemplifies the simultaneous feeling of closeness and distance typical of Surrealism. On the one hand, its production emerges, as Breton mentions, from an "interior transcendence": automatic techniques permit the flowering of a hidden unconscious that is close to us because it is actually "inside" us. On the other hand, Soupault's text celebrates the fascination that the oniric "other" – irrational and fanciful – produces in the observer. Our unconscious, although part of us, is also radically alien to us: we cannot appropriate it, and that is why the apparently senseless composition of Soupault's sentences intrigue us. We cannot deny that they are our productions, but at the same time their presence enthrals us, because we cannot completely identify them with ourselves.

Expansive architecture produces a similar aesthetic feeling. As Mario Carpo suggests, "the emergence of artificial intelligence in technology and in the arts already warrants a more than robust amount of natural discomfort and the feeling of 'alienation'", which is the result of the ongoing post-industrial separation of the minds of the thinkers from the tools of computation. In this sense, and from an aesthetic point of view, machine learning can be interpreted as the "strangement device" defined by Viktor Shklovsky in relation to poetic language[91]: it acts as a distancing apparatus that prolongs the process of perception. The "natural discomfort" and "alienation feeling" that Carpo relates[92] to the use of artificial intelligence in the arts produces, in expansive architecture, a remainder of alterity that breaks Walter Benjamin's "distracted perception"[93] by demanding a certain caution.

Özel's "Livef0rms" and RC3's "TARSS" are good examples of this: robot's coordinated movement follow a logic that is closer to that of a machine than to our own. The alterity and apparent capriciousness of the multiple trajectories are a reminder of a "technical logic that we may master and unleash, but that we can neither replicate, emulate, nor even simply comprehend with our mind"[94].

Beesley's "Hylozoic Ground" articulates this effect through the unrelatable sound and unexpected foldings that are constantly produced by its acrylic surfaces. At some point, viewers are essentially detached from what they are seeing, uncommitted to an experience that cannot be integrated into habit through a distracted mode of perception. Beesley's search for "another life" explains and develops the Surrealist's "deep nostalgia

_89. André Breton. *Surrealism and Painting* (London: MFA Publications, 2002), 68.
_90. Güvenç Özel, "Toward a Post-Architecture", *Log* 36 (2015), 101.
_91. Viktor Shklovsky, *Art and Device* (London: Bloomsbury, 2016), 14.
_92. Mario Carpo, *The second digital turn* (Cambridge: MIT Press, 2017), 81.
_93. Walter Benjamin, *The work of art in the age of mechanical reproduction* (London: Penguin Editions, 2008).
_94. Mario Carpo, *The second digital turn* (Cambridge: MIT Press, 2017), 81.

for archaic forms of existence," as well as their view of the creator as a "demiurge (alchemist and magician), who has the power to revolt against a hyper-conscious reality, and who is able to create a world which has its own logic"[95].

Paradoxically, these three projects also produce a feeling of radical closeness. This effect does not derive from the fact that humans are its coders and builders, but from the empathy produced by its hyper-specific behaviour. Artificial intelligence and sensorisation systems permit RC3's "TARSS" and Özel's "Livef0rms" to respond to the needs of their users with high precision. This hyper-accomodation to users' requirements facilitates their perception under a state of distraction – that is, through a vision that is more haptic than optical and, like everything that is mechanically developed, can easily be converted into a habit. In the case of Beesley's "Hylozoic Ground", the project is deeply intertwined with our human bodies through the chemical reactions produced by its forms. As its author suggests, the complicity evoked by this robotic forest forces us to ask "if it could know we are here, could care about us, could live with us"[96]. This robotic empathy, celebrated by the aesthetics of movies like "Her" (2014) or "Ex-Machina," (2014) fuels a dual regime in which expansive advanced architecture participates in a number of sequences that are increasingly present in our daily lives. As a consequence, the analysed projects are no longer perceived as the untouchable totems of modernity; rather their mode of perception is double: on the one side it relates to Antrobology's carnal familiarity characteristic of touch screens, facial recognition, voice orders, gestural indications, etc, while on the other side it relates to the unreachable distance posed by other's alterity.

Although the structural resonances in between 20th-century Surrealism and expansive architecture's Xeno-Surrealism, there is a decisive inversion in terms of content: the other presented by the latter is no longer constituted through the inner presence of an unconscious human agent but rather through the outer presence of an ecological, algorithmic or biologic agent. This point is relevant because while, traditionally, Surrealist approaches have been underpinned by theories of the unconscious developed by authors such as Freud or Lacan, expansive architecture's Xeno-Surrealism demands another theoretical background. Notions such as "psiche", "desire", "dream" or "impulse" are obsolete in order to approach this new form of Surrealism, which demands a new terminology less focused on the human being and more on its outer others: rather than reducing subjectivity to human subjectivity, Xeno-Surrealism assumes the presence of other non-human agencies: it breaks with the cosmological autism[97] characteristic of the modern *anthropos* by including in the equation other organic and inorganic subjects. According to the relevance that Xeno-Surrealism seems to have in expansive architecture, it is reasonable to predict that the aesthetic path developed by Surrealism in the first half of the 20th century will maintain, through a significant content renovation, a strong presence in the first half of the 21st century.

_95. James Williamson, "Acropolis, now!". In *Surrealism and Architecture*, edited by T. Mical. (London: Routledge, 2001), 320.
_96. Philip Beesley, "Hylozoic Ground". Youtube video, 4:15. Posted by "Vernissage TV", September 19, 2010. https://www.youtube.com/watch?v=v86B9Nz_LVU
_97. This expression has been coined by the antropolog Eduardo Kohn in the wake of its work in Amazonia.

_"Astrocyte", Philip Beesley, 2017.

MANUEL GAUSA

COLORARIUM
Autom-acting Agents & Performing Matters under an Actant Xenological Condition

1. PERFORMING MATTERS

The second decade of the 21st century opened with the exponential development of new technologies that have multiplied the potential for interaction between spaces, contexts, media and users. This has brought about a new phase of increasingly ubiquitous and augmented capabilities, embedded in a new material-virtual dimension called upon to define the "expanded" condition of contemporary reality.

The launch of new, more personalized devices (the appearance of the first iPads in 2010-2011 and new portable equipment like watch computers, iPads, augmented reality glasses, wearable devices, etc., with new interfaces that combine technological efficiency and new leisure-related, productive and interactive features) has translated into the progressive rise in the number of prosthetic devices that are coupled with (and inserted into or imbedded) a receiving body, associated with a new active, reactive (responsive) psychomotor skills, multiplying – in parallel – both features and portabilities.

The optimization of operating systems intended to expand the possibilities of interaction between media, means and users has favored the spread and increase (as of 2010) of mobile applications and open-source programs as anticipated corollaries of those processes.

At the same time, the exponential development of parametric programs for representation, modeling, design and algorithmic generation, and their combination with differential and three-dimensional production/simulation/representation devices, has contributed decisively to the improvement of robotic tools and tests using smart devices in the context of a possible association between space, architecture, artificial intelligence and automata agents (2007-2010, KUKA Robotic Knowledge & Technologies, Drones Big Data Records & Matter Performances, etc.).

These advances are directly or indirectly associated with the accelerated development of smartphones (the launch of 4G devices in 2010/2011 as a fourth generation of mobile phones with multiple features and interactions and the forecast for the 5G range in 2020, with a redesign of connection systems without fixed networks or poly-nets) and especially with the expansion of the Internet (the development, from 2010 to 2015, of Web 3.0 – the Internet of Things – was followed, in 2015, by Web 4.0 – the

Semantic Web or Internet of Intelligences, People connecting People –with web-apps aimed at integrating AI technologies and more sophisticated sensor elements able to understand natural language devices and Speech to text technologies (voice to text and vice versa), new "machine-to-machine" (M2M) communication models, location of specific networked parameters (GPS, heart rate, etc.) and new emerging models of user interactions.

The progressive step, Web 5.0 - Internet of Senses & Emotions? - must expand these capabilities to the field of emotions, a real and virtual sensory reality, processed in common and a more tangible and direct development of the AI itself, human-artificial intelligence, associated with the increase of nanotechnologies (ubiquitous and embedded) and of genetics itself (not strictly deterministic but modifiable with new information from the environment).[1]

On the other hand, the exponential spread of social and professional networks 2[2] – LinkedIn (2002), Facebook (2004), YouTube (2005), Twitter (2006), Instagram (2010), Snapchap (2011), Uber (2016) – and the spectacular growth, since 2009, of WhatsApp and other applications for mobiles and computers, like Skype, (decisive in promoting a direct – economic, productive, operative – interconnection among users) have combined to contribute to the consolidation of a new framework for recreational-relational, creative-rivindicative, exchanges, in a network, with new socio-economic and cultural – but above all productive and co-productive – effects, which are still coming to light and have been addressed in recent publications such as *The Third Industrial Revolution* or *The Zero Marginal Cost Society* (Jeremy Rifkin, 2011 and 2014), *Forty Ways to Think about Architecture: Architectural History and Theory Today* (Iain Borden, 2014) and *Open Source Architecture Manifesto* (Carlo Ratti, Joseph Grima, 2012) or in the theories of the actor-network of Bruno Latour (*Reassembling the social: an introduction to actor-network-theory*) in which the visions of a new "interactive, network intelligence" become apparent.

Chris Sugrue (2017): *Delicate Boundaries*. Action of virtual microbes happening from the screen to the agent's body at the moment he extends his arm, contacting with synthetic surface.

_1. 1– On the history and evolution of mobile telephony see:
https://en.wikipedia.org/wiki/History_of_mobile_phones

_2. On the history and evolution of the internet see: http://www.fib.upc.edu/retro-informatica/historia/internet.html
See also: https://en.wikipedia.org/wiki/History_of_the_Internet
See also: Mueller, Milton L. (2010). Networks and States: The Global Politics of Internet Governance, Boston, MIT Press.

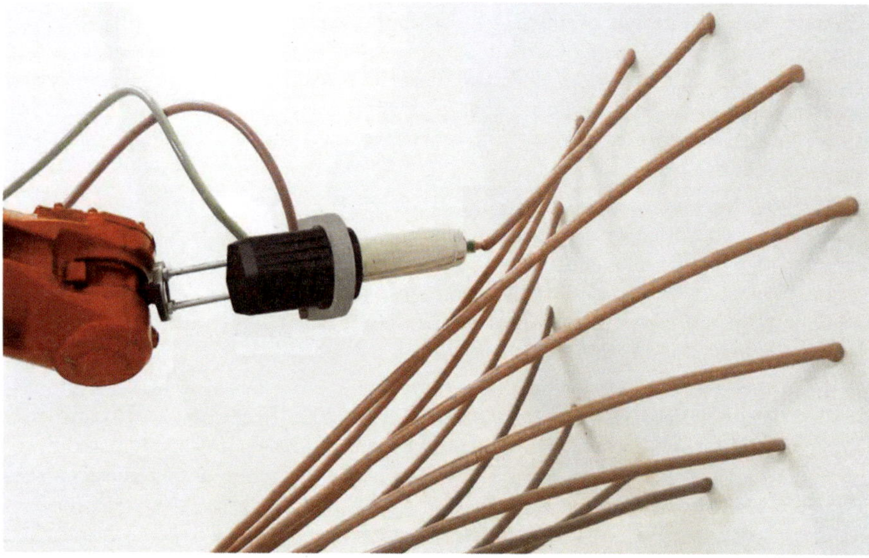

Mataerial (IaaC 2012, New Robot Construction Performances, Petr Novikov, Saša Jokić with Joris Laarman Lab)

The investigations developed in this third phase of research tend to delve into the exploration of these new capacities associated, on the other hand, with the accelerated progression of the meeting (and intersection) between reality and virtuality, materiality and digitality (integrated digitalization), associated with an increase in the interactions between (reactive) matter and (reactivated) environment but, also, between the (actuated) environment and the agents involved (actuators): agents and matters (Agents & Matters) suggest new points of interest.[3]

Researches that reinforce, increasingly, the capacity to interact with a múltiple socio-environmental información, optimizing it, taking datas and transforming them in co-productive and performative processes, working with new responsive devices (and prototypes) and with new digital and dynamic –composite and adaptative –matters (and materials) with vocation each time more reactive. The capacity for interaction between the new processor-devices gradually integrated into our body and an "augmented" culture of our living and relationship spaces, begins to be more and more obvious.

We speak, of course, of a progressive digital development of the Artificial Intelligence but especially of a new crossed (Inter)action with a new Collective Intelligence.

These dynamics are addressed, on the one hand, through the exploration of the new responsive and adaptive capacity of matter that has been augmented in its capabilities (Intelligent Matters) as a complementary paradigm associated with responsive (and/or reactive) systems and their new ubiquitous condition (distributed, simultaneous and sensitive) and, on the other hand, through an interest in the hyper-collective (and hyper-connective) condition of the new co-productive (co-participated, co-deciding) processes and their implicit empathic quality (new communities and new collective behaviors, Commons & Behaviors), as paradigms directly associated with a new system of exchange.

_3. Metter Ramsgard Thomsen, "The role of the news technologies", in *IaaC Bits*, no. 1 (2014), 2.

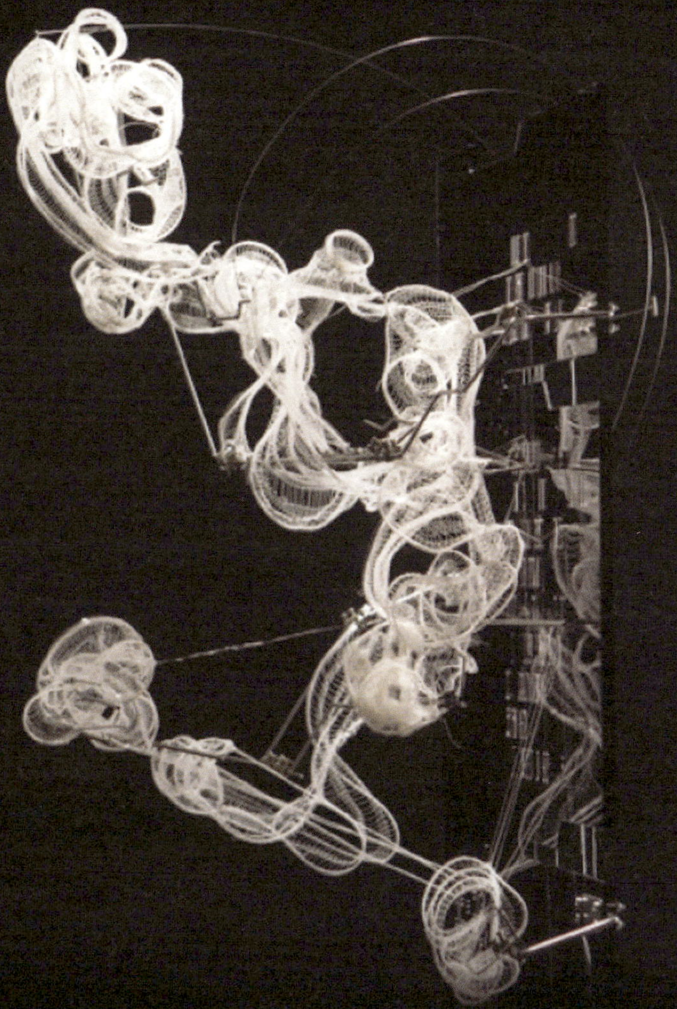

Strange Metabolisms (2007): research collaboration between Mette Ramsgard Thomsen (CITA) and Toni Hicks, Constructed Textiles, University of Brighton.

Moss Voltaic (IaaC- OTF-2014 by: Elena Mitrofanova. Faculty: S.Brandi, A. Dubor, L. Fraguada. Scientific development: P. Bombelli, University of Cambridge. In collaboration with Toni Cumella, Ceramica Cumella)

Bio Scaffold_ The Architecture of Decay (IAAC MAA 02, 2014/2015. Researcher: Natalie Alima; Faculty: Marcos Cruz. Photo Credit: Filipppo Poli)

The exploration of a new co-participated (empathic or eco-empathetic) definition for inhabited environments but also of a new endo-sensitive definition of/for a (ubiquitous, embedded) matter as it relates to the environment (nano-technologies, bio- technologies, etc.) is a common characteristic of much of the research produced in this new era.

Augmented Matters (new reactive and/or responsive capacities) but also Common Behaviours (new co-productive behaviors) are combined now, in both cases to delve into factors of interactivity and diversity: factors supported by multi-agency processes of exchange and interactivity, reactivity and ubiquity (informational simultaneity) rooted in synergistic mediations but also in new symbiotic operations.

Information understood as a (shared, cooperated) input-output or as a (supra-environmental) indicator-actuator gives rise to new formulations oriented towards the examination of new active and interactive responses, which are not only relational but decidedly synergistic (empathetic) with a milieu and with a reality that is – as we pointed out earlier – not only distributed but also ubiquitous, augmented in its own capacities for hyper-connection and sensorization; an expansive, systemic, responsive and co(ll/nn)ective condition, associated with an endo-technological definition, as a capacity for augmented relationships within and between systems.

It is an ongoing approach, which could be summed up in the operative optimization of a new "material intelligence" (Intelligent Matter[4]) and the consequent exploration of a new reactive nature of matter (nano-technologies, bio-technologies, etc.) materialized in new sensitive "endo-eco" definitions and new symbiotic operations (embedded matters, augmented matters) of – and for – space/form.

But, also, in the exploration of a new paradigm, that of the co-participated city or Co-City (cooperated, conjugated, co-responsible, convivial and co-decisional) and its translation into a new type of "collective intelligence" that is more holistic and intercommunicated (EmpathiCities, Common Cities, Smart Citizens), called on to address this new "co(ll/nn)ective" condition in/between spaces and behaviors.

– Similar experiences (and experiments) can be seen in many applied and/or laboratory proposals developed by research groups such as: Digital Matters (Areti Markopoulou, IAAC), BiotA Lab (Marcos Cruz, Bartlett) and Eco-logics (Poletto-Pasquero, Bartlett) Modelling Behaviours (Mette Thomsen, CITA), etc.

– Or by others more involved with the Spanish-American collective sphere, such as Eco-sistemas urbanos (Madrid), Basurama (Madrid), mmmm (Madrid), La Col (Barcelona), Recetas Urbanas (Sevilla), Al Borde (Ecuador), Elemental-Aravena (Chile), Urban Think Tank (Alfredo Brillembourg, Venezuela), Tomás Diez (Fab-Lab Barcelona), etc. Diversity and collectivity, affirmation and interaction, seem, more and more, to be combined in multi-agency processes with an increasing capacity for co-decision in governance and urban design, as well as spatial design.[5]

Today, a new type of direct social activism, OSBURT: Open Source, Bottom-up, Real-Time – at times informal, fresh and unencumbered and, at others, determined and engaged (somewhere between neo-atavic and supra-artisanal, between bio-environmentalist and neo-hippy) – is combined with a super-technology of connectivity and the open exchange of data, messages, experiences and information, which is widely varied but, also, mobilizing.

_4. Areti Markopoulou, "In(Form)ation- Architecture of Data & Code", in *IaaC Bits*, no. 1 (2014).
_5. Areti Markopoulou and Manuel Gausa, (eds). *Master in Advanced Architecture 2012-2014, Prospectus & Projects* (Barcelona: IAAC, 2014).

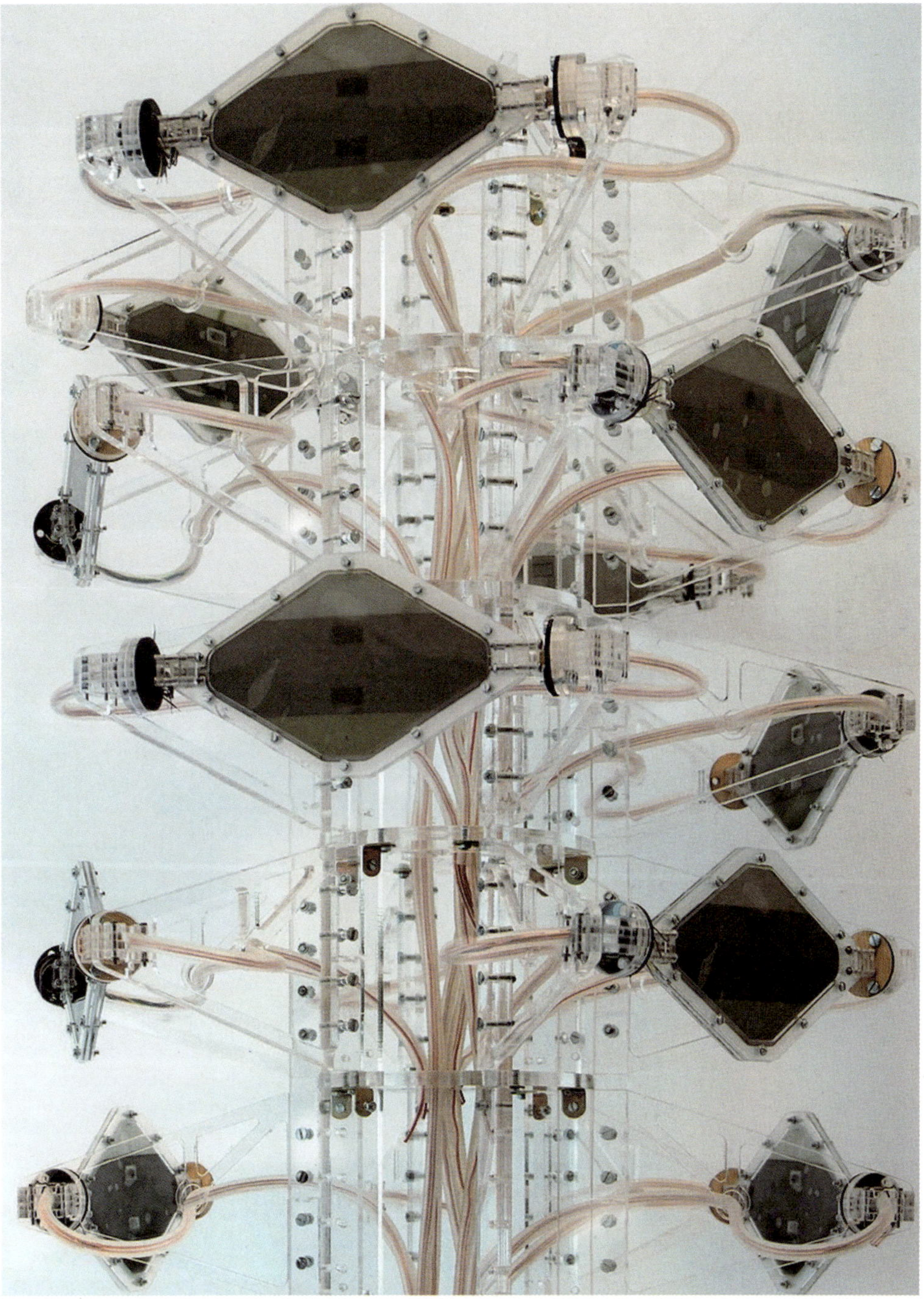

BioCatalytic Cell (IAAC-MAAA02, 2016/17. Researchers: Thora H. Arnardottir, Jessica Dias, Christopher Wong; Faculty: Chiara Farinea, Carmelo Zappulla, Paolo Bombelli, Maria Kuptsova; Guest Advisor: Claudia Pasquero; Biology Support: Nuria Conde Pueyo.)

Changing Adaptive Structure (IaaC- MAA 01, 2014/2015, Digital Matter Studio. Researchers: Ji Won Jun, Matteo Silverio, Josep Alcover Llubia; Faculty: Areti Markopoulou, Alexandre Dubor, Angelos Chronis)

Alejandro Haieck Coll–LBA.PRO.FAB (2007): *Nave Multiprograma. Sistema vertical de plataformas deportivas y culturales en las Lomas de Urdaneta*, Caracas

2. AUTOM-ACTING (ACTIVE/ACTIVATORS ANS NEW MEDIATORS)

In the second decade of the 21st century the multi-scalar (and a-scalar) complexity and transfer devices that had marked much of the research of the mid-1990s give way to a new type of more empathic, more "natural" approach and spontaneously called to combine not only "sense and sensitivity", but also "sensorization and awareness".

In the exploration of this new advanced logic of information and interaction, the pioneering advanced logics of simultaneity have been completed with the active notion of instantaneity. As an immediate response "in" and "for" the moment rather than "of" the event (or the monument) that seems able to combine a new "common logic" (active and activist, optimized or simply positive) generated beyond the exceptive (the singular, the episodic) but also confronted to the exceptional (the unpredictable, the indeterminate, the conflictual) .

We talk about the force of the new tools, related with the increase of intelligent and progressively autonomous (and strategically oriented) agents for interpretation, assimilation and data processing (from sensors to robotics or responsive matters).

But we also speak of an architecture of an "ordinary and collective activism" implicit in the culture of this time, not so much for its technological vocation but for its willingness to infiltrate new inputs in the system and/to re-inform it (resetting it, sometimes radically, provocatively or mischievously); reactivating it qualitatively and compromisingly.

An architecture correlated with a new sociocultural activism and / or mediation, in which natural and spontaneous agree directly to a processing (parametric or synthetic, but always dynamically efficient) of information, matter and context, combining (to beyond the aesthetic prejudices or stylistic filters) the optimization of the "simply necessary" (not of the minimum, not of the functional, not of the elementary but of the optimized - and qualitative - "just necessary", simply with a responsive vocation (reactive and responsible) without narrative or forcing claims aesthetic.

Many of the most common architectures that occur today (from the "field experience" to the experimentation with this new condition of "mediation") tend to make prevail the efficient management of information (in all senses, data, indicators, programs, conditions) and its immediate formal resolution/translation in possible (optimized) synthesized scenarios.

This direct, precise, immediate, "instantaneous" and resilient set of answers (where the old systemic definition of the "element" suddenly gives way to a new epistemic condition of the "elementary") continues to resort, today, to the abilities of craft and design (and, in this sense, it does not always require the technological apparatus to formulate direct answers) but, above all, favors the search of the shared process (co-produced, co-generated from a plural and informational exchange) encouraging, incontestably, a space definitely associated with the assumption of a new eco-medium and a new eco-mediation: a space called to exponentially expand these potential of exchange between situations and solicitations; but also the own ability to process and reprocess (in the form of parameters , indicators or algorithms, precise, recordable, traceable, re-editable in formats, trajectories or variable contexts, in real and deferred times) our relational environments, translating them into direct answers, as precise as elementary.

The development of the new information technologies brings us closer to a reality recorded in an increasingly precise and immediate way, opening up in real time an immense repertoire of possibilities in the field of the combination between materiality-informationality-spatiality, from a mutual collaboration (in and with the medium) more efficient and qualitative (recording data associated with urban mobility itself, energy efficiency, social economy, public space, collective self-organization, environmental response, etc.)

Hence the importance of the concept of interaction (of a positive exchange between environment, society and information) in relation to a more sustainable new development, not only as an ethical and socio-economic responsibility but also as a coherent consequence of the informational/relational revolution today in course.

The complementary appearance of a new type of sensitivity and social action linked to a mobilisation of the immediate, the unpostponable (the *improrrogable* [6])- of a precise (and precised) hyper-moment connected to the force of attack (*force de frappe*) of the active and activist - is marking the interest of the new generations, involved with this collective sensitivity, responsible and responsive at the same time. Self-generation, self-organisation, co-production and co-participation or multi-intervention architectures tend to combine operations, mediations and installations (more or less "instantaneous" and "economic", in ways and means) in possible live and relational spaces of urban reactivation or of exchange and collective affirmation.

Proposals that we have signified before such as those of Alejandro Aravena (Chile), Alfredo Brillembourg (Caracas), Alejandro Haiek (Caracas), David Barragán- Al Borde (Quito) and Eco-sistema Urbano (Madrid), Basurama (Madrid), mmmm (Madrid), La Col (Barcelona) and or Topotek (Berlin) and Arno Brandlhuber (Berlin) urban Eco-system, Alejandro Haieck, David Barragan-Al Borde, La Col, Basurama, etc., would be symptomatic of this time of direct operations, very close of the *Reagente Social Design* and the GIC-Lab performative experiential and convivial actions at the DAD-Unige in Genova..

Following - it is important to remember - the initial path of more conceptual, but no less committed, interventions, such as those of Lacaton-Vassal, Coloco (Paris), K Architectures (Paris) or, in particular, Santiago Cirugeda - Recetas Urbanas - at the beginning of the century. *Guerrilla boardings,* without formal pretensions, without rhetoric or spectacular gestures, but with a strong sense of commitment (of engagement) that, from the "elemental" they solve with imagination, and intensity proposals conceived beyond conventions. [7]

We can discuss whether this type of action is really "advanced "(not using, in general, new technologies). But it is evident that this strong sensitivity regarding the combination "information + interaction + integration" conjugated in social within reach performing" terms (not only digital or material processes but socio-collective actions and/or movements) taking advantage of imaginative and innovative resources and possibilities, arises from this assimilation of a processed, diverse and unprejudiced data-evaluation in synergy, typical of our informational time.

The exploration of this new positive mediation (synergistic) to define our habitats, but also of a new sensitive interaction (empathic or eco-empathic) to deal with increasingly complex scenarios, marks today many of the essays produced at a time when those inertias associated with global deficit situations related to conflicts, stresses and threats multiply, linked to critical geopolitical (and geo-economic) shifts, but also, of course, to climate changes with devastating effects on the most vulnerable populations (risks environmental problems, housing defects, pollution, ghettoization, increase in poverty thresholds, etc.). [8]

_6. With the title Improrrogable, was presented the very interesting central exhibition of the 2017 Biennial of Valparaiso, dedicated to social activism in Latin America curated by Felipe Vera and Jeanette Sordi

_7. Alfredo Brillembourg and Hubert Klumpner "Scarcity as Design Tool", in *IaaC Bits*, no. 2 (2014).

_8. See in this sense, the 15th Biennale di Architettura di Venezia, 2016 – Universes in Universe – curated by Alejandro Aravena

Alfredo Brillembourg, Hubert Klumpner (2011-2012): *Multifunctional public building, Fábrica de Música (music factory)*, Grotão, Paraisópolis Favela of São Paolo.

Alejandro Aravena (2016): *Half-houses. Elemental Social Housing*, Iquiqu, Chile

Boa Mistura (2005), Favela at Antofagasta, Chile. Co-generated painting self-affirmation expressions

Centre and down: Haas&Hahn (2005), Rio de Janeiro, Favela Sant Maria. Self-painting citizens project

Ecosistema Urbano (2007): *Eco Boulevard* in Vallecas, Madrid. A performance meeting space and environmental device.

Santiago Cigureda, Recetas Urbanas (1999): *Kuva*, Seville. A pioneer activist social intervention, dribbling the regulation of the urban container for denouncing deficitary playgrounds,

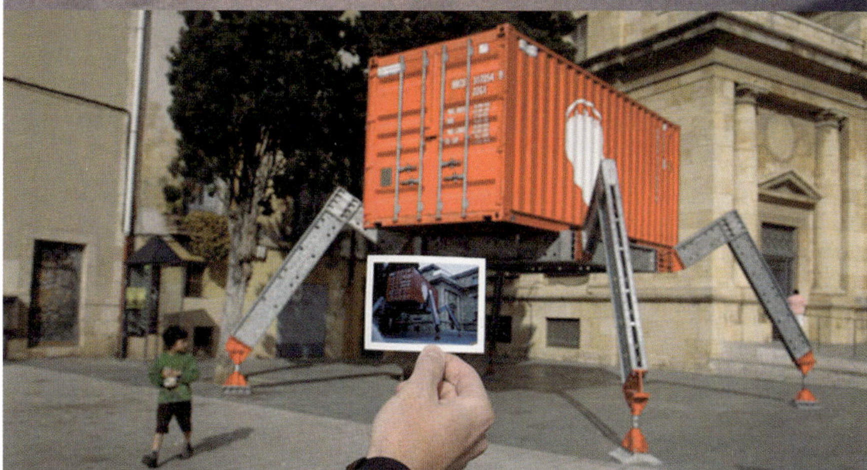

Santiago Cigureda, Recetas Urbanas (2011): *Araña [Spider]*, Seville. Portable space's social prototype.

Top: Lacaton et Vassal (Paris): Place Léon Aucoc (Bordeaux). The value of doing nothing with urgency!. A pioneer symbol of a responsible social and economic mediating attitude beyond "design".
Centre: Basurama (Madrid), *Autoparques* (Self-Parks), Malabo 2015.
Bottom: La Col (Barcelona) Community children's artefact in Vilafranca (Barcelona), 2016.

GIC-LAB, REAGENTE & RURBACT – DAD-UNIGE (Casa Gavoglio KAAU Summer Workshop, Genoa 2017:
Top: GIC_LAB: social and proactive Interventions in old militaries barracks.
Centre and Bottom: IAAAC- playground structures and Luis Falcon-IN ATLAS: interactive intervention.

Topotek & BIG, Bjarke Ingels Group (2016): *Superkilen Park*, Copenhagen. Co-participated public interactive space design

Agencia de Ecologia Urbana (in collaboration with IAAC, CTPFC and Alt.), *Poble Nou Barcelona Superblock*, Ajuntament de Barcelona, 2018.

Coloco (2016). Courbevoie, Jardins Mobiles (photo Estelle Pardon)

3. ACTANT XENOLOGICAL CONDITION

The researches conducted in this moment of exploration tend, in fact, to deepen in the new capacities associated with the accelerated encounter between reality and digitality (bio-technology, bio-materials, nano-technology, artificial intelligence, robotics, new interfaces, etc.); between matter (reactive) and environment (reactivated); but also, between environment (activated) and agents (activators) in progressively co-generated actions (co-produced, co-participated, co-decided, co-generated, co-activated) associated with the new collective processes.

The evocative lyric of the old designed "figuration" or the gestural and iconic strength of the objectual event, seem to give way, today, to the optimized management and efficient elaboration of a reality - potentially improved or re-activated - tackled immediately, in real time (precise data and concrete facts, for possible scenarios ... positive and / or proactive) giving priority - beyond predetermined aesthetics - to new *AST-ethics*[9] of action translated to the qualification/manipulation of matter, context, environment and inhabited space.

It therefore appears evident that in this new active, reactive and interactive logic (material and mental), a direct, essential and elementary, collective and shared architecture of the strategically adaptable, responds better to a new type of strange order of the responsively, unprejudiced, variable, adaptable and dynamic and unprejudiced in its manifestations.

In this new information age, adaptative (open) strategies prevail over static (predetermined) aesthetics, but not necessarily over *AST-ethics* visions, over creative and imaginative perception and over the ability to project "shared scenarios" - unexpected (and generally "hybrid") - understood as possible "horizons of action": not already symbolic or totemic but stimulators and orientators, conductors and inductors (catalysts) at the same time of better common habitats.

In fact if the informational notion of Program/Programmation has been one of the keys of our new time, in this new kind of approaches the program and the programmation of the operations through dynamic and digital software applications is so important than the programmed-prevision of actant-actions and user maneuvers.

The timing/evolving *program(actions)* more than the first open *formull(actions)* (or the simple data-managements) are now the big actors of these new advanced phase.

But is true, also, that terms as idea or concept, combined with others as representation or expression, continue to be necessaries and they are still needed to drive, guide or "design" processes.

As architects we work with a secular idea of design able to synthesize creation and technique, subjectivity and objectivity, rigor and intuition: to compress information and to transform them, to manipulate them, to reconvert them and to visualize them in creative and qualitative spaces: this spatial vision (which is a synthetic vision but which is able to translate a whole universe of analytical data manifested in the form of expressive, visual, perceptive bets), is our strength and our main quality.

However a big debate opens today to know if in our immediate future the notion of "spatial bet" of the 90s as an "open vision" (strategic answer) will tend to be substituted for the capacty to generate "open visualizations" (simulated answers of several optimized

_9. The *AST-ethics* neologism, similar in substance and semiotics to the term aesthetics, alludes to an overcoming of the "idealized" or "predetermined" aesthetic-form by a mixture, also aesthetic but more indeterminate and directly reactive, between processed learning (*AST*, Advanced Skills Teaching) and ethical factors (*ethics*).

IAAC BITS n. 9, 2019 (*Black Ecologies*). Photomontage for the cover

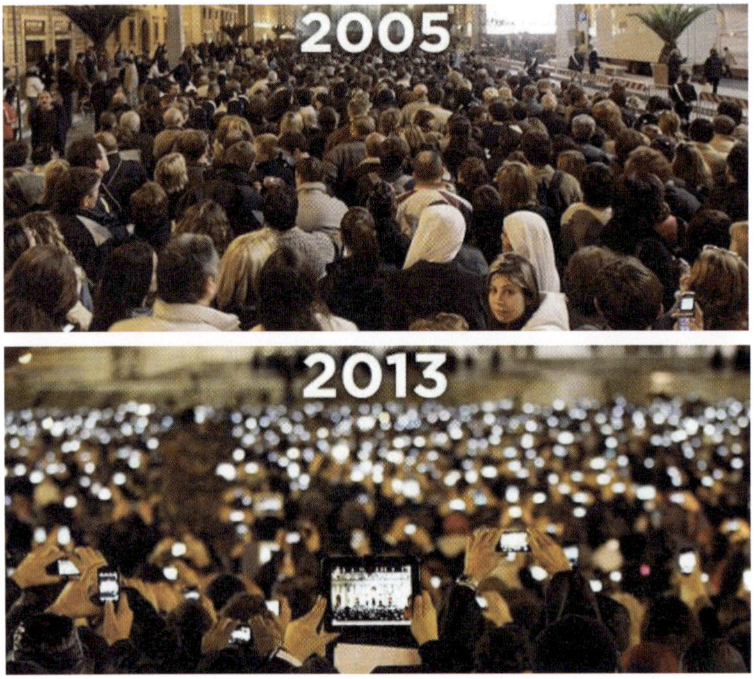

Two visions of a manifestation in Sant Peter´s Square: 2005 and 2013. We can see the evolution of the impact of the Smart pones as real-time intercommunication devices.

and possible scenarios, qualitative but indifferent to each other): possibilities linked to a certain spatial parameterization, in multiple options without "aesthetic" predeterminations, because they will depend, for the most part, on this *xeno-collective* intelligence of which we spoke beforehand.

The term Xenology refers to the study of strange phenomena (foreign to our nature or foreign) but also refers, in medicine, to the study of parasites (and in an architectural extrapolation, to that of a new type of infiltrated or integrated commensalism (embedded) in a way technology in our own human and / or post-human, urban and post-urban condition).

Despite the importance of the individual (in "singular", at all levels) probably the future calls to this cross-interaction between social users, technologies of inter-exchange(s) and temporal communions directed to concrete community goals and interests.

Like our own individual intelligence as humans, a new collective and artificial intelligence realized through statistical parameters (majorities determined in real time) and automata, natural and para-natural or pseudo-natural agents will be able to recognize, connect, react, adapt, structre and change our habits to "perform" collectively, spatial, urban and political actions, "empathic" and "experiential"; and here the word interactivity – more than interaction – will each time take over.[10]

_10. Areti Markopoulou, "Design Behaviors; Programming Matter for Adaptive Architecture", in ResearchGate, January 15, https://www.researchgate.net/ (2015).

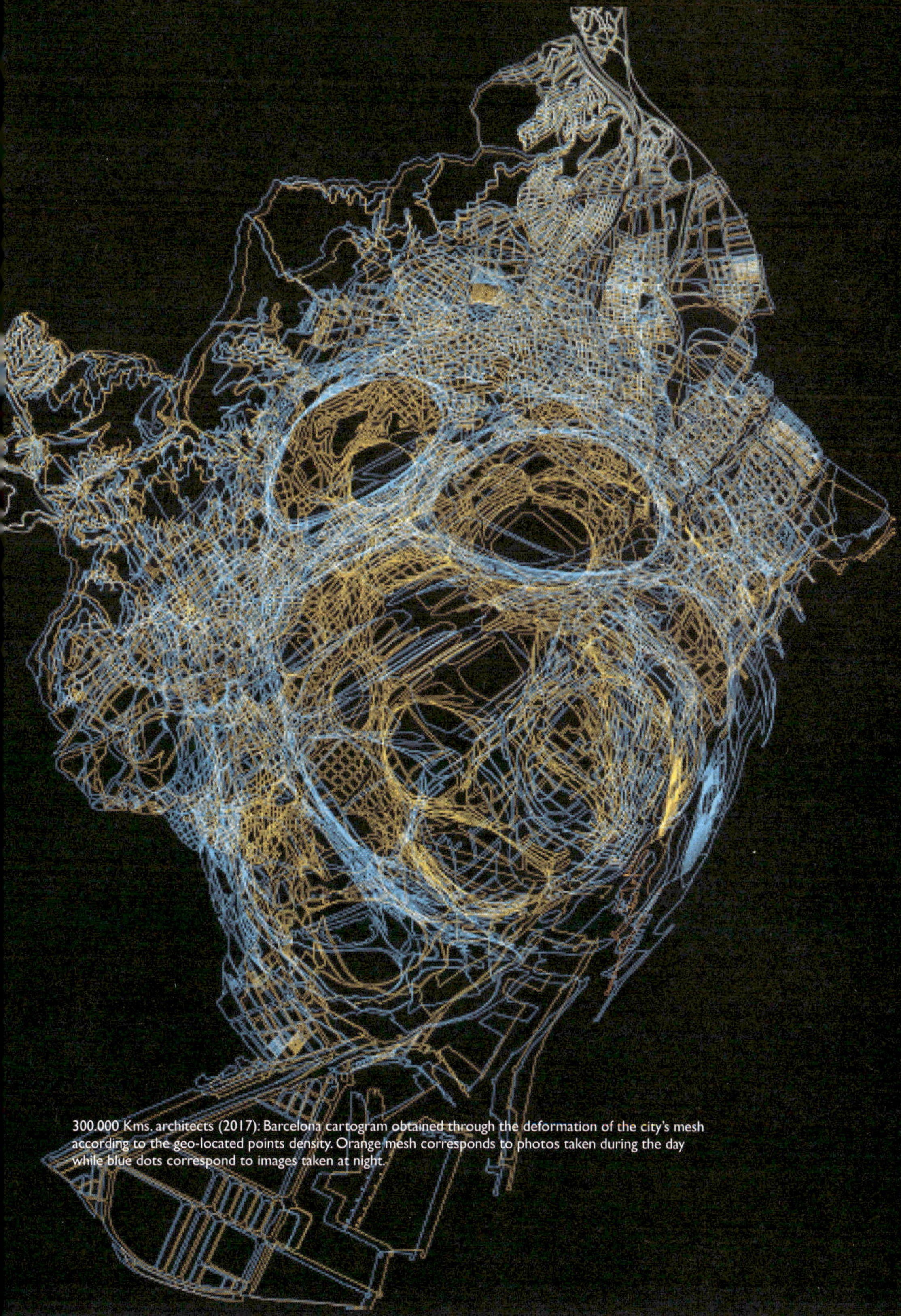

300.000 Kms. architects (2017): Barcelona cartogram obtained through the deformation of the city's mesh according to the geo-located points density. Orange mesh corresponds to photos taken during the day while blue dots correspond to images taken at night.

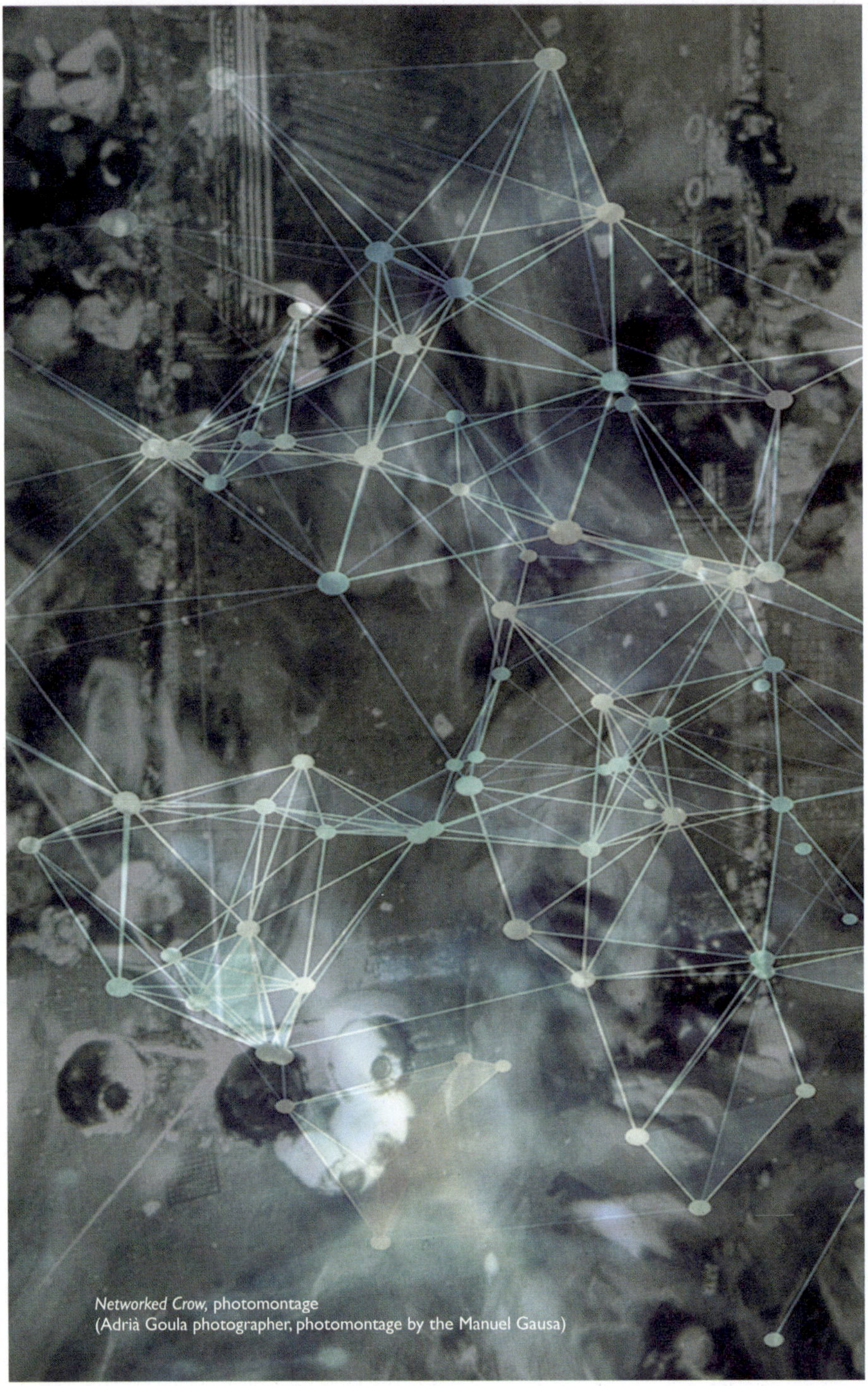

Networked Crow, photomontage
(Adrià Goula photographer, photomontage by the Manuel Gausa)

Élodie Nourrigat: *Social Clusters and Communities*, KAAU Symposium, Genoa 2016.

In this new Augmented Humanity that tends to have occurred with the digital revolution[11], it seems, in effect, that a new "Individualism of masses", as Alessandro Baricco calls it (or better, in my view, a new "Collective Individuality, in Common"[12]) is becoming increasingly important, thanks to the progressive networked applications (and actions), allowing us to reconstruct the "I",[13] not only as the traditional "ego/super-ego" but as a "n-ego" or "multi-ego ", as intentional and interested as an accomplice and (inter)active, capable of generating "millions of micro-movements that dismantle the work of the old guides".[14]

In this dynamic action, the complicities, the common actions, the "coagulations" or "clustering" of consensus, are formed and quickly undone, because they respond not so much to basilar or ideological sedimentations but to regrouping of "involved and organized" individuals (*impliqués* et *agencés*, to use the Deleuzian term of a new type of organization that is more open and interconnected[15]): "partners" of exploration, navigation and action, dynamically destined to "ungroup and /or to recompose in the next movement".

If the notion of homogeneous mass no longer exists (but episodically), it's therefore true that a certain collective actant capacity[16], individually and collectively involved (*engagée*)[17]

_11. Alessandro Baricco, *The Game* (Barcelona, Anagrama, 2018), 218.
_12. The importance of the new networked communities and/or in common is increasing in the last decade. It refers to the birth of new (inter)active communities and social collectives, but also to a (in) common creativity, obtained from the growing ability to share software and open programs (Open Source)
_13. Alessandro Baricco, *The Game* (Barcelona, Anagrama, 2018).
_14. Alessandro Baricco, *The Game* (Barcelona, Anagrama, 2018).
_15. Giles Deleuze and Felix Guattari, *Mille plateaux: Capitalisme et Schizophrénie* (Paris: Les éditions de minuit, 1980).
_16. "Actant": Literally the person, subject or thing that intervenes or has a necessary role in the history of an action, an event, etc. However, it is a term originally created by Lucien Tesnière and later used by semiotics to designate the participant in an active/narrative program.
According to Greimas, the actant is the one who performs or performs the act, independently of any other determination. We could speak of a new activism active and active, at the same time, for its provocative, mediating, narrative will ... to create awareness, implicated and / or affirmative, etc.
_17. Evidently "engagé" ("engaged, involved") in relation to the books Indignez-vous ! and Engagez-vous! of Stéphane Hessel.

– a new individual and collective intelligence at the same time, common and hyper-interactive, generated thanks to the exponential technologies of network exchange – call to share and act, at the same time, thanks, of course, to the progressive capacity for interconnection and digital interaction.

The progress of the transmission/communication/exchange technologies themselves has always allowed to facilitate socio-cultural, instrumental and mental revolutions and today this axiom is evident.

Baricco himself synthesizes later: "*(Today) the discipline of the study has been replaced by the ability to join points, the privilege of knowledge has dissolved in that of doing and the effort to think deeply has been invested in the pleasure of thinking fast.*"[18]

And, why not ?, in the ability to think "heterodox", to think "iconoclast", to think "hybrid", to think "provocative". Because in this new ability to join/combine/decline information(s) and solicitations (conditions and situations, mixtures and exchanges) crossing hybridations and operational paradoxes are generated in a way as direct as unprejudiced: paradoxes - as we indicated in the book *Open-Space-Time-Information*[19] - born of the informational union, apparently "against-natura", from/between "old essential categories" - secularly divided and taxonomically differentiated: architecture and landscape, matter and environment, reality and virtuality, realism and idealism, sciolism and knowledge, discipline and indiscipline, criticism and proactivism.[20]

It is true that doubts and perplexities have not yet disappeared, that the maneuvers and privileges of certain (old and new) elites seem to continue (and perhaps increase); that the old conventional systems (professional, academic, economic, cultural, etc.) are apparently still standing; that the multiple capacity of a potential and exponential knowledge seems - still - mostly installed in a hedonism of zapping/surfering, of mere indifferent navigation, of distraction or of spectacle; of the simple absorption of information (messages, news, statistics) manipulated and / or banalized, etc. But, nevertheless, this new "collective and interactive intelligence" - in network, of interrelation, complicities and interests - tends to emerge with power, here and there, and become an increasingly unstoppable promise, related, in turn, to the ongoing progress of a new humanism or post-humanism[21], reactive and artificial, as embedded as ubiquitous at the same time.

The emergence of this new hybrid intelligence (at once natural and artificial, individual and collective, physical and virtual, spontaneous and prosthetic, operational and relational, emotional and strategic, cooperative and dispositional) seems to invoke a new type of social subject that has come to be called post-human.

It is still too soon for us to know what kind of a new socio-spatial definition (post-human or super-human, post-social or super-social) these dynamics will tend toward.

Their translation into a new conception of the (co-produced) urban approach and (co-productive) architectural design will, no doubt, be the next great challenge we will face.

_18. Alessandro Baricco, *The Game* (Barcelona, Anagrama, 2018).
_19. Manuel Gausa, *Open, Espacio-Tiempo-Información* (Barcelona: Actar Publishers, 2010).
_20. Ibid.
_21. Ibid.

Glories Regenerative Systems (IAAC, 2015. Edouard Cabay with Rana Abdulmajeed, Tobias Deeg, Martin Hristov, Peter Magnus, Utsav Mathur, Nour Mezher, Jean Sebastian Munera and Lili Tayefi)

ENDING CONSIDERATIONS

SYNTHESIS:

Manuel Gausa

THE 4 (+1) IN FACTORS

Information, Interaction, Intelligence, Innovation

1. INFORMATION
2. INTERACTION
3. INTEGRATION (INTELLIGENCE)
4. INNOVATION
5. ANNEX. ANALYTIC AND COMPARATIVE WORKING-PROCESS MAPS

PERSPECTIVES:

Jordi Vivaldi

TOWARDS A LIMIT-SPACE

After the Architectural Rhizome

1. THE HOMOGENEOUS ANTI-SPACES OF CHORA AND TOPOS
2. SUBJECTLESSNESS
3. LIMIT-SPACE: LIMINAL, LIMITED, LIMITROPHE

MANUEL GAUSA

SYNTHESIS

THE 4(+1) IN FACTORS

Information, Interaction, Integration (Intelligence), Innovation

1. INFORMATION

Throughout this book, we have explored the various manifestations (intellectual and instrumental, conceptual and design-related) of a paradigm shift that is ongoing today, associated with a change of logic in our interpretation of space (and the idea of "order" and "organization" associated with it: classical (absolute) space and modern (relative) "space-time" have been replaced by an "interactive space-time" that has led to more indiscipline in our understanding of the universe. At the same time, it has made it possible to introduce the influence of information (combinatory and diversified, global and individual), and its effects, into the dynamic manifestations of processes.[1]

From architecture understood as a ritual-typological figuration, we have shifted, throughout the 20th century, to architecture understood as a functional machine (a mechanical artifact and iconic object at the same time) and now, well into the 21st century, to architecture conceived as a *(multi)relational* environment (an interface space, a multi-layer system, and an interactive scenario all at once), which is synthetic and systematic (global) while, also, unique and non-transferable (local).

The idea of design as an "operating system" – a flexible dispositive capable of processing the information received and transforming with it, capable of evolving and "mutating" according to general and specific demands – has emerged as paradigmatic.

The challenge of contemporary design, today, lies in exploring this operative and informational potential of architectural space, combining strategic decisions and synthetic data: simultaneous layers of processed information, intended to alter the primitive abstract definition of the "architectural object-box" to give it a new interactive purpose.

_1. Manuel Gausa and Jaime Salazar, "CASA-CAJA: ¿Objeto retr(o)activo o mecanismo reactivo?" in Manuel Gausa and Jaime Salazar, *Singular Housing–El dominio privado, Barcelona, Actar and Single-Family-Housing–The Private Domain*, (Munich: Ed. Birkhaüser, 2000).

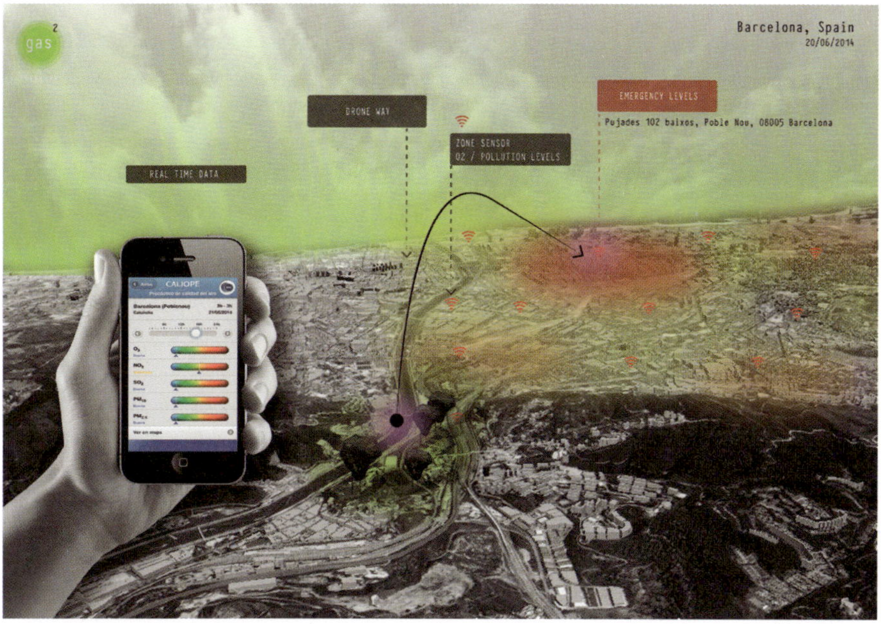

GAS (IAAC-MAA01 2014, Emergent Territories-Radical Regions. Researcher: José Díaz. Faculty: W. Müller, G. de la Camara, J. Vivaldi, M. Bravo, P. Ros,)

The "compositional-object" is replaced by the "dispositional-environment".

Geometric volume is replaced by an operating system.

"Retroactive" movement is replaced by "reactive" capacity.

The revolution that is underway today illustrates this shift from an eminently circumstantial action through architecture – a transformative (positivist) intervention in the milieu – towards an environmental (inter)action – a mediating (positive) relationship in/with/from/through and for the milieu.

This relationship is supported by the processing (reactive and reactivating) nature of architectural space, in an optimization of information (data and demands from the surroundings) as an essentially qualitative (re)qualifying response.

The digital universe has already given rise, indisputably, to an "informational" space that is full of possibilities and open to new spatial definitions capable of resonating with, tuning into, and "projecting" onto reality, within reality and beyond reality, all at once.[2]

A new period in architecture has emerged, linked in with different spheres of research and technological production: a period associated with new technical and formal, cultural and socio-spatial concepts, capable of responding to the challenges inherent in the new informational environments.

_2. Neil Gershenfeld, *When Things Start to Think* (New York: Henry Holt & Co, 2004)
Mark Weiser is credited with the concept of Ubiquitous Computing, toward which MIT has promoted significant contributions, such as Hiroshi Ishii's consortium *Things That Think* at the Media Lab and the CSAIL initiative.

2. INTERACTION

These new logic that is still emerging today is decidedly participating in the definition of its own technological development as well as those of a more innovative contexts in the construction and industry spheres (supported by more variable and flexible systems of conception, production and manufacturing); to the acceptance of a new *eco-milieu* and a new *eco-mediation* and its respective relationship with an approach to the landscape and to a (multi)city in balance with, in, and between, its territories; to the broad possibilities, ultimately, of computer programming and animation used in a new digital "genetics" – and "strategies" – of form and its possible concretion in more (private and collective) intelligent, sensitive and imaginative scenarios: real and virtual at the same time.[3]

The exploration of these dynamics has driven ongoing processes that underlie a whole generation of ideas, rooted in this paradigm shift that has left behind classical, modern and post-modern conceptions in favor of a new, more advanced informational logic.[4]

The digital world and new information technologies (the *Internet of Things*, *Smart Cities* and *Smart Citizens*, etc.) have exponentially expanded this potential for exchange among circumstances and needs, but also the parametric capacity to design and (re)design, to program and reprogram, to process and reprocess our own relational environments (in the form of precise, recorded, tracked and reedited algorithms in multiple and variable formats, trajectories and contexts).[5] Unlike in the 1990s, when digital computational development still seemed tied to the investigation of theoretical models and/in the virtual world, today we understand that the development of new information technologies and their translation into an efficient, multidimensional – and often nano-dimensional – *sensorization* brings us closer to a reality that can be surveyed in an increasingly precise and exhaustive way, offering an immense range of possibilities in the realm of combining *materiality* and *informationality*.[6]

We could venture, in this sense, that while the first stage of research (Conformative Protocols) would have tended to focus on addressing the new complex, fluctuant and topological-transversal condition (exchanged and interchanged as a first interaction step) of a new meta-urban and meta-territorial contexts, the second (Distributive Protocols) would have focused more on its progressive connective and interactive environmental capacity and the last one (Expanded Protocols) in its holistic, potential reactive and responsive (co-cognitive) dimension and vocation that would be not only interactive but inter-activated and "inter-activable".

– COMPLEXITY / INTERCHANGE in the first case,

– CONNECTIVITY / INTERACTION in the second and,

– CO-COGNITIVITY / INTERACTIVITY in the third,

would define possible synthetic IC or CI terms for the three stages indicated above, united by the same individual and collective will to explore – to investigate and inquire – about the current conditions of our own spaces and environments, about the new scenarios and places of exchange and the organization systems associated with them.

_3. Manuel Gausa, "Theoretical framework" published in Vicente Guallart, *Media House Project* (Barcelona: Actar, 2004).
_4. Manuel Gausa, Vicente Guallart and Willy Müller, *The Metapolis Dictionary of Advanced Architecture*, (Barcelona-New York: Actar, 2003)
_5. See LEACH, Neil (2014): "Adaptation", in *IaaC Bits* n. 1 (Barcelona, IaaC editorial, 2014), 1-2.
_6. Mette Ramsgard Thomsen: "The Role of the New Technologies" in *IaaC Bits* n. 1 (Barcelona, IaaC editorial, 2014). 2.

Digital manufacturing incorporates today the use of new composite materials and the opportunity to combine *sensorization* and manufacturing in new productive developments and new industrial systems – structures, constructions, products – that can be (re)active and (inter)connected, sensitive to a more efficient and qualitative mutual collaboration (in and with the environment): recording data associated with urban mobility, energy efficiency, the social economy, public space, collective self-organization, environmental response, etc.[7] Hence the importance of the concept of interaction (and a processed exchange and interchange of information, in any case) but also of interactivity in relation to a social and sustainable qualitative and benefactor development, understood not only as an ethical responsibility and a socio-economic necessity but also as a coherent consequence of the ongoing informational/relational revolution, which implies a shift from a merely aestheticist (and/or *functionalist*) urbanism and architecture toward a more "*(inter) activist*" approach – more relational, in short – with the potential to promote a positive (global and local) integrated interaction on all levels and between several systems: with the environment and with the surroundings, with the landscape and with the context, with the individual and with the community, with technology and with the economy, with culture and society.[8] These approaches are associated with a new increasingly widespread awareness of sustainability which, although it still displays a certain tendency toward accepted convention (technical-superficial solutions), demonstrates the potential of a new, more open and imaginative, sensitivity in traditional spatial disciplines.

And, thus, the need for determined innovation applied to a suitable combination of "Space-Habitat-Sustainability".[9]

In-Between Realities Towards a Socially Sustainable Urban Strategy for Beirut City
(IAAC MAA02 2014-2015, Researcher: Rasa Sukkari)

_7. Jeremy Rifkin, *La nouvelle société du coût marginal zéro,* (Paris: LLL Les Lignes qui Libèrent, 2015), 26.
_8. Manuel Gausa, ed. "Canvi climàtic: territori, urbanisme i edificació. nous models (mès) sostenibles" in ***AA.VV., II Informe sobre el canvi climàtic a Catalunya***, (Barcelona: IEC, CADS, Generalitat de Catalunya, 2009).
_9. Manuel Gausa, ed. ***Cap a un habitat(ge) sostenible***, (Barcelona: CADS, Generalitat de Catalunya, 2011).

3. INTEGRATION (INTELLIGENCE)

The recent evolution of networked informational and digital systems calls to the evolution of a new sort of (natural and artificial, singular and collective) *Informational Interaction* progressively related with a new integrated and integrative (transversal) Intelligence. The combination "Information + Interaction" talks about this idea of increased integral, integrated, integrative (embedded) "Intelligence" as a Relational and (Re)active and (inter) active capacity. These, theoretical positive progress, has a twofold effect.

– On the one hand, it is capable of optimizing the reading, management and specific (differential) elaboration of data, capacities and related stimuli in order to orient the different specific elements of the system(s) (users, buildings, sectors, matters, spaces) toward increasingly self-efficient, even self-sufficient (singularized) patterns of behavior, exchange, thinking and consumption, were differential individuality and solidary plurality (agenced diversity) could be declined together in new models of synergy.

– On the other hand, by integrating these differential elements into a larger transversal network, this increased capacity should be able to favor a collective solidary and synergetic distribution and management of needs and a progressive (and progressist) cooperation among networked energies, reducing potential weaknesses and deficits and/or the risk of absolute (widespread) dependence.

The elements should not be longer dependent on a centralized and global system (centralized, compact, guided and lineal model); rather, it is the system itself that should be, more and more, dependent on the local efficiency of its autonomous elements (distributed, heterogeneous, intentional and not-lineal model). The fundamental principle is that these new reactive and holistic elements resolve their own needs by optimizing their contextual (local) conditions, demanding from the (global) network those inputs, forces and/or services that they can not generated in – and by – themselves, calling for a new interactive sharing exchange (with all the synonyms that we can imagine: solidarity, relationship, interchange, interconnection, inter-linkage, reciprocity, conjugation, combination, etc., that have been always paradigms of an empathic reason and sensibility).[10]

This type of "*individual/collective interconnected and integrated intelligence*" [11] is what should allow, increasingly, a model of dynamic equilibrium model based on mutually supportive feedback and an interactive collaboration – and integration – of different multiplied (multi-layer and multi-level) systems and data-fields resulting from the logic of natural progress processes and/of this new networked interconnectivity (supportive, tolerant, irregular, multiple and plural, diverse and diversified).

The fundamental importance of singular-specific circumstantial factors (qualified as renewable) that must respond to different principles of adaptation to local and specific conditions (climates, topographies, urban metabolisms, cultures, economies, uses, etc.) combined with new forms of social and multi-connective collaboration (in processes of temporary and intentional complicity, integrated) should favor these dynamics of "(inter) connected increased condition", as a paradigm for new glocal organization models: i.e., models that minimize consumption and favor on-site – optimized – production rooted in a growing, weighted and processed capacity for *resili(g)ent* [12] *Interactive Intelligence,* declined

_10. Vicente Guallart, ***La ciudad autosuficiente*** (Barcelona: ed. RBA, 2012), 83.

_11. Juan Requejo : "Territorio y Energía: La autosuficiencia conectada." in http://www.atclave.es/publicaciones/descargas/pub_energia/27_territorio_y_energia_la_autosuficiencia_conectada.pdf

_12. The term *Resili(g)ence* (Resilience and Intelligence) is introduced by the author in several publications. See in particular the reports of the Forum, Meeting and Symposium Resili(g)ence, Intelligent Cities, Resilient Landscapes, Genova, DAD-UNIGE, October 2016. Manuel Gausa, C. Andriani and R. Fagnoni, *Med Net 3 Resili(g)ence, Meeting Proceedings* (Barcelona: Paper Docs 2017).

Human embedded Matrix: Matrix digital rain, Matrix code or sometimes *Green Rain*, is the computer code featured in the Matrix film series. (Wikipedia, Matrix)

in all the senses, between citizens, users, environments, cultures, matters… and between all of them. The paradox is that, at the same time, we are assisting to all the last perplexities, and resistance behaviors of the old ego-social models (egoism and ego-centrism, superficiality, xenophobia, mono-leaderships, distraction and evasion, indifference, etc.), that curiously, seem to be augmented in this the digital era.

Probably they are the last manifestations of the *present-past refusals*.

But it is also true that, despite the confidence in progress and the human need to continue developing a progressive equation between technology, thought, creativity and a sensitive culture, sensible to the demands of our time, that proactive vocation cannot fail to be combined with a critical gaze capable of detecting perplexities and conflicts. This publication appears at a time marked by the technological progresses and the creative potentials but also by a succession of crises in the last decade, economic (crash of the financial bubbles, since 2008), environmental (awareness of the threats of an undeniable climate change, since 1997 and specially, since 2007), socio-political (fragmentation and xenophobia, lack of solidarity in the face of forced immigration flows and local armed conflicts, increasing since 2008) and finally, health emergencies such as the great viral and universal Pandemia (Covid, 2020) similar to that Spanish Fever produced at the beginning of the 20th century, in full industrial and energetic progress.

Crises that seem unrelated to this exponential technological change but that, nevertheless, have gone hand in hand, parallel to it and curiously leading – more and more - an increase not only in super-connectivity but also in multi-productivity, in a "time without times, without *tiempos* ... or *tempos*" ; a single overlapping and overlapping hyper-time, with immediate responses, productive stress, on-line bureaucratic tides, big and little data controls, and obligated requirements in/by the telematic connections; with absence of rigor and spaces (in the sense not only literal but temporal) for concentration, for reflection, for interpretation or knowledge and contrast of what implies and surrounds us.

The "multiplication" of a strange conductive "homogenization" and of a disciplined collective "acceptation" that the recent economic, pandemic and epidemiologic stresses has produced in the reasoning processes and the massive use of telecommunications and new pre-5G digital technologies, the exponential dynamics of online multi-work, the physical and social distancing, the crisis (if not demonization) of the old ludic-unproductive hedonism and its replacement by a new leisure-work simultaneity, but also by a new hyper-connectivity without apparent intimacy or capacity for "desertion", surely will be subject of attention (on a sociological, anthropological and even philosophical level) to analyse and to reflect.

A hyper-time of acceptances, requests and obligations; of immediate responses and mediate actions; a time of common experiences that, being able - potentially - to be increasingly free, tolerant, complicit, shared and spontaneous, seem to tend to confinement, segregation, self-affirmation, more prosaic selfish pragmatism and pure submission to the universal media and medial messages.

4. INNOVATION

A lot of perplexities are emerging today – more than 30 years ago – about the future of this expansive, ubiquitous, omnipresent and embedded digital universe, which is consolidated today in a way that is not always as idealistic and propositional as we initially thought. The informational interaction that was to bring tolerance, diversity, socio-environmental respect, freedom of thought and action, creativity, complicity and research and knowledge on the net, ludic and enjoying informality and, therefore, a new type of democratic and *glocal* (global and local) *AST-ethics* and politics of progress, seems to be crossed, today, with a new type of universal control; with a new productive "slavery" – without schedules, or reflexion, concentration and relax timing –... a rapid consumption of stimuli, thoughts and anecdotes, a selfish hedonism more than really playful, a standard bureaucracy in the collection of personal data, efficiency indicators or statistical lists, a certain unexpected xenophobia and a socioeconomic unbalanced and distanced inequality, without mediations or clear intellectual orpolitical responses.

We hope, however, that the emergence of this actual new era, digital and computational – but also procedural and relational – will allow not only an increase in the level of global (and informational) connectivity, but also in sensitive and human exchanges, while a increase degree of local qualitative response to the needs, potentials and resources of each context; but that also allows - thanks to the increase not only in Digital Development and *Artificial Intelligence* but in a new *Collective Inter-diligence* – a substantial improvement in matter/material answers (responsive), environmental conditions (reactive), and socio-cultural behaviors (interactive).

This conjunction between *information* and *informationality*, *interaction* and *Interactivity* buts also between *independence* and *interdependence*[13] is what can guarantee a possible evaluation and balance between a responsible desire for ethicsl and individual integral freedom (autonomous, singular, local) and the need for collective integrated and integrative responsibility and solidarity (shared, plural, global), both convoking a new transversal, holistic and innovative intelligence. All these factors can support, in effect, a qualitative leap in our socio-cultural and socio-environmental relationship with the medium and between

_13. The term 'Interdependence' derives from the definition used for the first time by Gandhi in 1929: interdependence, understood in turn as self-sufficiency, allowed for combining individual independence and social interrelation.

media, in which *nets* systems (and *sets* systems), smart conditions and slow conditions, globality and locality, connectivity and disconnection, can coexist at the same time, taking advantage of proximity, interrelation and distribution, beyond totalist and deterministic industrial models based on maximum material concentration/centralization – material and materialistic – not only of goods but power and knowledge; and in the standard universalization of exchanges, thoughts, and consumptions.

We might say that the pursuit of greater *Interactive Integrated Intelligence* in our habitats also implies urban synergy and empathy (positive and processing informational exchange).

And that combination between *self-efficient city* (in ecological, social, creative and economical-productive terms) and *empathiCity* will be fundamental in the future.

Reactive environments and proactive environments, in innovative networked conditions.

Whereas the industrial era of the 20th century favored a paradigm shift in the city and architecture, based on the development of new systems – new technologies and new materials – for construction and production (mechanical and functional developments, synonymous with progress but net consumers of resources and gross producers of urban waste), the information age of the 21st century seems poised to enact a new paradigm shift based on the development of new "infra"-, "socio"- and "eco"- structures – both material and immaterial – for social and environmental management, interaction and co-production. At the same time, this informational condition, progressively open, uncertain and variable, must be combined with the ability to create "horizons of certainty", shared criteria of action, visions and forward-looking strategies capable of orienting (driving and induce) qualitatively the new urban developments, especially in Europe, combining advanced technology with new relational models, spatial and social strategies, innovative and sustainable at the same time: susceptible to combine "sensing" and "sensitive" logics.

SENSORS AND SENSIBILITIES

City–Senses and sens(c)ivilities.

Responsive contexts and responsable societies.

Processing attention and creative innovation.

Precise DATAS & holistic VISIONS.

Such combination "*information + vision*" (processing capacity and prospective, strategic and relational capacity) lacks today of suitable reference areas and ambitious programs of inter-disciplinary innovative exchanges.

If we understand the new logics –associated to a new urban thinking – in relation with the challenges of a new informational era –and the capacity, in this one, to multiply the interactions between conditions and information(s) understanding "information", not only as a data-parameter or a data-indicator but as a more enlarge concept associated to other assimilated key-terms (programs, solicitations, messages, patterns, identities, matters, cultures, types, *behaviours*, senses, networks, natures, morphologies and metabolic contexts) able to be combined in (and from) new – and more – open, flexible and resilient (urban) systems. The next generation of urban planners will be challenged to find solutions to complex problems related to population, energy, environment, food, water, security, housing, health, and transportation. These challenges will be to provide new scenarios no longer productive or reproductive but "co-productive", capable of generating open and resilient models, orientated and co-participated at a time, from which address:

– The new complex recognition and expression of the contemporary Multi-City and its many informational levels (data-maps and intentional-maps) and the new *geo-urban* articulations and translations in new "eco", "intra" and "infra" structural networks.

– The new demands of urban re-naturalization and recycling, rational land-use and "inward growth" and the new active dimension of landscape (and public space) as operational, relational and co-productive space at a time.

– The new sustainable agendas (energetic (self)sufficiency, intelligent management of resources, etc.) and their translation into new types of eco-habitats able to mix uses, functions and programs in a new kind of multi-layer repertories and hybrid typologies.

– The increase in telecommunication of real-time data and its relationship with a new type of actant-citizens more autonomous and incidents in urban self-organization itself.

– The new phenomena of co-participation and transformation "bottom-up" of spaces and collective scenarios, more or less reversible linked with the new technological – and digital – interactive capabilities and their translation into new processes of intelligent fabrication and the research of new materials, more reactive-responsive in/into the medium.

The notion of Advanced Architecture and Urbanism wants to contribute to address - from the exchange of researches and explorations- such multiple approaches to the complex conditions of the city in the new century.

Approaches capable of combining data processing, modelling of variables, integrated mapping records (analytical and synthetic, relational and structural), economy of resources, new urban entrepreneurships and innovative governances, in a new type of transversal urban thought, strategic, creative and interactive. With the aim of combining "data" and "visions" in/for the city – information and prospection: sense, sensuousness and sensibility- in a new type of more efficient and relational habitats: informational and convivial, at the same time.

We are in a time of exploration and obviously of research but the architecture must be especially a great cultural adventure. Culture is that: search, create and share. Current research related to technological development requires ever more scientific answers, but it must also become a culture that can be understood by citizens: as architects we have the ability to create a specific and expressive spatial culture of the time, and to transmit it by looking for one's own abilities but also by celebrating one's own ideas: to create a new "better" living space; a certain idea of habitat resonating with our own time.

Architecture is no longer envisioned only as a "machine for living" but as an "environment" for (in)habi(lita)ting ...and cohabi(lita)ting.[14]

_14. This text is based on reflections and premises previously presented in the text "City Sense: Territorializing Information," suitably revised and updated.
Manuel Gausa, "City Sense: Territorializing Information" in *AA.VV: City Sense, 4th Advanced Architecture Contest* (Barcelona-New York, IaaC –Actar Publishers, 2012), 6.

Living Screen // Robotic Fabrication of Algae based Gels
(IAAC-MAA02 2015. Researcher: Irina Shaklova, Tutor: Marcos Cruz, 2015)

V. ANNEX

ANALYTIC AND COMPARATIVE WORKING-PROCESS MAPS

The various tables and maps that accompany these lines attempt to understand, compare and relate the various parameters associated with a new era in architectural logic and technique, technology, science, creation – and thought, in general – and which we have wanted to argue throughout these pages in their different periods and under the name of Advanced Logic (Informational, Complex, Digital, Intelligent or Holistic for various authors).[15]

A logic clearly associated with an experimental and operational will linked to a new interpretation of our relationship, exchange and space-temporal and informational environments, still in the process of being defined. These tables allow us to observe the various lines of action and work that have accompanied the thesis presented here and their various systematizations, more or less schematic and/or taxonomic, in said cartographies or synthetic maps.

Throughout this work, we will return repeatedly to this notion of the "map" understood not only as "representation", but also as "interpretation" and/or "translation" of an anticipatory (resonating) and projective (transferring) action with respect to reality.

Both approaches let us present the idea of the notational map not only as a synthetic representation of reality but also as a set of beacons indicating possibilities; i.e., as a mental framework for anticipating movements. This not only relates to the aforementioned capacity for exploring new territories (with an attentive gaze), but also to the ability to propose new definitions for them and new keys as "*interpreta(c)tions*".

Keys" in the sense of ("guidelines") – rather than strict classifications or taxonomies – meant to recognize a new reality by indicating it through different voices; with the understanding that re-naming things (suggesting new associations, new readings, new messages and signs) allows for creating new mental maps. Recognizing a triple meaning in the very notion of "map":

– the map as a cartography of expression and representation (as a tool for recording and reading – for analysis and understanding – for the purpose of action).
– the map as an anticipatory mechanism (as an outline for (other) possible actions and movements)
– the map, lastly, as a mental and operational translation key (for codes and meanings, but also for possible interpretations and interpreta[c]tions).

Based on these considerations, this work can be understood also as a possible "map" of contemporary experimental design and the city and its new advanced dynamics of change: a map – or reconnaissance cartography – that can be used to explore, analyze, describe and design all at the same time: proposals that are formulating new "key-terms" (plays on words, neologisms, hybrid voices like hypothetical "beacon-messages" or conceptual "ideograms") intended to encourage the possible exploration of limits that are subject to constant redefinition and change.

_15. For this part connected with the final corollary see the introduction to the book: Manuel Gausa: *Open(ing): Space-Time-Information & Advanced Architecture. Underlying Architectonic Logics in the Turn of the Millennium* (Barcelona: Actar Publishers, 2018), 11-13.

TRANSFERS
EARLY 20TH CENTURY
MODERN LOGIC

Contributions to holistic knowledge

The birth of cinema
1895/1900

Sigmund Freud
The Interpretation of Dreams
1900

Max Planck
Energy quanta
1900

E.S Potter
The Great Train Robbery

Wright brothers
First manned flight
1903.

Albert Einstein
Theory of Relativity
1905

Henry Ford
Launch of the Model T
1906

Pablo Picasso
Les Demoiselles d' Avignon
1907

Arnold Schoenberg
Irst atonal composition
1909

Vasili Kandinsky
First abstract watercolor
1910

Technological, intellectual, and scientific changes

A new functional, objectual and objective or"positional" interpretation of space

Space-Time Link

Rational, material and industrial thought.

Rational, abstract, universal Modern logic

A SHIFT IN LOGIC
MID 20TH CENTURY
INFORMATIONAL/ADVANCED LOGIC

Contributions to holistic knowledge

Televisions appear in homes
1960

Marshall McLuhan
Understanding Media

Guy Debord
La société de l'espectacle
1964

IBM
Computational system based on "Windows"
1965

Murray & Gellmann
Development of quantum physics

Discovery of the structure of DNA
1961

Edward Lorenz
Chaos Theory
1963

Jay Forrester
The formulation of System dynamics
1969

Benoit Mandelbrot
the formulation of Fractal Systems
1969

Birth of the Internet
1968

Birth experimentations in Silicon Valey
1970

Technological, intellectual, and scientific changes

A new dynamic, procedural and relational or "dispositional" interpretation of space

Space-Time-Information Link

Complex, transversal and digital thought

Complex, transversal, informational Advanced logic

This work is not intended as a "summary" or a "compendium" of that research, but as an attempt at an "overall re-formulation" (in a new conceptual corpus) of many of the reflections and experiences that have been developed – in parallel, simultaneously and coinciding although they were undertaken in separate contexts and areas – combined with others that are meant to provide structure and fill out the theoretical framework that we are attempting to build up.

This territory of exploration and research, of trials and distant, interconnected experiences – which are both familiar and distant at the same time... – would define a framework for a network of concerns (and explorations), based on far-off exchanges, intersecting stimuli, shared reading, mutual interests, feeding and feedback, which are more or less conscious and/or convergent. It is obvious that this new desire for exploration would be coupled with a new desire to observe, to listen and to transmit ... to generate new references, in any case: i.e., to create new imagery and new "mental maps" capable of connecting (and interconnecting) with a new universe of ideas and concepts specific and global, singular and plural, individual and cosmopolitan at the same time.

This intellectual and cultural effervescence (which is also prospective and propositional) and present in many fields of knowledge (economy, art, science, technology) require, so, a new theoretical construction very close to an operational action" able to "take an ideological position" –ethical, political, social, close to the attention to the environment, the human and social progress, the believing in the cultural and technological innovation, the bet for the creativity, the respect and the adaptability to the common welfare– more than to continue with the simple description (glossist, erudite, or simply historiographical) of neutral chronicles, "listed" brands or panoramic visions.

In this sense, we could talk about a certain "para-theory" developed by aware "para-theoreticians" who, aside from "producing" and "designing" – doing – would also talk, write and debate – think – about urban, spatial, formal and even moral issues ... concerning architectural attitudes and ethics ...

The conscience of a change of paradigms can explain the boom in forms of expression, transmission and dissemination that have being so important at the turn of the century, especially in Europe. We could say that in the 1990s, while in Holland these diversified group of convinced and innovating teams were directly building, in France they were debating about the new ideas, in Italy they were trying to renew the Old Academy, in United States they were exploring a new universe of technological possibilities and in Spain they were proposing, envisioning, disseminating and diffusing internal and external inputs.

As we have pointed out, publications like *Quaderns, Fisuras, A+T* or *Circo* in Spain, *Arch+* in Germany, *Archis* in Holland, etc.; platforms like Actar Ediciones (Barcelona); meet-ups and forums such as Europan or Archilab in France; centers like the Berlage Institut in Rotterdam, Columbia in New York and MIT in Boston or SI-ARC in L.A, or research units at the AA or Bartlett in London or CITA in Copenhaghen would be fundamental in this scenario of fledgling propositional appearances.

In this context, the importance of collective actions like the work done by Metapolis in Barcelona (meetings, publications, spaces for debate and teacher training) would express, perhaps like nothing else, this desire to communicate and celebrate a new experimental thinking, made explicit in the Metapolis Dictionary of Advance Architecture and at the IAAC (Institute for Advanced Architecture of Catalonia) launched at the beginning of the XXI Century.

ORDER FORMAL
UNIVERSAL
LINEAR
DETERMINIST
CLOSED

SPACE AND TIME	SPACE-TIME	SPACE-TIME-INFORMATION
CLASSIC	MODERN	ADVANCED
<AB>: ABSOLUTE	**<RE>: RELATIVE**	**<IN>: INTERACTIVE**
FIXED	***STABLE***	***DYNAMIC***
META-PHYSICAL AND PHYSICAL	PHYSICAL-REAL	REAL-VIRTUAL
ESSENCE (ESSENTIAL)	**MATTER (MATERIAL)**	**INFORMATION (INFORMATIONAL)**
UNIQUE	DIVERSE	DIVERSIFIED (MULTIPLE)
ANALOGICAL	MECHANICAL	DIGITAL
RITUAL	***FUNCTIONAL***	***OPERATIONAL***
SYMBOLIC	DOGMATIC	STRATEGIC
HARMONIOUS	AUTONOMOUS	UBIQUITOUS (EMPATHIC)
EVOCATIVE	CONCEPTIVE	REACTIVE
HIERARCHICAL RELATIONSHIP	**POSITIONAL RELATIONSHIP**	**PROCESSUAL RELATIONSHIP**
CONTINUOUS	DISCONTINUOUS	SIMULTANEOUS
COMPACT	***FRAGMENTED***	***FRACTAL***
UNIFORM	VARIABLE	EVOLUTIONAL
EXACT	***PRECISE***	***COMBINATORY***
PREDICTABLE	MESURABLE	DIFFERENTIAL
NORM	**TYPE**	**DATA (INFORMATION)**
PROTO-LOGICAL	TYPO-LOGICAL	TOPO-LOGICAL
FORMAL	ABSTRACT	MIXED
FIGURATIVE	***STRUCTURAL***	***INFORMATIONAL***
SOLEMN	SEVERE	EXTROVERTED
CEREMONIAL	STRICT	UNINHIBITED
PURE	PURIST	CROSSBRED (HYBRID)
REGULATION (CODE)	**RELATION (PLOT)**	**COMBINATION (MATRIX)**
CONTROL (FORMAL)	**ORDER (OBJECTUAL)**	**SYNERGY (ENVIRONMENTAL)**
PLANE (2D)	**VOLUME (3D)**	**FIELD (4D)**
COMPOSITION (CODIFICATION)	**POSITION (CORRELATION)**	**DISPOSITION (INTERACTION)**

NEW DEVICES: BEYOND LINKS-RESPONSIVE FORMS

<IN>FORMAL ORDER
MULTIPLE
NON-LINEAR
IN-DETERMINIST
OPEN

<IN> PROPERTIES	
<IN> DETERMINATION	<IN> FINITENESS
<IN> STABILITY	<IN> TERACTION
<IN> TERCONNECTION	<IN> DISCIPLINE
<IN> COMPLETION	<IN> FORMALITY

SPACE-TIME -INFORMATION AND NEW ARCHITECTURE

Comparative Table "SPACE-TIME-INFORMATION" published in *Quaderns* n. 222, 1999 and reviewed for the publication GAUSA, Manuel (2018), *Open(ing). Space-Time-Information 1990-2000. The Beginnings of Advanced Architecture.* New York-Barcelona, Actar publishers, p. 293. An initial approach to many of the considerations that are discussed in these pages.

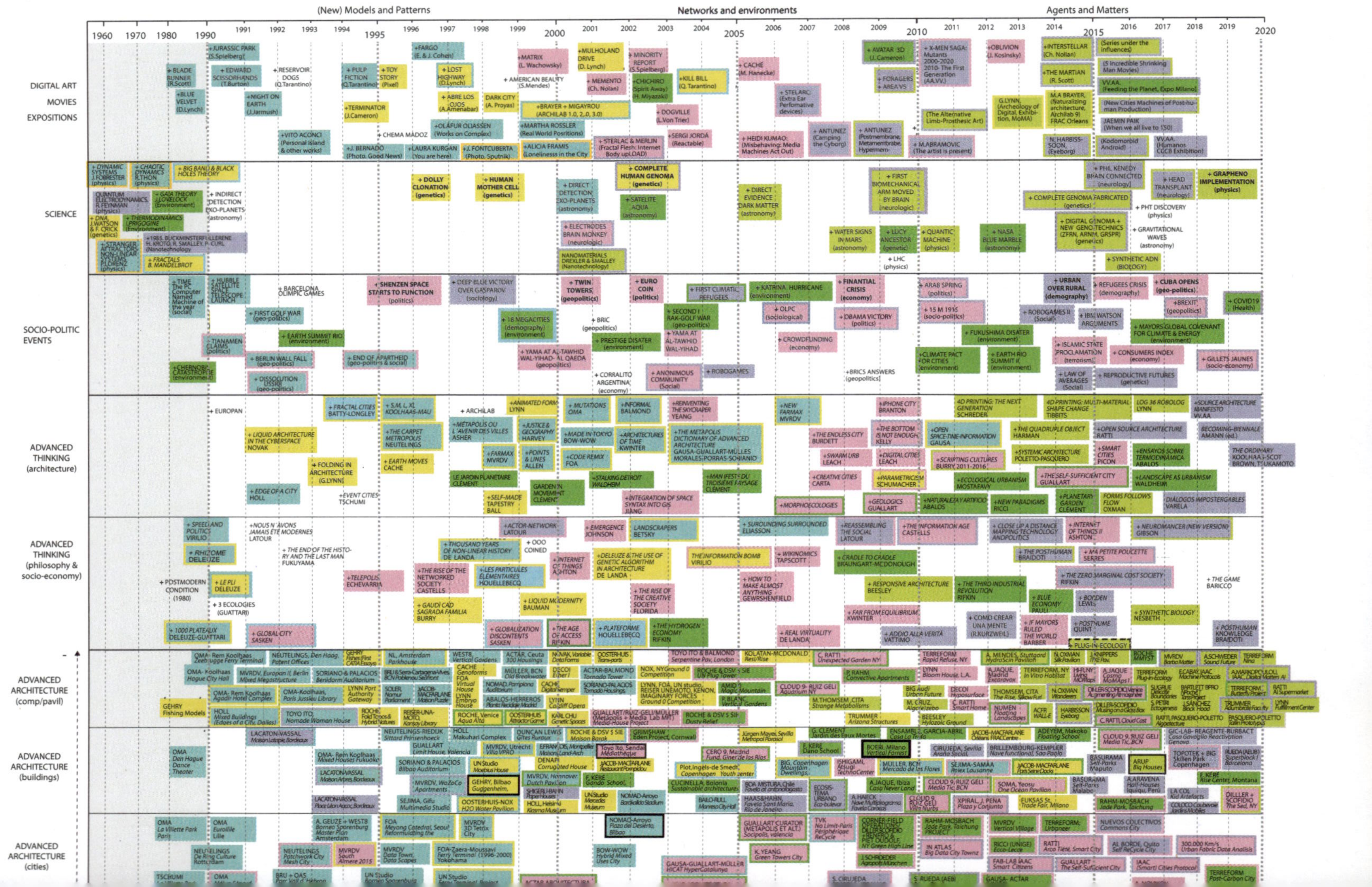
(New) Models and Patterns
Networks and environments
Agents and Matters
DIGITAL ART
MOVIES
EXPOSITIONS
SCIENCE
SOCIO-POLITIC EVENTS
ADVANCED THINKING (architecture)
ADVANCED THINKING (philosophy & socio-economy)
ADVANCED ARCHITECTURE (comp/pavil)
ADVANCED ARCHITECTURE (buildings)
ADVANCED ARCHITECTURE (cities)
1960
1970
1980
1990
1995
2000
2005
2010
2015
2020

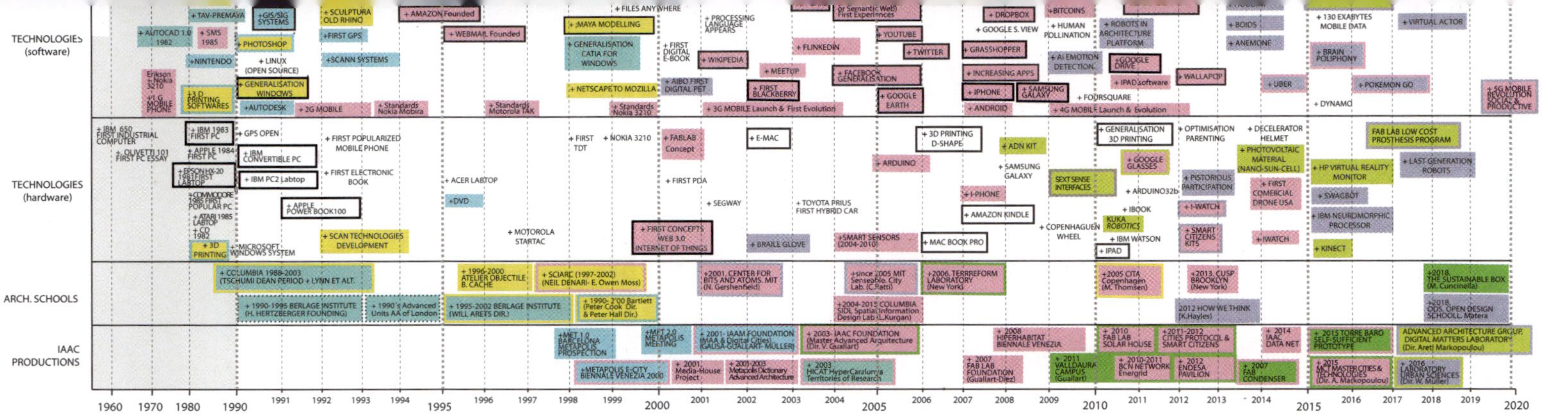

advanced architecture through
CONFORMATIVE SYSTEMS
Aprox 1990-2000...

- **FRAMEWORK** -> Topologies (system of relations)
- **INFORMATION** -> Combinatory geometrical parameter
- **RESOURCES** -> Layers & Folds/Bends
- **OPERATIONS** -> Overlapping & Modelling
- **KEY WORDS** -> Configuration, Strata, Yuxtaposition, Deformation, Mesh, Stretch, Combination, Simultaneity, Co-existance, Formulation, Field
- **CITY** -> n-City, Complex-City or Multi-City

advanced architecture through
DISTRIBUTIVE SYSTEMS
Aprox 2000-2010...

- **FRAMEWORK** -> Ecologies (relation among systems)
- **INFORMATION** -> Connective/Collective Real Time Indicator
- **RESOURCES** -> Networks & Environments
- **OPERATIONS** -> Connecting & Propagating
- **KEY WORDS** -> Ambient, Atmosphere, Diffusion, Web, Inter-connection, Multinodal, Glocal, Bidirectional, Planetarian, Eco-system, TICS
- **CITY** -> Network City, Sense-City or Intelligent City

advanced architecture through
EXPANSIVE SYSTEMS
Aprox 2010-2020...

- **FRAMEWORK** -> Xenologies (relations between foreign systems)
- **INFORMATION** -> Materic and Sensorial responsive & AI inputs
- **RESOURCES** -> (AI)Agents & X-Matters
- **OPERATIONS** -> Mediating & Augmenting
- **KEY WORDS** -> Post-humanism, Machine thinking, Deep learning, Drones, Grapheno, Robotics, Cyb-org, Augmented Reality, Artificial Intelligence, Nano-technology, Devices Behaviours
- **CITY** -> Co-City, Responsive-City, Ubiquous City, EmpathyCity

LOGIC	CONDITION	APPROACH	VOCATION	DEVELOPMENT	ORDER	CONSTITUTION	QUALITY
Informational (Complexity)	Interactive (Interactivity)	Holistic (Transversality)	Integrative (Mixicity)	Evolutive (Dinamicity)	Open (Adaptability)	Heterogeneous (Diversity)	Responsive (Reactivity)

advanced architecture through
CONFORMATIVE PROTOCOLS
aprox 1990-2000

- **FRAMEWORK** -> Topology (system of relations)
- **INFORMATION** -> Combinatory geometrical parameter
- **RESOURCES** -> Layers & Folds/Bends
- **OPERATIONS** -> Overlapping & Modelling
- **KEY WORDS** -> Configuration, Strata, Yuxtaposition, Deformation, Mesh, Stretch, Combination, Simultaneity, Co-existance, Formulation, Field

advanced architecture through
DISTRIBUTIVE PROTOCOLS
aprox 2000-2010

- **FRAMEWORK** -> Ecology (relation among systems)
- **INFORMATION** -> Collective real time Indicator
- **RESOURCES** -> Networks & Environments
- **OPERATIONS** -> Connecting & Propagating
- **KEY WORDS** -> Ambient, Atmosphere, Diffusion, Web, Inter-connection, Multinodal, Glocal, Bidirectional, Planetarian, Eco-system, TICS

advanced architecture through
EXPANSIVE PROTOCOLS
2010 - 2020

- **FRAMEWORK** -> Xenology(expanding relational systems)
- **INFORMATION** -> Sensitive personal application
- **RESOURCES** -> Agents & Matter
- **OPERATIONS** -> Mediating & Performing
- **KEY WORDS** -> Post-humanism, Machine thinking, Deep learning, Drones, Grapheno, Robotics, Cyb-org, Augmented Reality, Artificial Intelligence, Nano-technology, Devices Behaviours

ADVANCED ARCHITECTURE LOGICS
THE 8 (7 + 1) FACTORS

In this sense, the end of the first decade of the 21st century has been characterized –as we pointed out in this publication – by the appearance of decisive new technological advances and of new conceptual contributions; new sensibilities that have grown according to a formation that is open to reflecting on complexity and the importance of the interactivity that we have described here.

A new generation of concerns and proposals called on to set off this fundamental digital revolution – associated with the assumption of an informational interaction as an undeniable part of a new space-time-information that is less lineal in its behavior – approaching it from parameters not just of synergy with the context, the landscape, the place or the city (or among structures, types and programs) but from a positive exchange with the medium, with society, with the use and the user; between the city and the citizen; between the polis ... and, why not? ... the politics, understood as the possible construction and administration of a common horizon for collective actions. *Sensorization* and *parameterization*, data optimization, design of intelligent interfaces and of responsive and responsible answers: today, the a-scalar transfer devices that were characteristic of much of the research in the mid-1990s are no longer so necessary; rather, there is a more empathic and imbedded, more "natural" and spontaneous approach to the environment, called on to combine "sense and sensibility". In this individual and collective desire to research, to explore, to investigate and to delve into the current conditions of our own environment, the new scenarios and areas for exchange – and the organization systems associated with them – we can observe a clear desire for an implication in the culture of our time, reclaiming the active role of architecture in understanding, interpreting and designing our contemporary spaces. Reclaiming, in fact, the historic role of architecture as a benefit mediation and an endeavor that is cultural, intellectual, creative, technological, scientific, social and political at the same time: a collective adventure (and not a mere record of individual brands or personalities) with the ability to connect ethics and aesthetics of our time... expressions and approaches ... combining implicated professional activity, engaged intellectual action and proactive design interaction.

With the capacity to continue defining our environment qualitatively, in order to create a better habitat, i.e., a type of habitable space, in consonance with the ambitious preoccupations and expectations – rather than the contingent inertias – of society itself.

Not according to its tastes, but in keeping with its ambitions (i.e., with the capacity to encourage intellectual curiosity, social interaction, a creative stance, and cultural projection) based on new types of spaces and habitats (planned or built) more imaginative, more empathetic, more open and, ultimately, more expressive and stimulating.

Previous Table: Manuel Gausa and Jordi Vivaldi (with the collaboration of Mohamed Atab).
Up: Comparative Time-Field with different items – technological, socio-cultural, intellectual, artistic, academic and urban-architectural – chromatically and chronologically positioned according to the different protocols derived from the cluster-densifications presented in this publication.
Down: synthetic framework of the three systemic protocols that have marked these 30 years of Advanced and Experimental Knowledge.

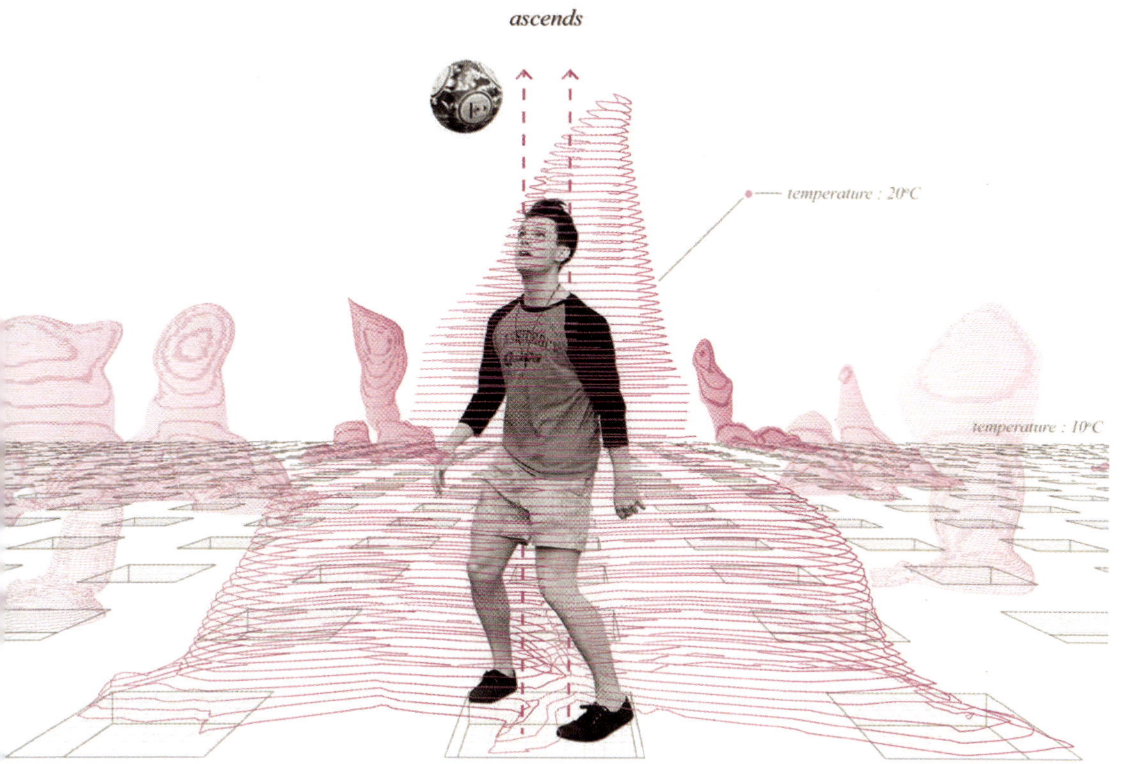

°*ATMOSPHERA* (IAAC MAA02 2015-2016. Researcher: Asya Guney)

JORDI VIVALDI

PERSPECTIVES

TOWARDS A LIMIT-SPACE

After the Architectural Rhizome

Daring dwellers of the world's confines, the *limitanei* inhabited the Roman Empire without occupying its interior. Belonging to the *civitas* but alluding to the *barbarie*, a suffocating and malleable territory flourished between the Roman Empire and the Gothic tribes: the *limes*. Rather than a clinical edge or a border wall, the Roman limit was a narrow and oscillating territory, a carnal space of junction and disjunction, an unstable land of conflict whose bustling diversity by no means could take place within the mathematical abstraction of the Euclidean line. Placed at the intersection between law and anarchy and fluctuating between world and mystery, the limes constituted a spatial oxymoron and a territory of friction, an isthmus susceptible to colonisation, cultivation and worship, a land whose horizon was always threatened by the otherness of the barbarian armies, whose incursions insistently re-wove the *limes*' limits. Under its jurisdiction, Roman soldiers, local families, exotic merchants, friendly tribes and hostile troops populated vivacious and eclectic poles of activity, effervescent zones of multitudes irreducible to any single identity.

The Roman notion of *limes* constitutes, in its "differential sameness and autoreferential difference"[1], a spatial logic whose architectural modulation is defined here as Limit-Space. Its threefold nature – liminal, limited and limitrophe – blossoms surreptitiously as a form of spatiality that aims at modulating the coming years of advanced architecture. Limit-Space is thus an architectual spatial speculation; it is a propositive conceptual construct, a hypothetical spatiality resonating with current's subjectless condition and partially anticipated by some contemporaneous experimental projects. It is animated by a primary vocation: that of defying both the Promethean flatness of the Platonic *chora* and the baroque fluctuations of the Aristotelian *topos* by opposing their common anti-spatial conditions: that of being generic, that of being continuous, that of being homogeneous.

_1. Eugenio Trías, *Los límites del Mundo*, (Barcelona: Ariel Filosofía, 1985), 121.

1. THE HOMOGENEOUS ANTI-SPACES OF CHORA AND TOPOS

Peter Eisenman situates[2] the origin of the concept of homogeneous space in Alberti. It appears as a space in which all objects exist in a consistent and calculable medium, defined by Mark Wigley as total and non-hierarchical[3]: a notational space associated with Alberti's allographic conception, but, above all, intimately related to the notion of *anti-space* coined[4] by Steven Kent Peterson to differentiate the modern movement's spatialities (flowing, continuous, universal and infinite) from the *space* of the Renaissance (static, discontinuous, singular and finite). Kent's homogeneous *anti-space* corresponds to Plato's *chora*. This term was used in ancient Greece[5] to evoke an occupiable expanse without referring to a particular location. In the Timaeus, Plato describes a "third type" of existence, beyond the world of ideas and objects: "And the third type is space, which exists always and cannot be destroyed. It provides a fixed state for all things that come to be. It is itself apprehended by a kind of bastard reasoning that does not involve sense perception."[6] This type of existence consists of a medium that is unchanging and inmaterial, yet in its eternity it allows everything to happen. The *chora* is a receptacle for all generation – invisible, amorphous, open to everything, an interval between being and not-being in which forms (eidos) are originally held and from which they receive their spatiality.

Modernity's homogeneous anti-space of transparency and domination exalts many of *chora's* attributes: fluidity, uniformity, secularization, continuity, openness, universality, infinity, etc.[7] Le Corbusier's "free plan" and Mies van der Rohe's "open plan" constitute, in opposition to Renaissance architectural distributions, an "ineffable space" navigated by independent forms. This process can already be observed in "Sir John Soane's Museum" (1824), where paintings and sculptures flow through a slippery space that no longer resonates with the centralized rigidity of Renaissance architecture. The gridded plans by Jean-Nicolas-Louis Durant and the transparency and lightness of Joseph Paxton's "Crystal Palace" (1851) announce the arrival of this limitless space, culminating in the typical space of the International Style: uniform, universal, eternal and unlimited, framed by a discrete set of horizontal planes that simply encircle a fraction of that space. Its Platonic roots give it an ideal, theoretical, generic and indefinite condition, which can only be approached through mathematization: modern space has been measured and calculated by the rigor of science and the efficiency of industry.

While the term *chora* refers to a receptacle, the term *topos* refers to a place. In contrast to the flat spaces of modernity, the three-dimensional variability of 1990s spaces produces topographic surfaces in which every point is singular. This results in "a constant modification of the space that leads to a changing reading of the place"[8], implying the shift from Plato's *chora* to Aristotle's *topos*. Unlike the universal abstraction of the former, in the Physics, Aristotle "identifies the generic concept of space with another more empirical concept, that of 'place', always referred to with the term *topos*. In other words, Aristotle

_2. Peter Eisenman, "Brief Advanced Design Studio", last modified October 2014, https://www.architecture.yale.edu/courses/advanced-design-studio-eisenman-0#_ftn3

_3. Mark Wigley, in conversation with Peter Eisenman, "Eisenman/Wigley X: The Problematic of Homogeneous Space", YouTube video (56:00), conversation on August 8, 2013, posted by "Columbia GSAPP", September 11, 2013, https://www.youtube.com/watch?v=0_b5COTxHuc&t=125s.

_4. Steven Kent Peterson, "Space vs Anti-Space", *Harvard Architectural Review: Beyond the Modern Movement.* (Cambridge: MIT Press, 1980).

_5. Keimpe Algra, *Concepts of Space in Greek Thought*, (London: Brill, 1995), 36.

_6. Plato, *Timaeus*, trans. Peter Kalkavage, (New York: Hacket Publishing, 2000), 52b.

_7. Josep Maria Montaner, *La modernidad superada,* (Barcelona: Gustavo Gili, 2011), 33.

_8. Alejandro Zaera-Polo, "Nuevas topografías. *La reformulación del suelo," in Otra mirada: posiciones contra crónicas*, ed. Manuel Gausa and Ricardo Devesa, (Barcelona: Gustavo Gili, 2010), 116-17.

looks at space from the point of view of place. Every body occupies its specific place, and place is a fundamental and physical property of bodies"[9]. This is very clear in the following text by the Stagirite: "Again, place (topos) belongs to the quantities which are continuous. For the parts of a body which join together at a common boundary occupy a certain place. Therefore, also the parts of place which are occupied by the several parts of the body join together at the same boundary at which the parts of the body do."[10] Aristotle defines topos as a continuous and three-dimensional underlying substratum, but above all as an empirical and localized substratum.

The difference between the spatiality of the Mies van der Rohe's "Lake Shore Drive" (1949) and the one of Rem Koolhaas' "Jussieu Libraries" (1992) plays out in parallel to the difference between the *chora* and the *topos*: whereas the former engages an indefinite, generic, abstract and ideal condition, the latter has an empirical, specific, articulated and defined character. As opposed to Modernity's tabula rasa and its understanding of the floor as a "datum", the rhizomatic floors of the late 20th century are a continuum of artificial "places" whose topographic structure resonates with Parent's "inclisite". In opposition to modernity's chora, the topological space of projects such as the "Yokohama Ferry Terminal" (2002) or the "Rolex Learning Center" (2009) is not constituted as the universal *support* for an accidental *circumstance*; rather, it is *support* and *circumstance* at the same time.

The rhizomatic twists associated with these projects and underpinned by the intensive use of computational tools seem to oppose homogeneous anti-space. According to Eisenman, "while Alberti's notational systems transcribed a single design by a single author, computation has the capacity to produce multiple iterations that the designer must choose from."[11] Computers function as generators of variability, a fact that seems to promote inconsistent multiples, calling into question Alberti's homogeneous spatiality. However, the rhizomatic constitution of projects such as the "Jussieu Libraries", the "Yokohama Terminal" or the "Rolex Learning Center" is reducible to one single formula or equation, that is, a consistent and calculable single medium (parametricism). Thus, in spite of the visual heterogeneity evoked by the three-dimensional vibration of these projects, the unitary surfaces that characterize their spatiality cannot be described in terms of heterogeneity. Their rhizomatic nature is reducible to Alberti's single notational system, a fact that intimately associates chora and topos by unveiling their common homogeneous nature, and, above all, their common rejection of limits through Kent's infinite anti-space.

Thus, what anchors the notion of *topos* to a homogeneous spatiality is its rhizomatic vocation. Following Gilles Deleuze, a rhizome "has no beginning or end; it is always in the middle"[12], and, as claimed by the topological space of these projects, the rhizome "extends without limits or center"[13]. Precisely because of this, the logic of the rhizome is additive; as Deleuze affirms, "the fabric of the rhizome is the conjunction, "and ... and ... and..."[14]. This endless conjunction, so celebrated by the French philosopher, is, in the end,

_9. Josep Maria Montaner, La modernidad superada, (Barcelona: Gustavo Gili, 2011), 32.

_10. Aristotle, *Physis*, trans. W.A. Pickard, (Cambridge: The Internet Classics Archive, 1994), Section 2.

_11. Peter Eisenman, "Brief Advanced Design Studio", last modified October 2014, https://www.architecture.yale.edu/courses/advanced-design-studio-eisenman-0#_ftn3

_12. Gilles Deleuze and Felix Guattari, *A Thousand Plateaus*, translated by Brian Massumi, (Minneapolis: University of Minnesota Press, 1987), 25.

_13. Byung Chul-Han, *La desaparición de los rituales* (Madrid: Editorial Herder, 2020), Kindle Edition, Pos 499.

_14. Gilles Deleuze and Felix Guattari, *A Thousand Plateaus*, translated by Brian Massumi, (Minneapolis: University of Minnesota Press, 1987), 25.

destructive: according to Bhyung Chul-Han, it "leads to a carcinomatous proliferation of sameness", that is, it leads to the foreigner's eviction. Although Deleuze insists on affirming that "the middle is by no means an average"[15], he states that "between things [...] designates a stream without beginning or end that undermines its banks and picks up speed in the middle"[16]. This absence of shores is characteristic both of the endless flatness of modernity's *chora* and of the fluctuant topologies of 90s *topos*.

Thus, both spatialities share three key attributes associated with Kent's *anti-space*. First, they are *homogeneous*; both can be subsumed to one single notational system. Second, they are *generic*; both are open and indeterminate, that is, formulative. Third, they are *continuous*; both avoid the cut and the interruption, that is, they form a whole with no jumps. It is precisely in this threefold sense that the spatialities of *chora* and *topos* can be considered as *subject to something*, that is, as operating under the gravitational field of a single subject – a privileged object to which other entities can be ontologically reduced.

2. SUBJECTLESSNESS

Both modernity and late 20th-century (post-)structuralisms celebrate the notion of subject. While the former associates it with the figure of the human being, the latter instrumentalizes relational fields for this purpose, in their linguistic, ideological, psychological or political registers. In both cases, there is a particular entity, the subject, whose ontological structure subjugates a set of objects by absorbing them into its gravitational field. However, as we analyzed in the third chapter, the autonomy recently deployed by zoological, algorithmic and geological beings calls into question the presence of any underlying entity claiming a privileged ontological position, that is, claiming being considered as a subject.

Thus, rather than an underlying master figure or field around which all objects would reverently orbit, what we have in contemporary philosophies like Object-Oriented Ontology are fleeting, distinct and horizontal poly-pluralities, i.e., ephemeral groups of collections and sub-collections constituted by multispecie agencies. This is a far cry from the continuous and holistic fields of Deleuze's ontologies; rather than a rhizomatic network of forces crystallizing in different beings, what we find are collections of autonomous entities whose local and ephemeral intertwinings constitute clusters and sub-clusters. As such, there is no world understood as a unified and unifying super-object; there are only sets of emancipated objects. This radical decentralization of the subject deprives it from any ontological favor, converting it into just another object; there is no longer any element acting as a universal point of reference, i.e., there is no single notational system within which entities are framed. Rather, each entity is, in itself and by itself, an independent notational system.

The overlapping of multiple notational systems emancipated from any single meta-system resonates with Eisenman's architectural concept of "inconsistent multiplicity". Under this conceptual umbrella, Eisenman lucubrates a type of space opposing the homogeneity characteristic of *chora* and *topos*. He identifies it with the expression "heterogeneous space", that is, an architectural space of non self-same repetition.

Andrea Palladio and Adolf Loos are put forward by Eisenman as two of the first architects linked to this type of spatiality. In the first case, Eisenman argues that "the articulated architectural elements – portico, transition space, and central space [...]

_15. Ibid.
_16. Ibid.

become dislocated from their supposed normative location as well as their meaning and become noniconic spatial inscriptions. These inscriptions often produce conditions where two or more notations become overlaid in a single space. The resultant space no longer has a simple or singular conceptual valence, as in homogeneous space, but rather takes on indeterminate characteristics."[17] In Palladian villas, heterogeneous spatiality is built up through the superposition of different notational systems in the same space. Consequently, it appears as "different" or "other", particularly in its notational reading. Thus, the ideal condition of the uniform and universal space conceptualized by Alberti disappears, making way for spatial conditions that Eisenman describes as virtual.

Something similar happens with Adolf Loos's Raumplan. Eisenman introduces the Viennese architect using the evocative nickname "Mr. Heterogeneous"[18]. Unlike the *chora* or the *topos*, the superposition of different geometries within the same space provides the Raumplan with conditions of spatial heterogeneity based on an idea we mentioned above: that of an inconsistent multiplicity – i.e., multiplicity understood as a set of elements that cannot be reduced to a single universal notational system (Alberti), a set of extensive inconsistencies (Postmodernism) or a group of incomplete wholes (Deconstructivism). Instead, an inconsistent multiplicity provokes heterogeneity within a set of intensive cohesions that have limits. Precisely because of their liminal nature, these cohesions cannot be totalized or totalizing; they cannot become a meta-system, that is, a subject. Their limits keep them local, ephemeral, plural, distinct and autonomous, capable of the associations and dissociations, junctions and disjunctions, pressures and tensions that characterized the Roman territories of the *limes*.

3. LIMIT-SPACE: LIMINAL, LIMITED, LIMITROPHE

Unlike the *chora* or the *topos*, the Roman *limes* described at the beginning of this text stands in opposition, in its architectural modulation, to Kent's *anti-space* by taking on some of the attributes associated with Eisenman's heterogeneity. It does so by instrumentalizing the notion of limit from an affirmative point of view. Rather than an infinitesimal and dividing Euclidean line operating as space's enclosure, the limit is spatialized: it is conjugated as a territory in itself, as a land outside of land, as a *limes*. Thus, in the Roman register, the limit is not an entity enclosing space, but rather it is space, or, better, it spaces (verb).

The notion of limit is actually at the core of architecture. If we understand the architectural practice as the production of interiorities, that is, as the production of spaces within spaces, the idea of a border distinguishing them is decisive. In this sense, the etymology of the term "temple" is particularly revealing: its root "-tem", present also in the terms "témenos", "templum", and "time", indicates the idea of a cutout, a demarcation, a frontier, a limit instrumentalized in order to separate the sacred realm of the gods from the profane territory of humans. In ancient Rome, the construction of a temple began with the *cumtemplatio*, the contemplative observation of a demarcated zone of the sky by the augurs. Through the attentive observation of birds, the sun and the clouds' trajectories within the selected celestial area, the augurs interpreted the auspices of the city that was about to be founded. Once the observation was completed, the demarcated zone of the

_17. Peter Eisenman, *Palladio Virtuel*, (London: Yale University Press, 2015), 10.

_18. Mark Wigley, in conversation with Peter Eisenman, "Eisenman/Wigley X: The Problematic of Homogeneous Space", YouTube video (58:00), conversation on August 8, 2013, posted by "Columbia GSAPP", September 11, 2013, https://www.youtube.com/watch?v=0_b5COTxHuc&t=125s.

sky was projected onto the ground in order to trace the contours of the future temple, germinal cell of the coming city. *Cumtemplatio* was thus cum-tem-platio: the tracing of the limits through which the cosmos took on meaning and signification by being projected onto the earth and establishing the ambit in which the humans could purposively inhabit the world. Thus, the temple instrumentalized the limit not just as a border between what is sacred and what is profane, but as a defined frontier space, as a contoured isthmus mediating between the celestial realm of the gods and the terrestrial realm of humanity.

The spatialized register of the limit evoked by the Roman temple and the Roman limes lays the foundation for a type of spatiality defined here as Limit-Space. It opposes the homogeneity characteristic of *chora* and *topos* by opposing its homogeneous, generic and continuous nature. Limit-Space resists reduction to one single notational system; it unfolds a subjectless spatiality in which the participation of algorithmic, biological and geological agents overlap distinct notational systems while producing sets and sub-sets of distinct spatialities. As we will see in what follows, the heterogeneity, specificity and discreteness of the Limit-Space is paradoxically closer to the spatialities associated with the Renaissance and identified by Kent as *space*, than those referred to by the same author as *anti-space* and related to modernity. The Limit-Space aims at modulating the coming years of Advanced Architecture by developing this subjectless condition through a threefold spatial nature: that of being *liminal*, *limited* and *limitrophe*.

3.1 Liminal: Interplays of Notational Systems

Limit-Space is *liminal* in its overlapped and promiscuous interplay of notational systems, opposing thus the homogeneity characteristic of *chora* and *topos*. The notion of liminality is instrumentalized here in the anthropological register developed first by Arnold Van Gennep[19] and later by Victor Turner.[20] Van Gennep divided the rites of passage in three phases: separation (detachment of the individual from an earlier fixed point in the social structure), liminality (ambiguous phase in which the individual has attributes both of the past and the coming state) and aggregation (reincorporation of the individual to the social group, but with the rights and obligations characteristic of his/her new status). On this basis, Victor Turner developed the notion of liminality emphasizing its ambiguity and its capacity to elude the network of classifications that usually locate states and positions in cultural space. Liminal entities are neither here nor there; they are "betwixt and between the positions assigned and arrayed by law, custom convention, and ceremonial"[21]. Liminal states are thus states of overlap: during the liminal period, the individual exists in a situation of in betweenness, that is, a situation in which s/he possesses attributes of both the previous state and the coming state.

It is in this sense that Turner's notion of liminality qualifies Limit-Space: while liminal periods overlap attributes coming from different socio-political positions, limit-space overlaps spatial frameworks coming from different notational systems. Thus, the notion of limit, in light of the architectural register orchestrated here, is no longer the Euclidean divider line that is at the core of the Modern Movement's programmatic zonification. The limit is, instead, in its territorial register, a daimonic space whose nature is that of "differential sameness and autoreferential difference"[22]: if the limit is in itself and by itself

_19. Arnold Van Gennep, *The Rites of Passage* (Chicago: University of Chicago Press, 1961).
_20. Victor Turner, *The Ritual Process* (London: Routledge, 2017).
_21. Ibid., 95.
_22. Eugenio Trías, *Los límites del Mundo*, (Barcelona: Ariel Filosofía, 1985), 121.

internal differentiation, if in its re-flection the limit separates and divides, then the limit necessarily joins and disjoins, or, more accurately, the limit joins what it disjoins. Under this register, the Limit-Space is liminal precisely because of being a *locus* composed of multispecie encounters and dis-encounters: it is constructed and inhabited by a mixture of entanglements among organic and non-organic agencies that, in resonance with the Roman *limitanei*, coexist under a constant interplay of pressures.

However, the liminality associated with the Limit-Space does not consist in a pre-conceived receptacle occupied by a myriad of different agencies. What provides spatial heterogeneity to the Limit-Space is not the mere coexistence of these biological, algorithmic, human or geological agencies, but the promiscuous superimposition of the notational systems associated with the spatial logic characteristic of each one of them. We cannot sense this "inconsistent multiplicity" in the *chora* of projects such as Mies van der Rohe's "Barcelona Pavilion" or Le Corbusier's "Ville Savoye", nor in the *topos* of projects such as FOA's "Yokohama Terminal" or Ben van Berkel's "Mercedes Benz Museum". Even recent experimental projects such as Oxman's "Silk Pavilion" or Bartlett's RC3 Unit "TARSS" do not relate to Limit-Space, in that the zoological agents of the former or the algorithmic agents of the latter still respond to preconceived homogeneous formal structures, like the former's dome. Rather than replicating well-known homogeneous spatialities, the overlapping of these different systematics has the capacity of producing a kaleidoscopic spatial regime, a heterogeneous spatiality irreducible to any meta-system operating as a transcendental subject: there is no single parametric formula or calligraphic gesticulation acting as a unified and underlying field of forces, that is, as a subject, as a privileged element capable of comprehending the resulting spatiality. This does not mean that the final result is simply the random juxtaposition of a litany of solipsistic monades: in their symbiotic intertwinings, the different agencies involved in the spatial production establish clusters and subclusters of performative transfers that are constantly sewing and resewing the "limit's limits": their operativity is not always structured by harmonic consensus, but their different spatial notational systems engage in constant resistance and deviation. They produce spontaneous symbiotic interlacements that overlap without any preconceived agreement and certainly not without décalages, displacements and misfits – in other words, the dissensus, the collections of com-pressions and ex-pressions that we find between the different agents involved in experimental projects such as Maeid's "Pahoehoe Beauty". In this context, the Limit-Space aims at unfolding its liminal heterogeneity by overlapping the different spatial notations characteristic of each of the organic or non-organic species participating in the construction and co-inhabitation of its common architectural spatiality.

3.2 Limited: Plastic Determinations

The Limit-Space is limited in the Hegelian understanding of the notion of limit: "The limit is the essentiality of something, it is its determination."[23] It opposes thus the generic vocation characteristic of *chora* and *topos*; to limit means to define. The latin term *definire* signifies the act of tracing with clarity and precision the borders of something in order to separate it from its neighbors. *Definire* is thus *de-finire,* the establishment of *finis*, ends. However, the term finis should not be read here only under the light of its topological or chronological sense, but it should also be approached in its ontological register: to

_23. Georg Wilhelm Friedrich Hegel, *The Science of Logic.* Cambridge: Heidelberg Writings, 1996), 249.

define means to specify the qualities of an object that make an object this object and not that object. To define is thus to shed light on the object's thisness, on "what an object is", on what Scotus alluded to with the term *haecceity*. To define consists of tracing an ontological contour in order to limit the object's in-finite possible variability under a single framework that distinguishes it from the rest of objects while avoiding the generic. De-finition implies con-fination; to illuminate the object's thisness means to isolate it from its exterior, to enclose it, to mark its quantitative and qualitative borders, to cut continuity's homogeneity by accounting for the object's double discreteness: the object's mathematical countability and the object's individual distinction.

Thus, a limited spatiality is not a fragmented spatiality referring to an absent whole or a contoured spatiality equipped with a prominent physical border. A limited spatiality refers to a distinct spatiality that has been individuated. It is defined and specific, contrasting with what is open and generic.; is determined, but not predetermined, that is, it is not determined *avant la lettre*: its radical distinction opposes the generic openness characteristic of the Modern Movement, but also of projects such as Archizoom's "Non Stop City" (1972) or Kasuyo Sejima's "Rolex Center" (2010). In a context where the power of today's supercomputation makes it possible to notate the inherent discreteness of reality, it is obsolete to operate with simplified spatial formulas (fields), or repetitive spatial blocks (particles), that is, it is obsolete to operate with *generics*. Today's computational power applied to architectural design allows an emancipation from reductive laws, whose standardisation is at the core of the homogeneous architectural spatialities referred to with the terms *chora* and *topos*.

The limited spatialities associated with the Limit-Space do not align, thus, with the notion of the generic, nor with derivative concepts such as flexibility, adaptability or resilience, attributes particularly common in the spatialities of *chora* and *topos*. Only with a certain dose of generality can something be flexible enough to assume modifications without becoming something else. Thus, rather than flexible, a limited spatiality is *plastic*: it varies, that is, it is ephemeral, evanescent, but at the price of gaining a new specificity (*plastiquage or plastiquer* are terms whose french utilisation is associated with the concept of explosion) and cancelling the previous one. In this sense, the notions of adaptation, flexibility or resilience are understood as reactionary: its common capacity to assume transformations without breaking is precisely what permits the persistence of what is established, rather than its replacement.

3.3 Limitrophe: Foliated Sets of Figures

The Limit-Space is limitrophe in the sense used by Jacques Derrida, opposing thus the continuity characteristic of *chora* and *topos*. Rather than effacing or ignoring the limit, Derrida attempts, through his use of the term "limitrophy", "to multiply its figures, to complicate, thicken, delinearize, fold, and divide the line precisely by making it increase and multiply"[24]. The limit is thus thickened, which is the literal sense of the greek term *trepho*, to nurture. Under this umbrella, the Limit-Space reverberates with Eisenman's "inconsistent multiplicity" by acquiring a foliated consistency and becoming an edgy, plural and insistently folded frontier.

_24. Jacques Derrida, "The Animal That Therefore I am (More to Follow)" translated by David Wills, *Critical Inquiry*, Vol.28, No. 2. (2002), 398.

We can find a wide range of experimental formal strategies in architecture working in this direction. Daniel Köhler's and Rasa Navasaityte's Hyper-Nollie (2019) take advantage of the unprecedented power of processors in order to compute a collection of different floor-parts whose complicit discreteness constitutes a foliated montage, a spatiality constantly demarcated and multiplied.

In spite of a general systematicity that precludes Eisenman's "inconsistent multiplicity", collections of differentiated floors as the previous one have relevant disciplinary consequences: rather than favoring a vertical circulation based on an efficient spine ("Lake Shore Drive") or on a Baudelairian wandering ("Jussieu Two Libraries"), it promotes a navigation by "jumps"; it is more like a syncopated movement – i.e., a movement that is not completed in a single gesture: it requires jumps, the presence of which signifies that there can no longer be a defined trajectory (discrete floor) or an indefinite trajectory (continuous floor). Instead, there is a cluster of movements, interruptions, starts and stops, turns and dislocations that make the overall circulation through the set into a heterogeneous experience.

However, the "continuous connection" of its spaces and the fact that "each one of them is accessible from each part" seem to formally evoke the logics of a relational field, particularly through the homogeneous granularity revealed by a general overview. Nevertheless, the project's tension between the distinct discreteness of its close-up view and the texturised continuity of its far-away view precludes any attempt to simply reduce its parts to an underlying material substratum: each part positions the interpretation of its own context through a complex balance between identity (inherent distinction) and relationality (local complicities). The Limit-Space is thus not an abyssal and discontinuous limit: it does not form the single and indivisible line characteristic of Modernity; rather, it produces "more than one internally divided line"[25]. The Limit-Space is thus a limit that grows and multiplies into a plethora of edges. Precisely because of its limitrophe condition, the Limit-Space is not just one, like the spaces associated with *chora* and *topos*; it is not reducible to a single universal notational system but it is formed through a collection of territories that implies the superposition of different frameworks. Thus, rather than the formulative and open spatiality characteristic of both *chora* and *topos*, the unprecedented power unfolded by supercomputation lets us operate with massive sets and sub-sets of distinct and promiscuous figures that are no longer totalised by any underlying whole.

4. IN-BETWEENNESS

The Limit-Space is thus liminal in its promiscuous interplay of notational systems (heterogeneity), limited in its plastic determination (specificity), and limitrophe in its massively foliated figurativity (discreteness). A set of spatial conditions that opposes the homogeneous, generic and continuous nature characteristic of the modern spatialities of Plato's *chora* and the rhizomatic spatialities of Aristotle's *topos*, whose presence is still prevalent in the contemporary landscape of Advanced Architecture. The Limit-Space, in its liminal, limited and limitrophe vocation resonates with the subjectless condition embraced by the 21st century and its myriad of multi-specie agencies, human and non-human, organic and non-organic, natural and artificial; subjectless objects liberated from the absolute subject of modernity and the relational subject of postmodernity, emancipated beings overlapping their own spatial logics in order to produce a massive foliated montage of hyper-specific figures that avoids any attempt at unity. The unbounded anti-spaces of *chora*

_25. Ibid., 398.

and *topos*, characterized by their common desire to be universal, continuous, open-ended and unimpeded, are surreptitiously being eclipsed by a type of spatiality whose subjectless contemporaneity paradoxically rekindles certain attributes characteristic of pre-modern spatialities defined by Kent as *space*, in opposition to *anti-space*. Thus, the heterogeneous, specific and discrete spatialities of the Limit-Space recover something of the figurative, closed and finite spatialities of the Renaissance and the Neo-classic, but replacing their unified order under a central dominant motif with the computation of massive sets of figures; the Limit-Space does not support the generic and its limitless flexibility, but rather the specific and its demand for compromise: it produces spaces of tension, spaces that escape the tender dictatorship characteristic of harmony, inclusivity, and consensus. Instead, the Limit-Space aims at being permeable to conflict and dissensus precisely because it is determinate, that is, precisely because it is limited, because it is *this* rather than *that*. They are spaces, thus, characterized by processes of individuation that oppose the harmonic flexibility and adaptability characteristic of what is indeterminately open. Instead, they consist in the massive computation of promiscuous, plastic and distinct contours which conjugate the term "in-between" under a very specific register: rather than being articulated only as a preposition, it is also approached as a noun. The liminality evoked here proposes not just spaces in between spaces, but also spaces of in-betweenness: what matters is no longer only what is adjacent to the two sides of the limit, but also what occurs within it. It is only under this light that the limit becomes *limes*: a bustling space of junction and disjunction, a land of deviation and pressures, a strange territory of multitudes whose fluctuant co-existence is not merely positional. It is operative, it is ideological, it is critical. It is subversive and performative, it is intimate. It is constituted as a carnal liminality that by no means can be exhausted in abstraction or lyricism. It is precisely this Faustian desire for an embodied entanglement that makes advanced architecture's design into an experimental practice of what Donna Haraway has defined using the term *worlding*. *Worlding* as an active and ontological process of creating worlds, that is, stories, tales, fictions; worlding not only as the result of our passive encounter with events, locations, circumstances or scenarios, but as a vectorized practice, informed by our attention, our critical sensibility, our active engagement with the materiality in which we are enmeshed. Advanced architecture aims at proposing, above all, embodied processes of *worlding*, liminal practices designing spaces within spaces under the very act of attending to the world.

ARETI MARKOPOULOU

AFTERWORD

Collective Intelligence Design

Throughout this rigorously written, sensationally rich and evolutionary narration of Gausa and Vivaldi's *The Threefold Logic of Advanced Architecture*, one can observe the experimental nature of architectural discipline - unfolded, constructed or emergent - through a continuous field of action in resonance or in contrast with the variation of its surrounding socio-technological framework. History indicates that any profound social change enters into a circular feedback with a technological revolution, meaning that one is both fueling and being fueled by the other. With the revolution of the printing press, we distributed information and knowledge. With the revolution of the steam engine, we physically connected people with places and generated massive amounts of energy at will. With the revolution of the personal computer, we digitally connected people to people and places, while with the Internet and the Internet of Things we democratized information and connected the physical with the digital world.

And, although it is of great value to our discipline to observe how architecture is continuously evolving and responding to these profound social changes and technological advancements, it is only when we understand the magnitude of architecture to affect society in turn - its ecological environment and its surrounding economic and political regimes - that the real power, relevance and responsibility of our discipline unfolds.

As an epilogue to this work, there is a relevant discussion around the notion of how a new design paradigm becomes a cultural one.

Let us first try to define the emerging design paradigm.

As we have seen throughout this text, a series of advances in disciplines including material science, synthetic biology, aerospace engineering and computer science, among others, have profoundly affected the protocols of an "informational practice" in architecture, as the title defines it. And although the territory that can defined be "informational" may be misinterpreted and limited to the computational logics of our digital era ("information", "informed"), I believe we should perceive it in its augmented (or "expanded") view.

Predictive modelling of future biodiversity zones based on big data of satellite images, biological growth and environmental forecast. P.G Magnus and J. Irawan, Intelligent Cities Research Studio, Master in Advanced Architecture, IAAC, 2016.

Contemporary designers are participants in and witnesses to an accelerated digital society in the Anthropocene;[1] a society aware of its expanded and critical impact on the planet. We are part of a society that consists, in 32%, of digital natives,[2] while it is populated by cultures of open source or digital commons, and it is immersed in virtual, augmented or synthetically engineered and biological environments and products. We are both citizens and designers of a society whose operation, interaction, health and safety mainly rely on, or are formed by, vast data sets that feed evolutionary algorithms capable of analyzing, learning and eventually predicting behaviors or urban and environmental phenomena. Finally, we are part of a society whose species are constantly being redefined or even relocated. From sensorially augmented bodies and cyborgs to built spaces and products that are edible, compostable or symbiotic with other species, our practice cannot be merely seen as "informational" but rather as "experiential" and, more than anything, "collectively" created by a variety of intelligences including cognitive, machinic, geological and biological kinds.

Within this context, we observe that the advances from material sciences, manufacturing and synthetic biology, coupled with computational design, human-computer interaction and artificial intelligence, open up unique opportunities for the creation of responsive,

_1. Efforts to label the expanded human impact on the planet have created a scientific debate between geologists and environmentalists. Many environmental experts support evidence that suggests that we have entered into a new geological age, called the "Anthropocene", which defines a human-influenced time period where the Earth's system processes are highly altered by humans. The Anthropocene is distinguished as a new period either after or within the Holocene, the current epoch, which began approximately 10,000 years ago (about 8000 BC) with the end of the last glacial period. The term was popularized by the atmospheric chemist and Nobel laureate Paul Crutzen in 2000, and it is used by many environmentalists. Although it is not totally accepted by all geologists, one can clearly identify the urgency for the environmental community to raise awareness about the multi-layered human impact on the planet.
_2. Aa Bloomberg analysis based on United Nations data, showcases that, in 2019, 32% percent of the global population wais born after 2000, while 31.5% wais born between 1980 and 2000. The first, called the Generation Z, have never known a non-digital world, while the latter, called Generation Y have experienced the digital shift before the age of 20. For more, sSee more: Bloomberg, Rise of Gen Z Over Millennials, 2019. https://www.bloomberg.com/news/terminal/PDMAV0T25UKH, (accessed February 2020)

collectively created and intelligent environments. The protocols and processes of the creation of these spaces define a new emerging design model which - as seen in many of the examples in the expansive chapter of this book- is essentially collective and evolutionary: a Collective Intelligence Design model.

Through the applications and implications of the Collective Intelligence Design model, we are crossing a threshold in design where physicality follows and reveals information through time and through dynamic configurations, rather than static and rigid geometries. This technologically enhanced design process represents a new design paradigm, where users and the environment are participants in unique exchanges and dialogues, facilitated by all human, material, biological and computational intelligence. Materials become bits and information, uniting with the digital world, while computational processes, such as algorithmic control, circular feedback, input and output, both drive and are driven by the morphogenetic capacities of matter (active or alive), uniting, therefore, with the material world.

Buildings, landscapes and spaces are able to reconfigure themselves, on both an atomic and macro scale, to support ecological/biological changes and multiple users' needs, as well as behavioral and occupational patterns. At the same time, the Collective Intelligence Design paradigm emerging from symbiotic processes of co-creation places not only matter and the environment at the center of design and morphogenesis, but also the users, who become active participants in their built environment and play the final creative role. This paradigm shift boosts new relations between the built space and humans, or among inhabited space, non-human agents and human body and perception.

This new design paradigm is also a new cultural one, in which accuracy, statics, repetition and Cartesian grids – traditionally associated with safety, control, orientation and comfort – give way to motion, unpredictability and organic principles of evolution. In the architectural model promoted by Collective Intelligence, principles of safety, passive occupation, or orientation and control employed by the traditional model give way to dialogue, co-existence and indeterminacy (or surprise). In the same way as humans coexist with, are mutually affected by, and affect natural and geological elements, including rivers, forests or rain and storms, they will co-exist with buildings and public spaces, as well as with other species. This new relation and co-existence are characterized by an increased awareness that human behavior affects ecologies and environments, changing them, and that this change then affects human behavior in return, in a cyclical way. Although, one could argue, that the principle of mutual affection and collective evolution is the essence of natural co-existence, it is also true that the increasingly artificial and hierarchical (top-down) design and construction of our environments have been consistent in excluding nature or organic principles in their operation. This has created a micro-cosmos in which artifice suppresses the natural sphere and people translate the notion of protection to mean a disconnection from natural forces or other species. The notions of separation, dualism or dichotomy are all symptoms of a traditional hierarchical understanding of the world, in which artifice and nature are disconnected and opposites. In the highly digitized world of today, the traditional and strict lines of dichotomies start to blur, revealing a unique merging of organic and inorganic atoms, and digital bits. This merging, present in all actions and interactions of our everyday life, expands to define a new cultural paradigm.

Zygmunt Bauman defines it as the paradigm of "liquid" modernity, a society in continuous change placing importance on notions of "forever becoming", "blurred limits" and "undefined" states and shapes.[3] Rosi Braidotti asserts that the subject inof the emerging society

_3. Zygmunt Bauman, *Liquid Modernity*, (Cambridge: Polity, 2000), 82.

Urban Simulator of networked buildings for predictive modelling in urban planning. The simulator processes data related with all environmental, human, and technological intelligence. It is fed by (i) infrastructural big data such as mobility and contamination, (ii) user's emotions, opinion or desires and (iii) phenomena including viruses spread, urban floods or ecosystem's growth. Project developed at Internet of Buildings, Master in City &Technology, IAAC, 2018

becomes "a nomad assembly in a shared life space that it does not control or own". S/he just occupies it, always in community with biological, technological and cultural others.[4] Ray Kurzweil, in a more futuristic view, predictsforesees that this unique merginge will drive us towards a state of technologically enhanced human nature, callnamed the "technological singularity",[5] while Timothy Morton introduces the term "dark ecology" to highlight the paradigm shift from a natural celebration towards a more complex interconnection, today, of all forms of life and all natural and technological expressions that introduce areas of uncertainty, unpredictability and hesitation, rather than a clear and clean separation and dichotomy.[6] Finally, Donna Haraway emphasizes her notion of multispecie players, approaching them as "partial and flawed translations across difference";[7] mixed entanglements looking not for reconciliation or restoration, but for being "deeply committed to the more modest possibilities of partial recuperation and getting on together".[8]

Within this context, Collective Intelligence Design contributes into a unique architectural paradigm shift, that is not only related towith design logics and aesthetics. Aligned with the aforementionedabove philosophical views on contemporary culture and society, its most significant contribution lies in the redefinition of architectural "environments" and "ecologies" understood as agglomerations and continuous interactions that extendgo beyond the mere interaction between humans and built space, between humans and other humansamong them, between humans and nature, or between artifice (technology) and

_4. Rosi Braidotti, "Posthuman Critical Theory", *Penn State University Press, Journal of Posthuman Studies*, vol. 1, no.1, January (2017), 9-25.
_5. Ray Kurzweil, *The Singularity is Near: When Humans Transcend Biology* (New York, Viking, 2005), 136
_6. Timothy Morton, *Dark Ecology: For a Logic of Future Coexistence* (New York: Columbia University Press, 2018).
_7. Donna Haraway, *Staying with the Trouble* (London: Duke University Press, 2016), 10.
_8. Ibid.

nature. The emerging design paradigm defines uniquely enhanced "environments" and "ecologies" that are dynamic and reconfigurable, in whichand where humans, nature, artifice, technology and other species collectively and evolutionally co-exist within a framework of increased consciousness and awareness.

The operations required for this reconfiguration usually take place in non-perceivable material or biological scales, as well as in the absence of hard mechanical parts. In that sense, they promote organic and soft forms that can merge with the landscape or the natural environment. Architectural behavior can be designed on different scales – from small-scale component-based skins to larger urban configurations – and applied to different mediums: from building structures and skins to human bodies, organic matter and landscapes. Such architectural space is the expression of a unique merging of physical and digital, as well as a unique collaborative creation among humans, matter and the environment; a space loyal to the current cultural evolution related to "liquid" and soft states, unpredictability or continuous change.

Going one step further, Collective Intelligence in architectural design consolidates a more direct connection between users and built space, presenting unique possibilities for enhancing the identity of places, strengthening place making and bringing humans closer to what has been traditionally considered as an "artificial" or "non-natural" environment.

The new architectural model surrenders its status as a background-related model and enhances our sensory, perception and bodily experience in relation to the inhabited space. It enables a shift in our relationship and our connection to it, and we become capable of influencing it actively, co-creating it, co-existing with it, personalizing it and eventually being responsible for it. The new architectural environment becomes an extension of human needs and desires, an extension of the natural surroundings and eventually an extension (expansion) of the human body, while materially mediating between the virtual and the real.

Although, in today's highly digitized and monitored world, many sustain views that the excess of both data and efficient (predicted) decisions might harm the adventurous, playful and emerging character of our cities, fosteringenhancing a culture of routine and repetition, Collective Intelligence in architecture presents a significantly different view. The fact that it is founded on, and promotes physical rather than purely digital changes and operations, might be a significant way tof bringing back the crucial aspects of co-formation, co-action, and, eventually, collective intelligence back into the arena of architecture and public space, - where social interaction in fact takes place.

This unique merge of organic evolution, crowd wisdom and digital technologies marks a significant design and cultural milestone in the creation of the future of our built environment and the society that inhabits it.

Collective Intelligence Design Practices. Research projects exploring morphogenetic capacities of matter for responsive and adaptive architecture developed at Digital Matter Research Studio, Master in Advanced Architecture, IAAC, 2016-2020

Manuel Gausa Navarro (Barcelona, Spain, 1959) is a PHD architect and critic, author of several awarded projects and publications. From 2017 he has the Chair of Planning and Urban Design as Full Professor at DAD-UNIGE (Università degli Studi di Genova) where from 2008 to 2017 he was successively Associate Professor of Design and Full Professor of Landscape Design. Since 2015 he is Director-Coordinator of the ADD-UNIGE (PHD Program in Architecture and Design). Co-founder and Senior Professor of the IAAC (Institute for Advanced Architecture of Catalonia in Barcelona), he was its Dean from 2012 to 2015 and currently he is Lead Professor in Theory and Advanced Knowledge and Member of the Scientific Committee. From 1991 to 2000 he was Director of the magazine *Quaderns d'Arquitectura I Urbanisme*. Founding Member (2000) and Principal Advisor (from 2008) of Actar Publishers and Actar Arquitectura, in 2000 he was honoured with the *Médaille de l´Académie d´Architecture de France.*

Jordi Vivaldi is a writer, philosopher and architectural theorist based in Vienna. PhD Architect and PhD Philosopher (cand.), Jordi works as theory faculty at the Institute for Advanced Architecture of Catalonia in Barcelona, at the Bartlett University College of London and at the Institute of Urban Design in the University of Innsbruck. His areas of investigation include 20th and 21st century's theory of experimental architecture, art and technology, as well as various forms of Speculative Realism and New Materialism. His research capitalizes on the notion of "limit", both as an ontological device of definition/ perception and as a contemporaneous architectural form of space. Besides several essays and lectures, his recent work has crystallized in a forthcoming book with Actar Publishers (2021): *In-Limit. Space and Agency in a Xenological World.*